14

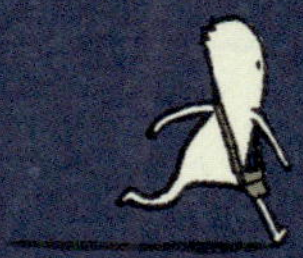

manix abrera

For my family,
KASAMA KONG MAHILIG
MANOOD NG ULAN. ☺

For you, dear reader,
MAY YOU ALWAYS BE AMAZED
BY LIFE'S BEAUTIFUL
MYSTERIES. ☺

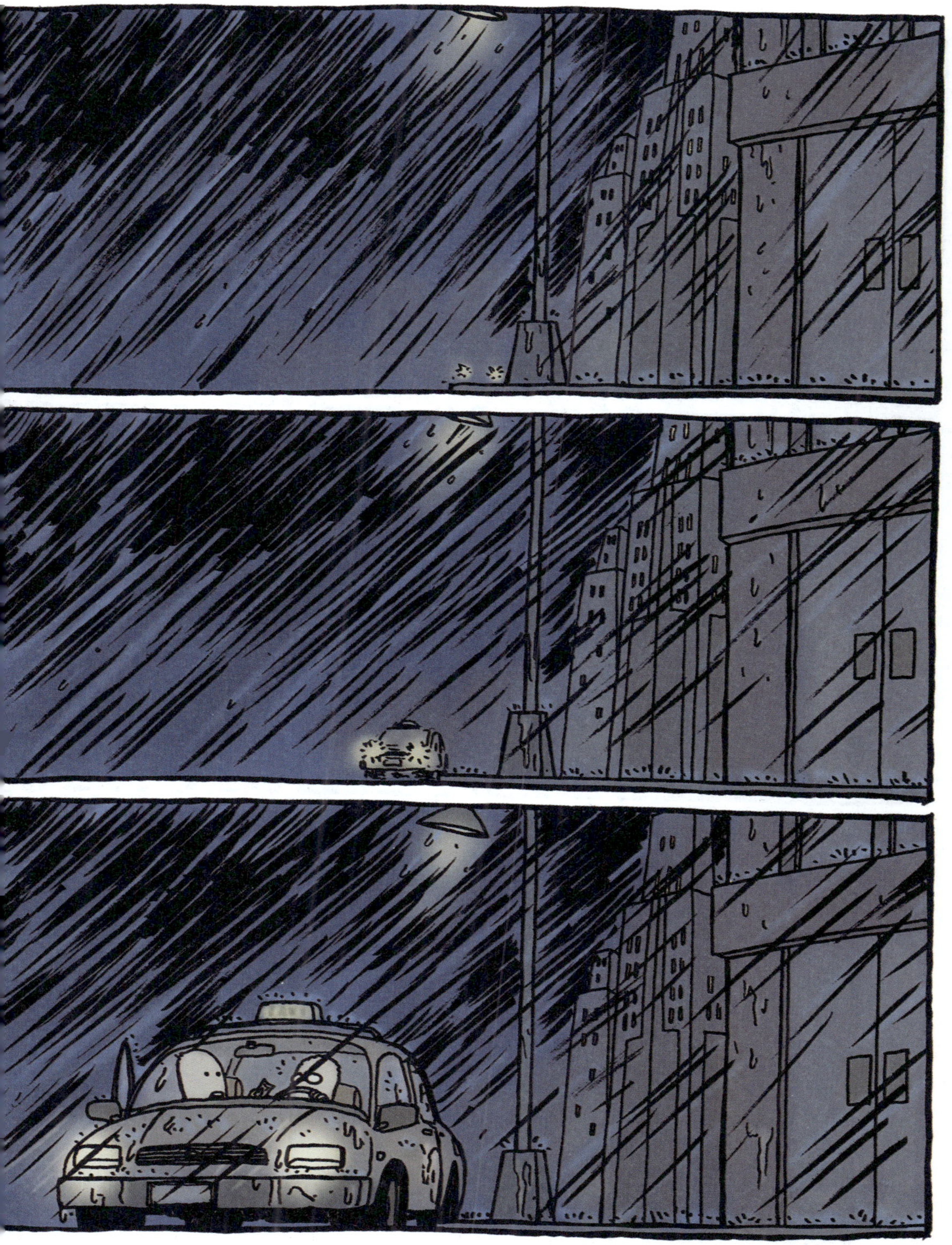

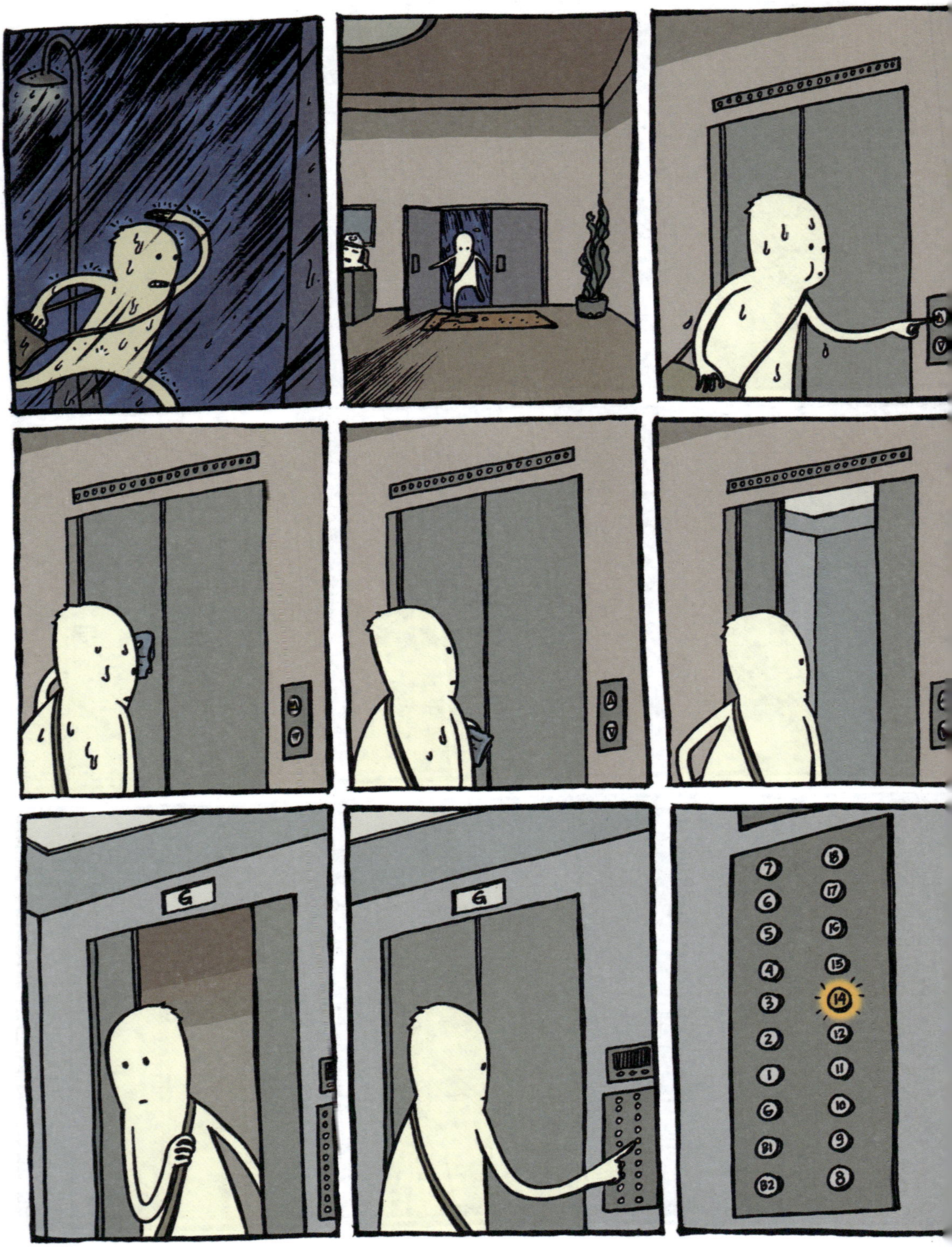
G
G

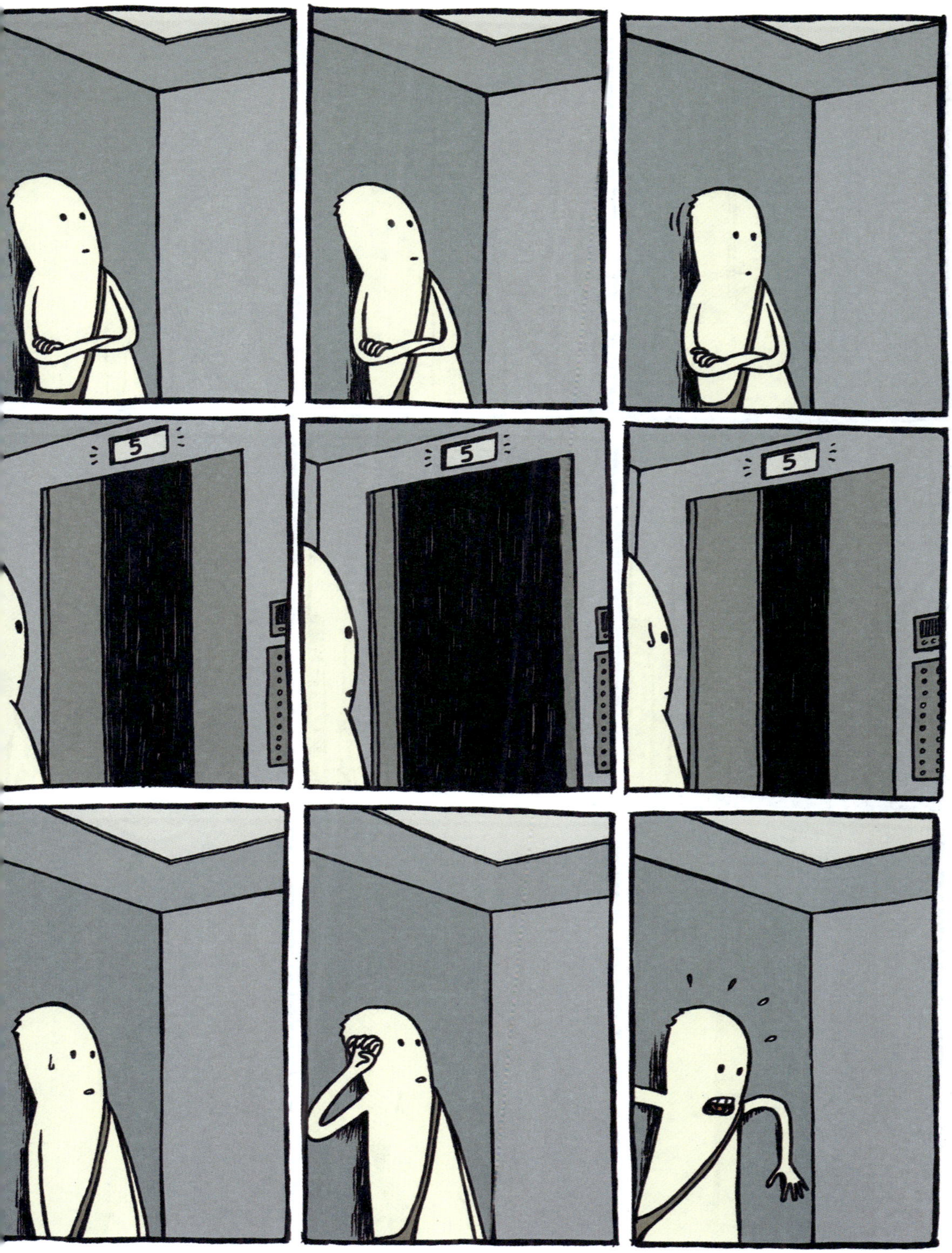
5
5
5

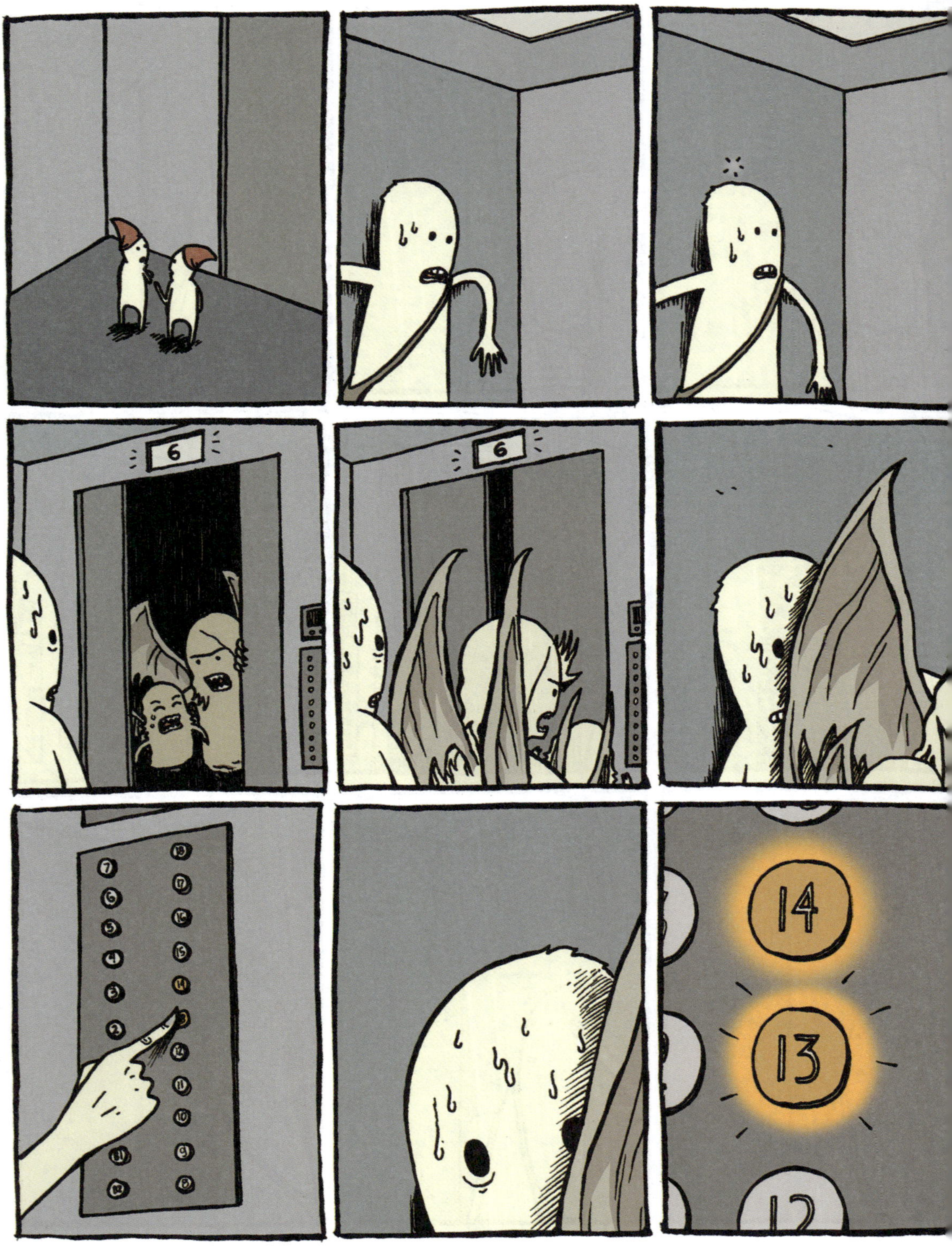
6
6
14
13
12

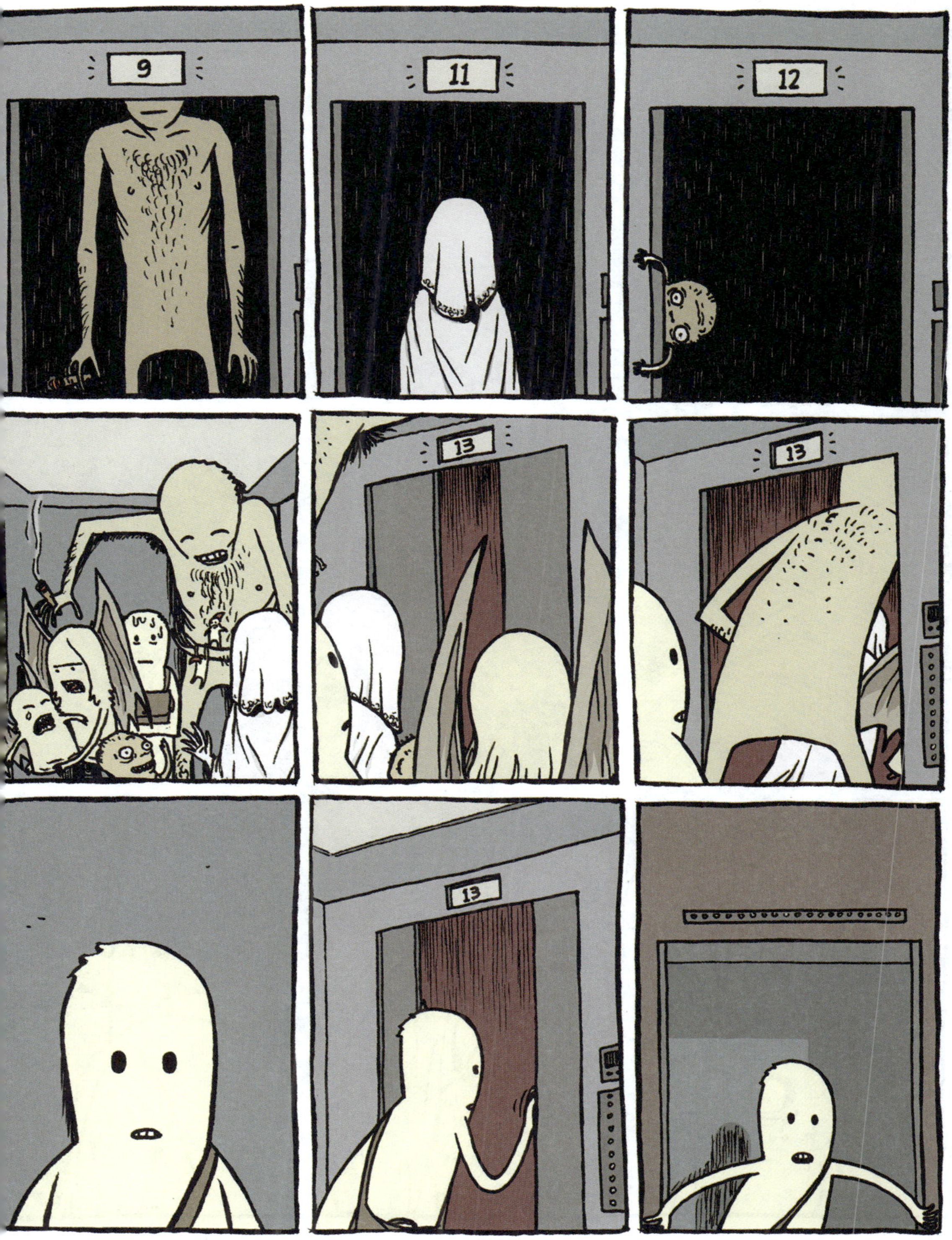
9
11
12
13
13
13

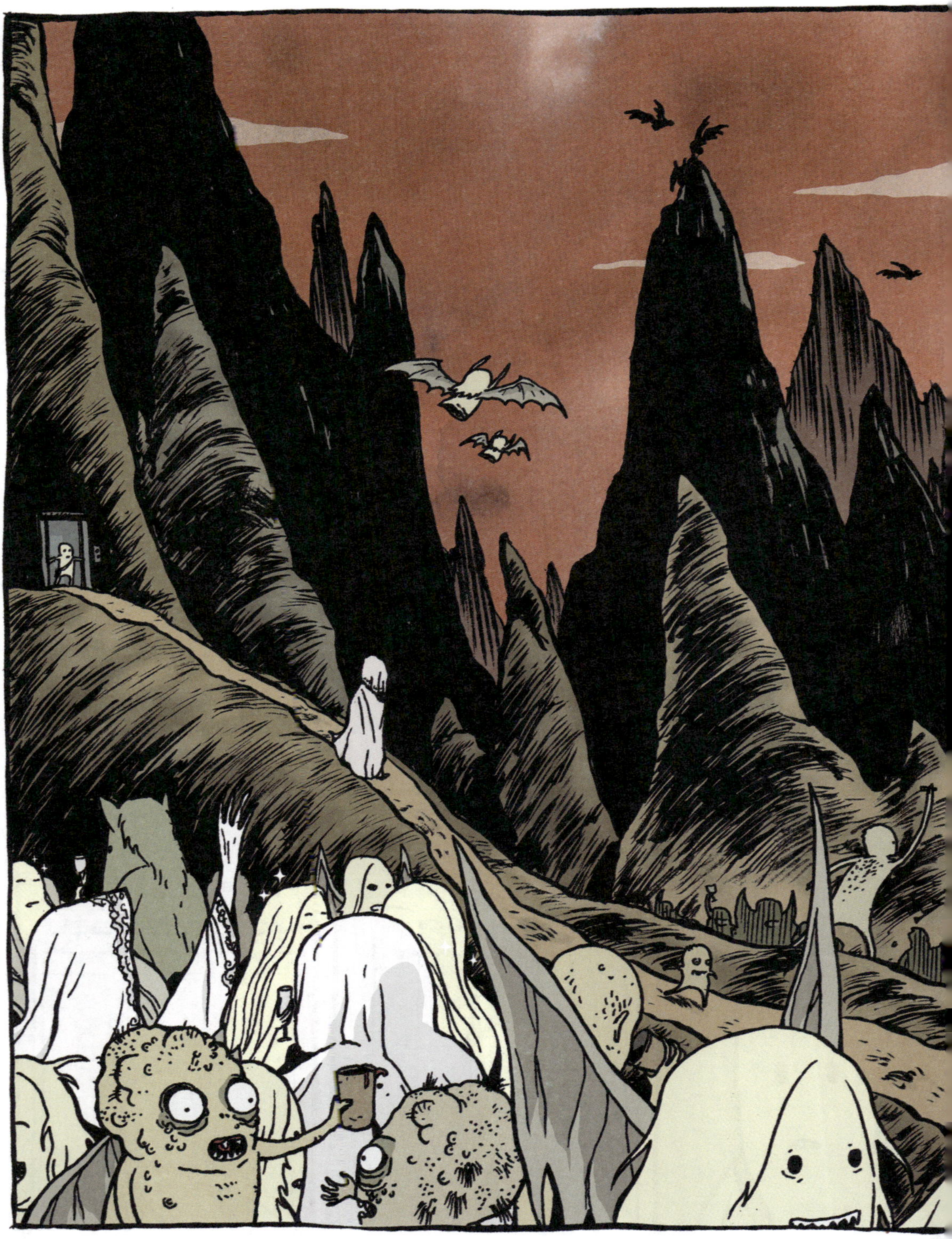

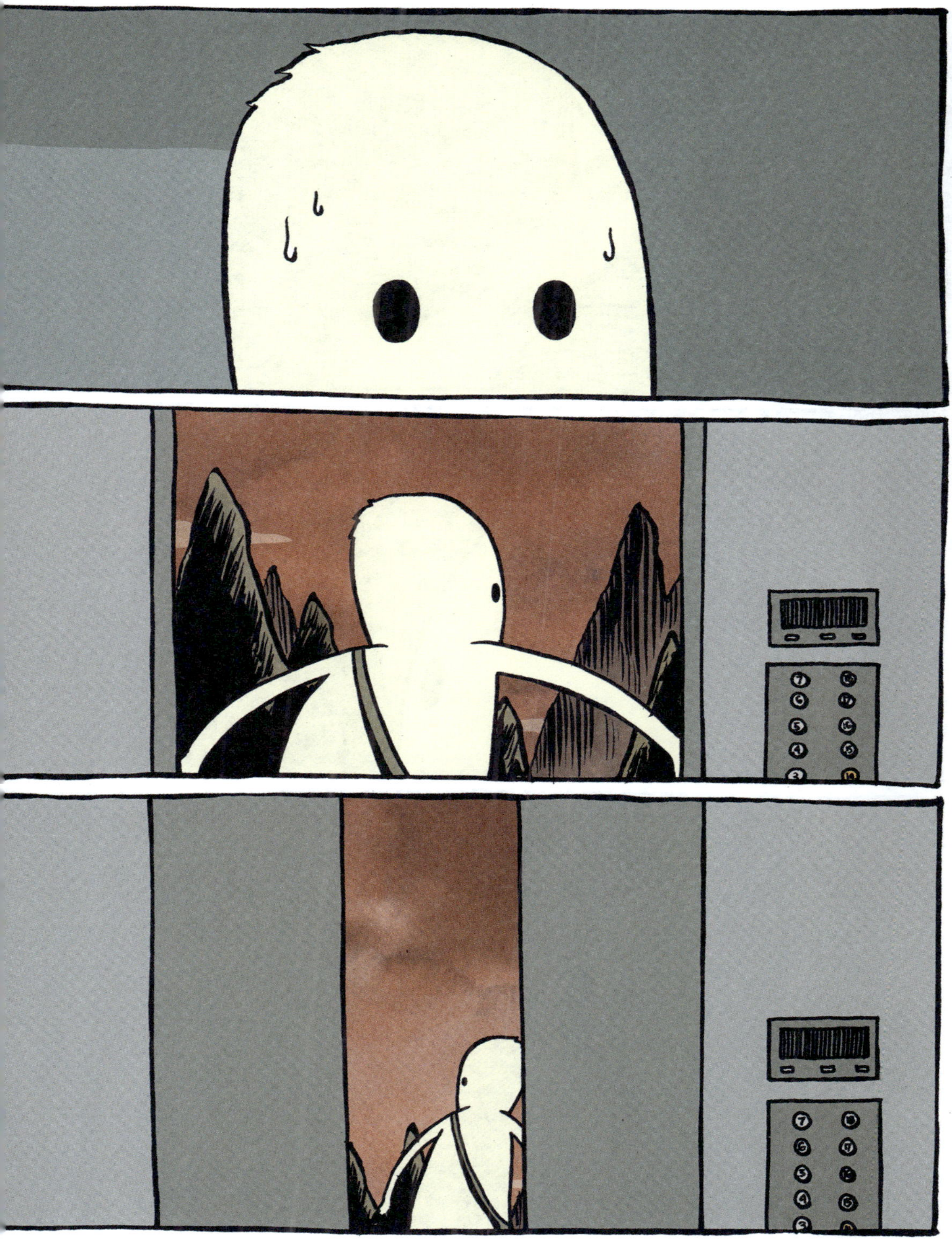

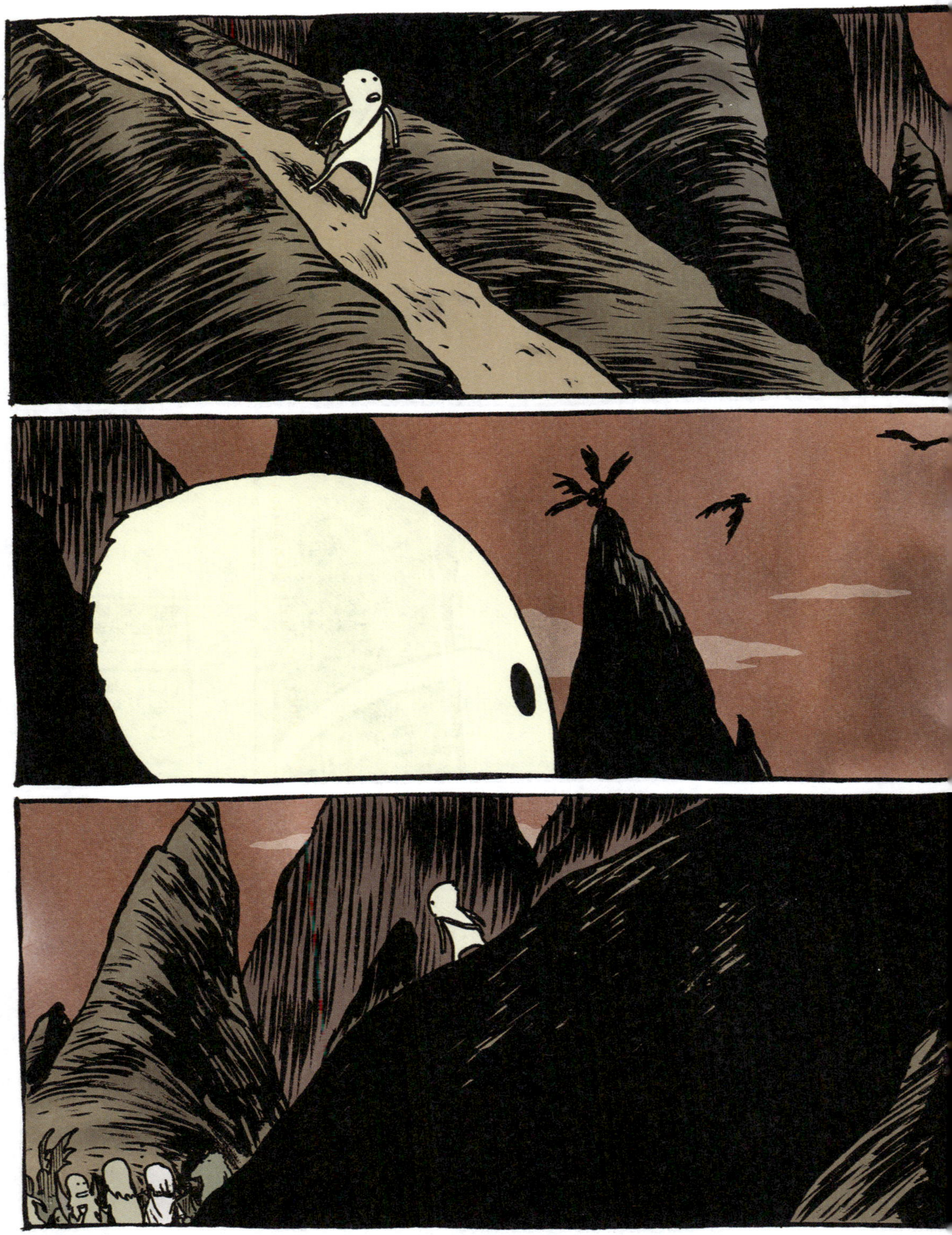

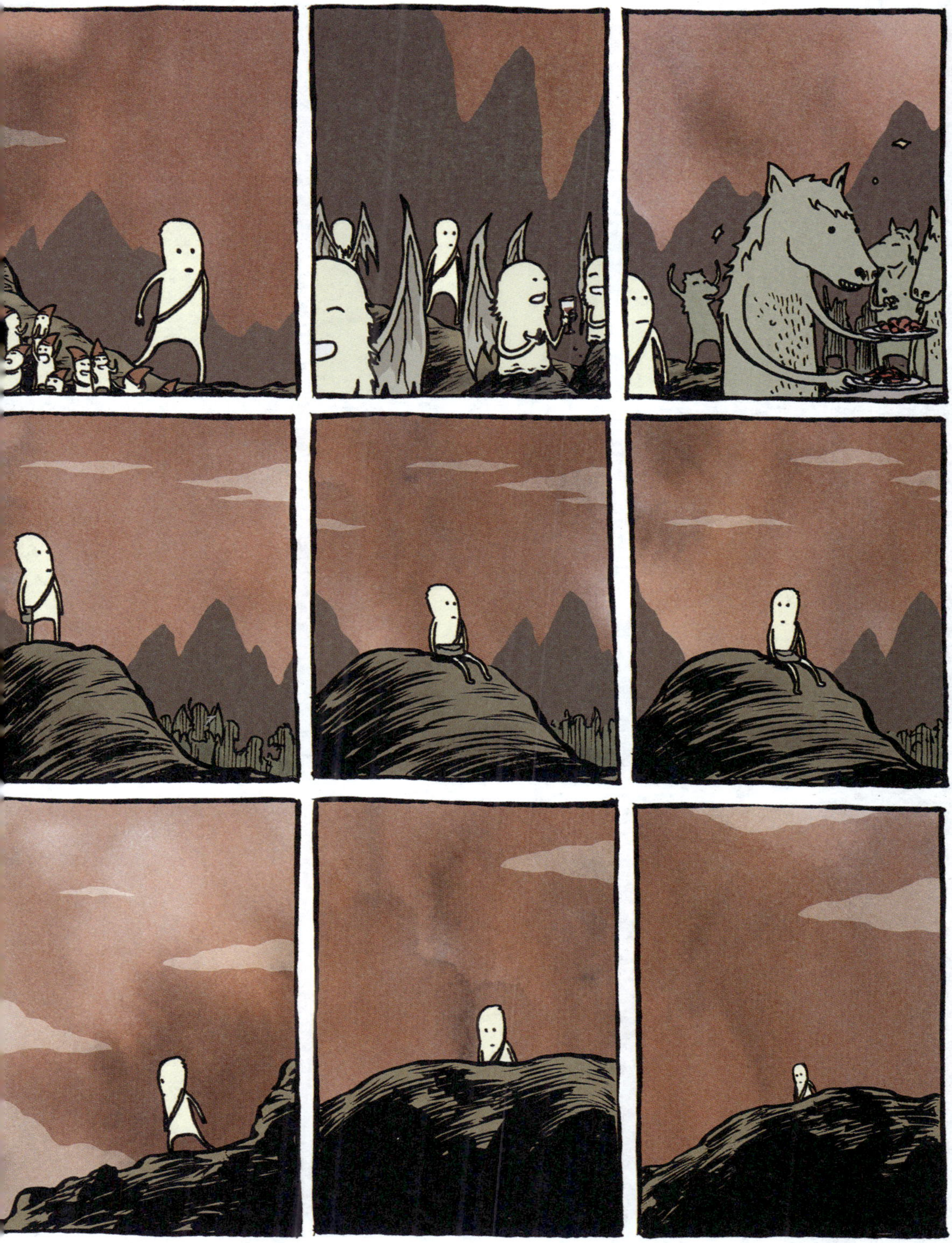

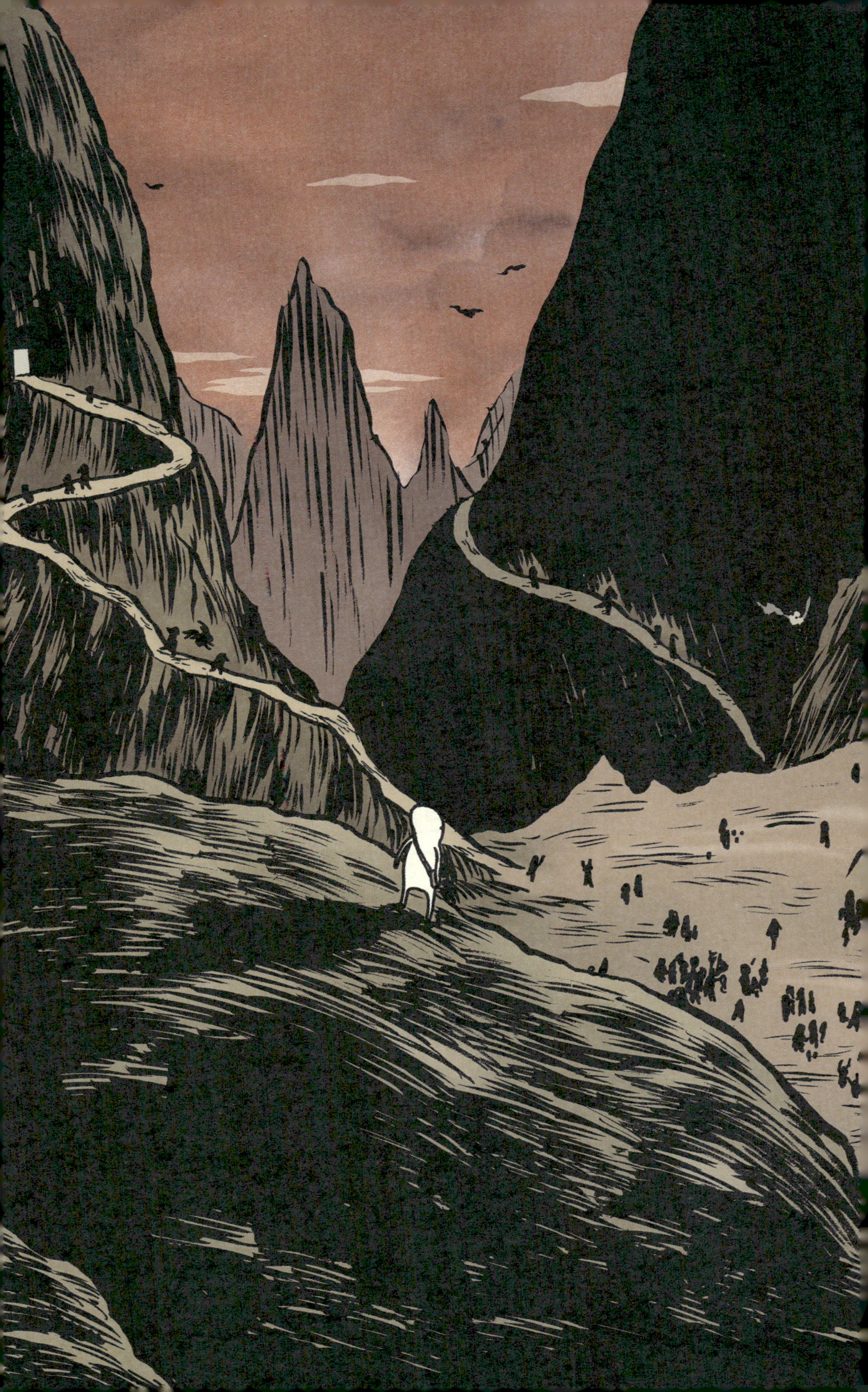

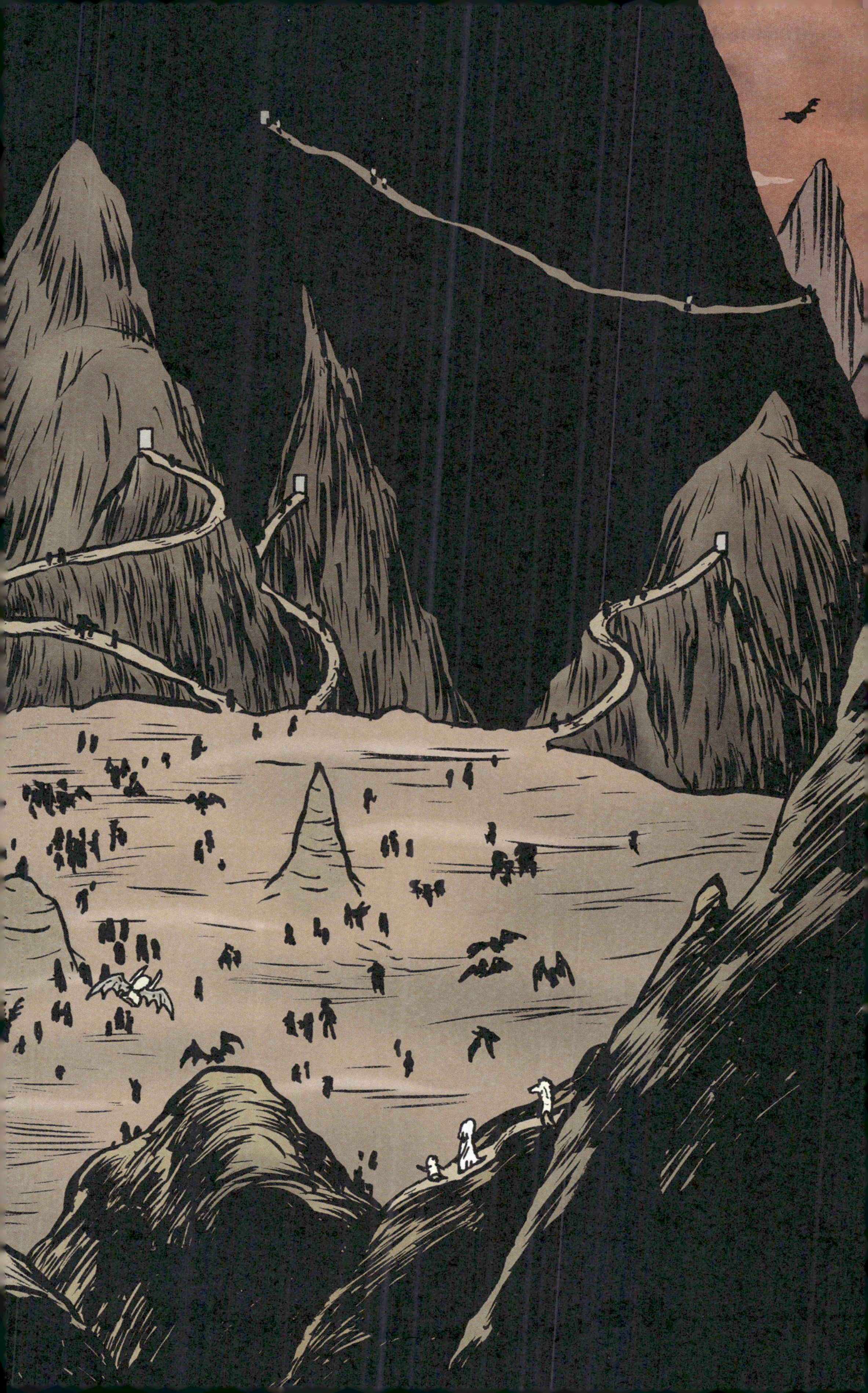

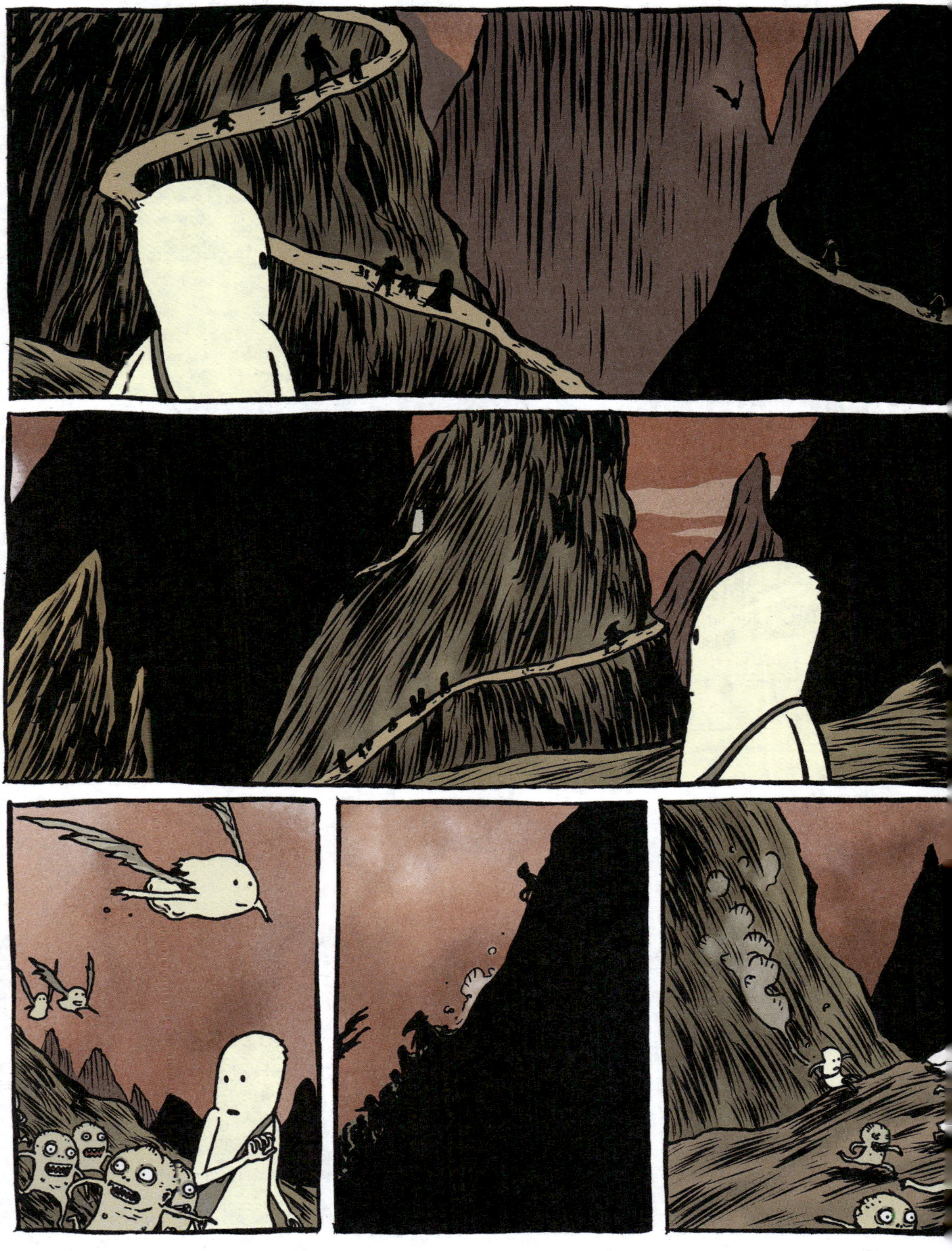

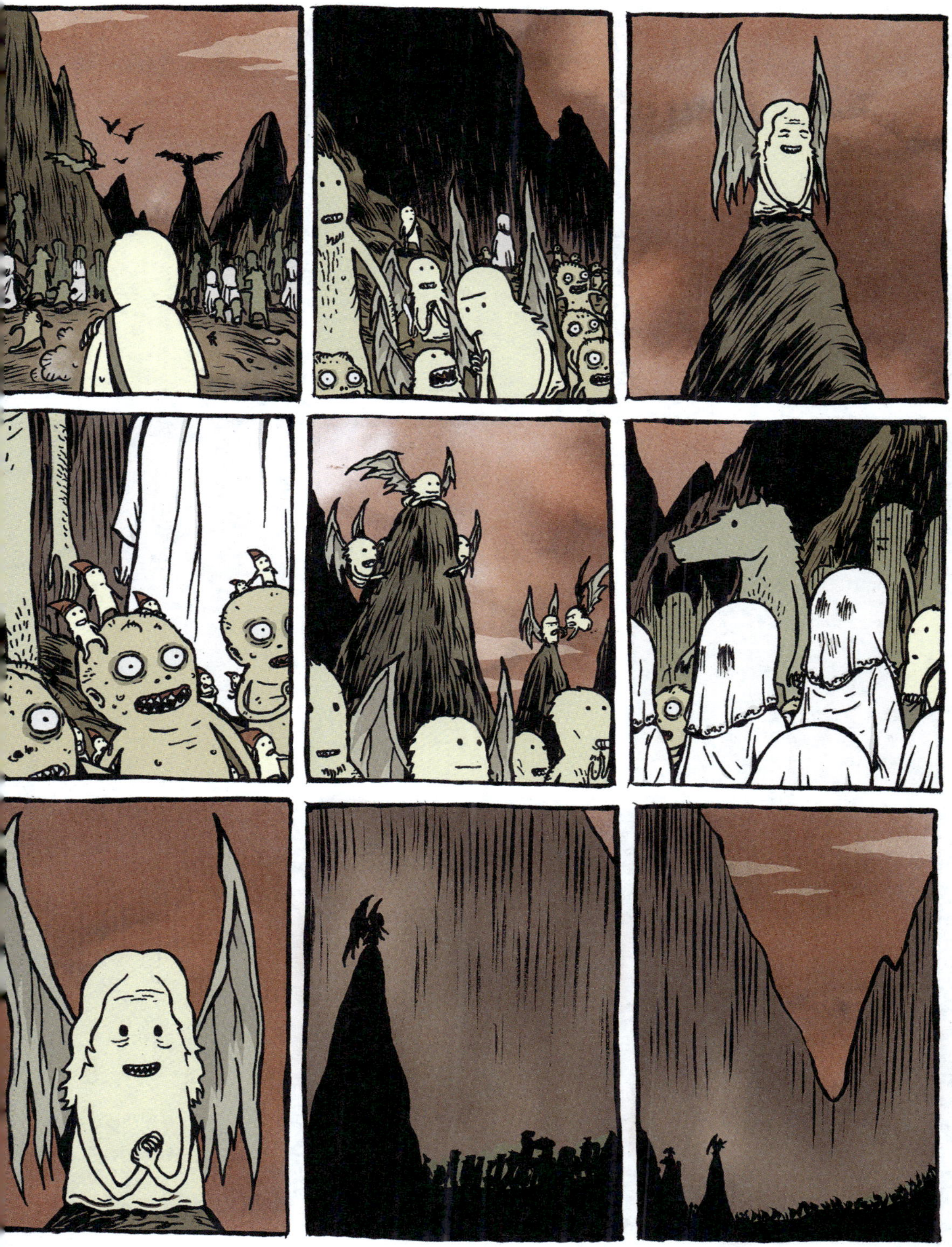

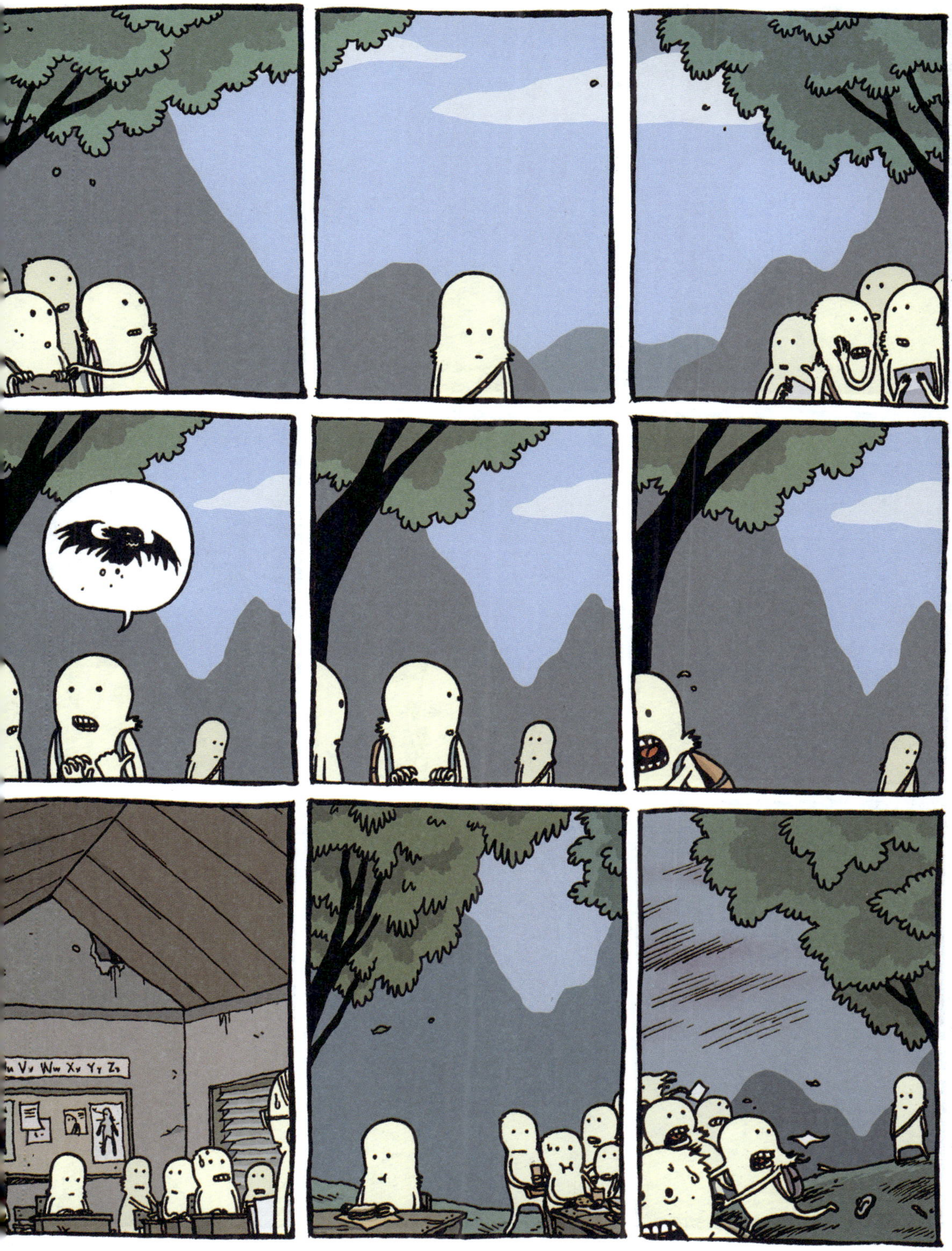
Vv Ww Xx Yy Zz

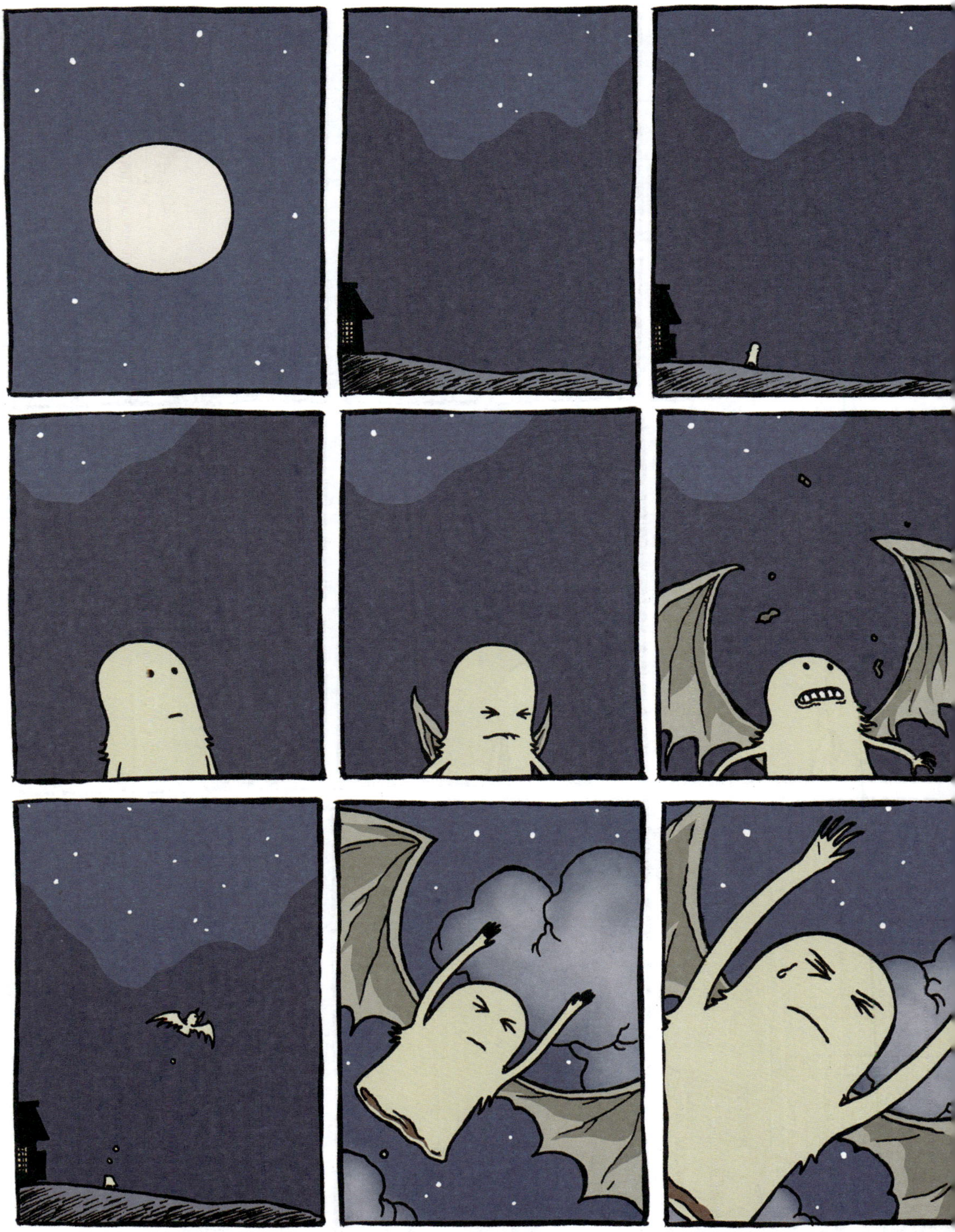

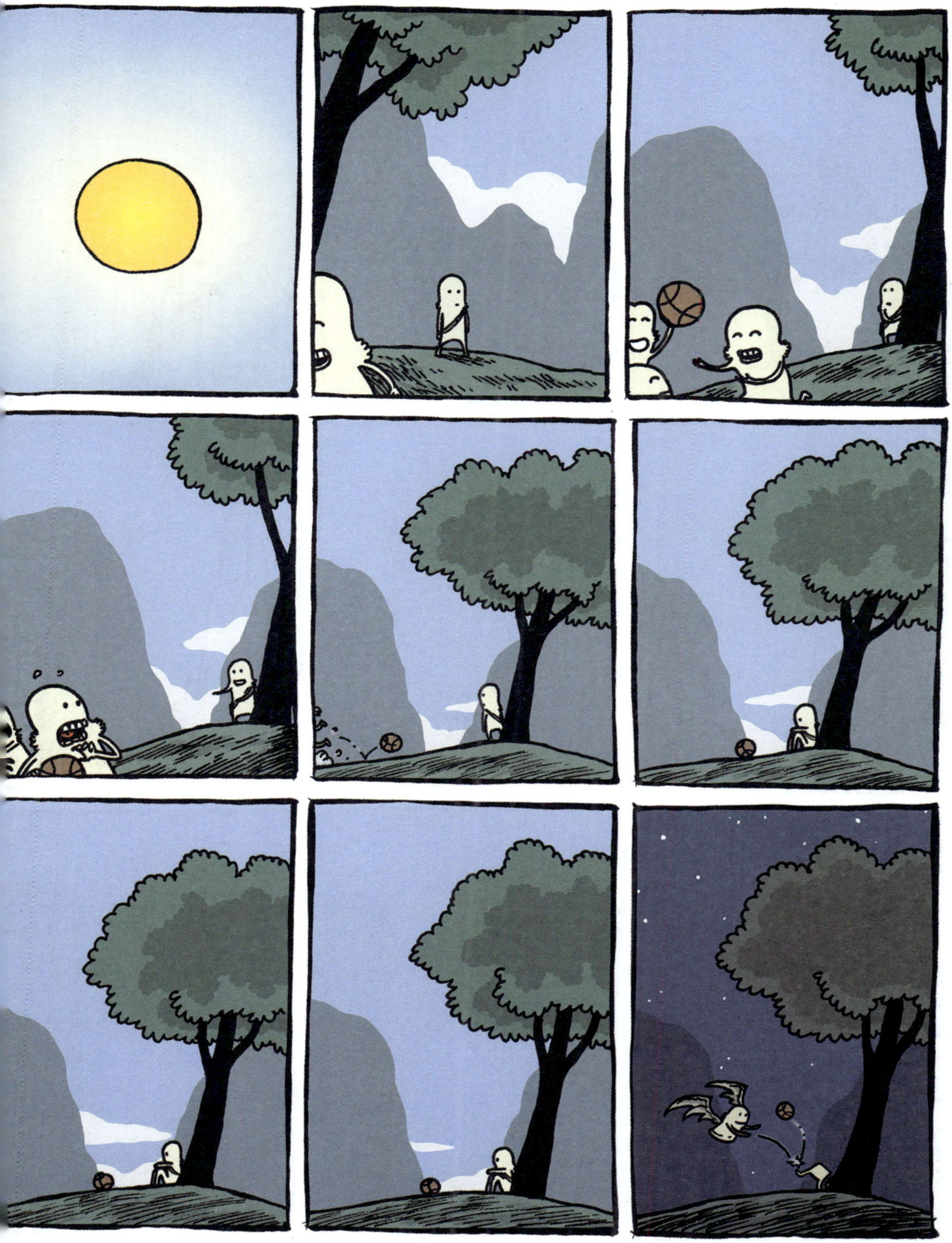

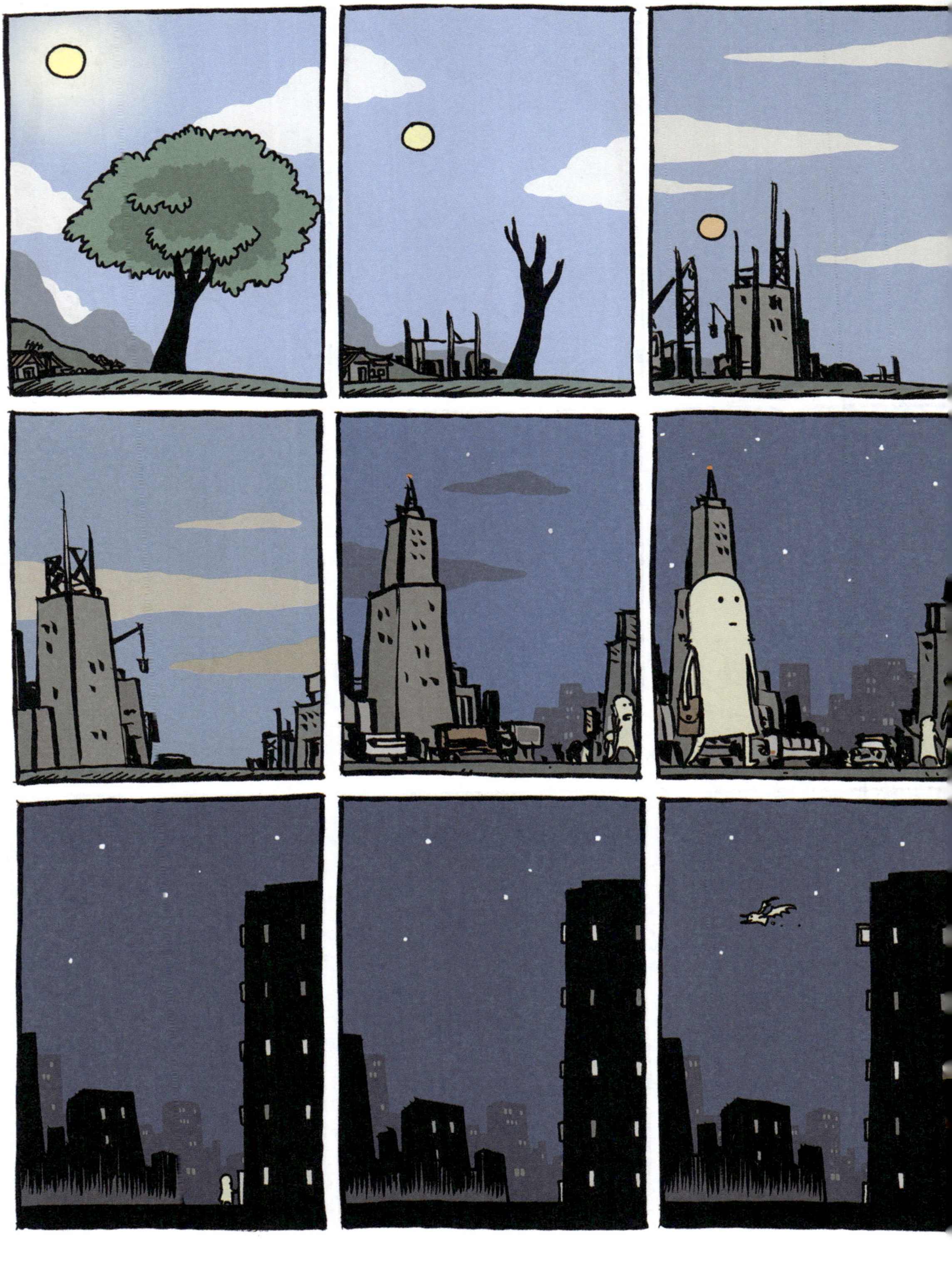

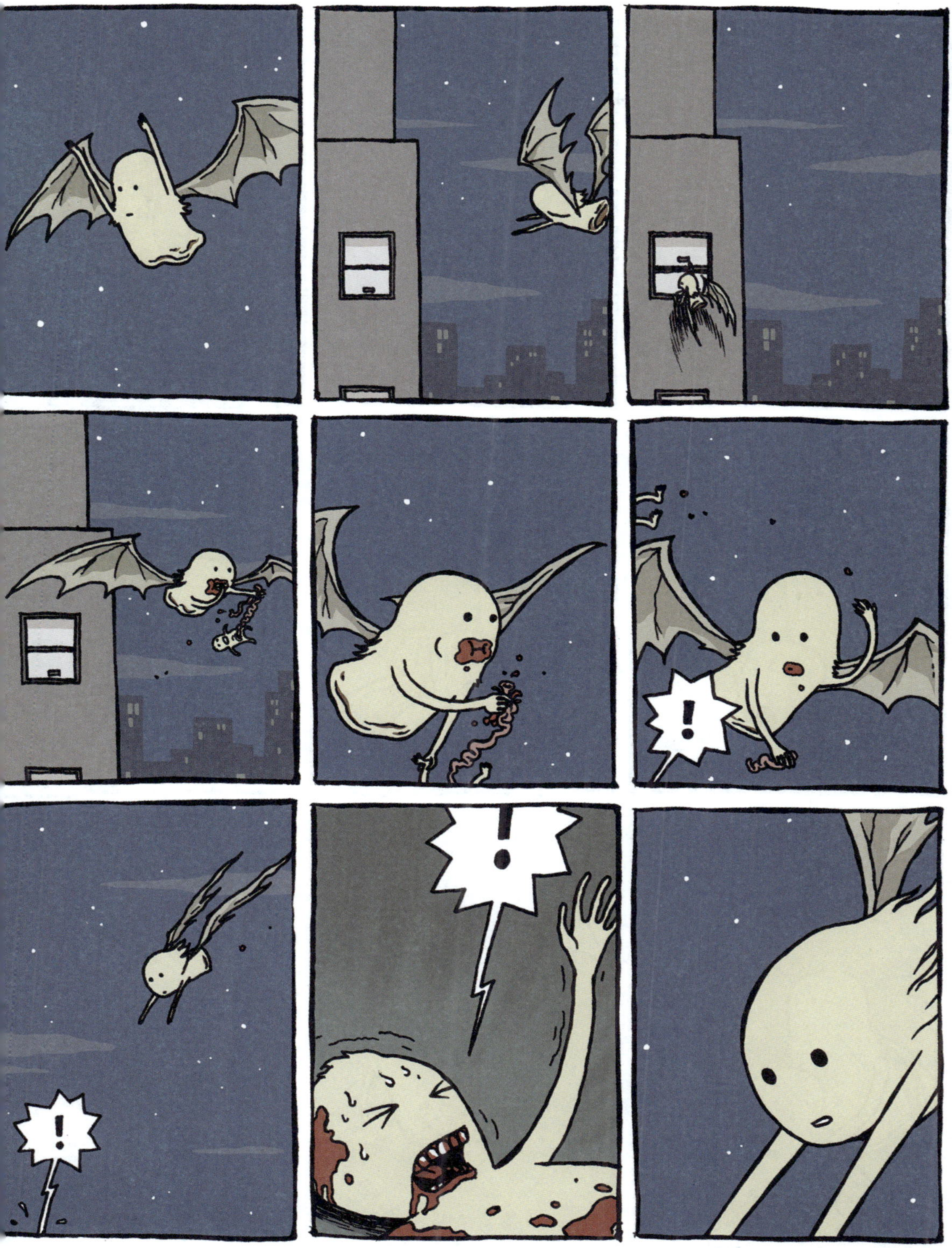
!
!
!

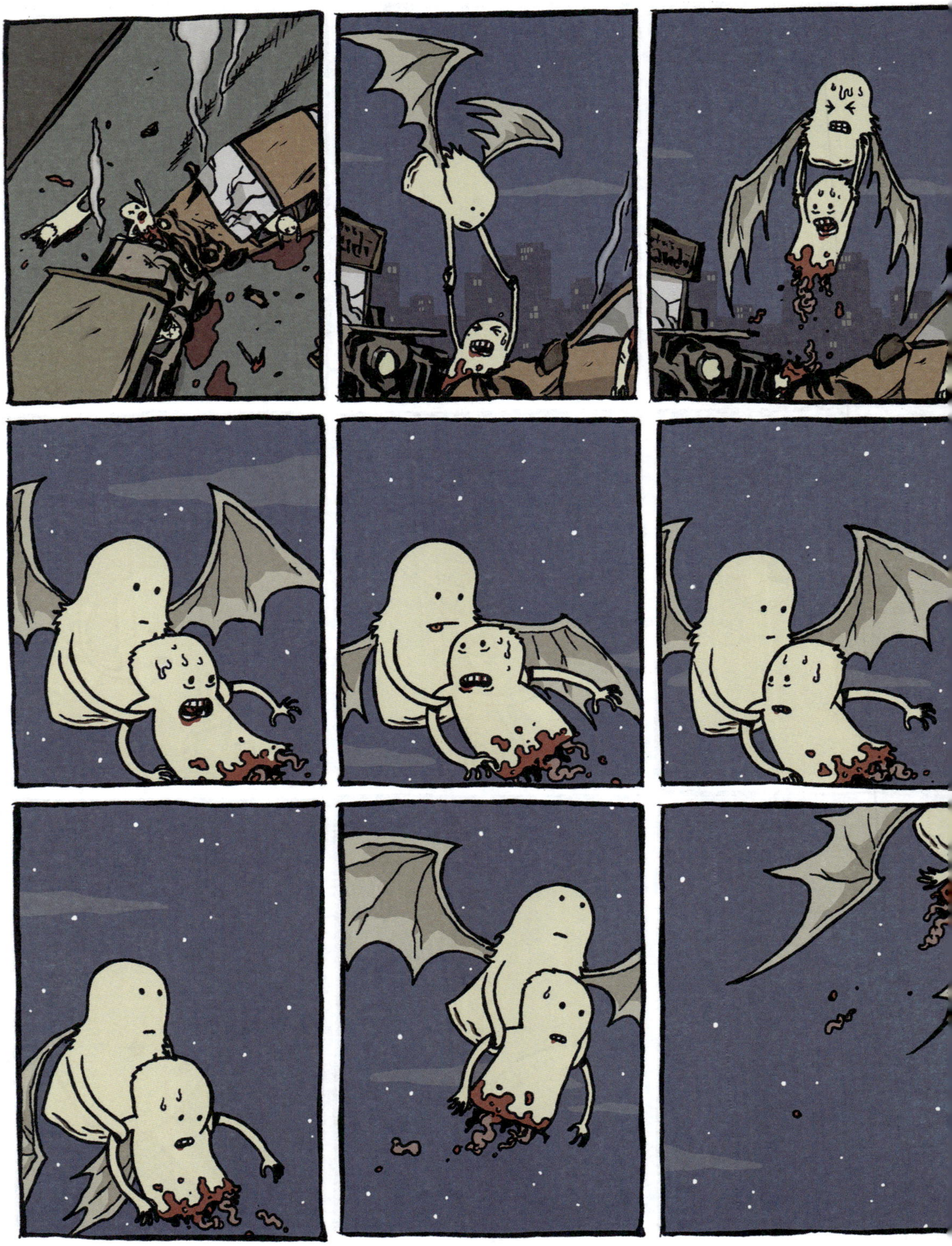

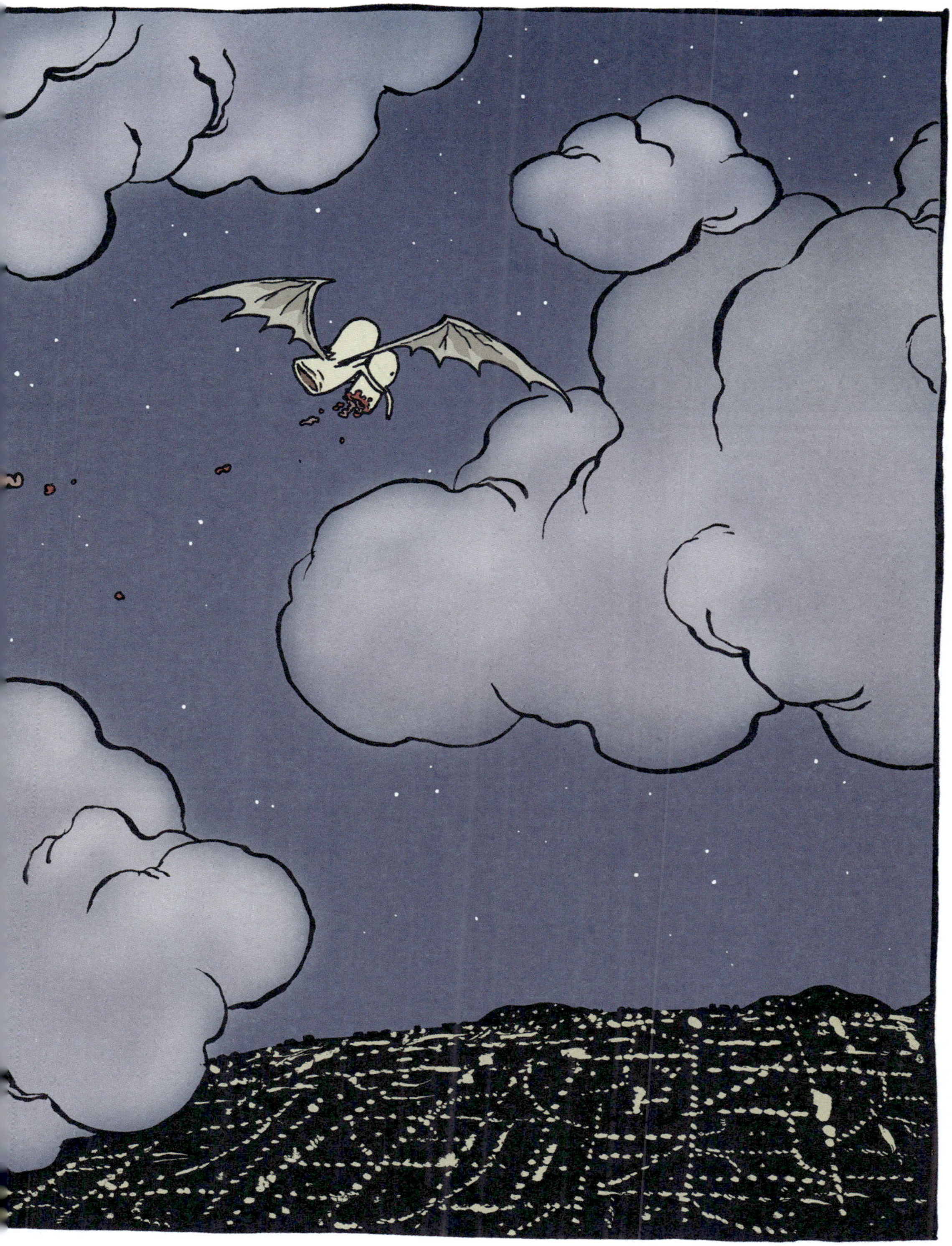

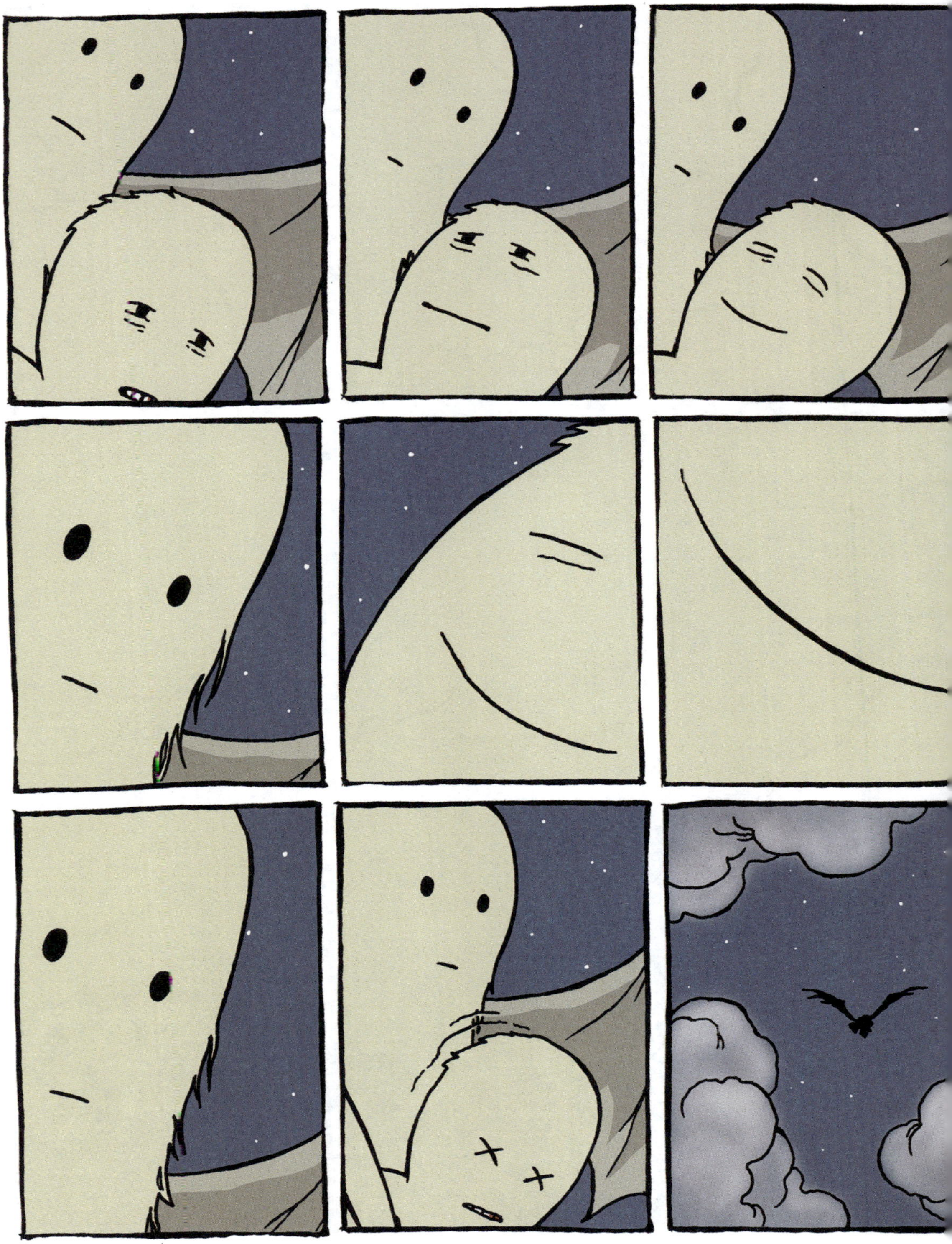

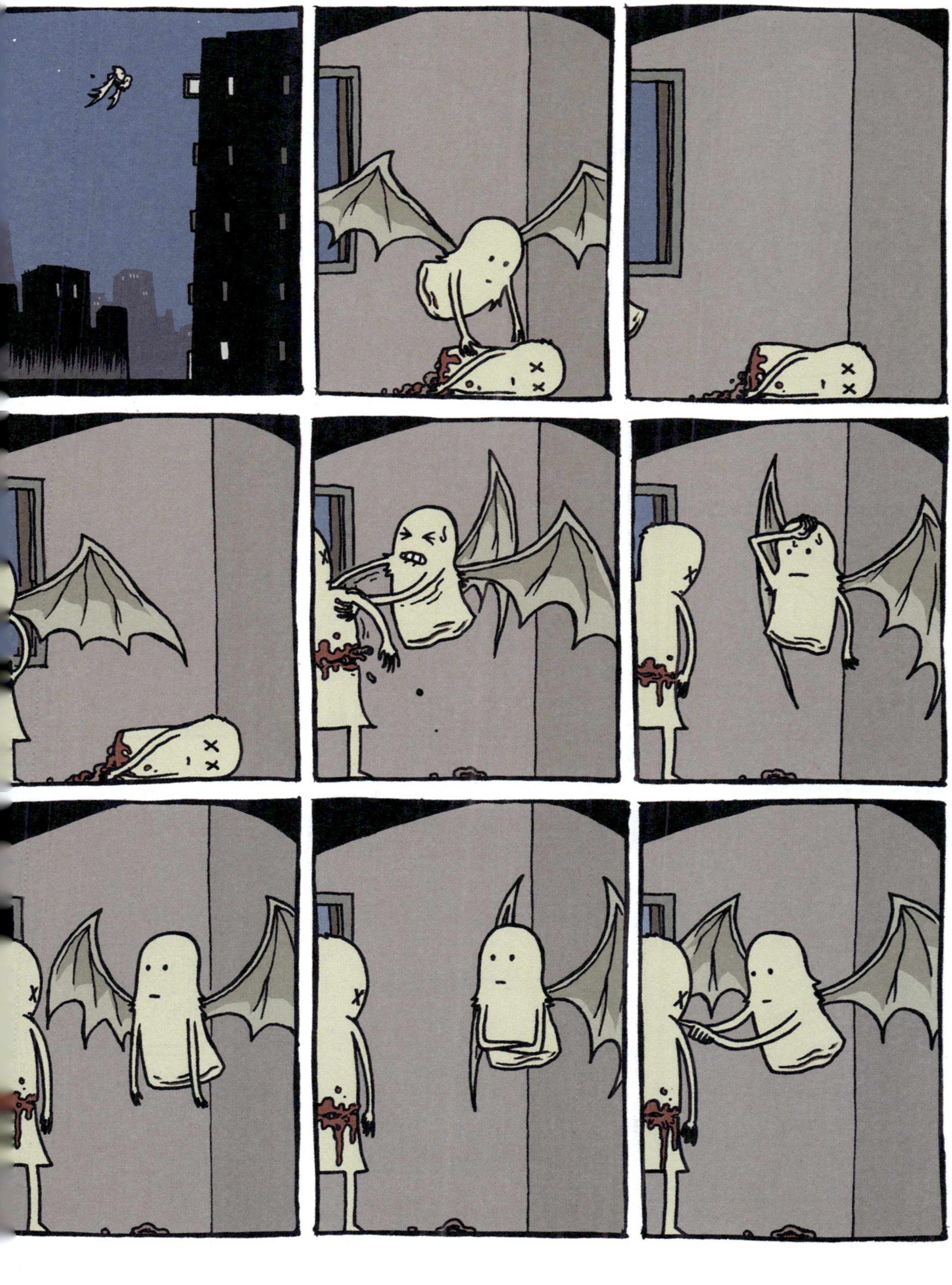

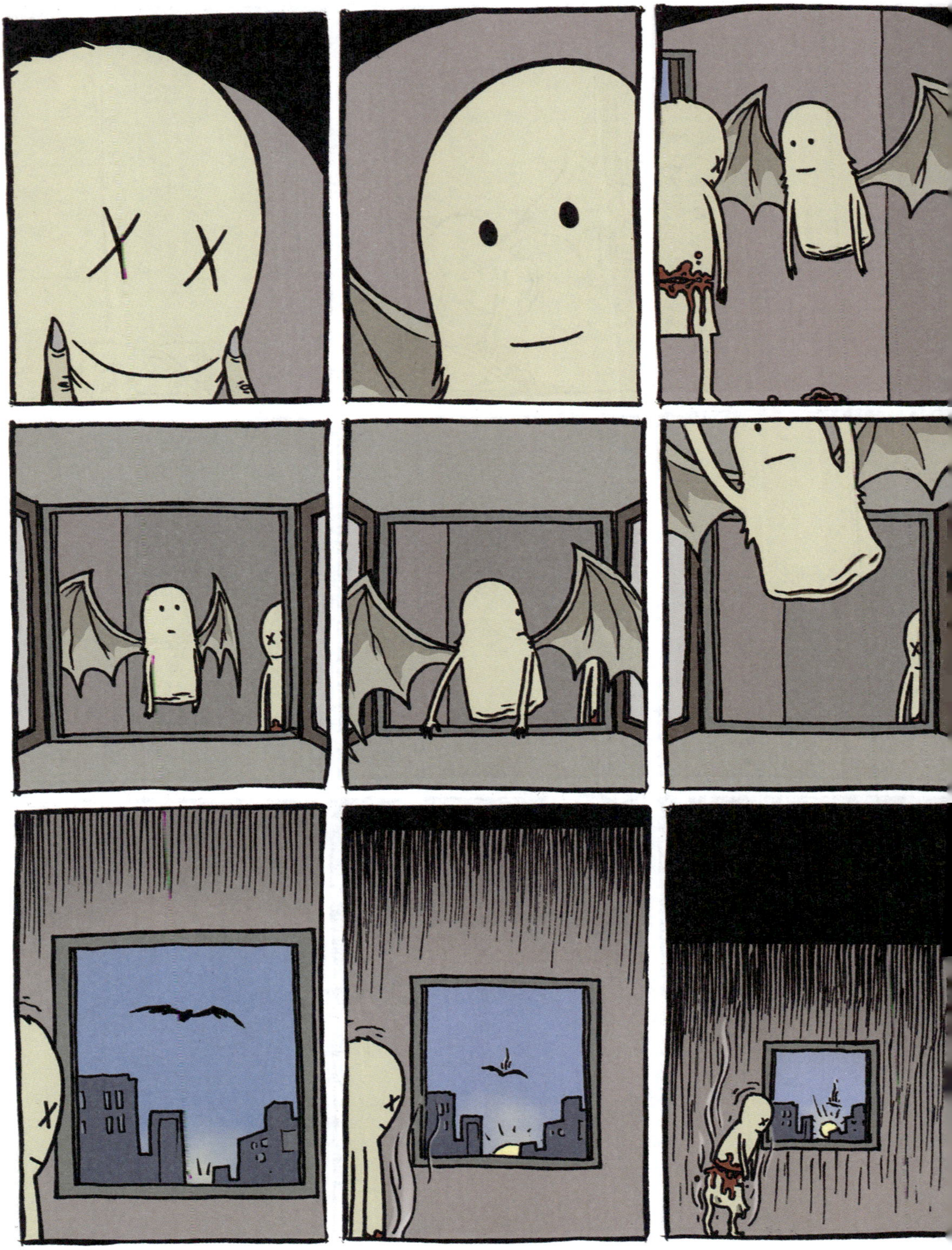

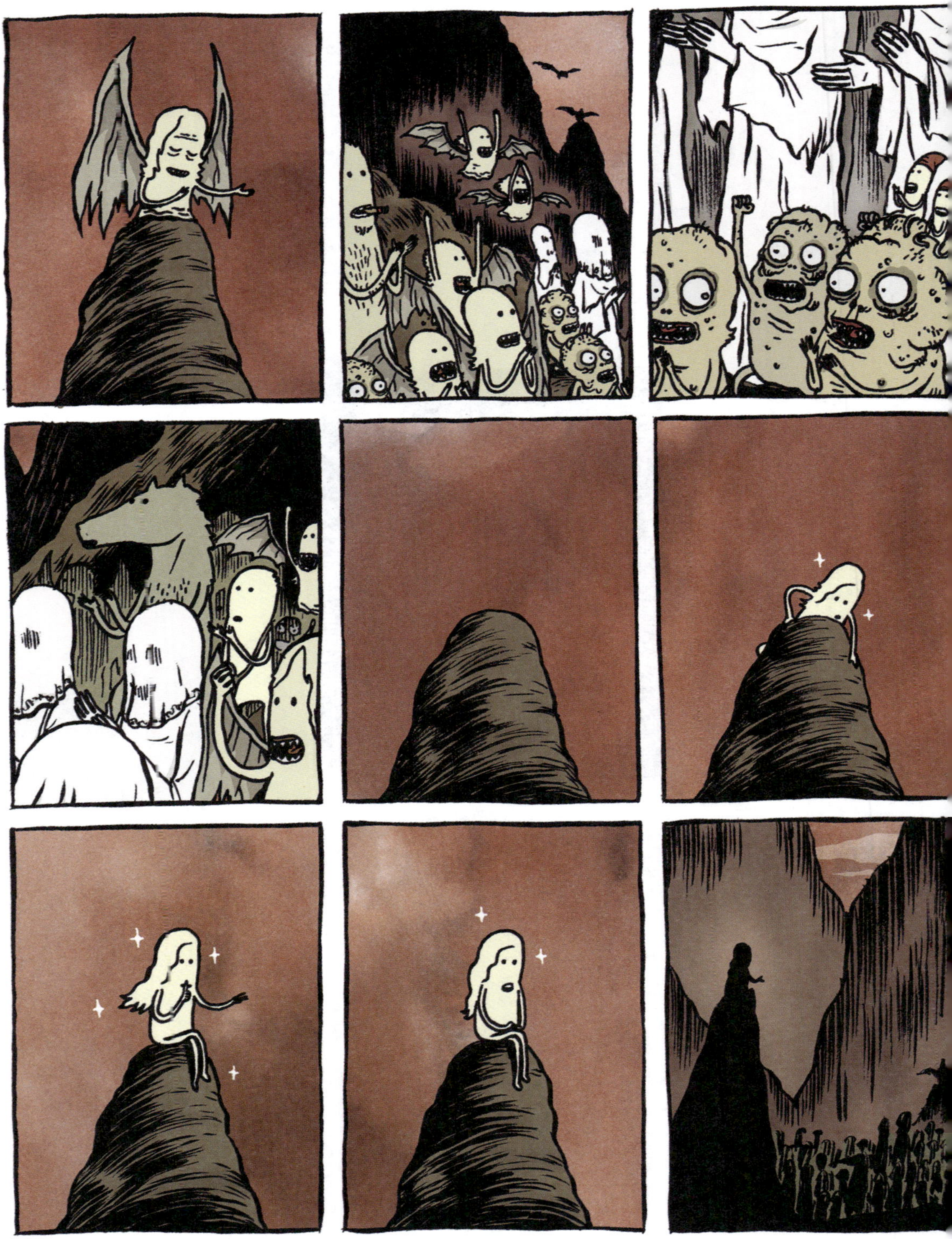

I

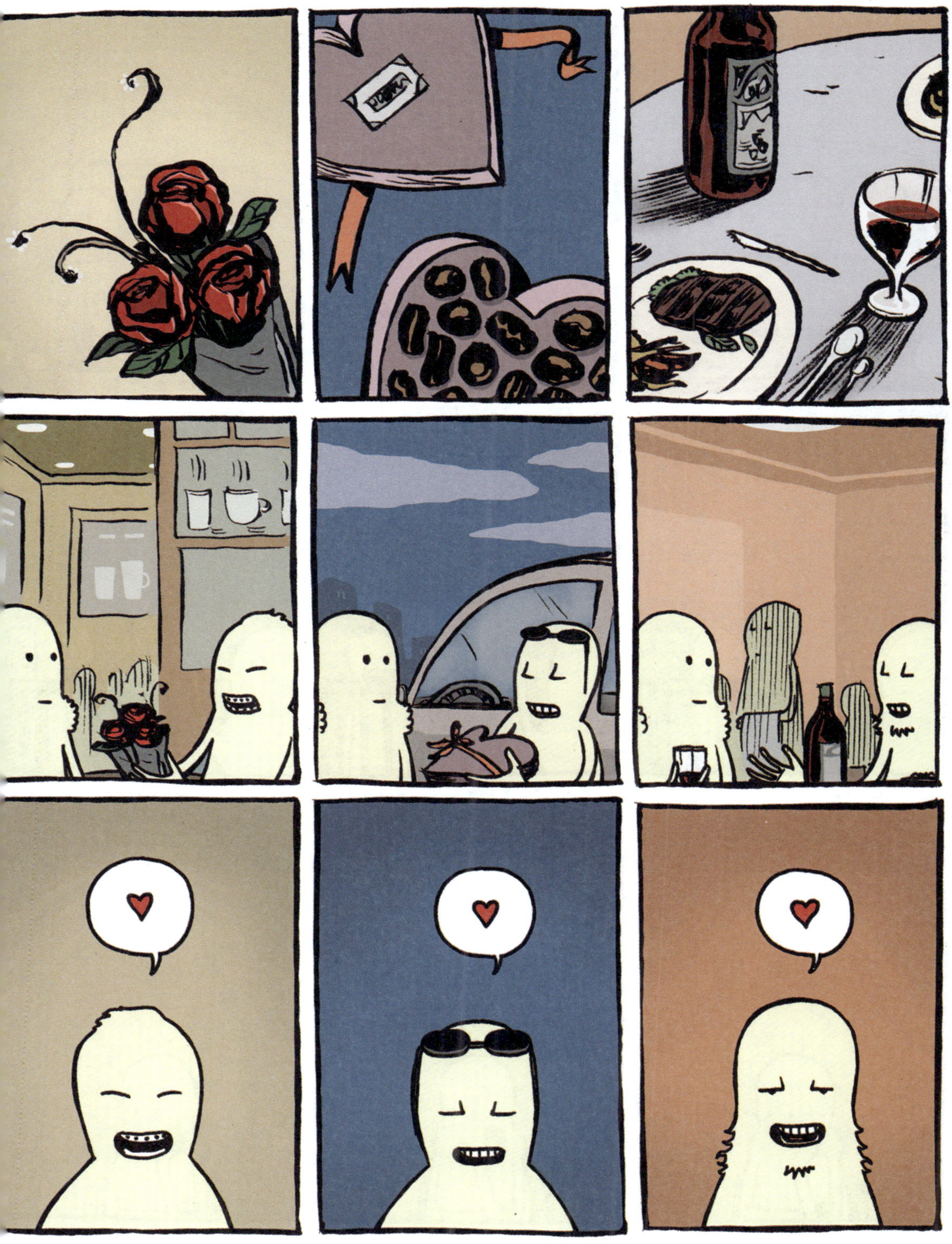

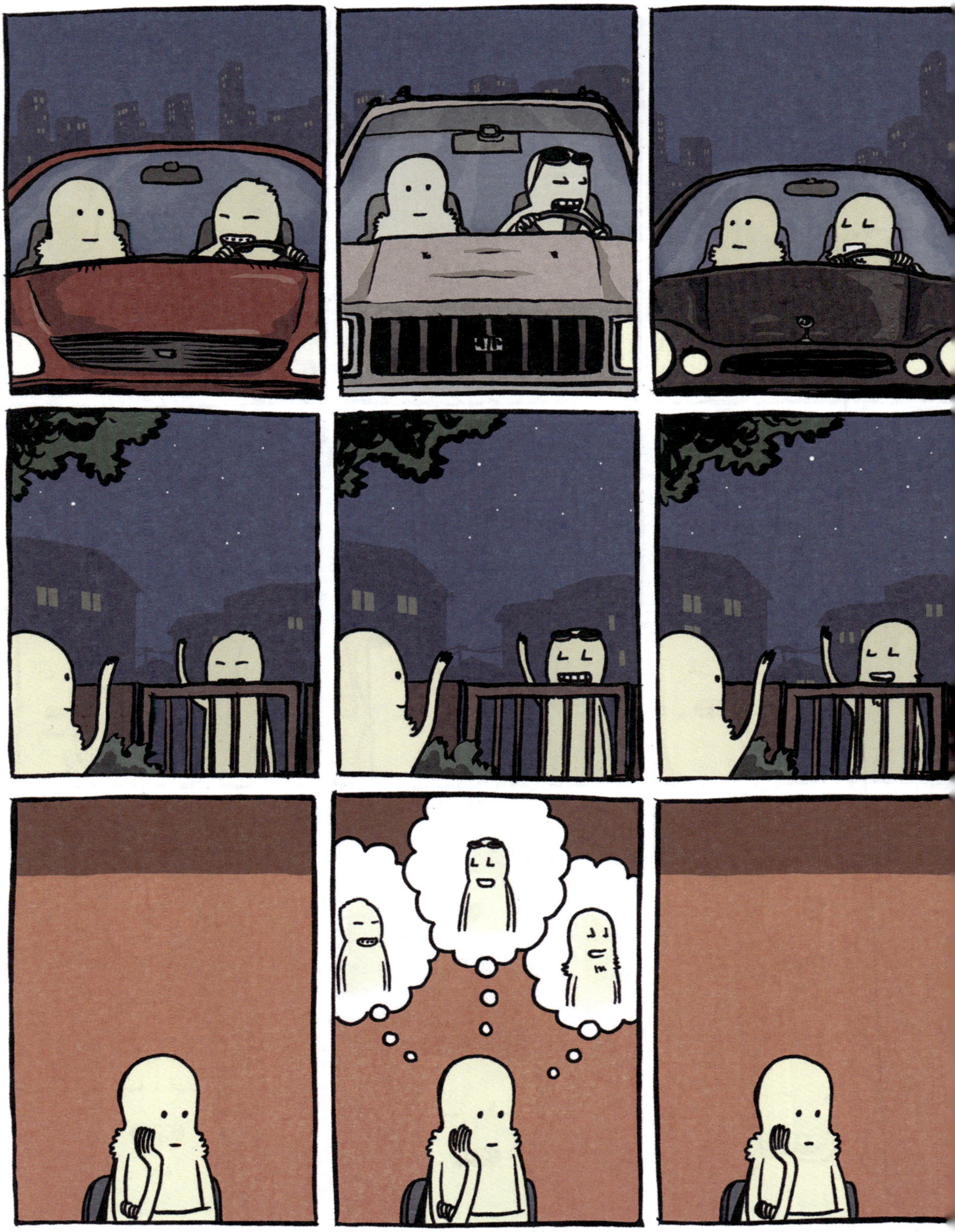

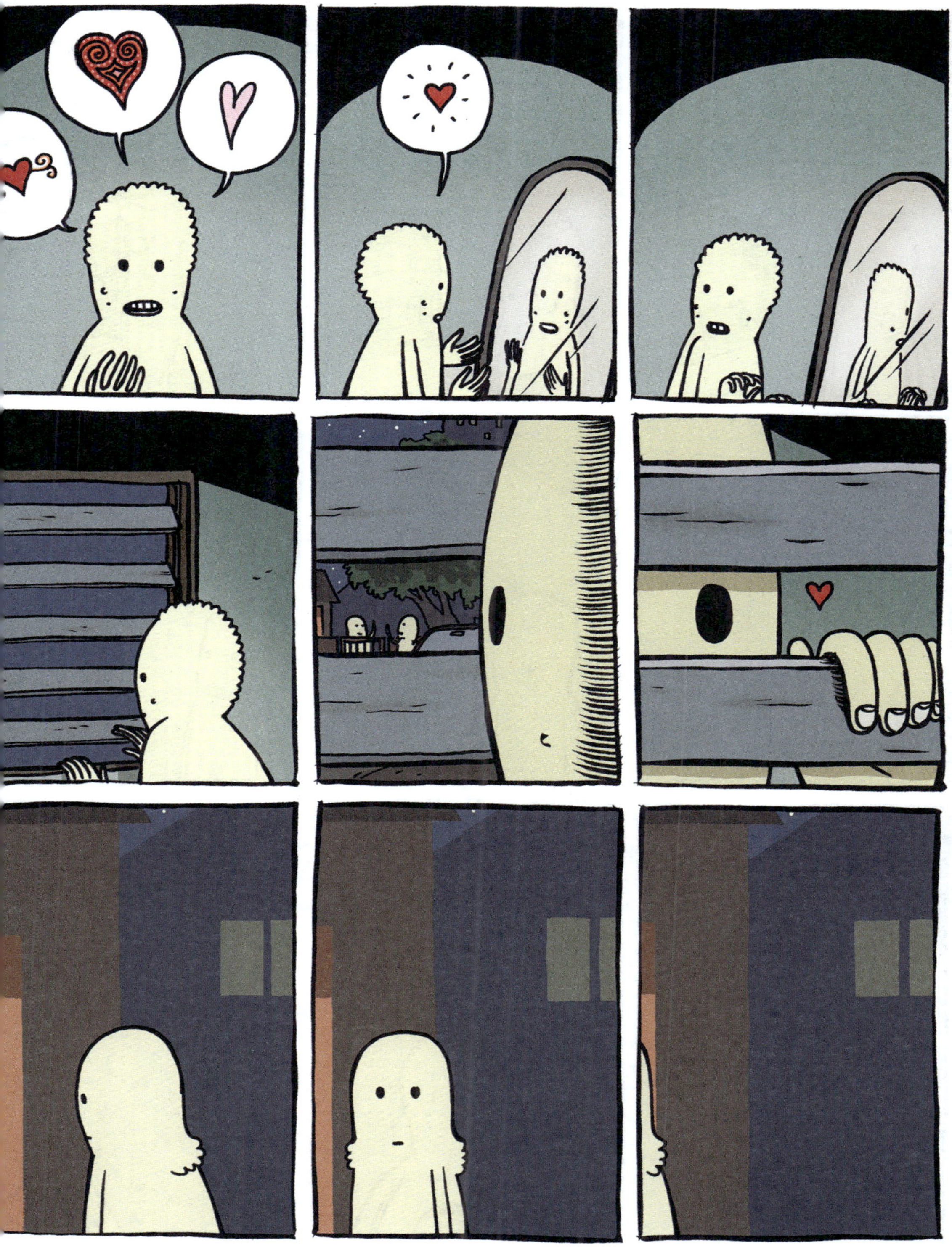

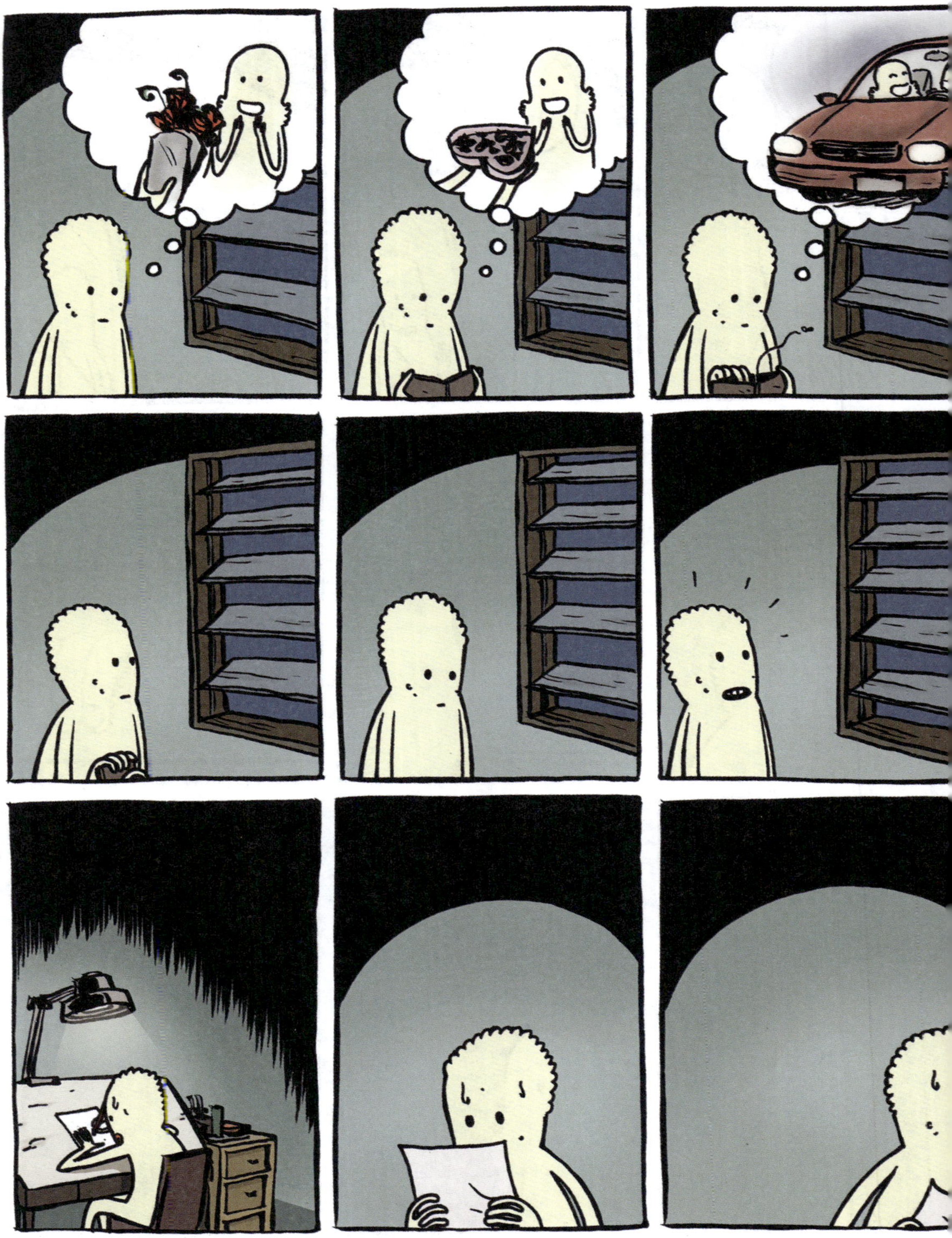

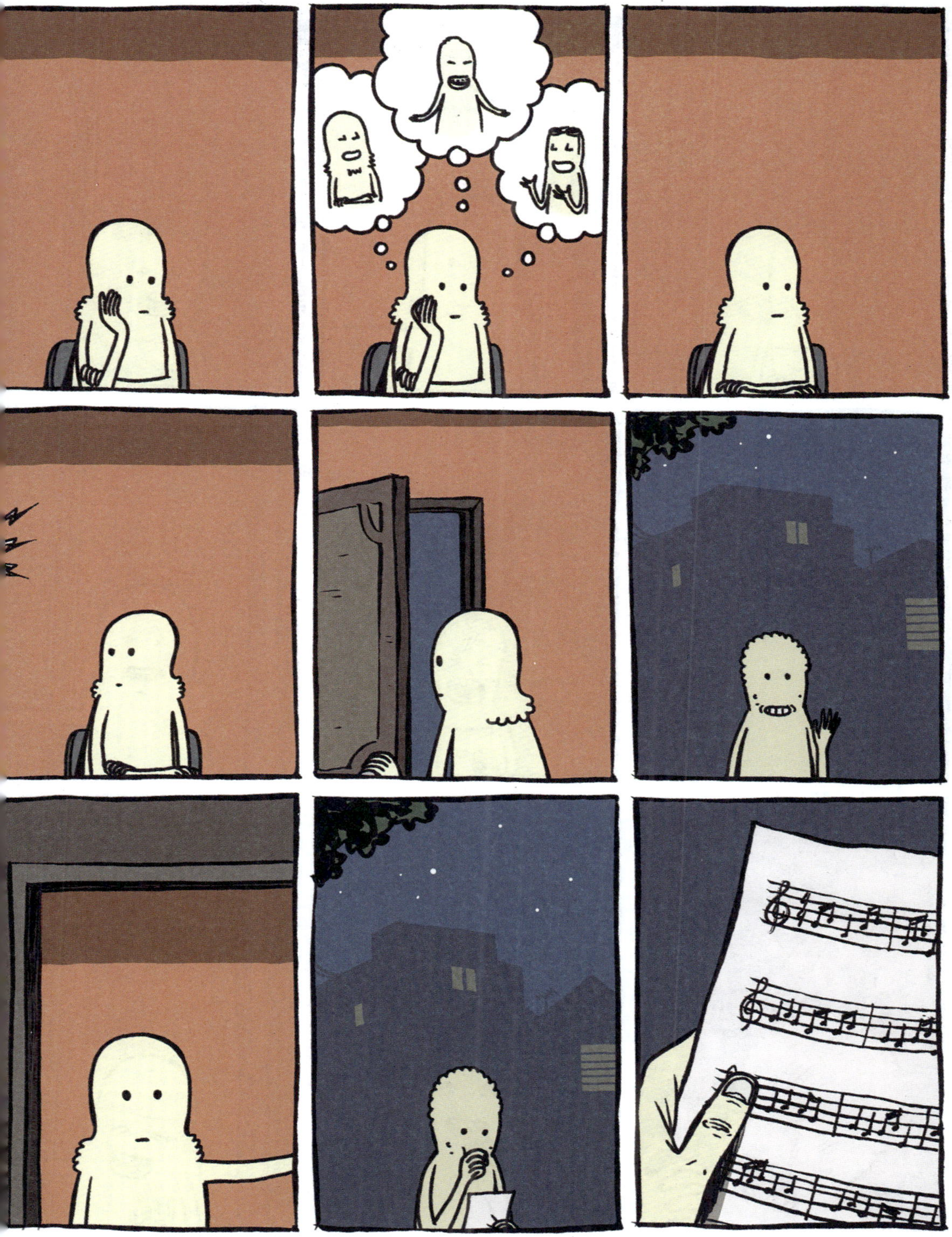

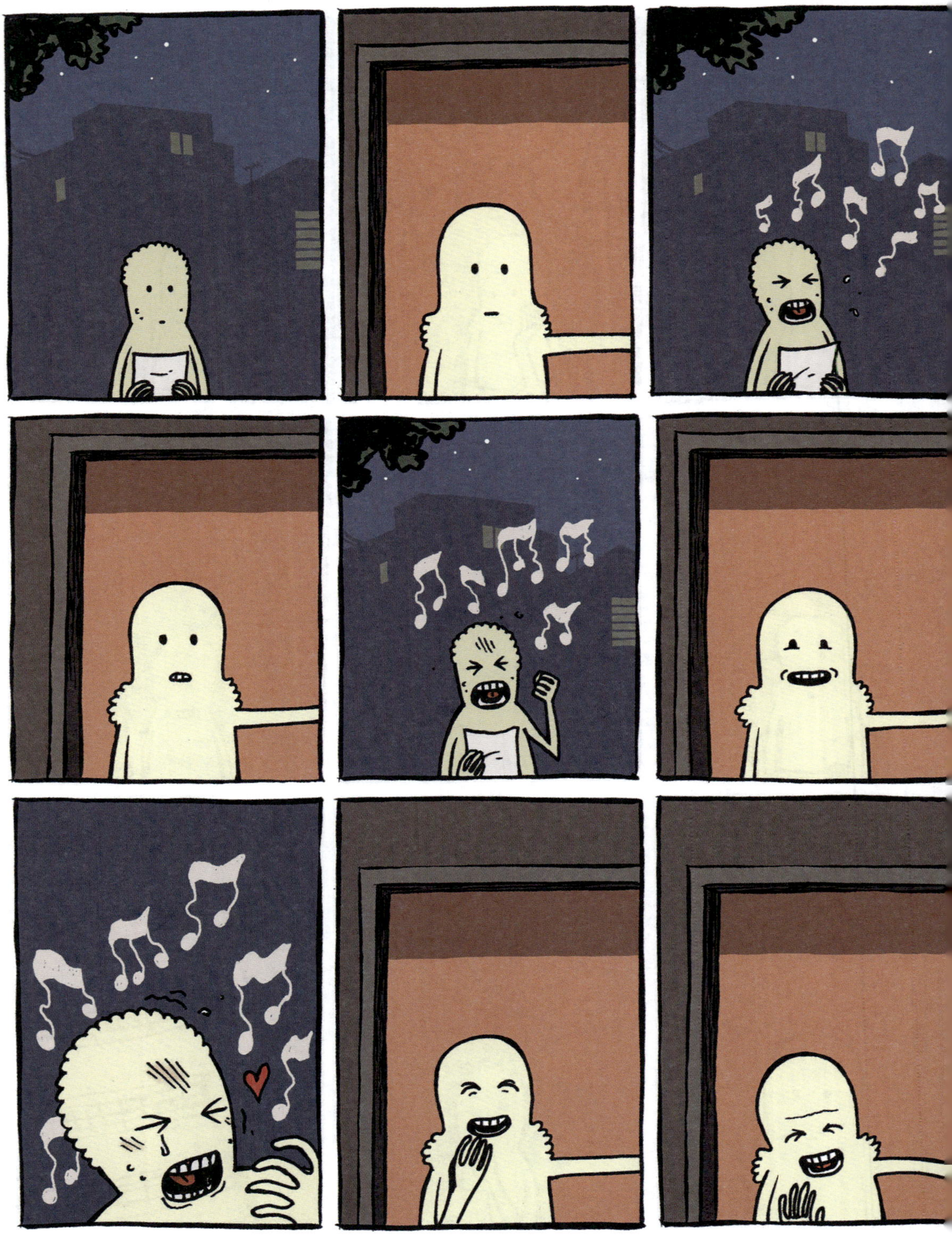

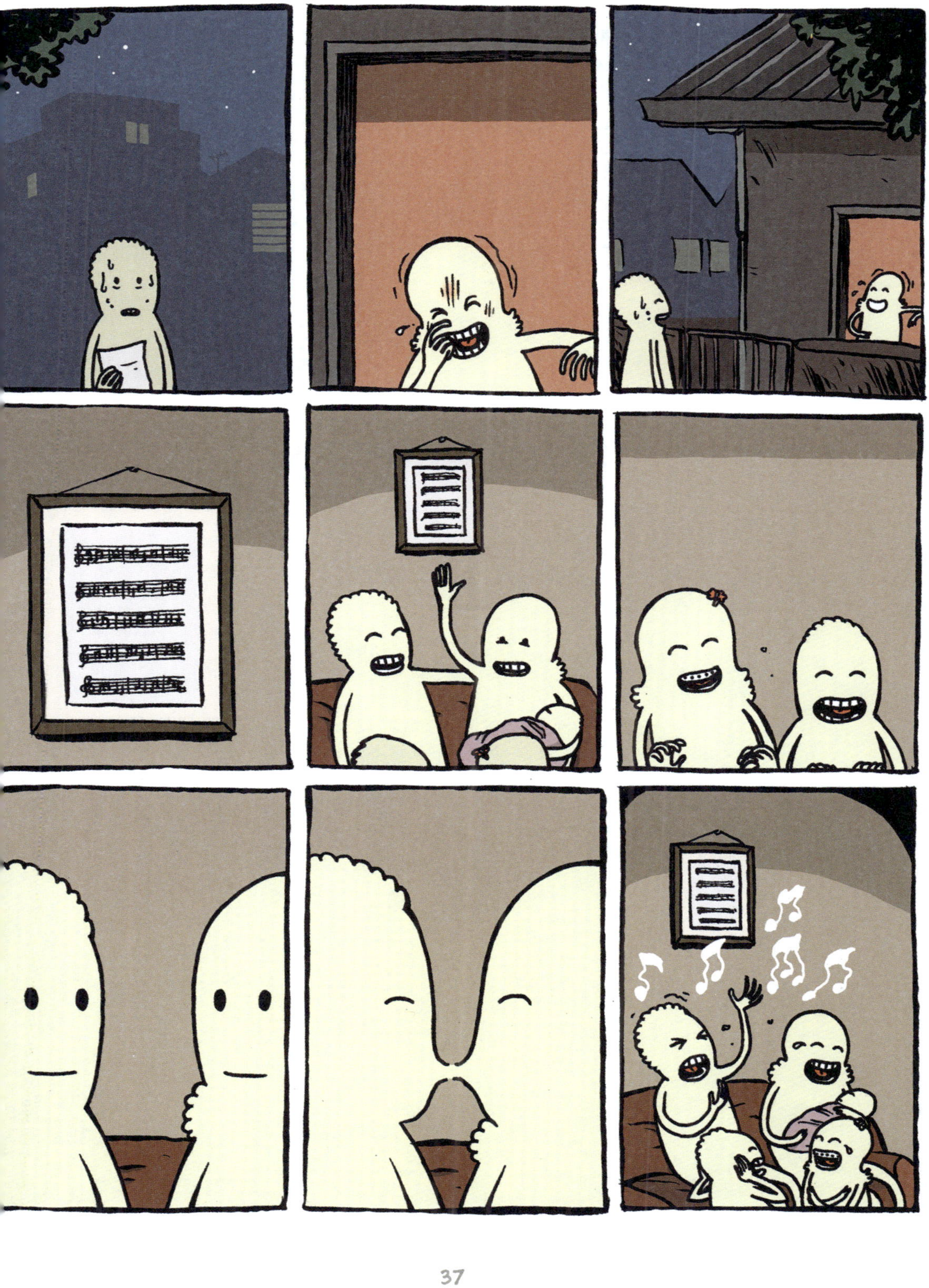

II

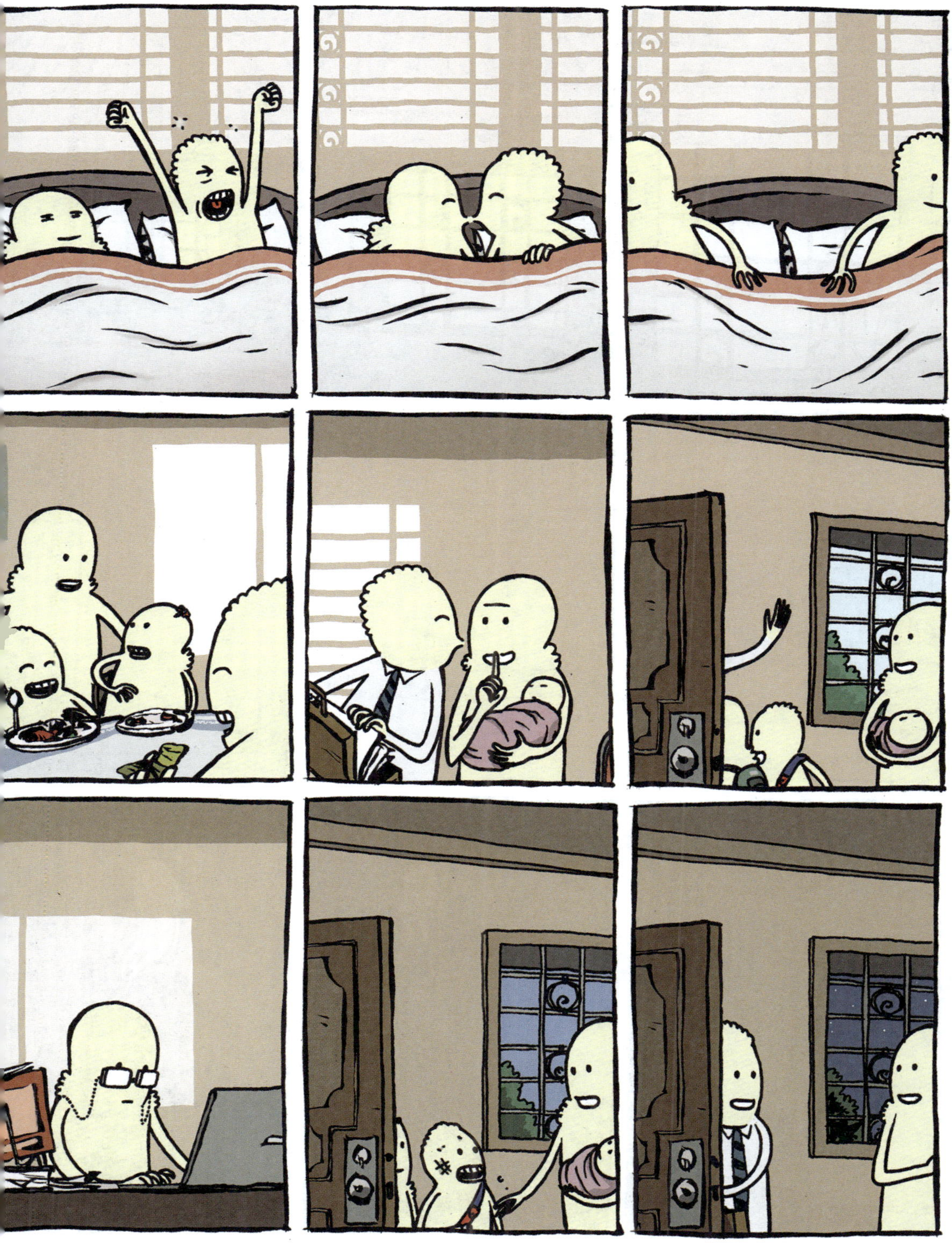

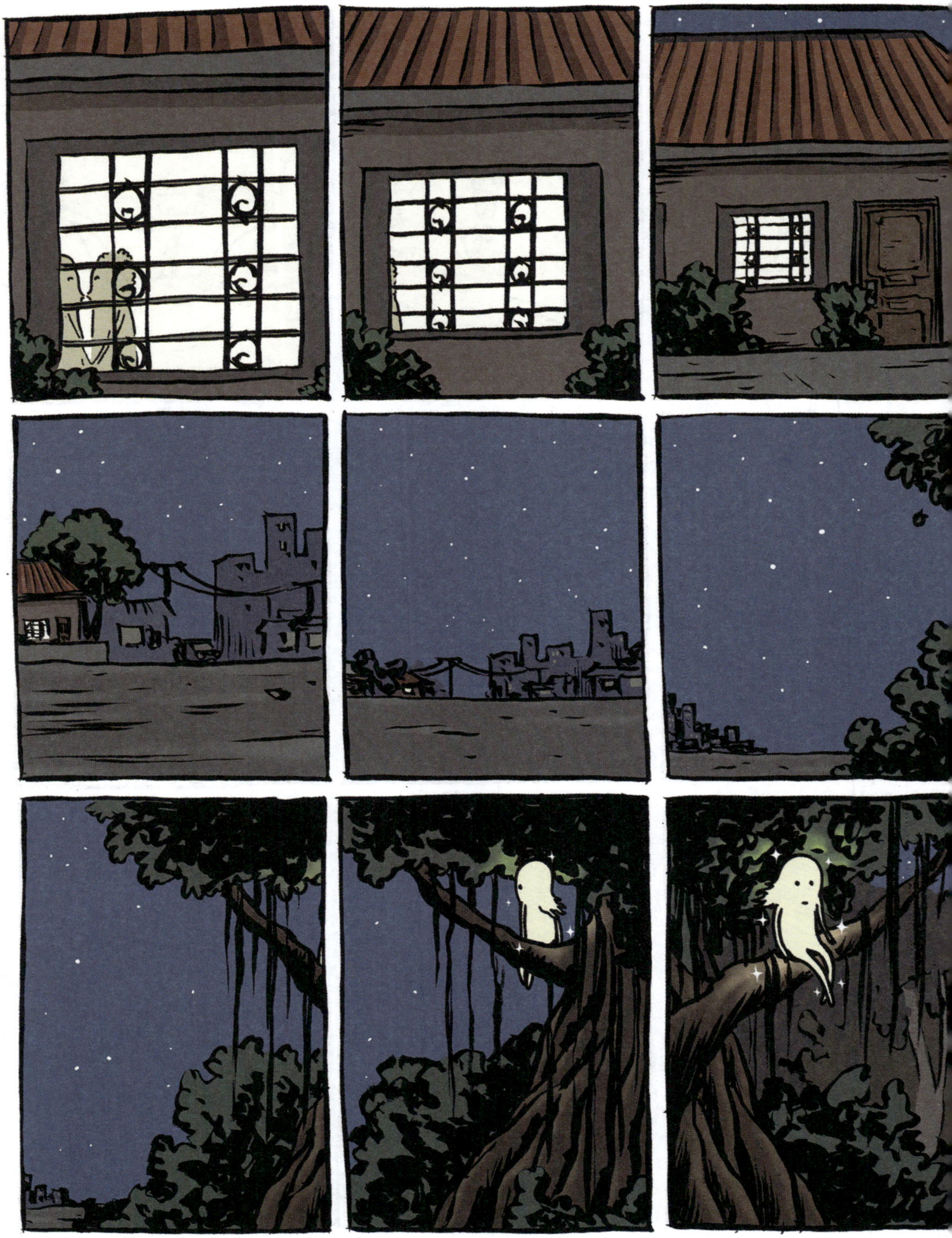

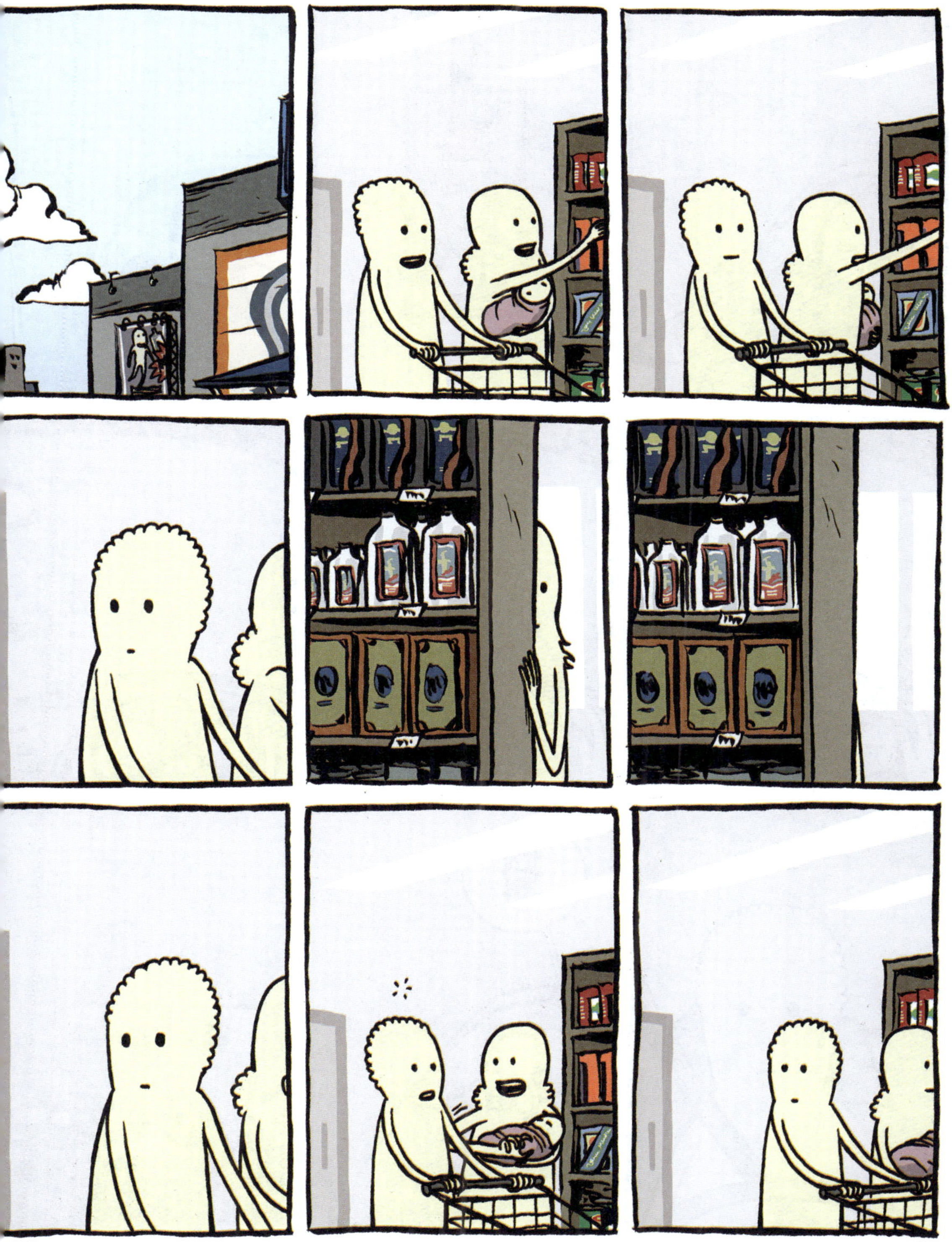

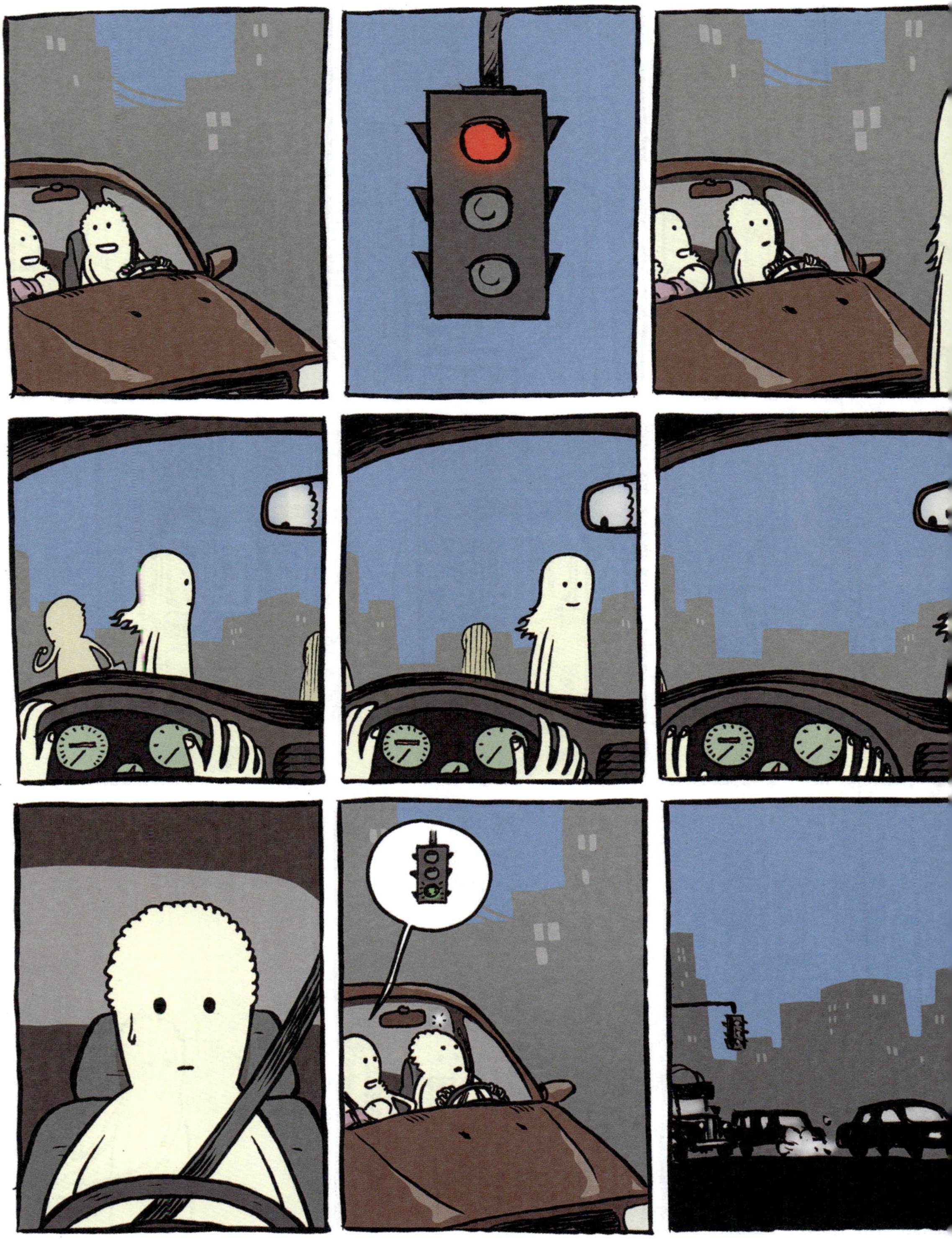

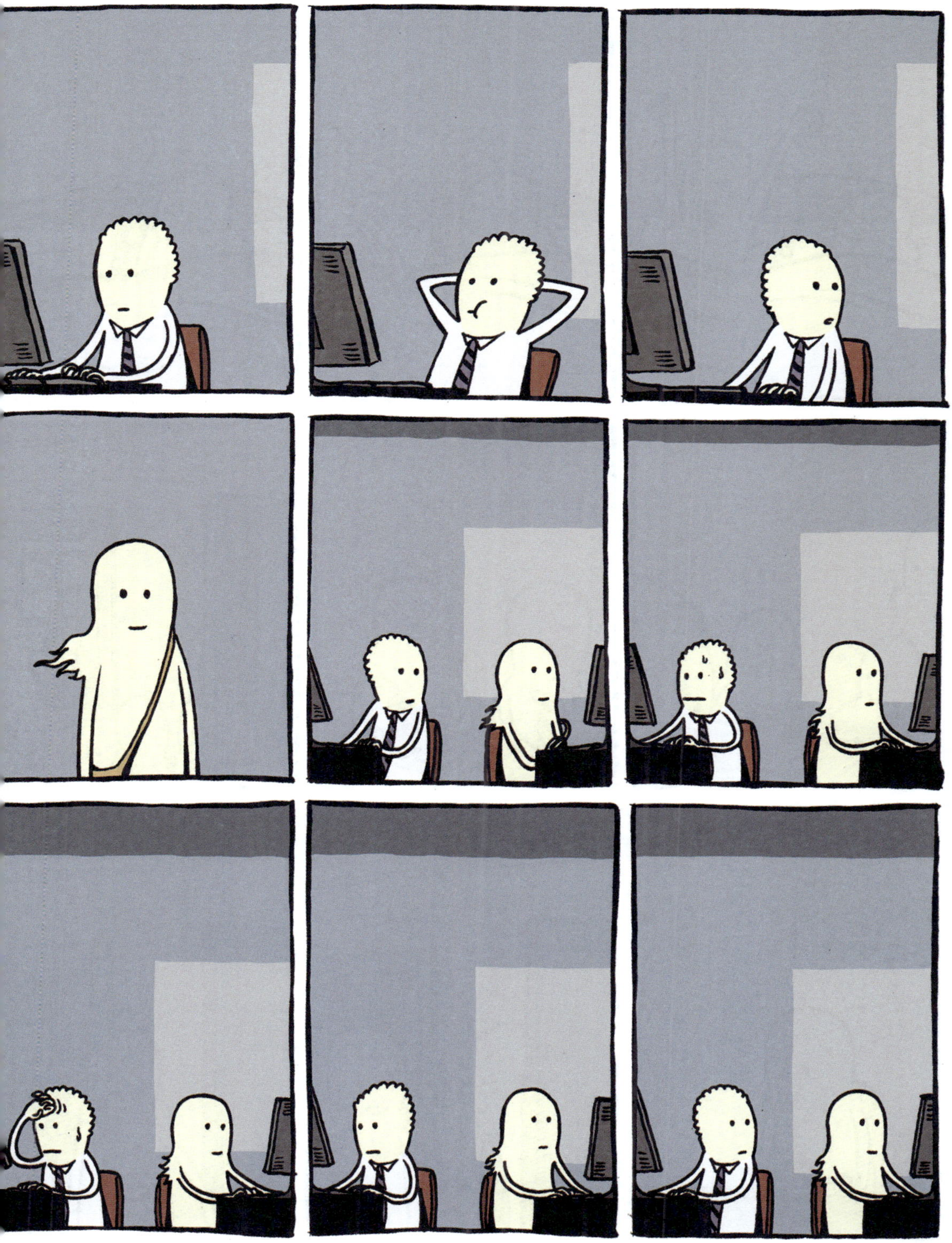

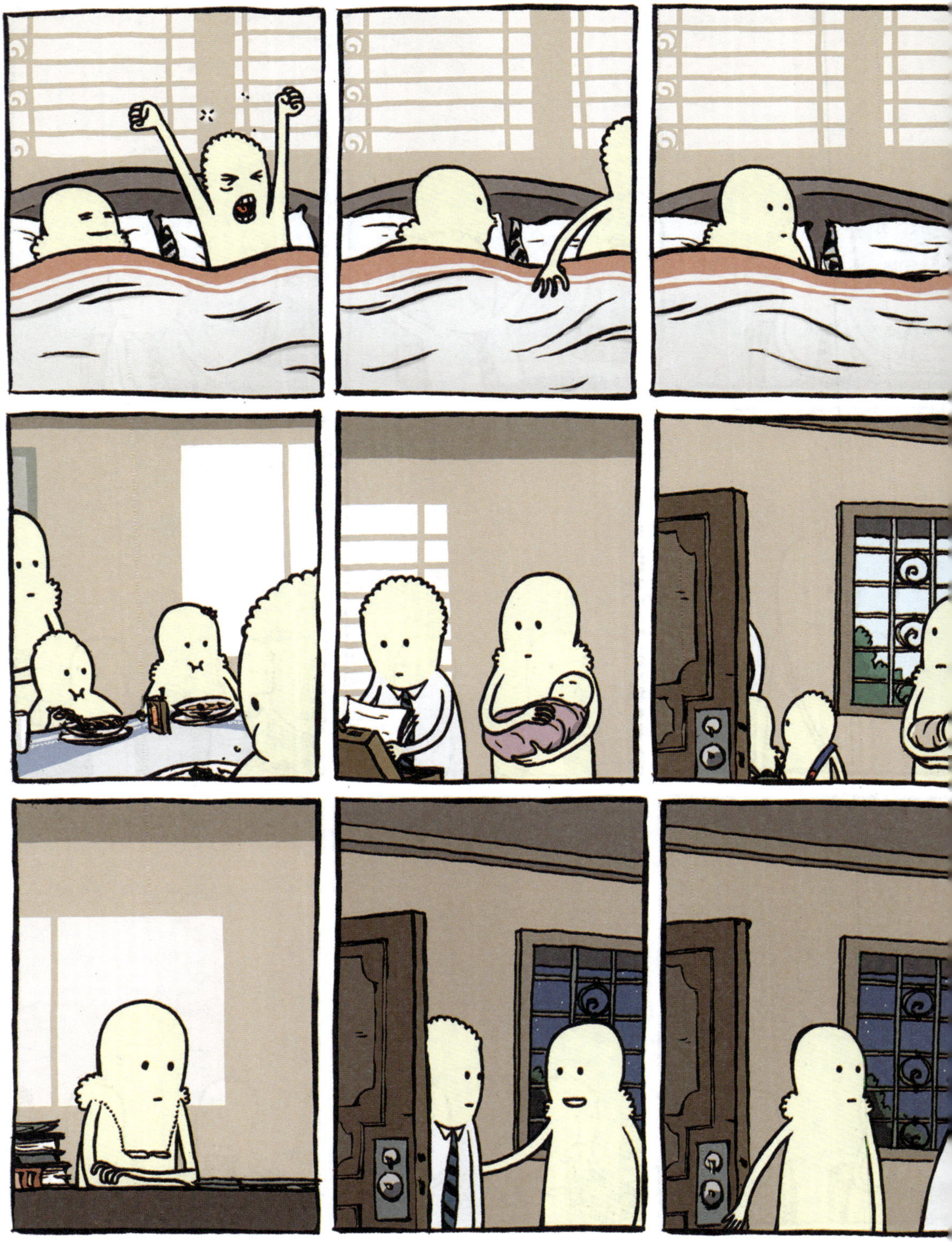

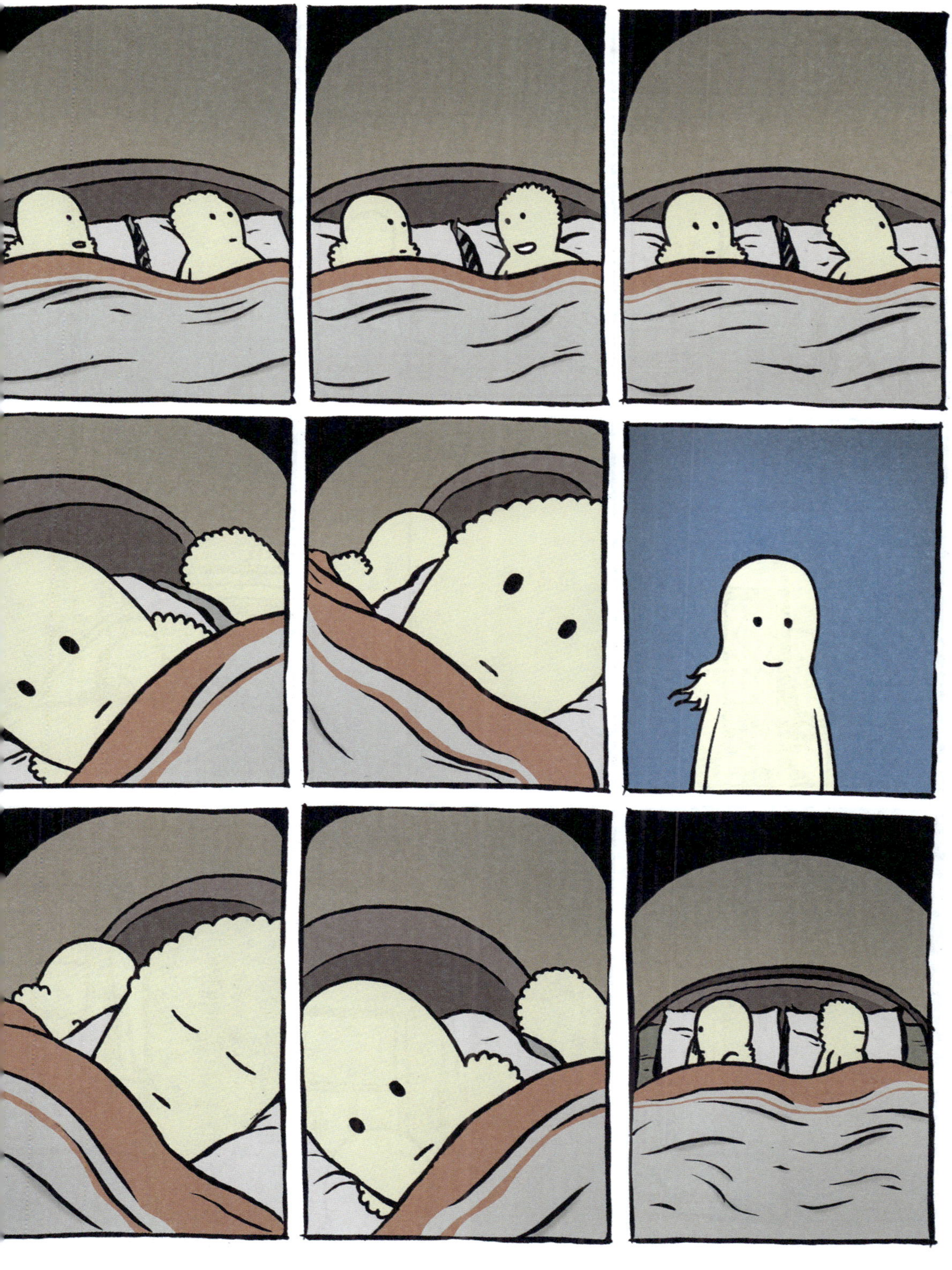

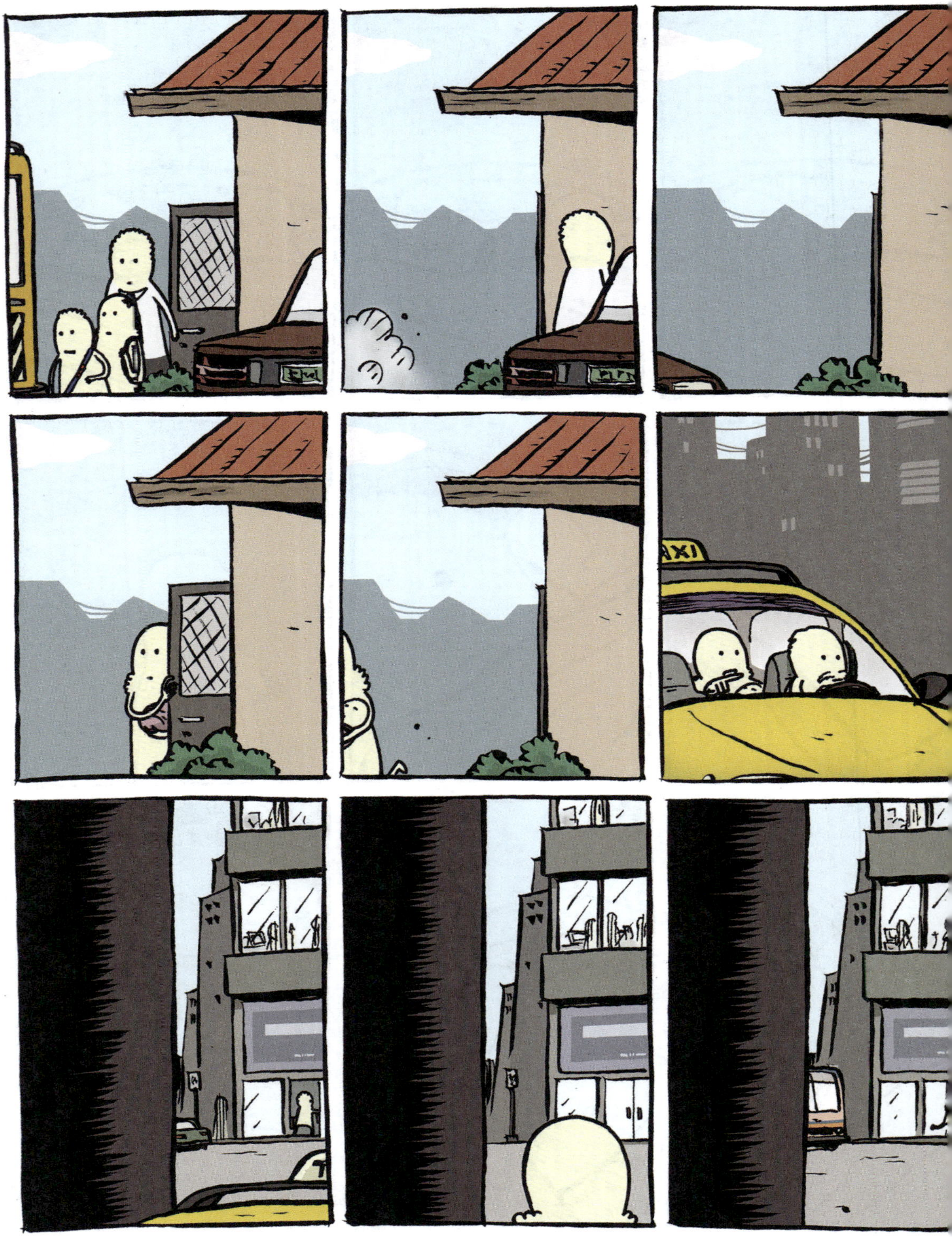

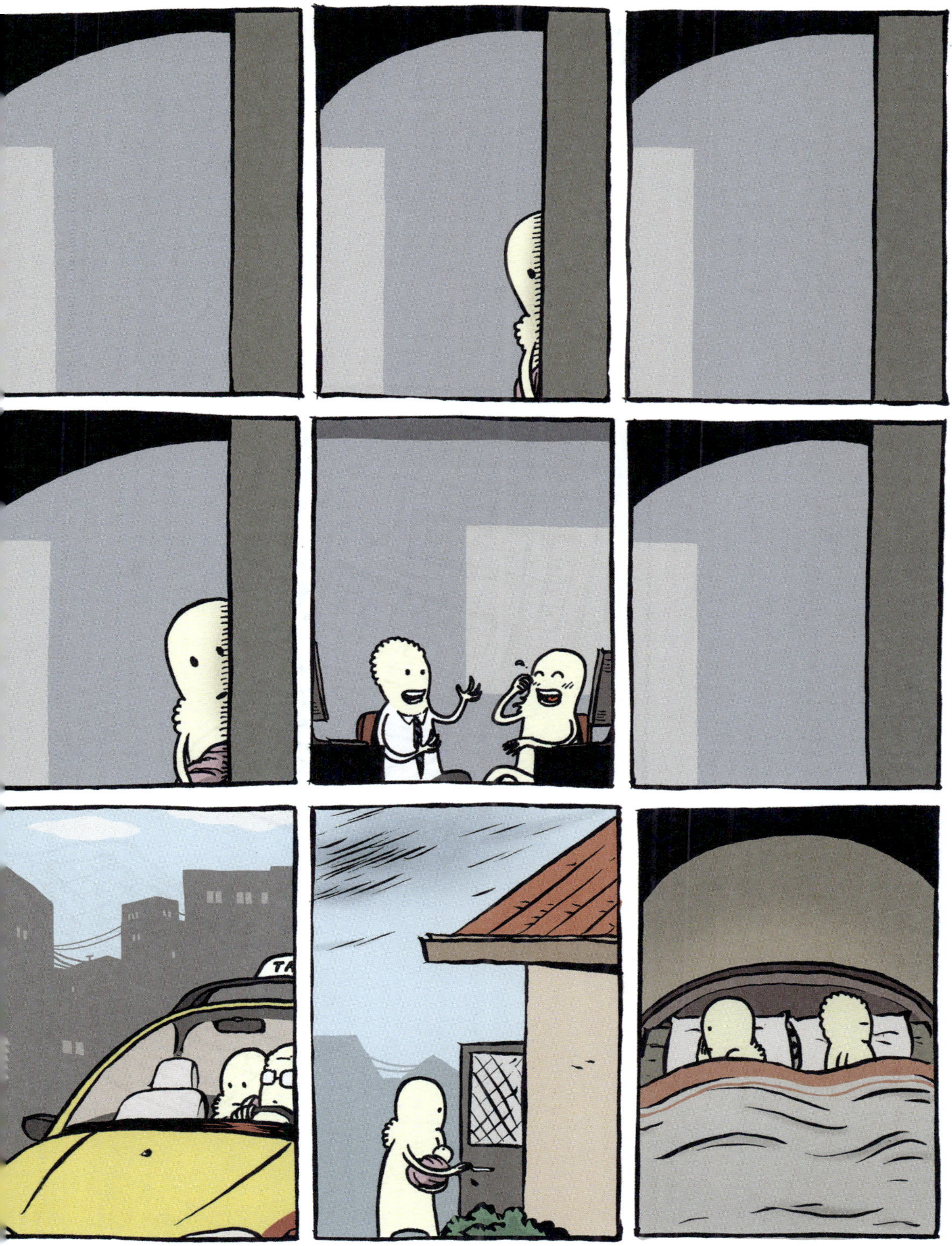

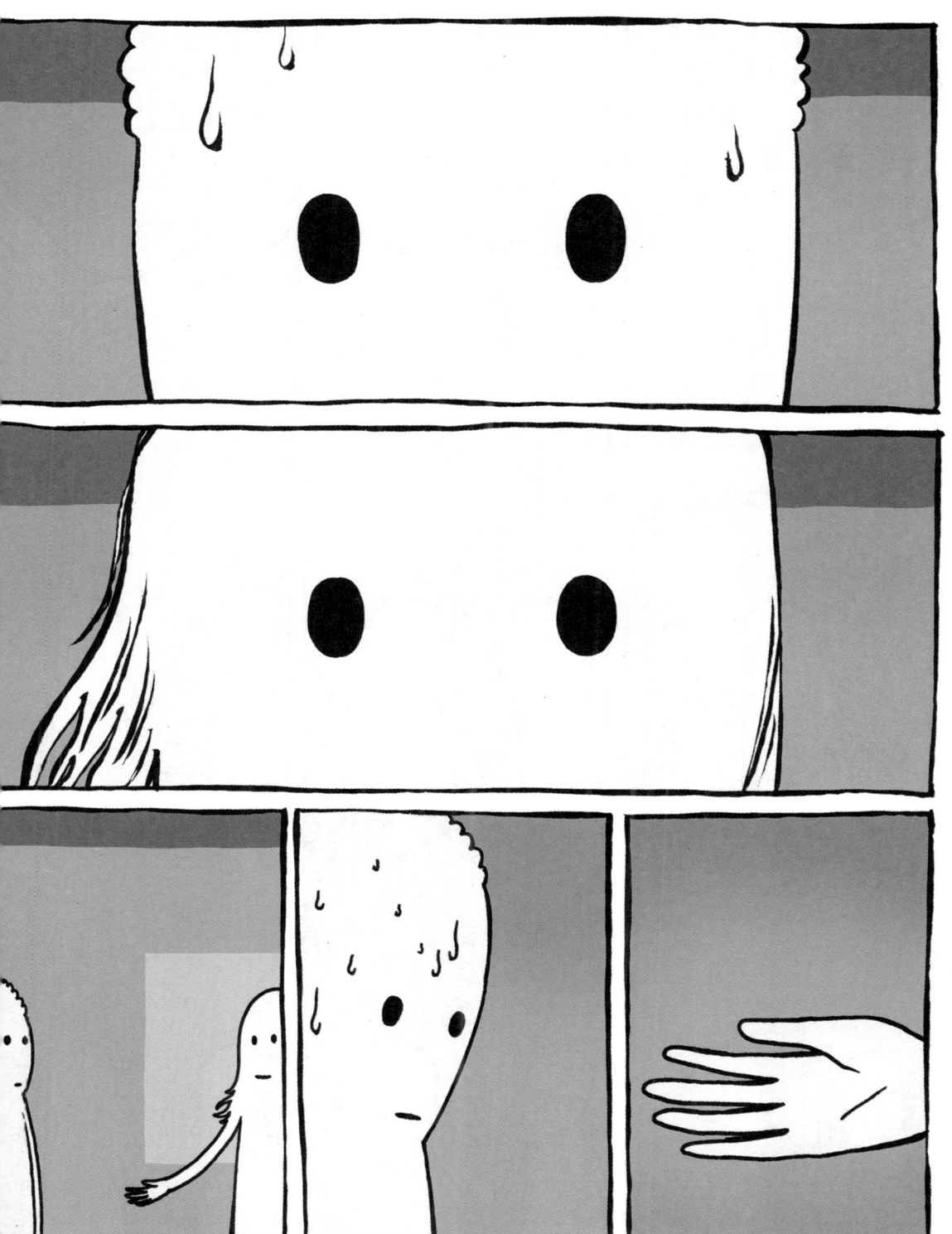

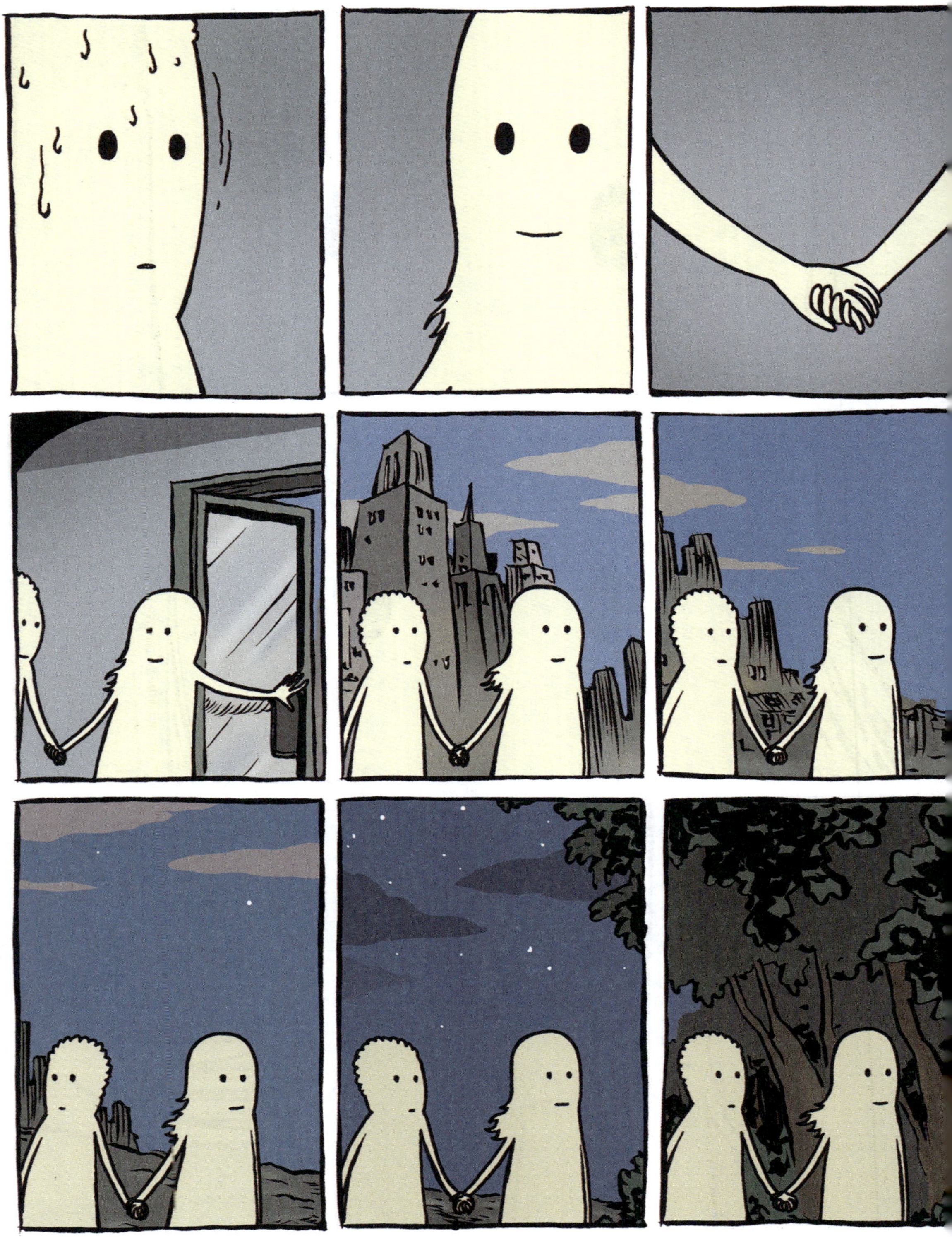

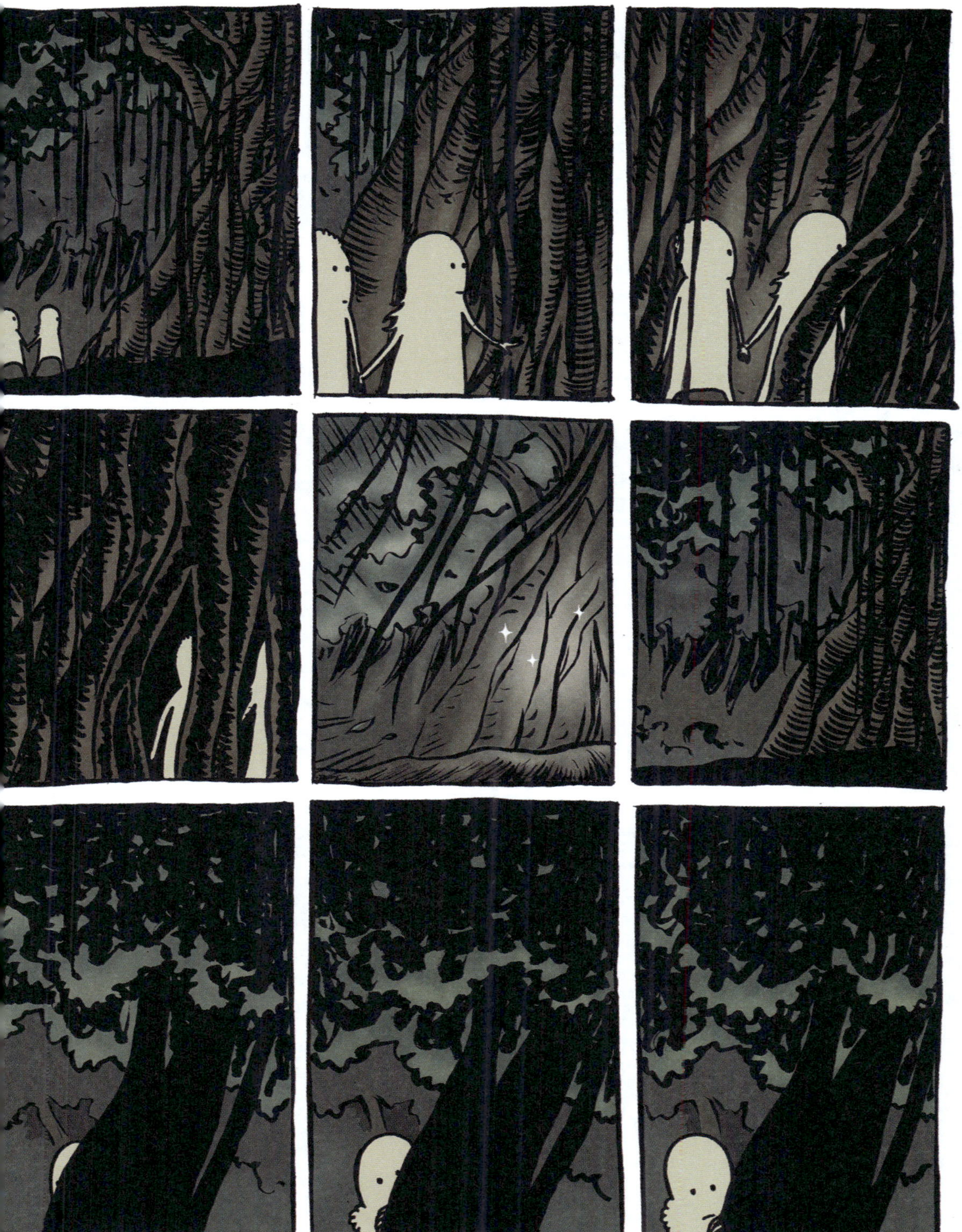

III

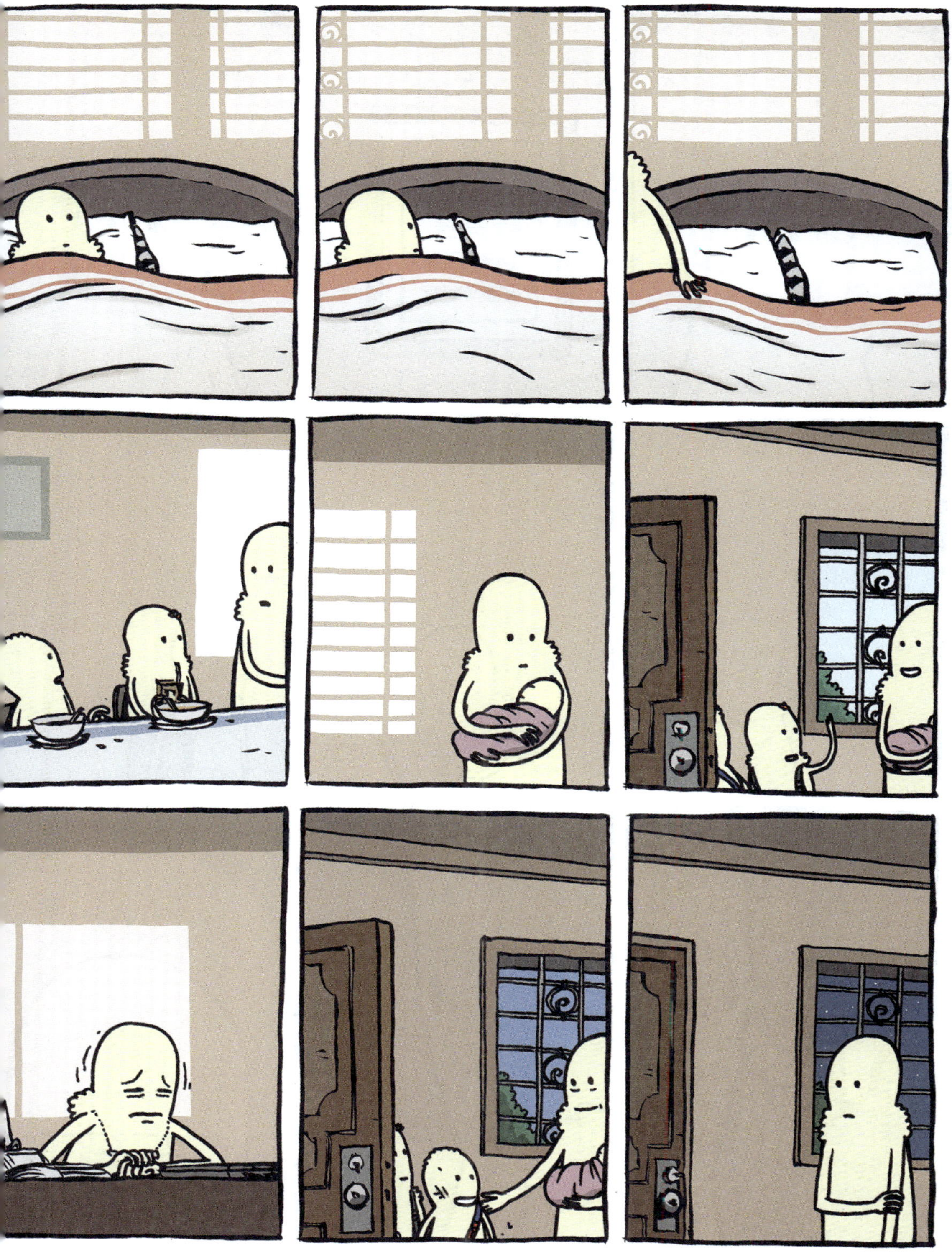

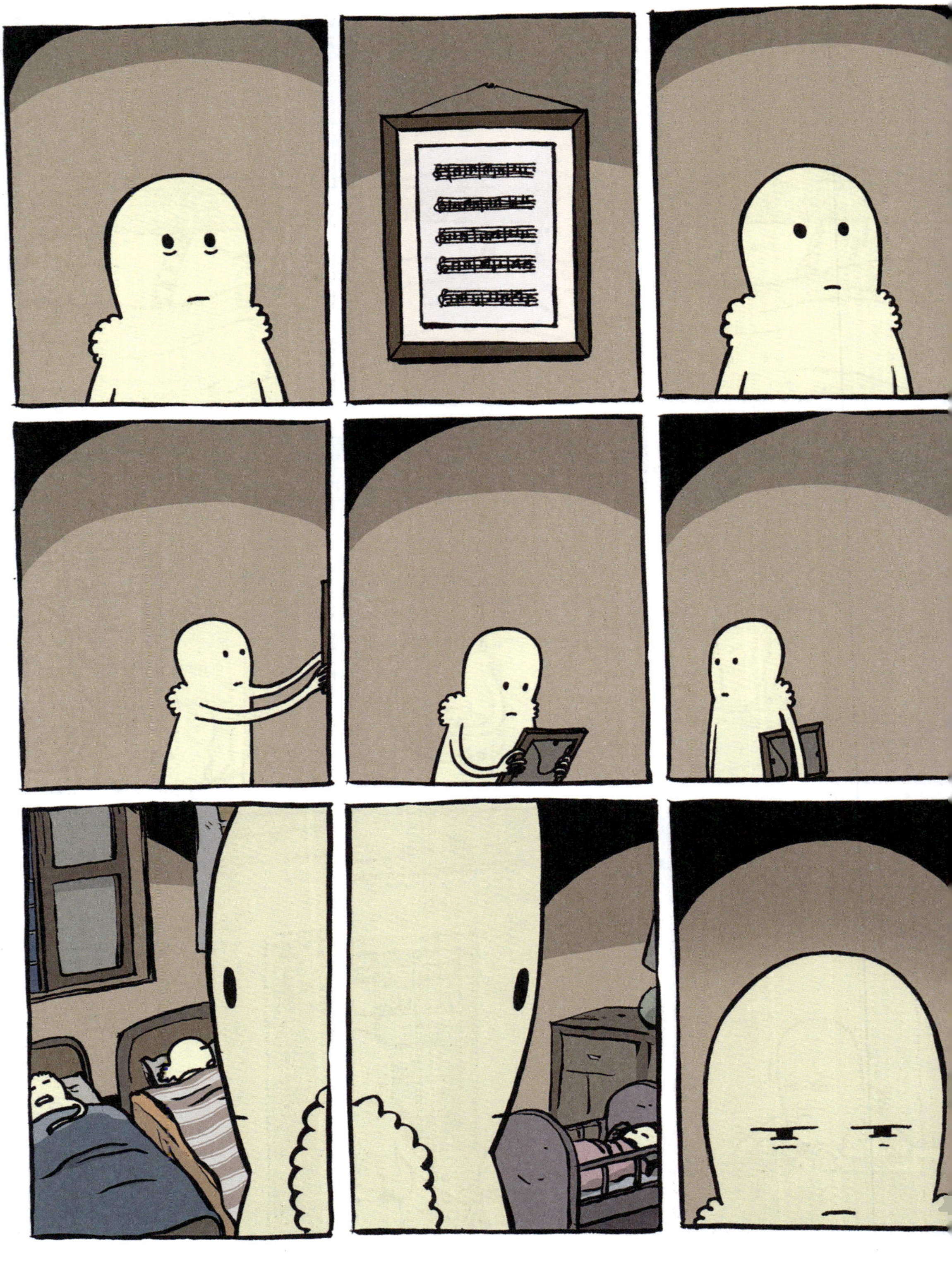

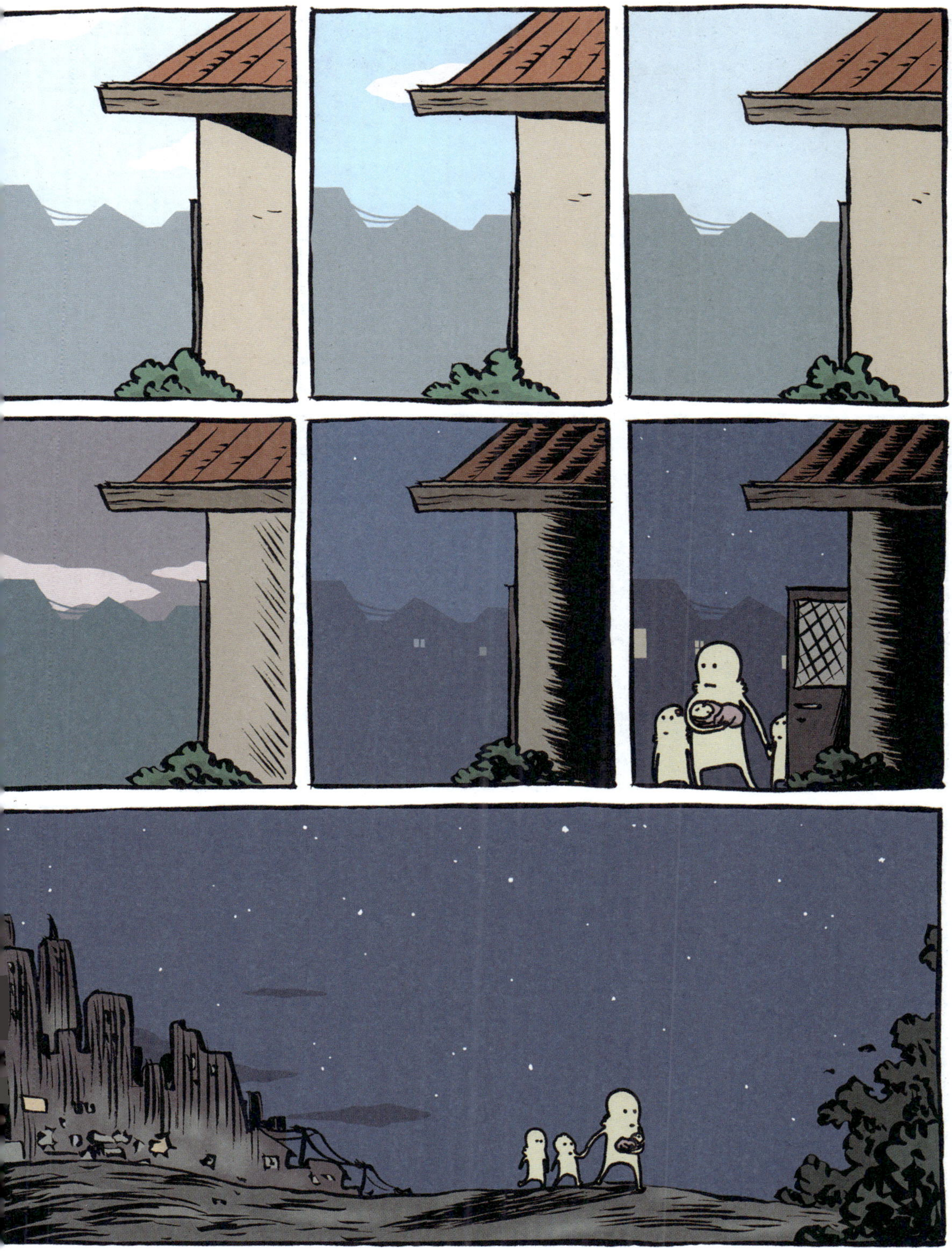

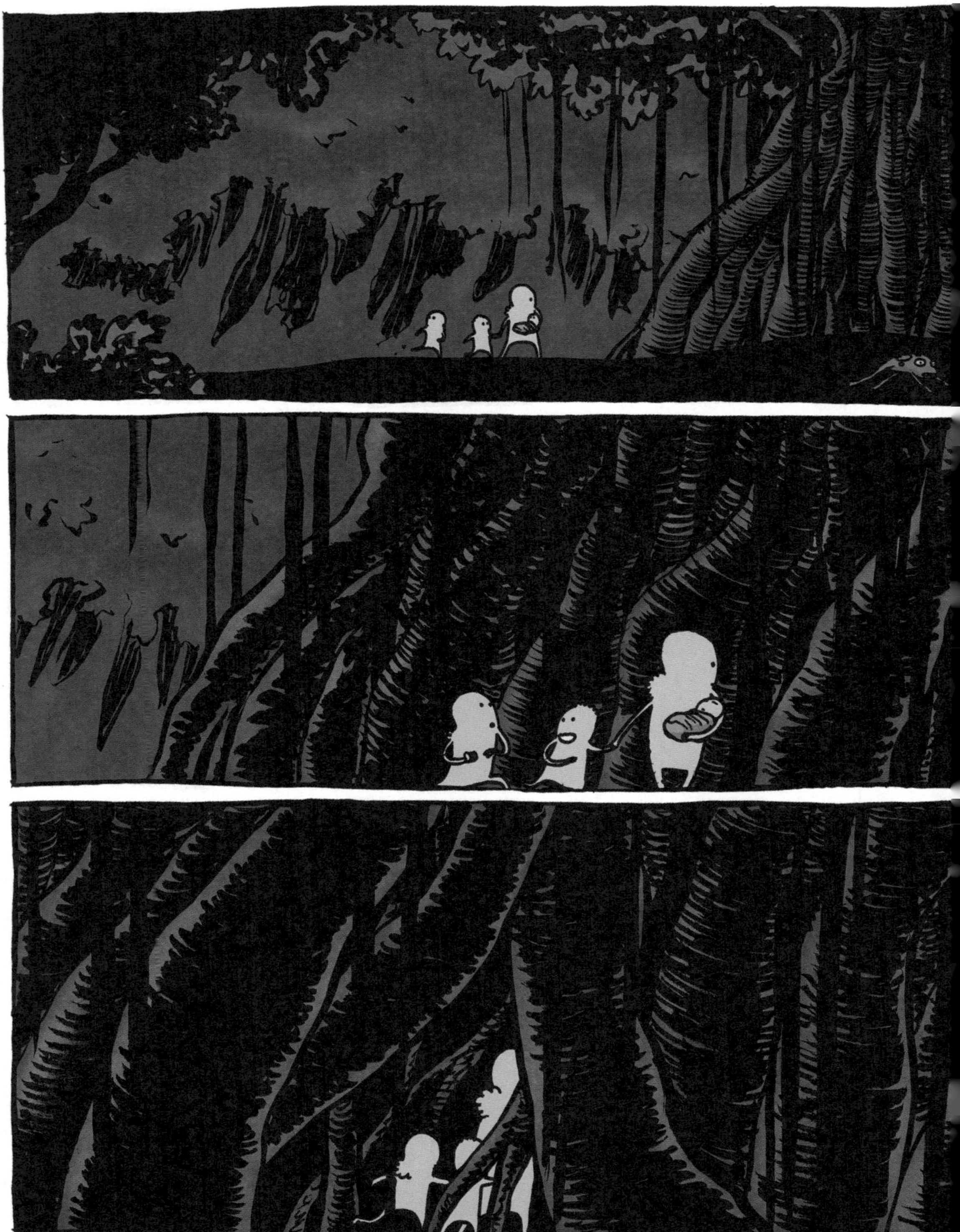

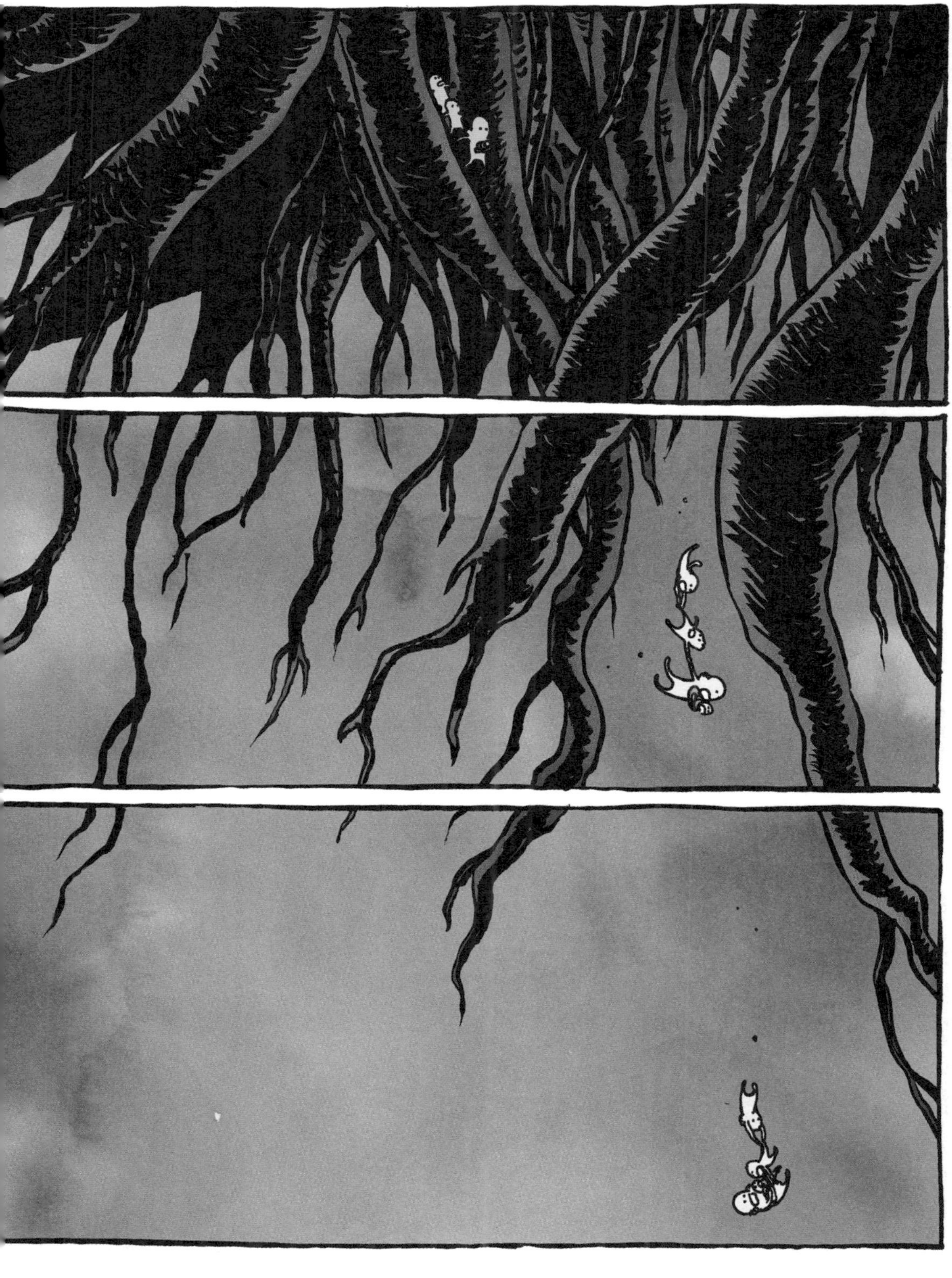

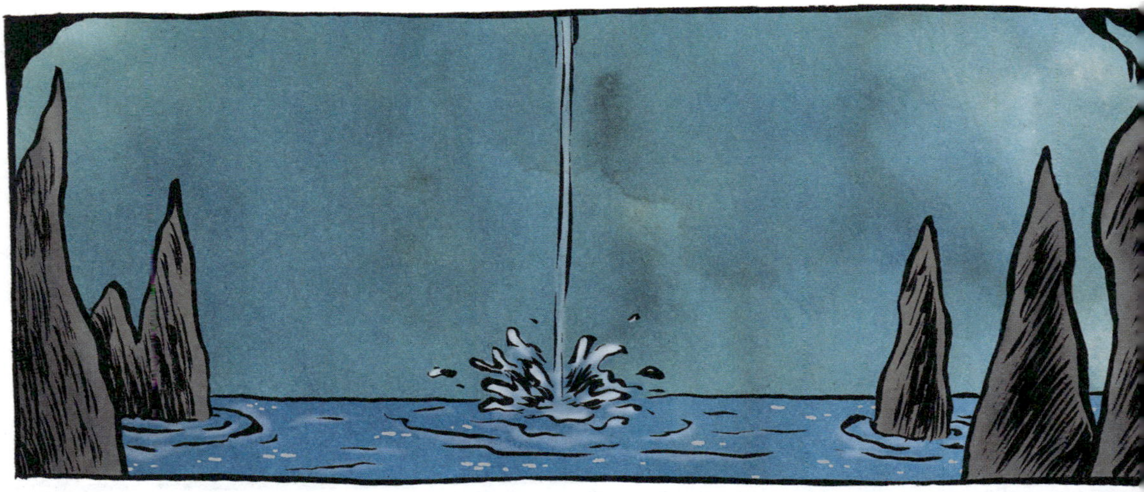
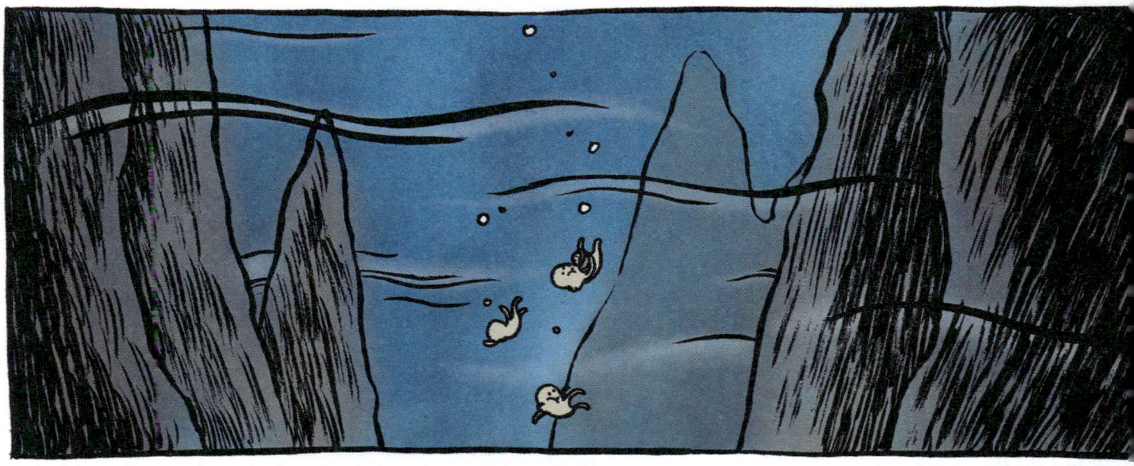
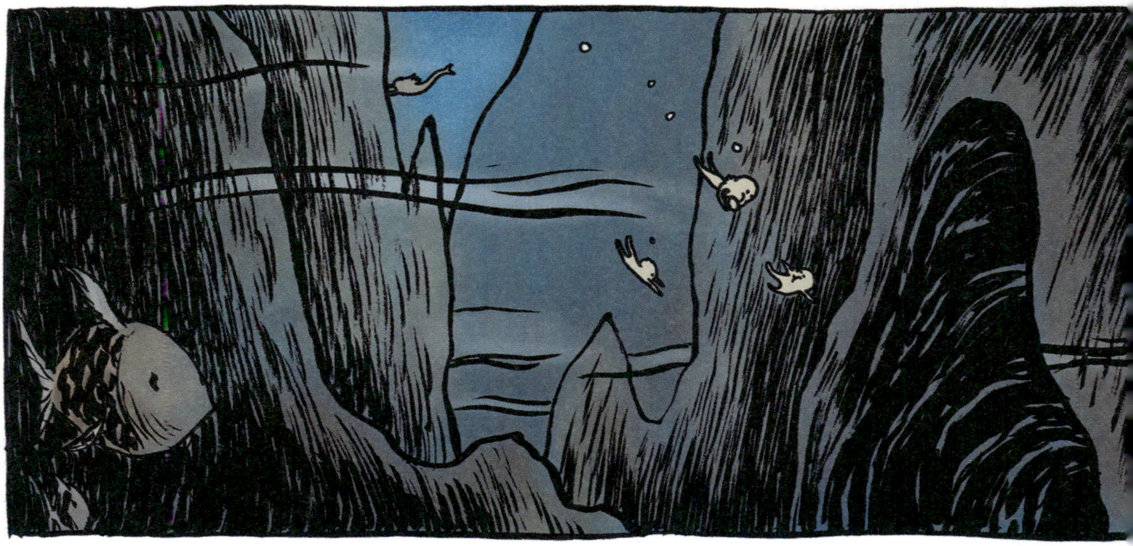

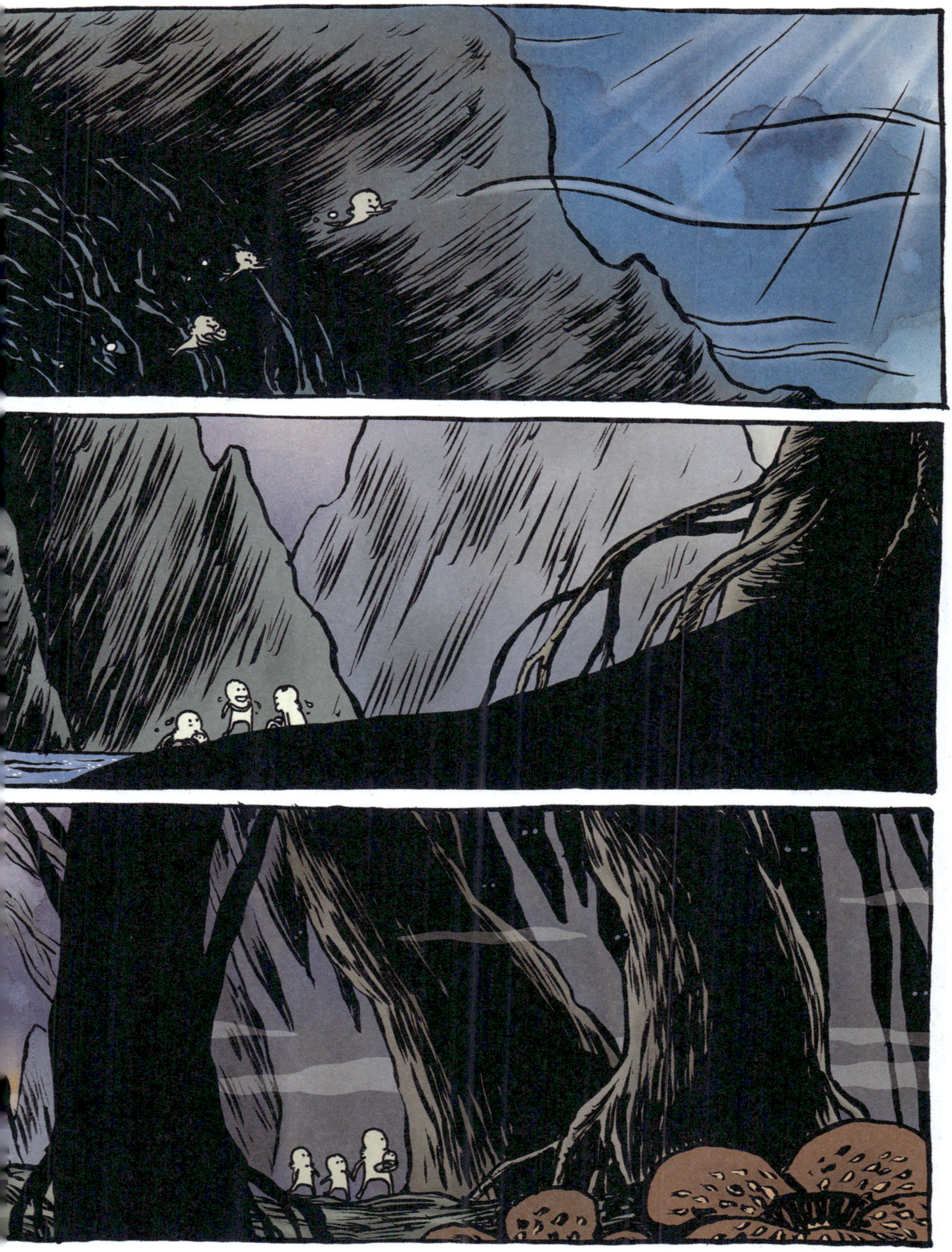

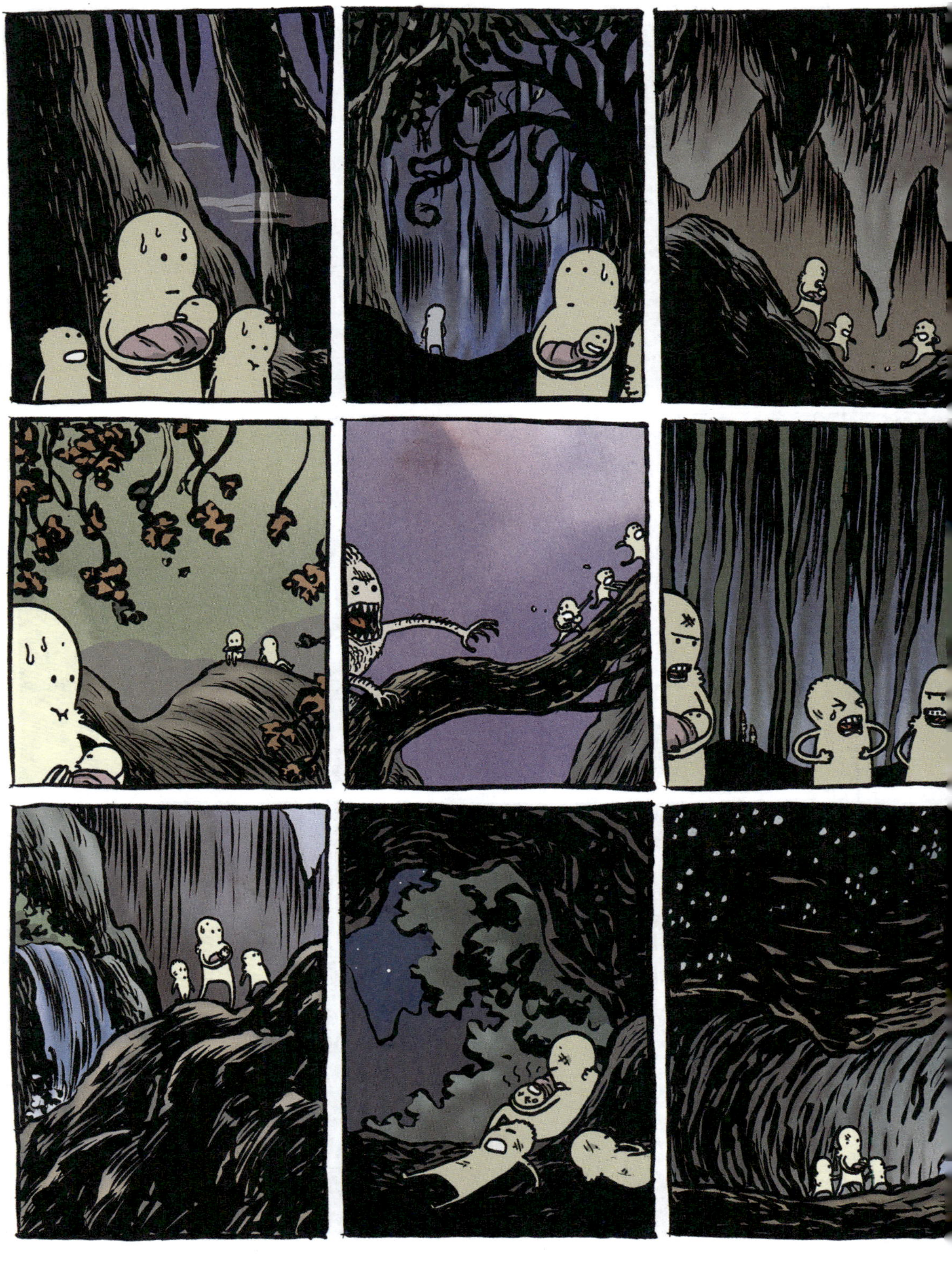

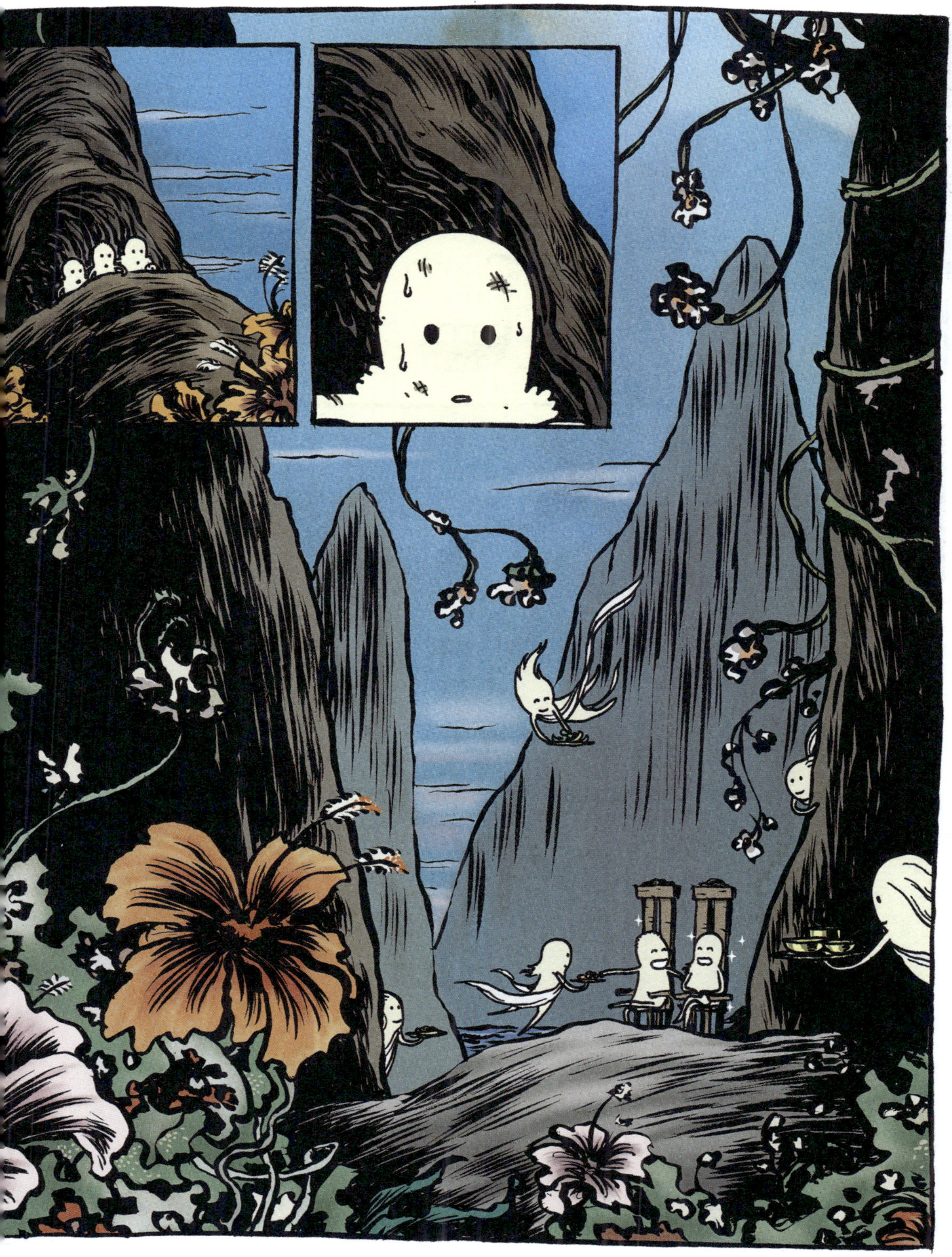

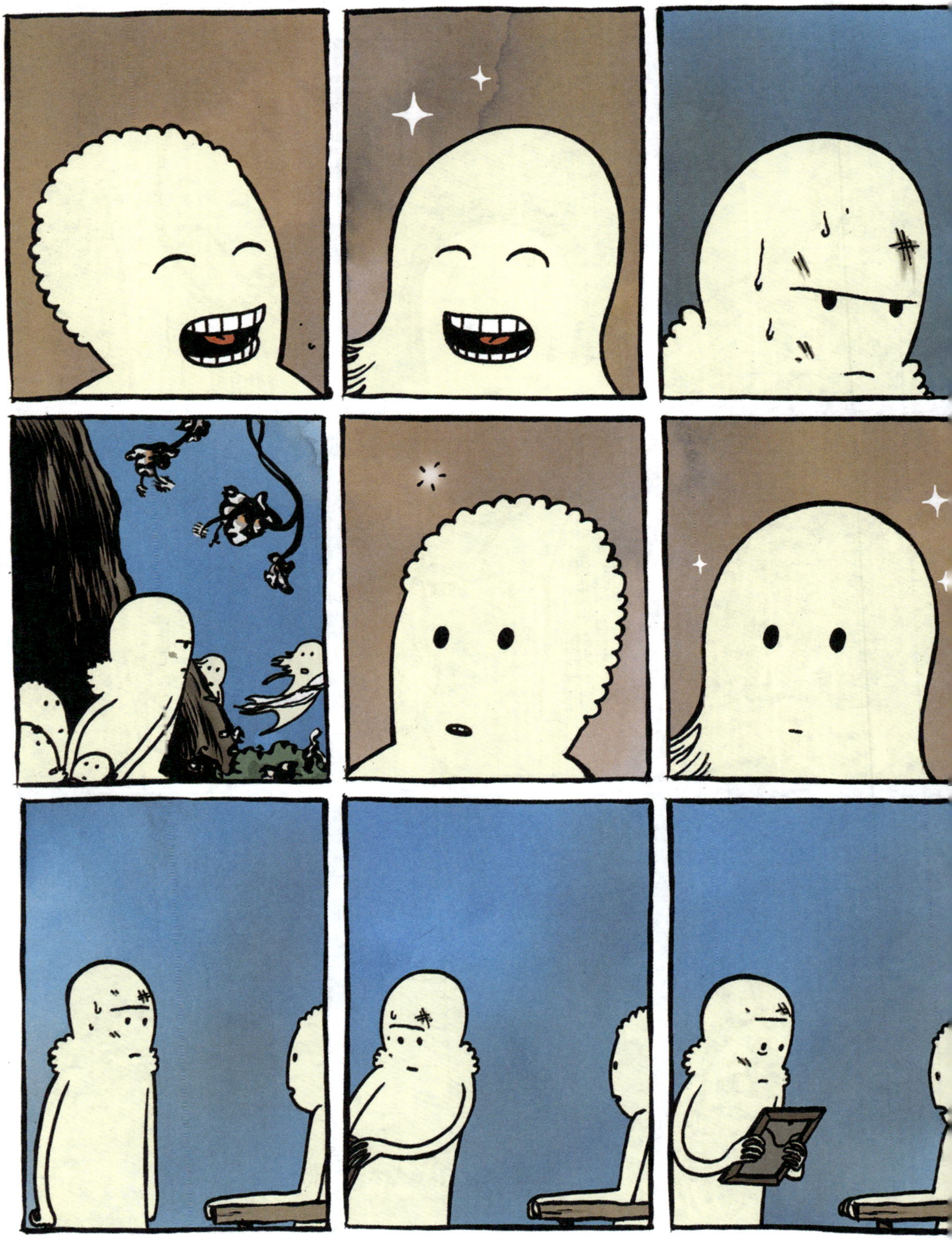

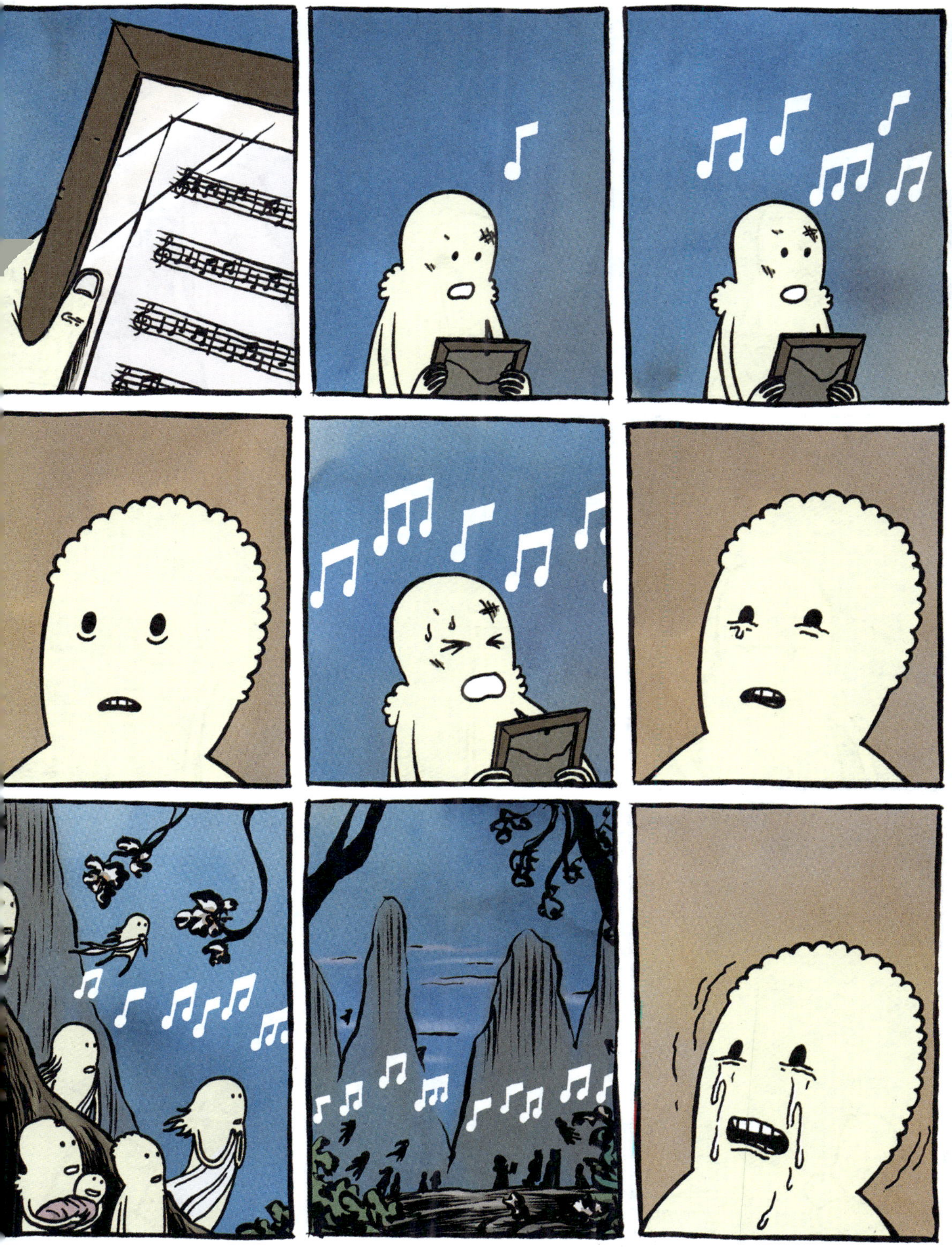

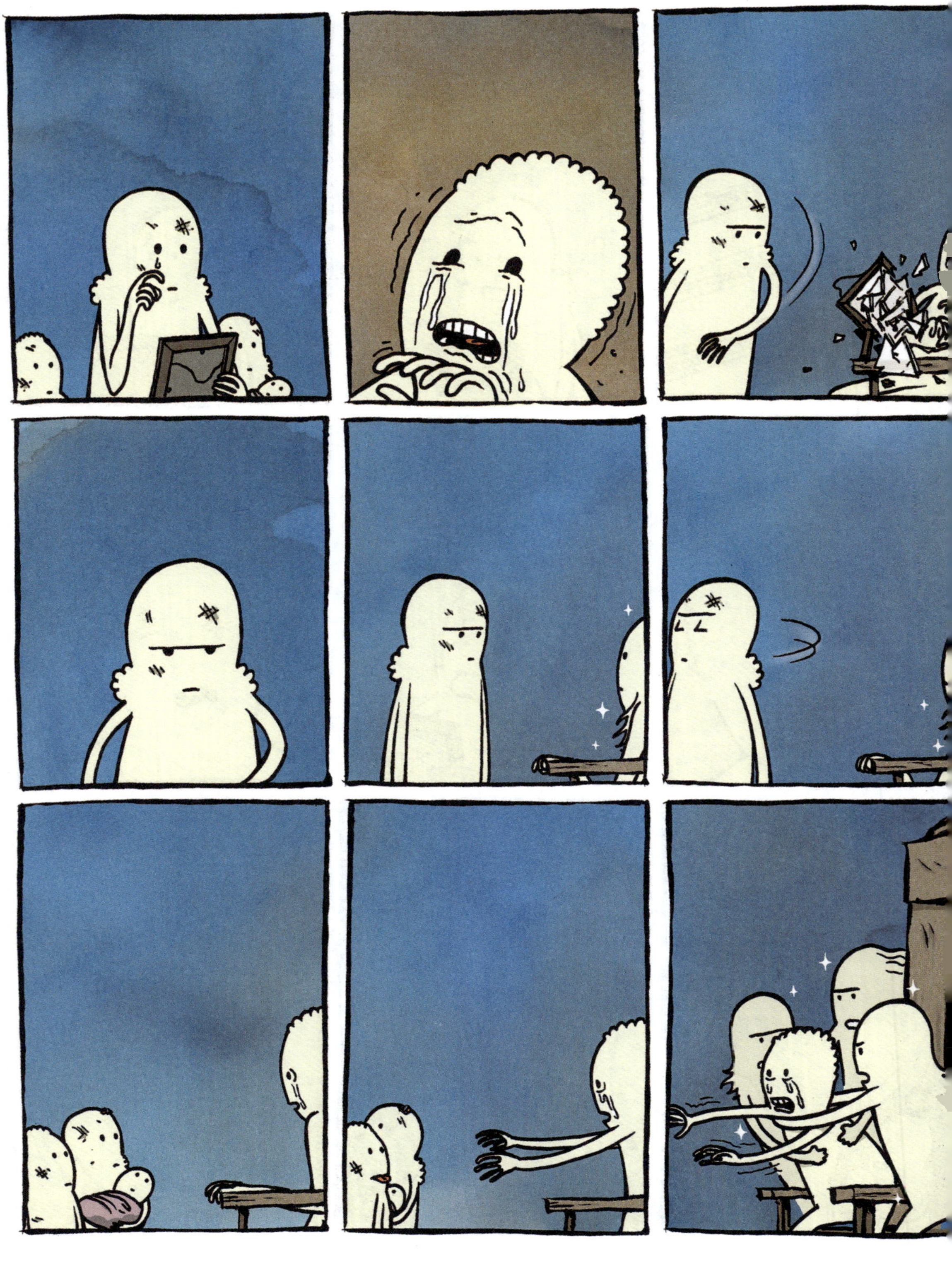

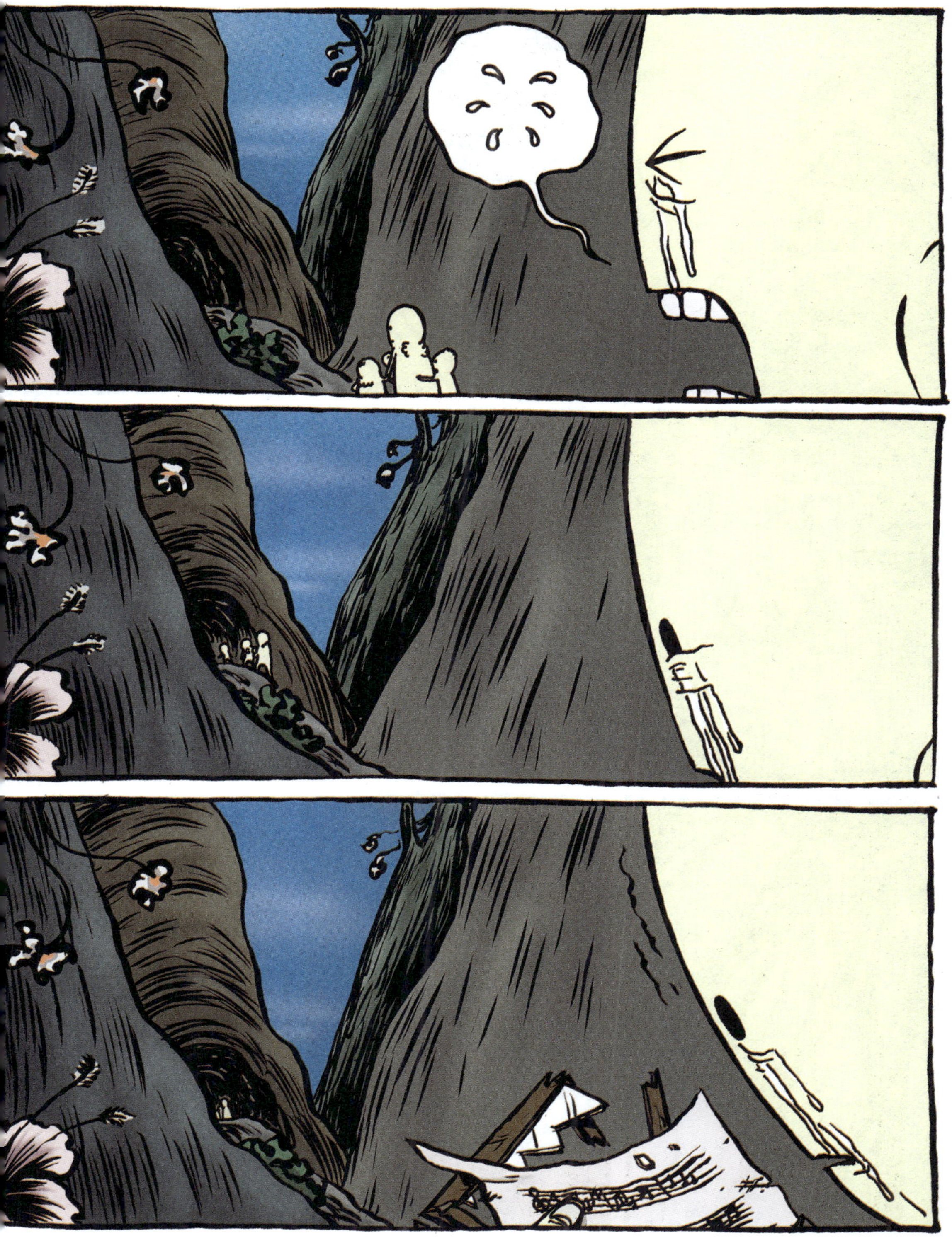

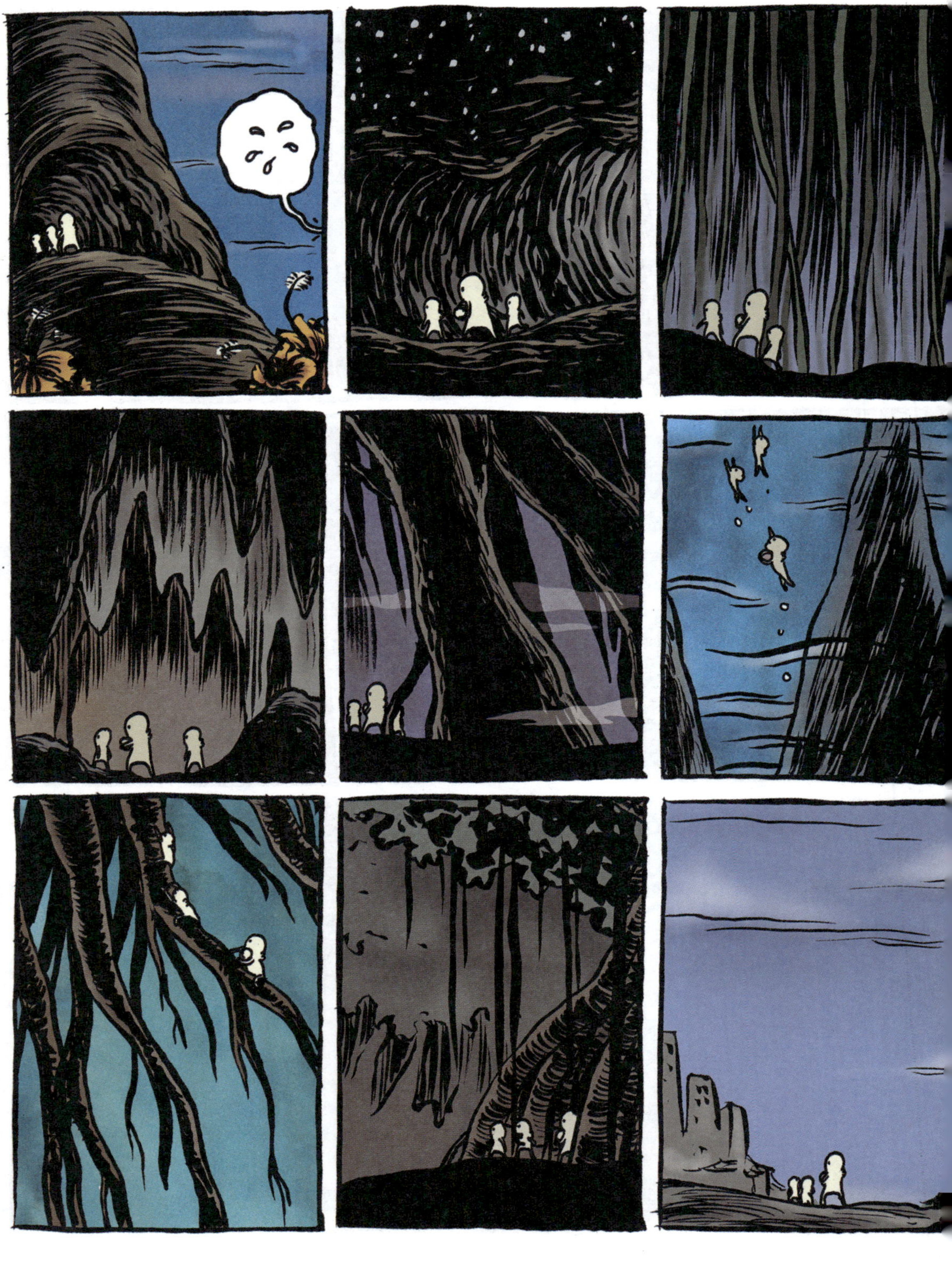

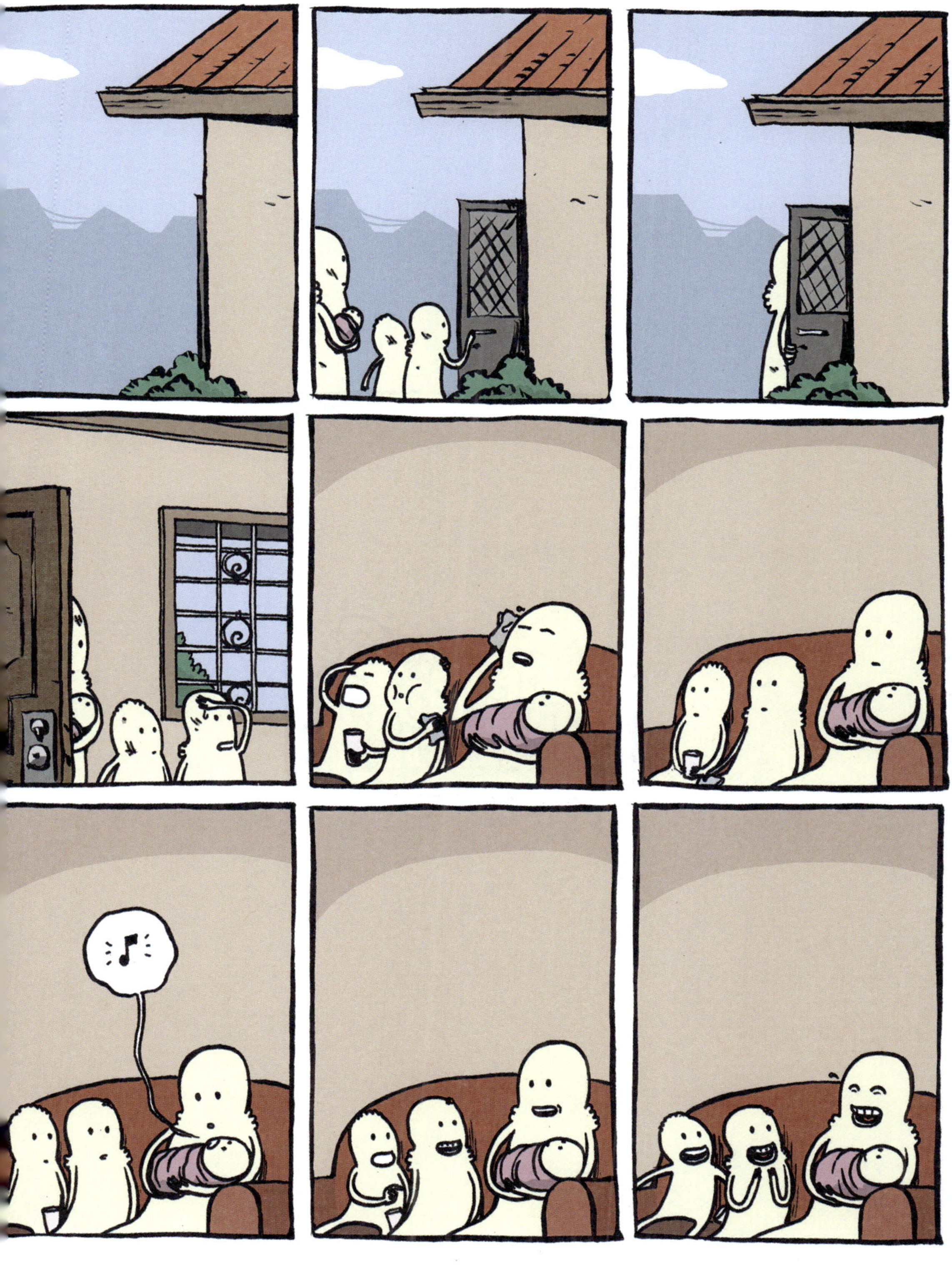

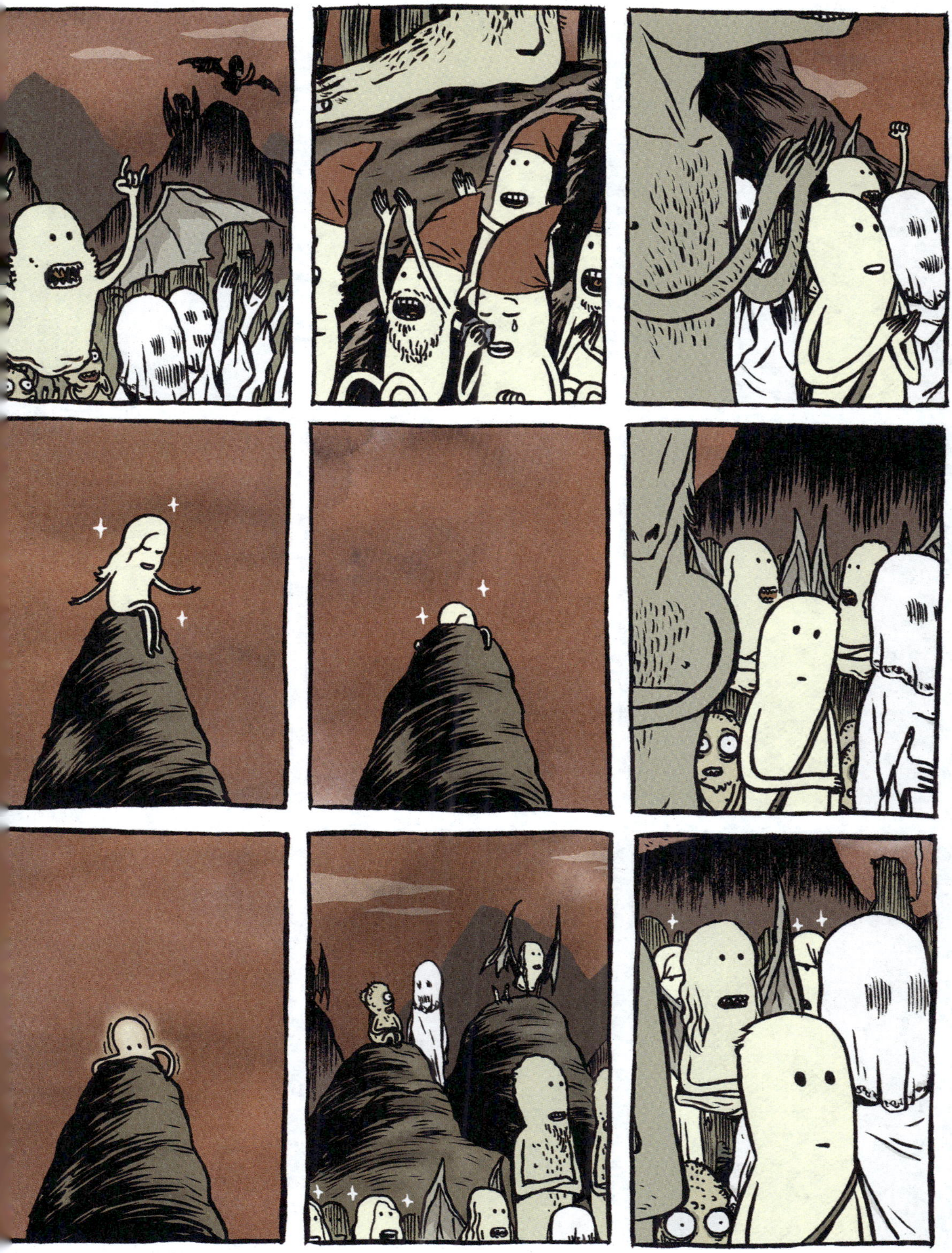

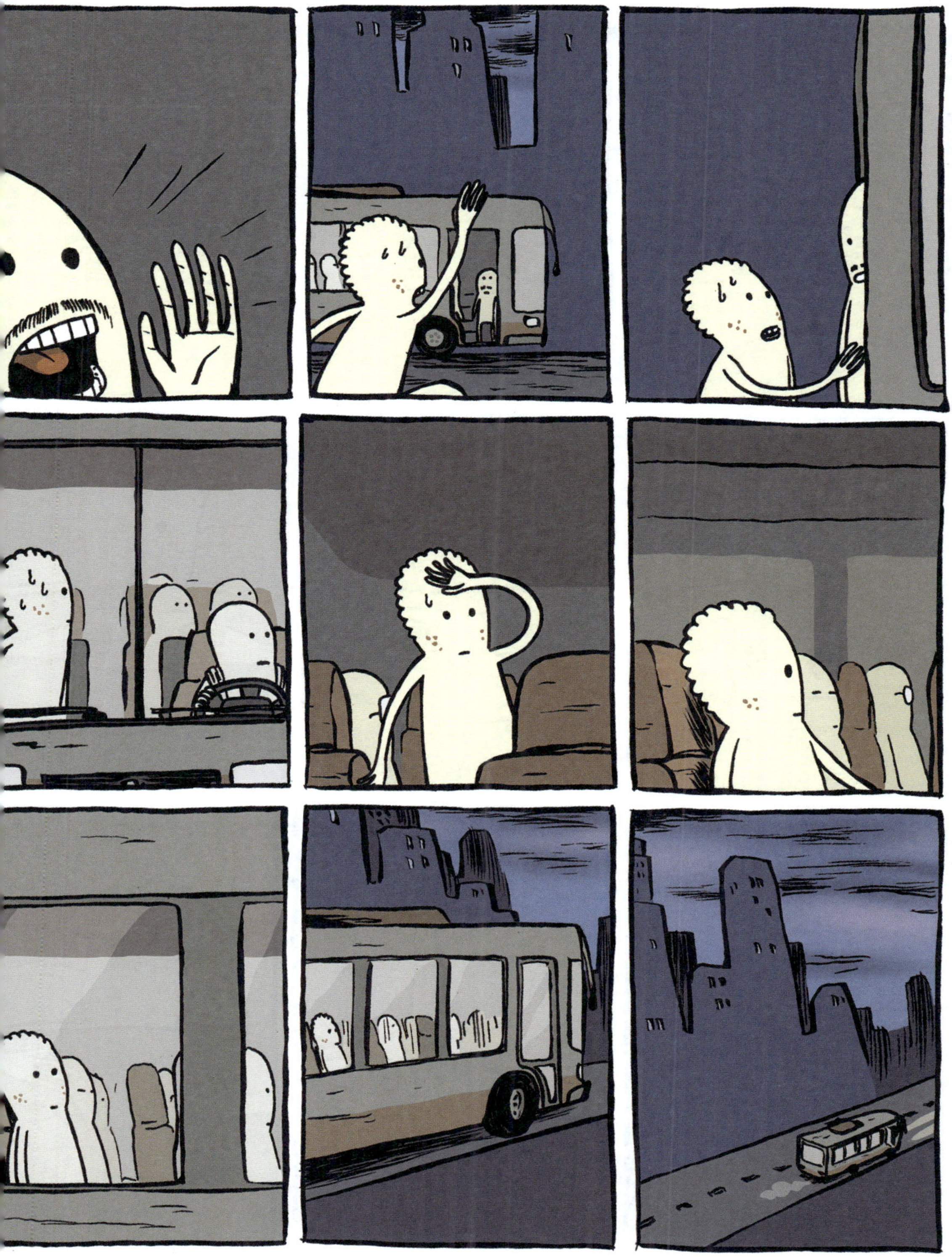

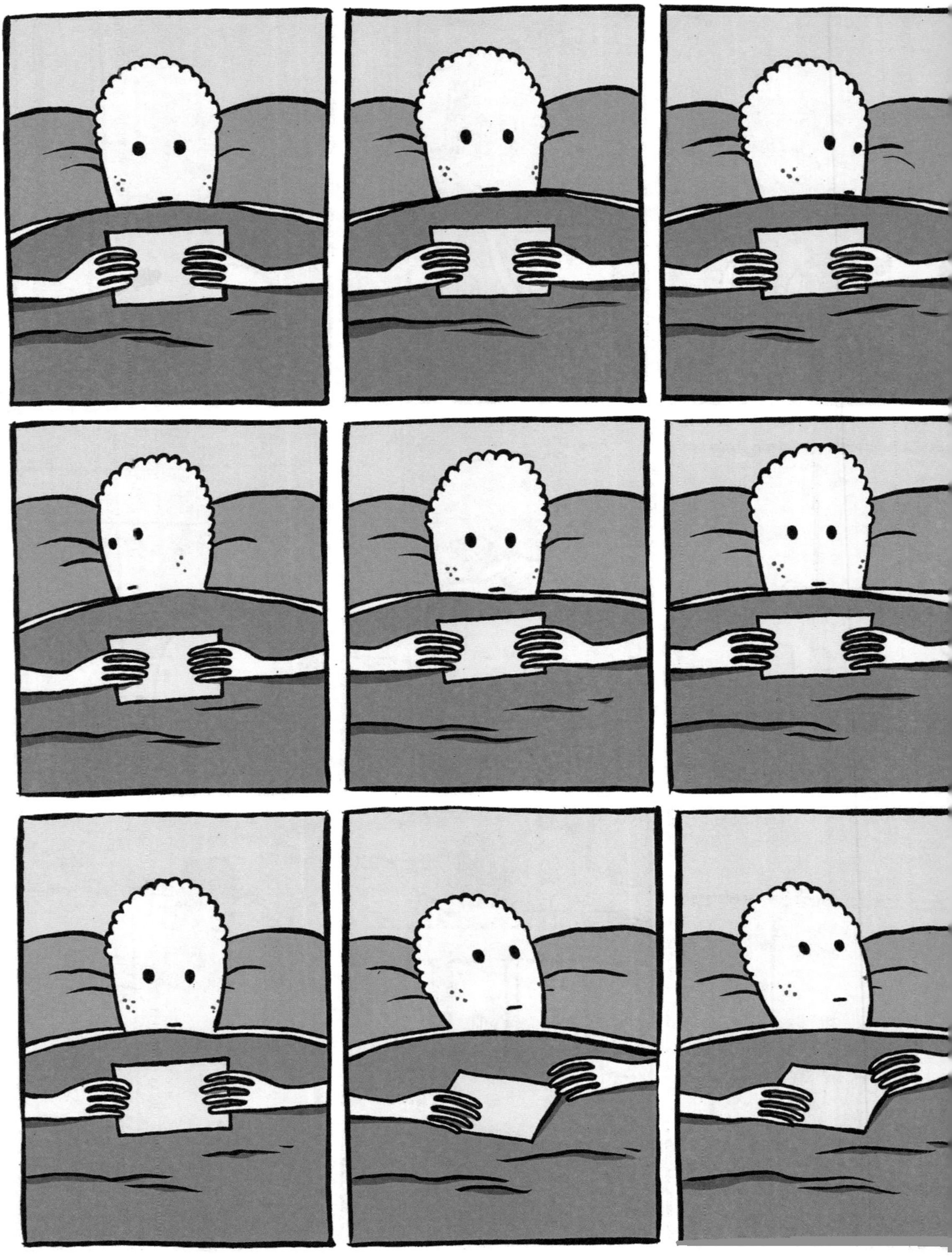

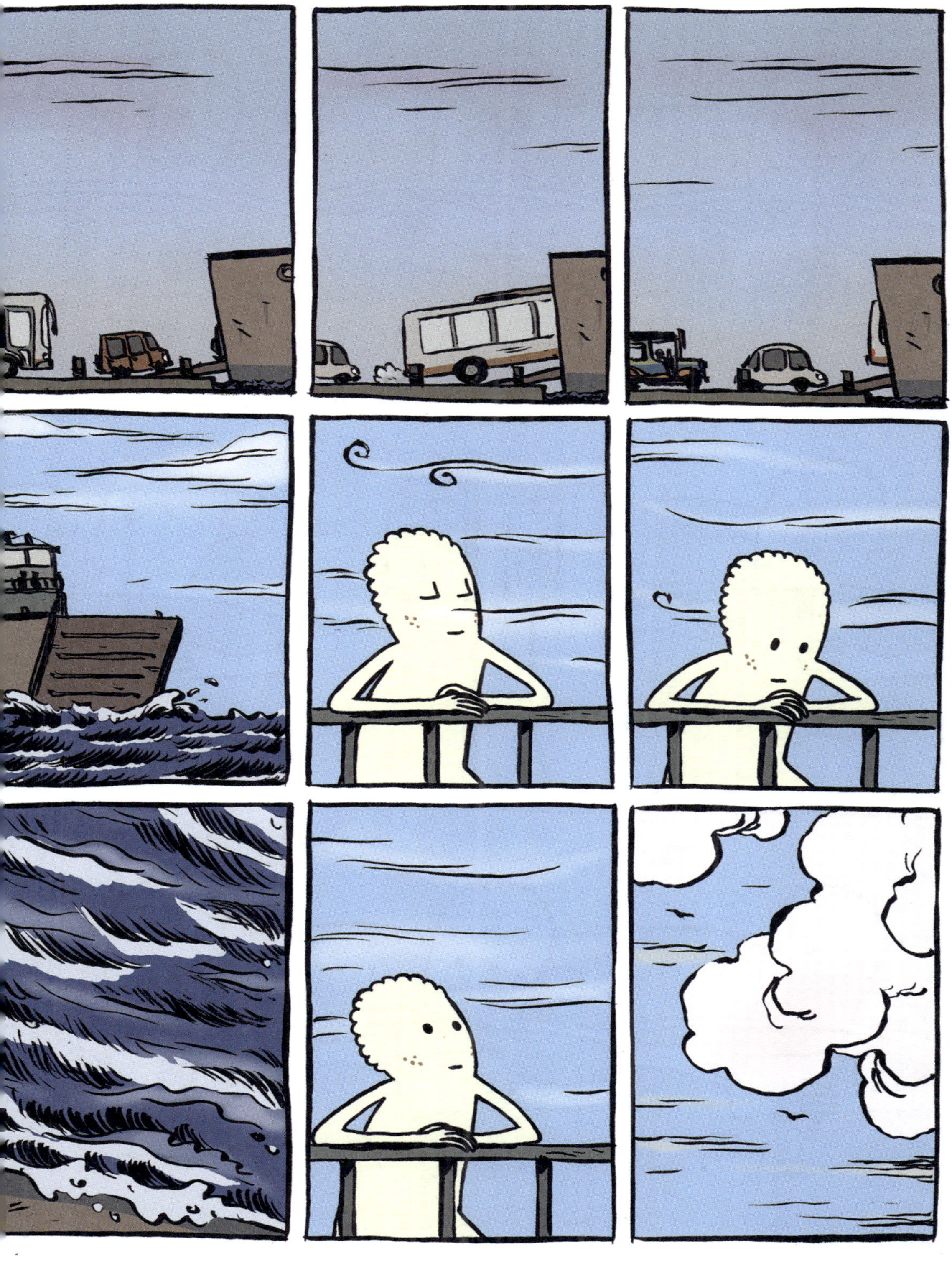

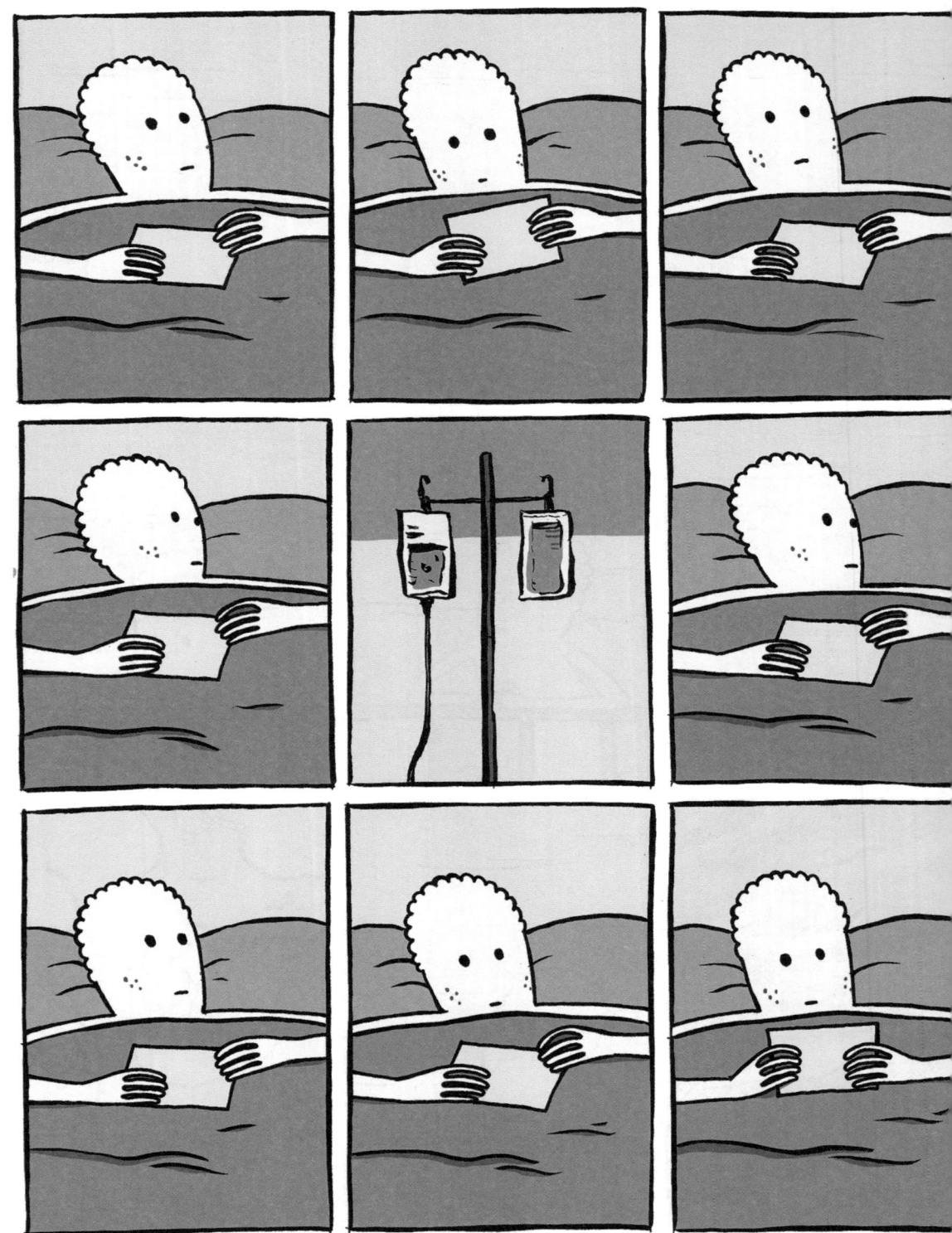

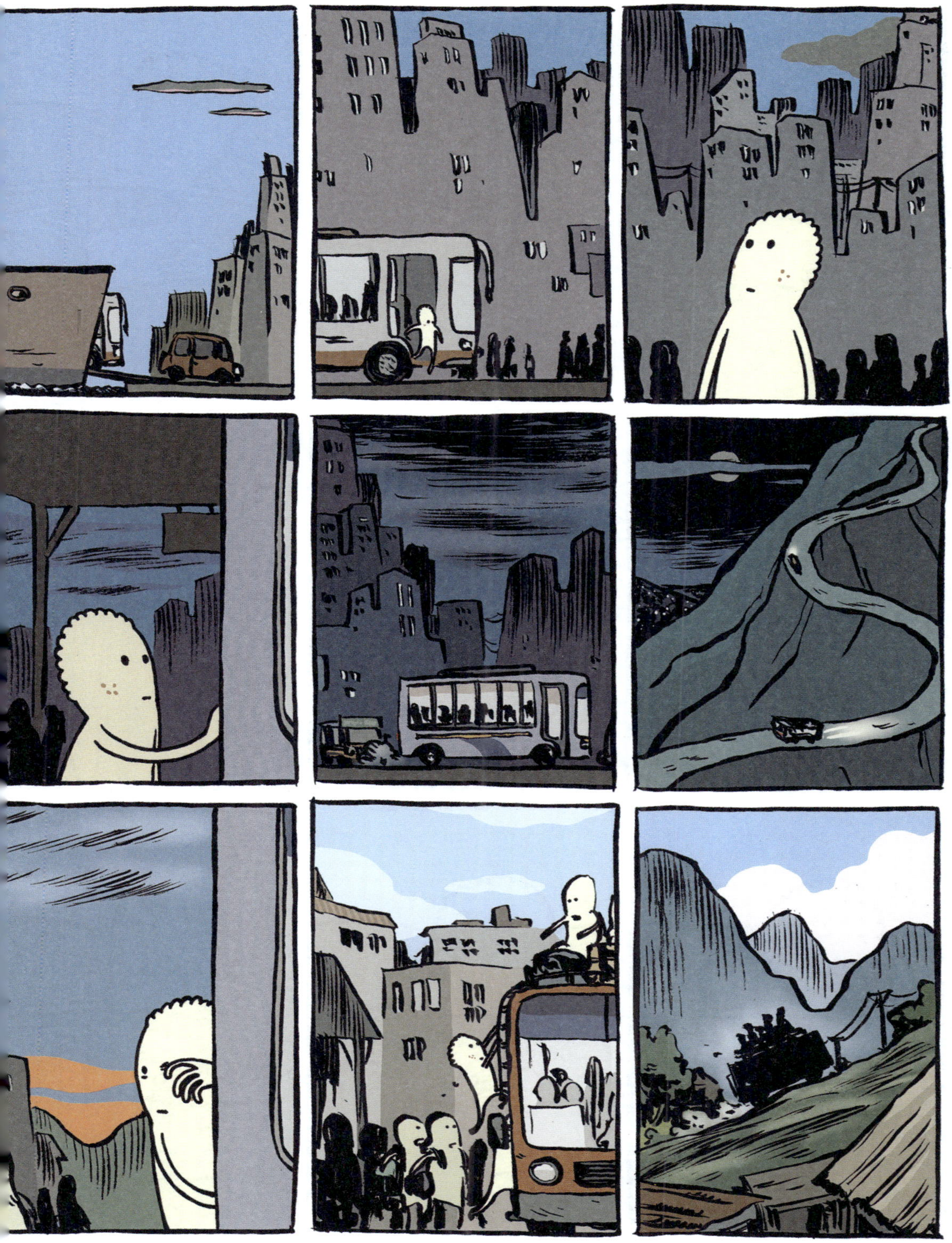

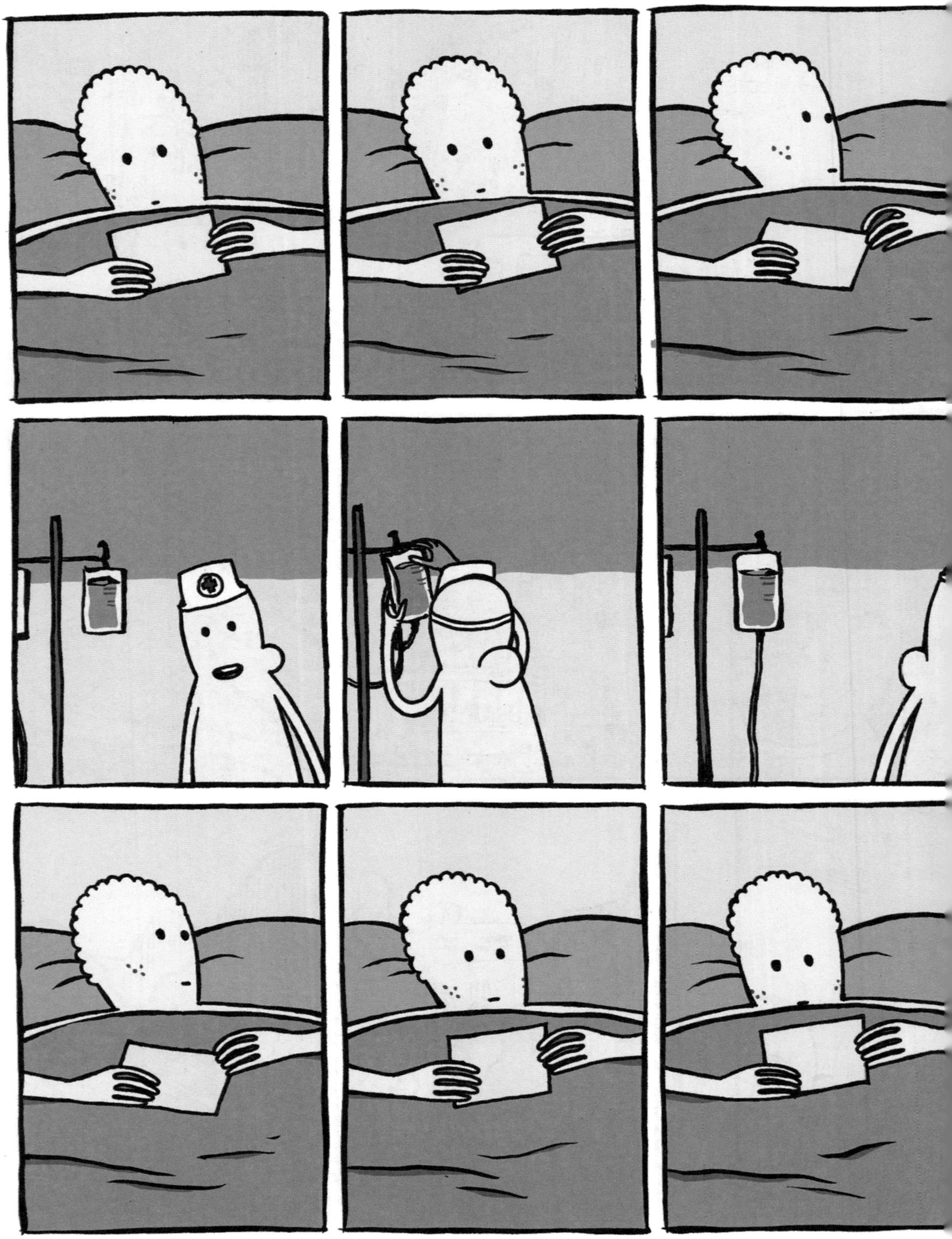

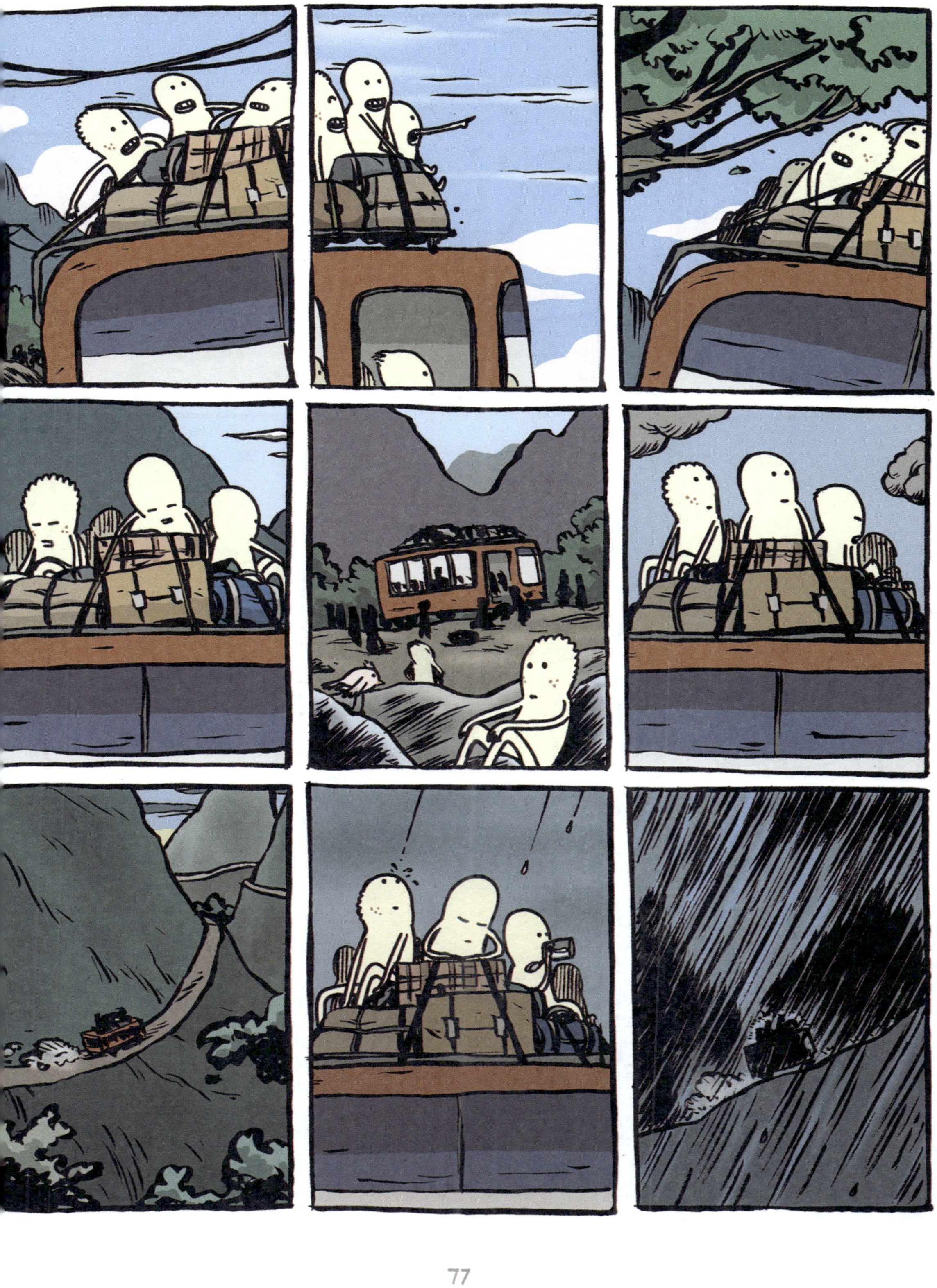

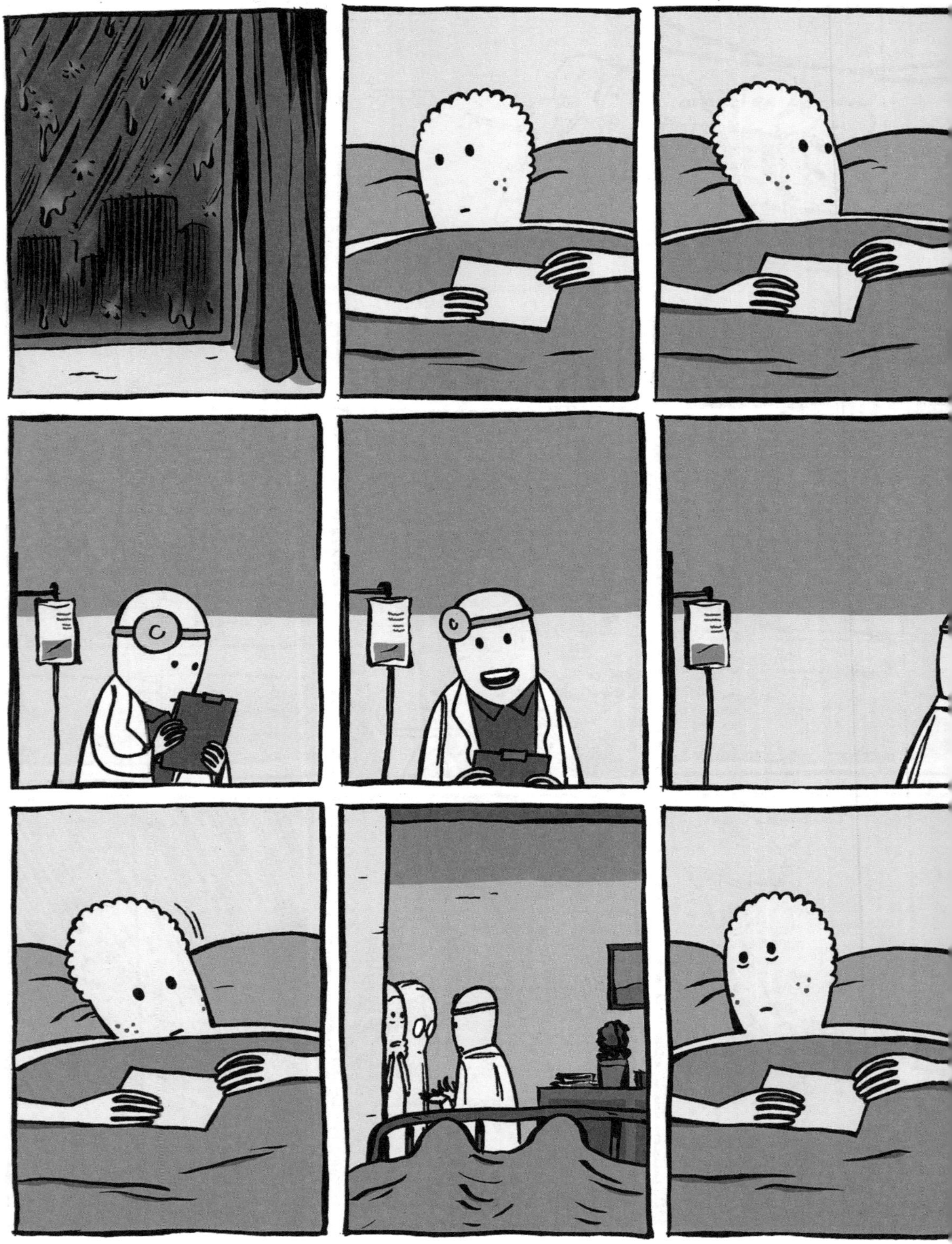

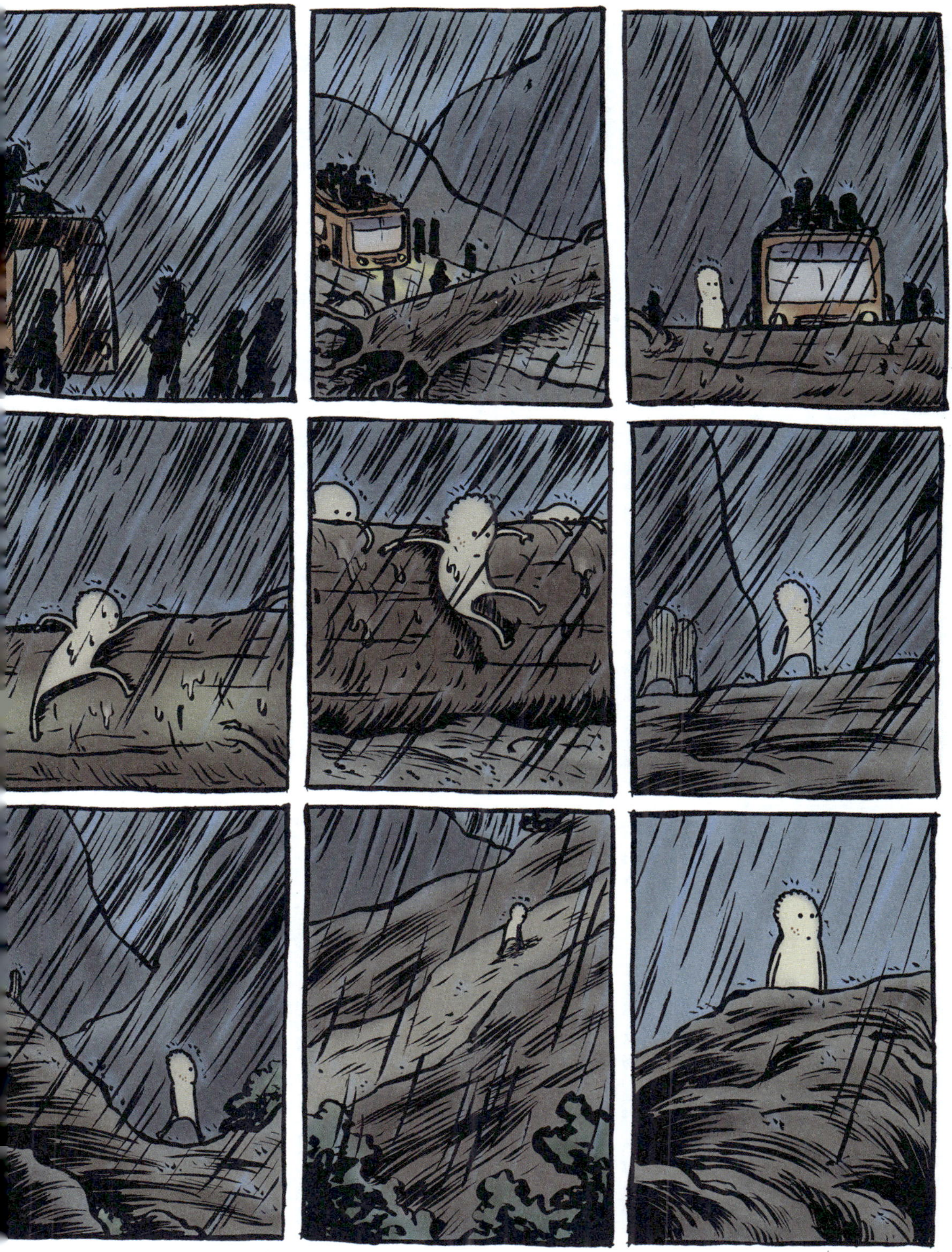

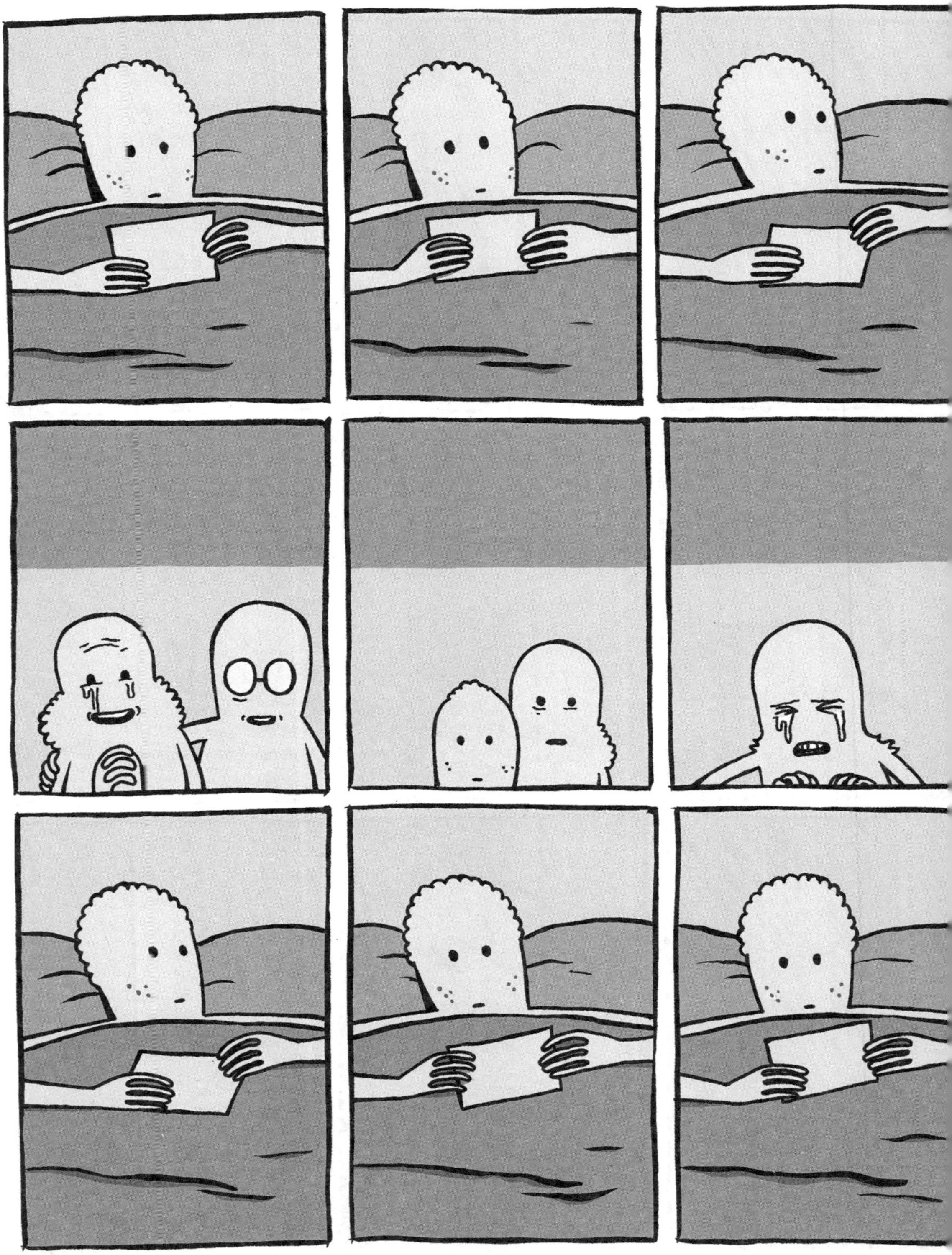

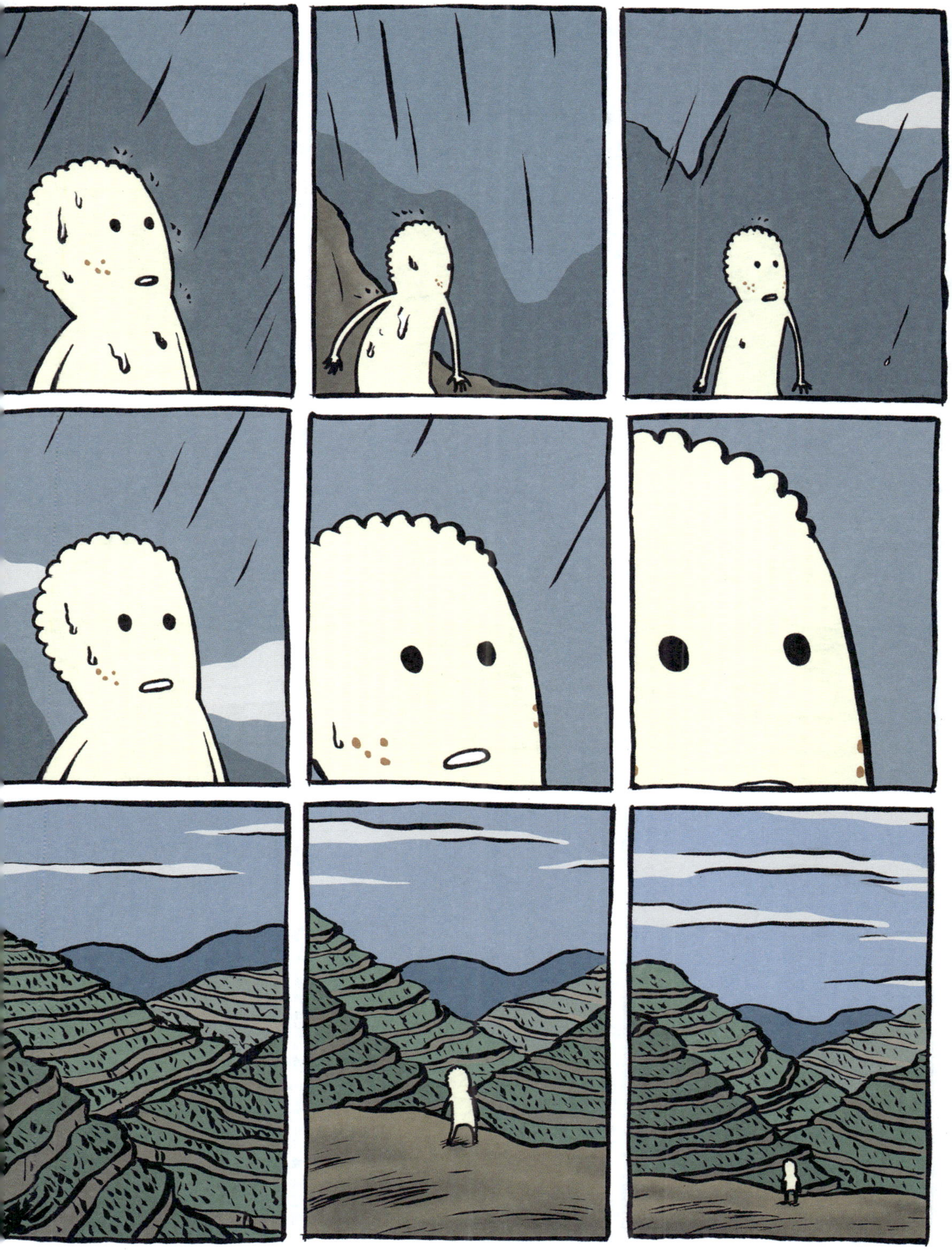

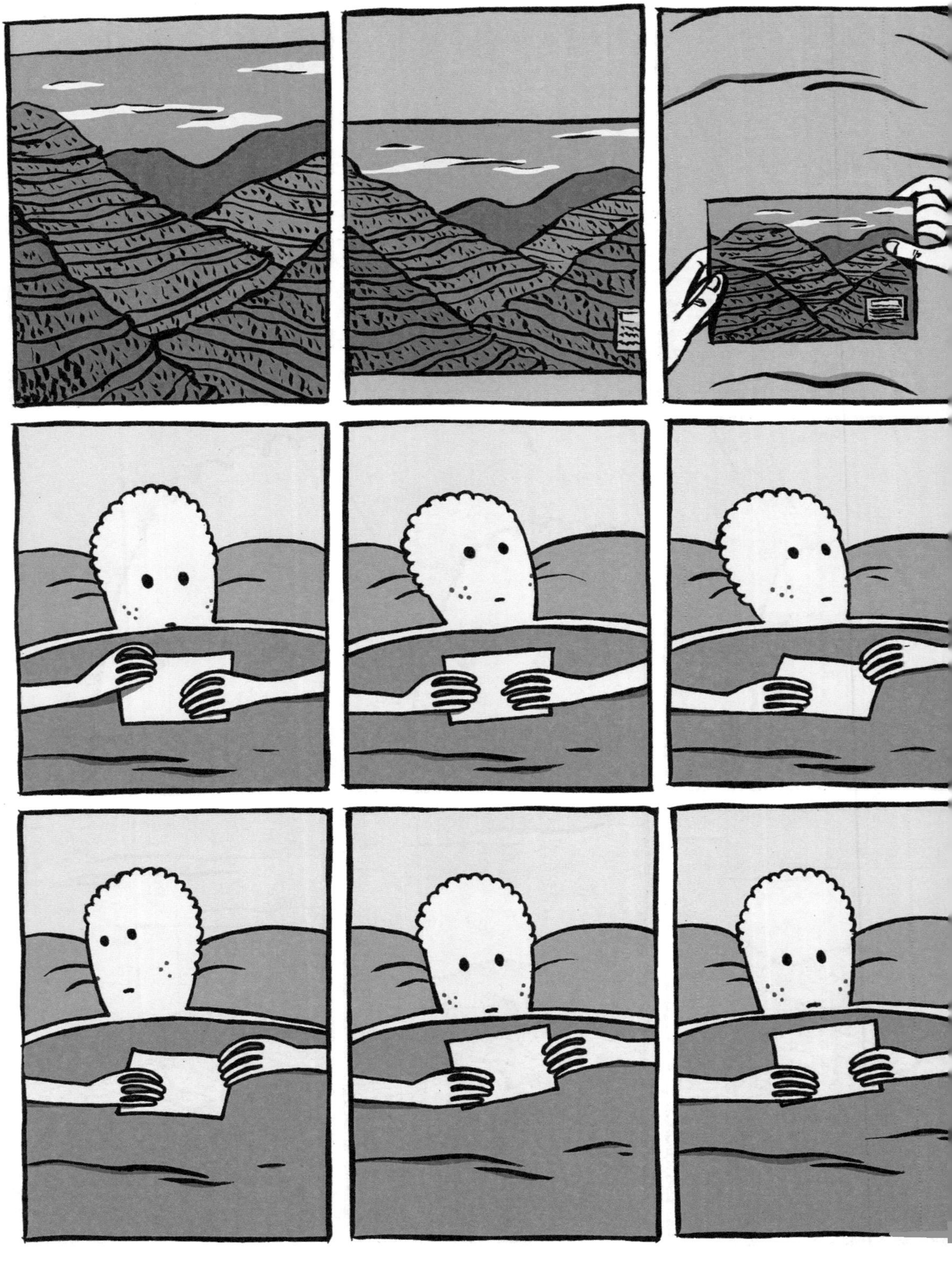

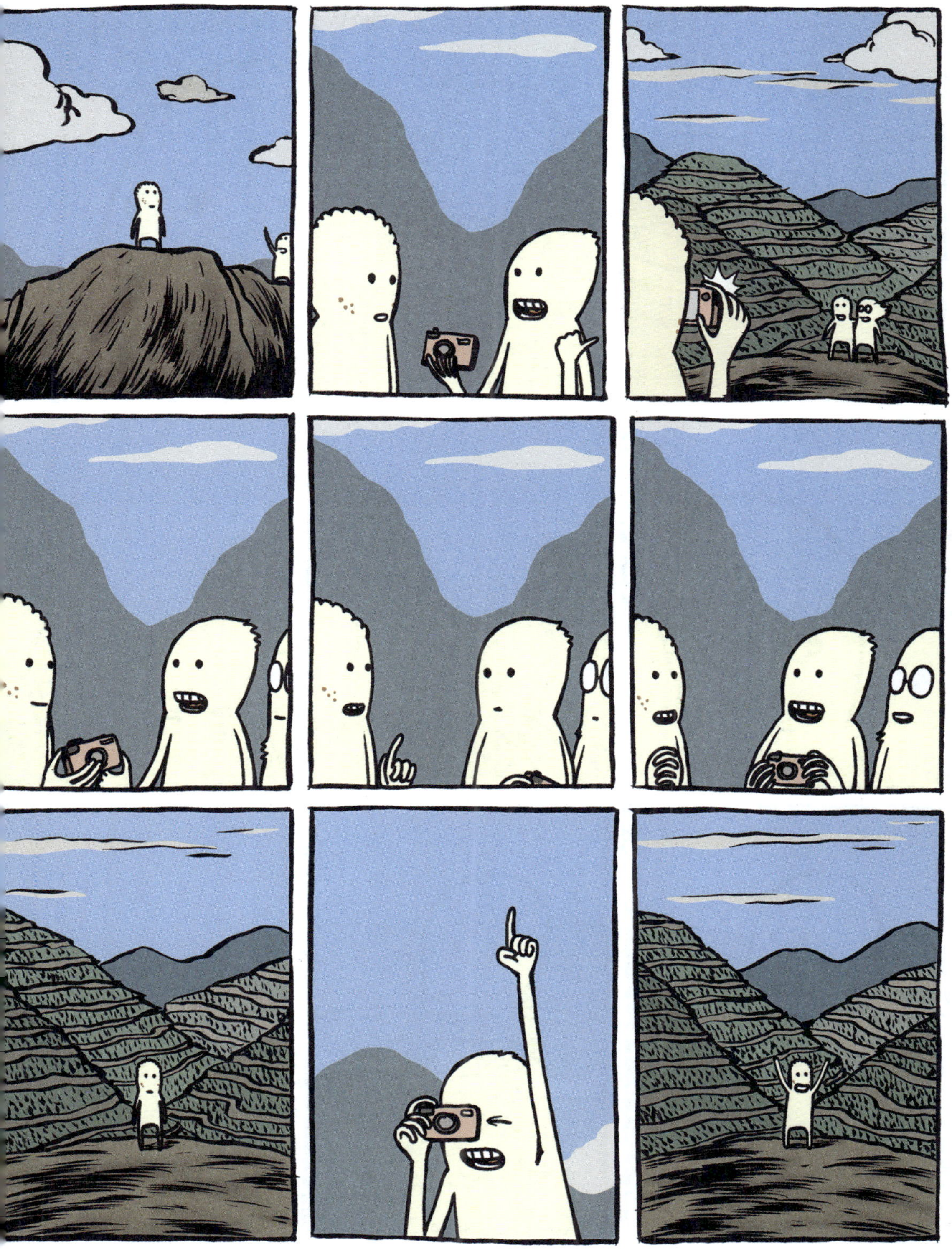

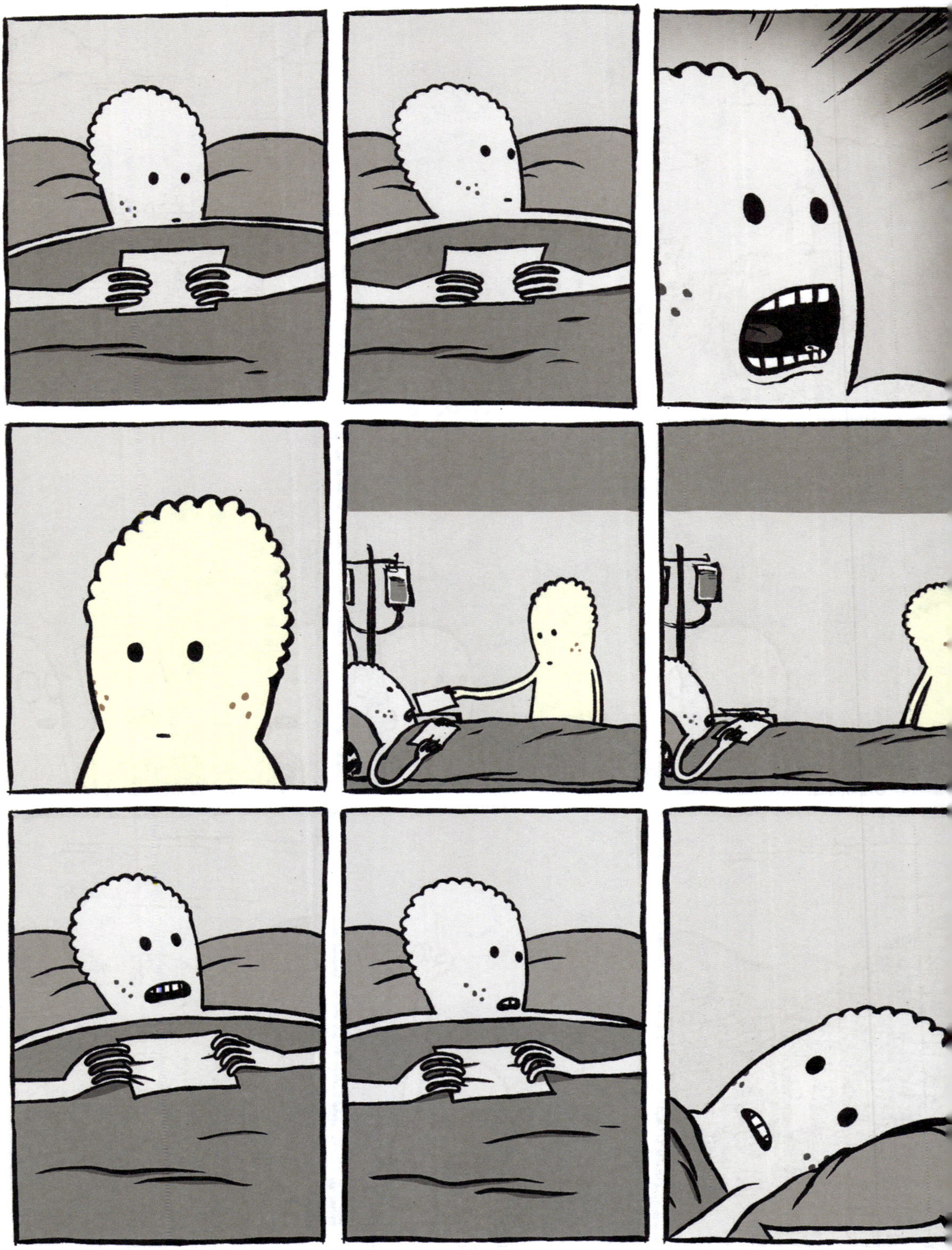

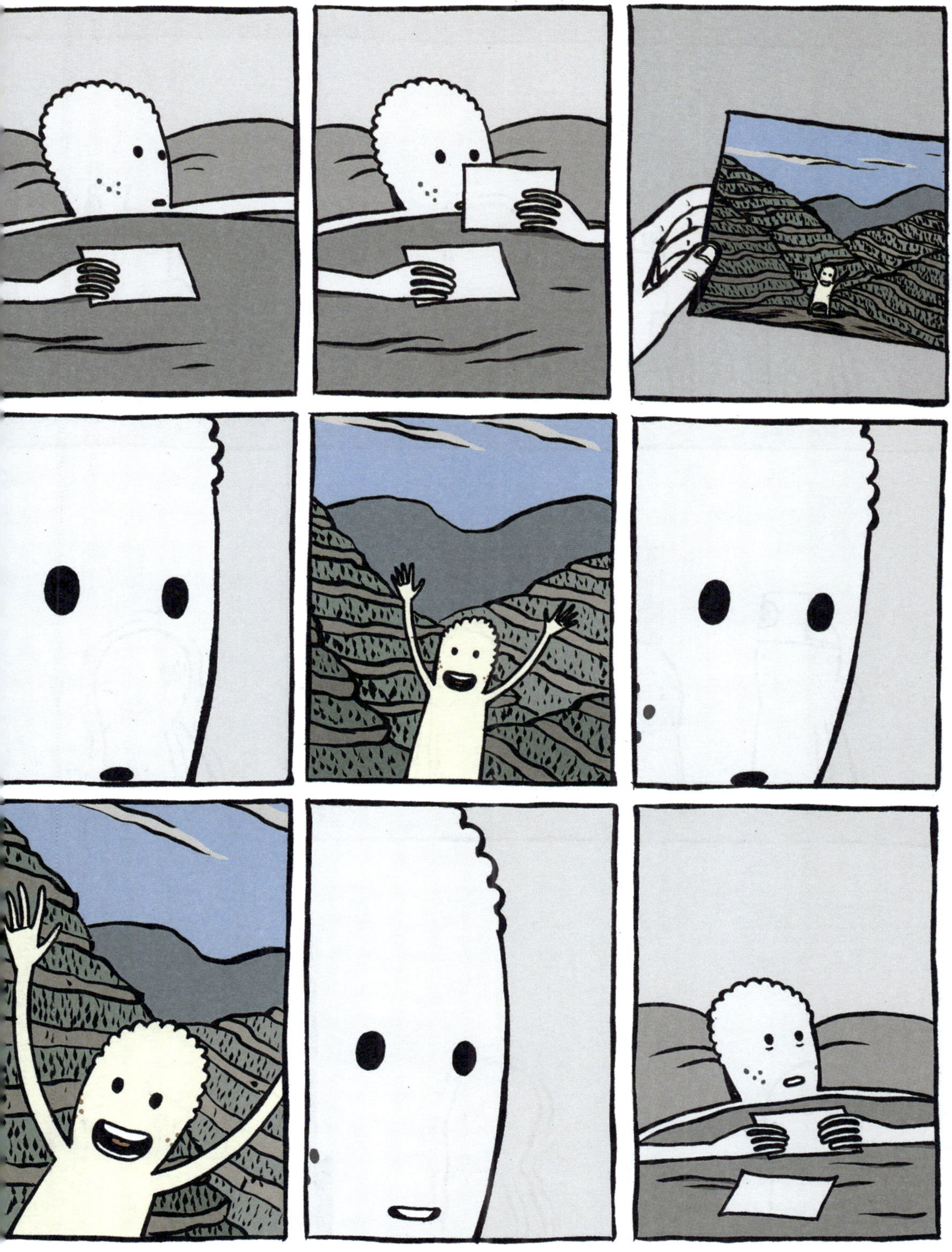

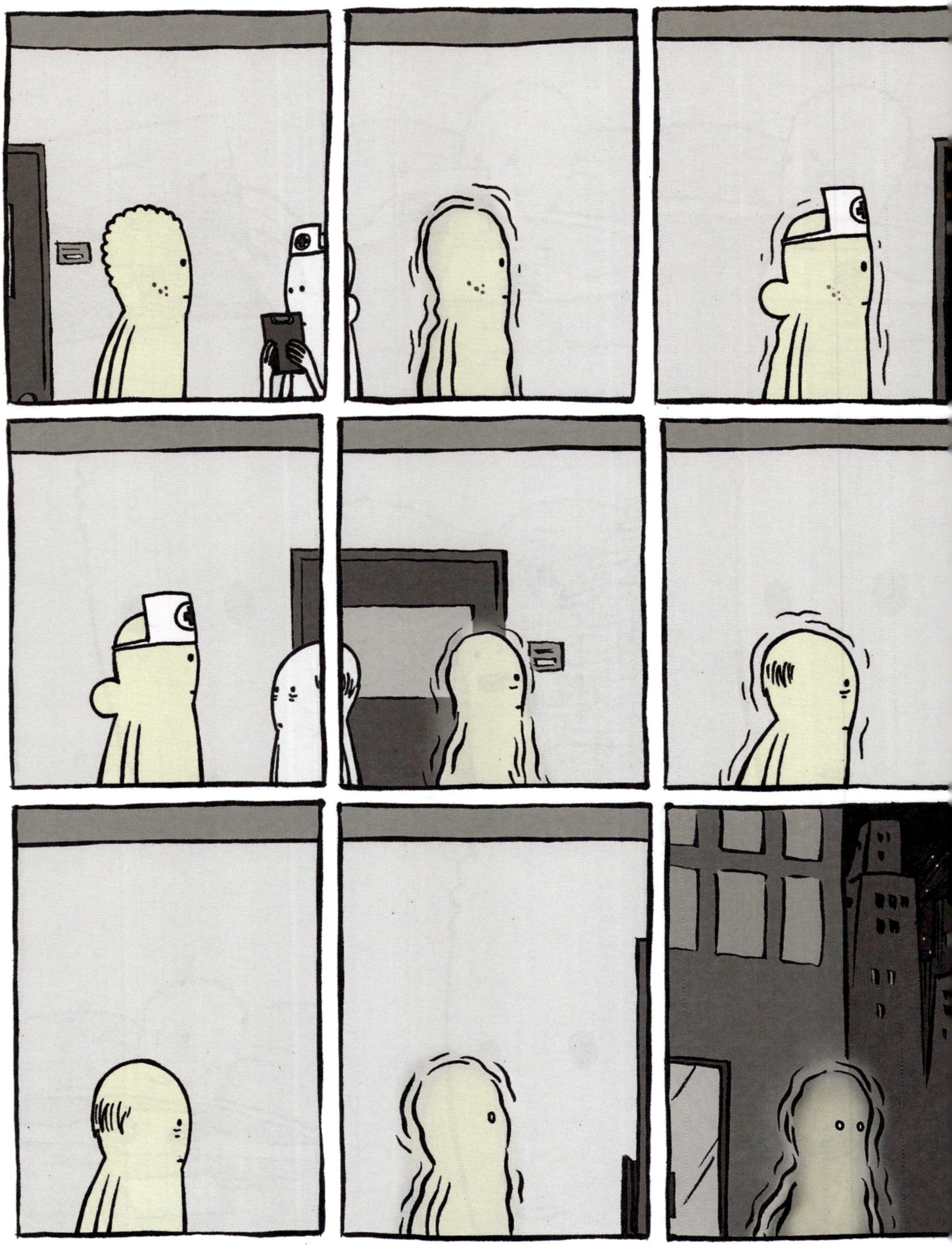

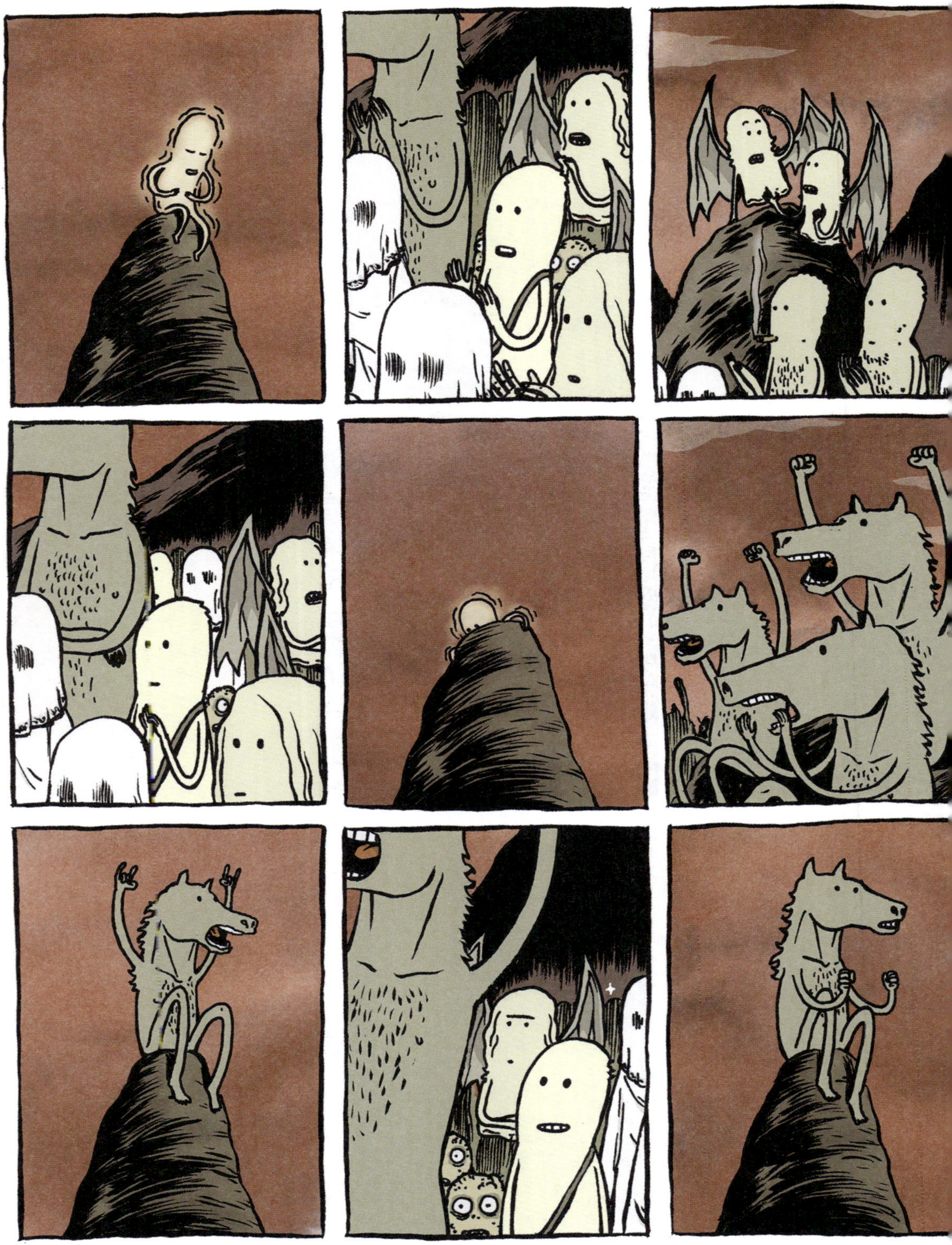

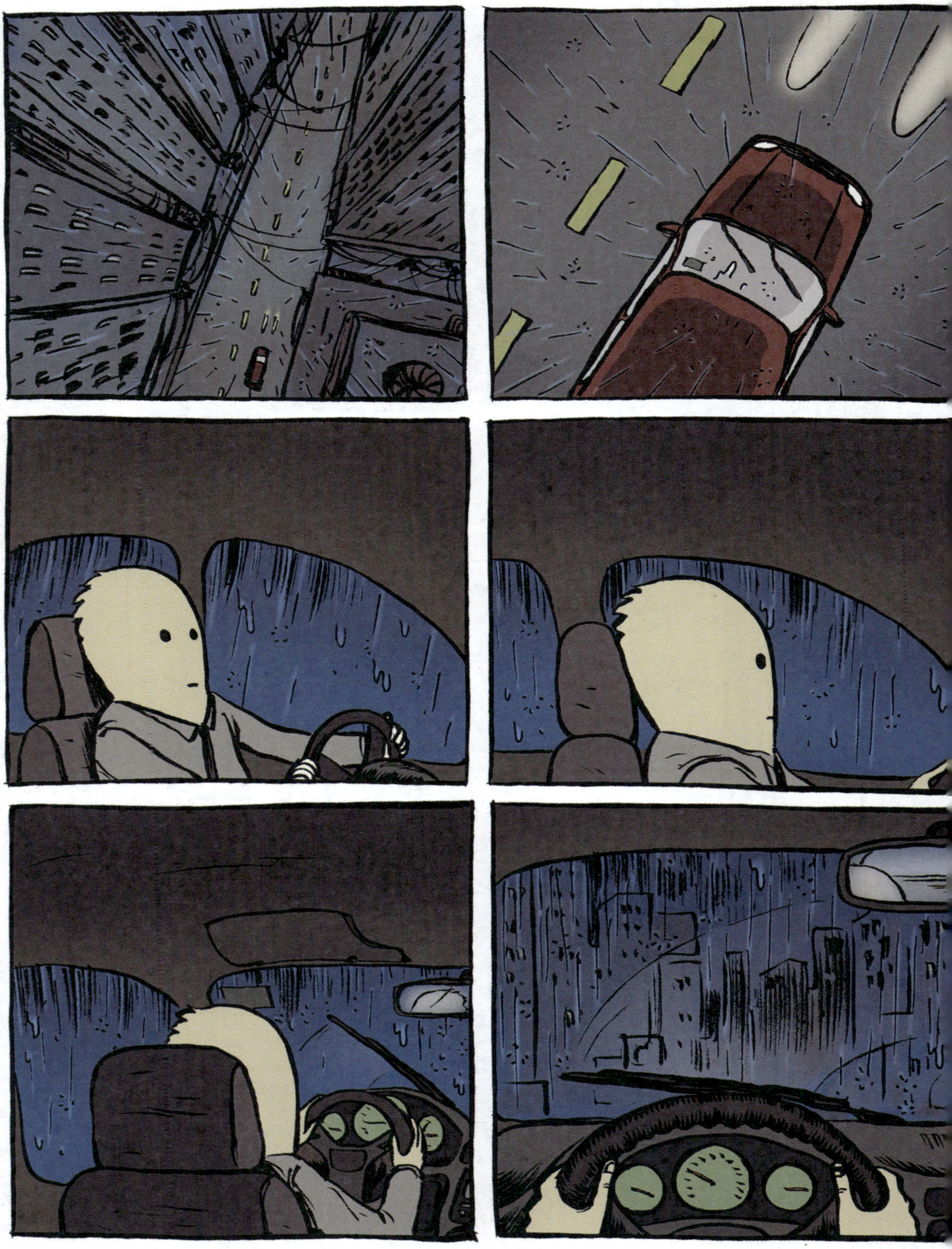

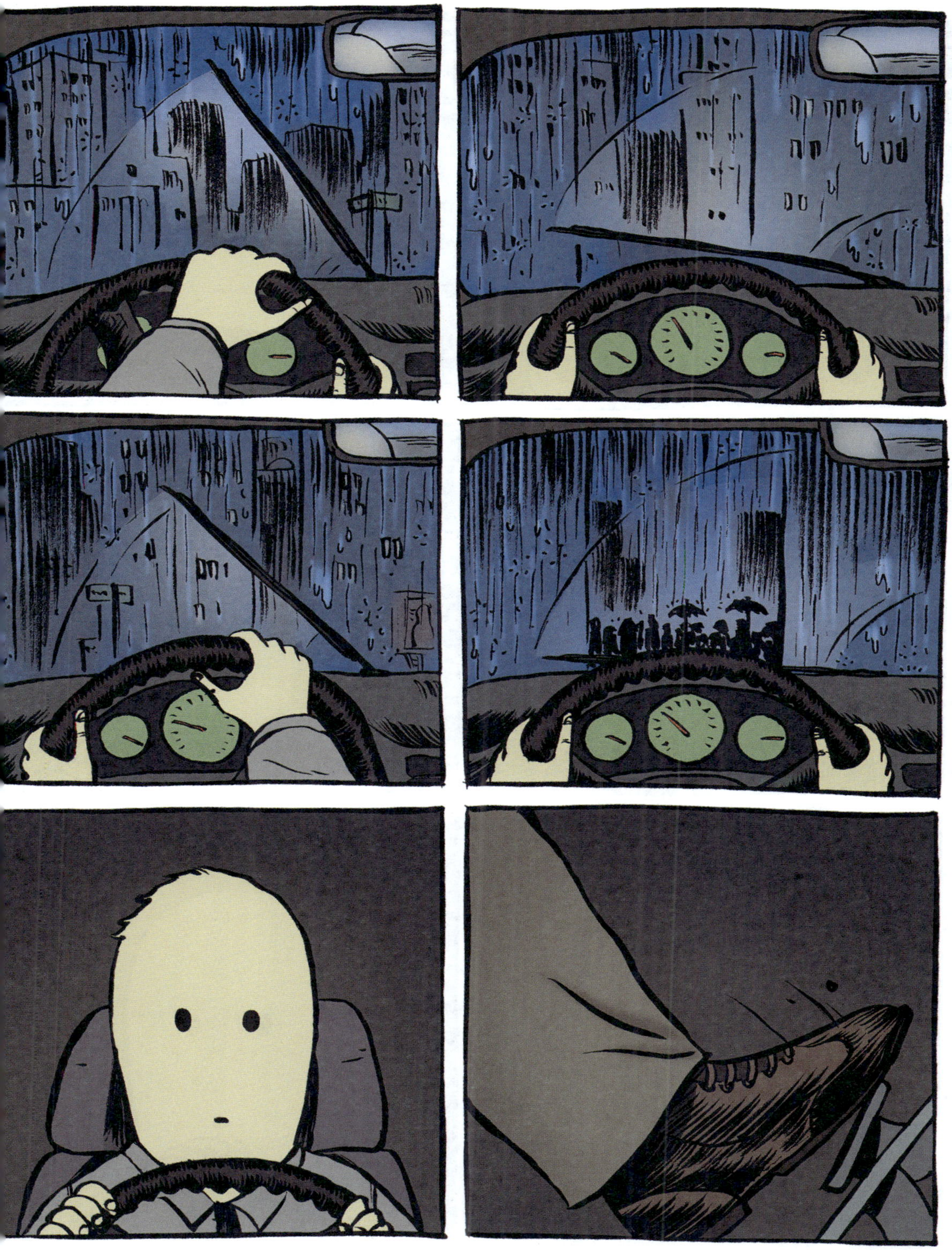

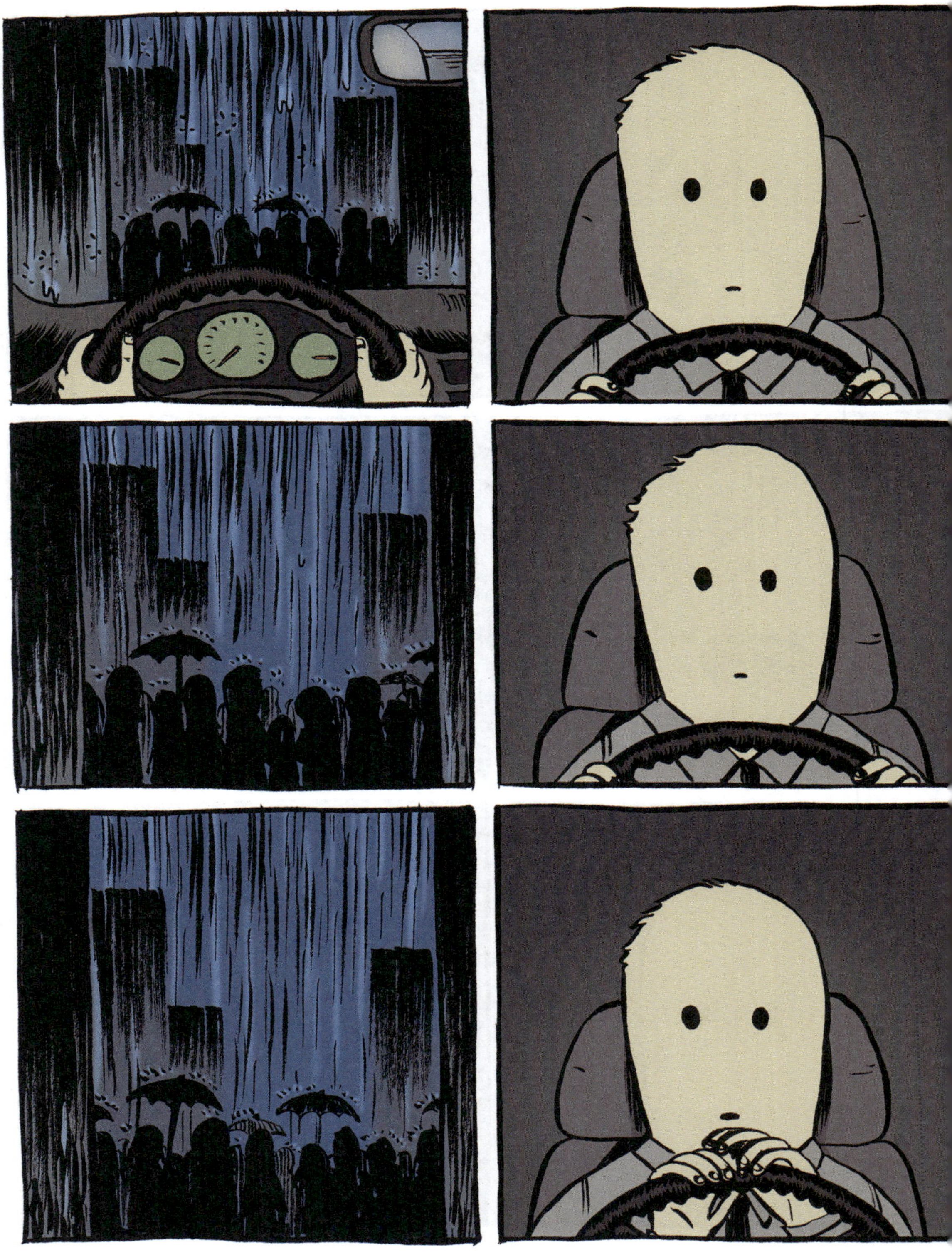

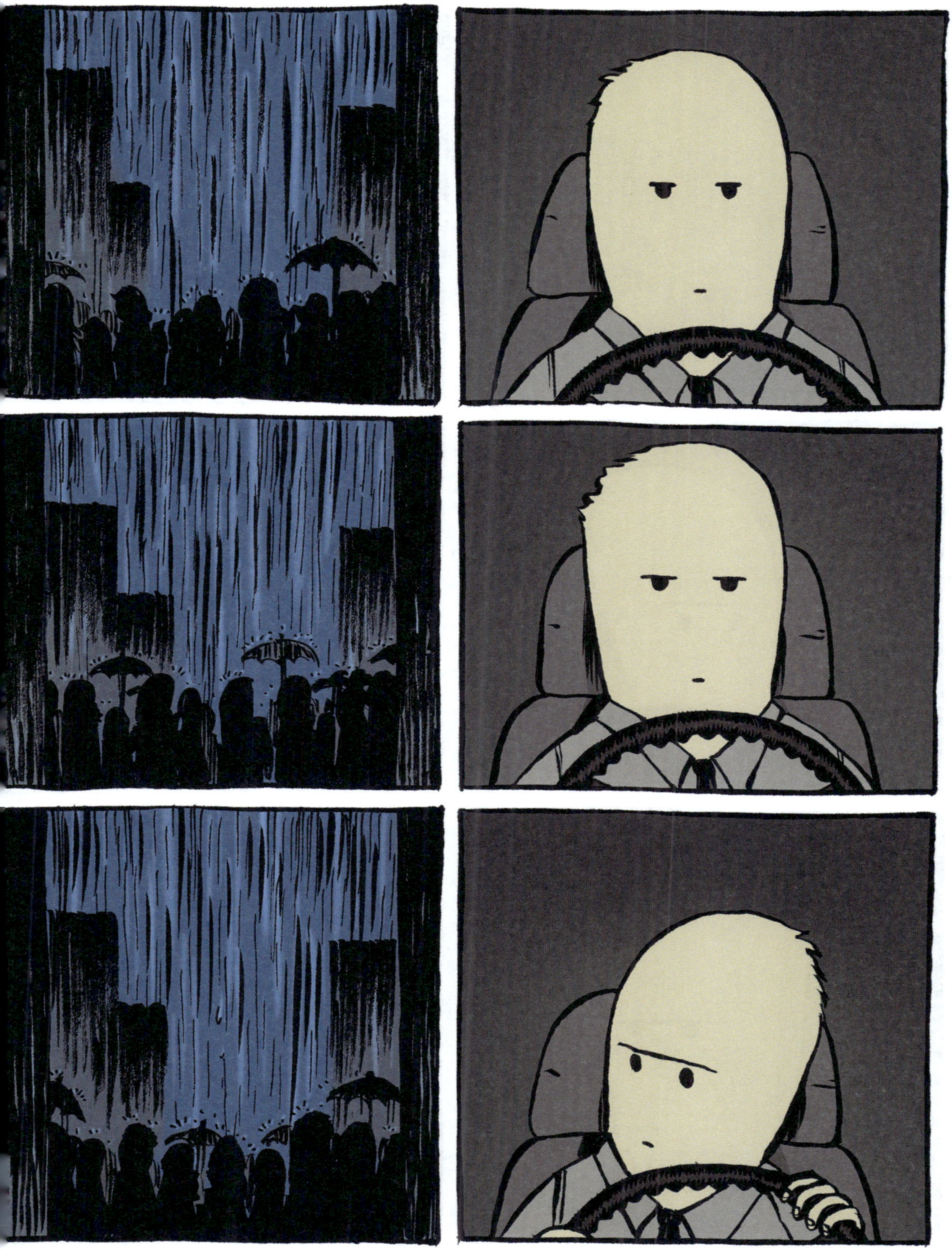

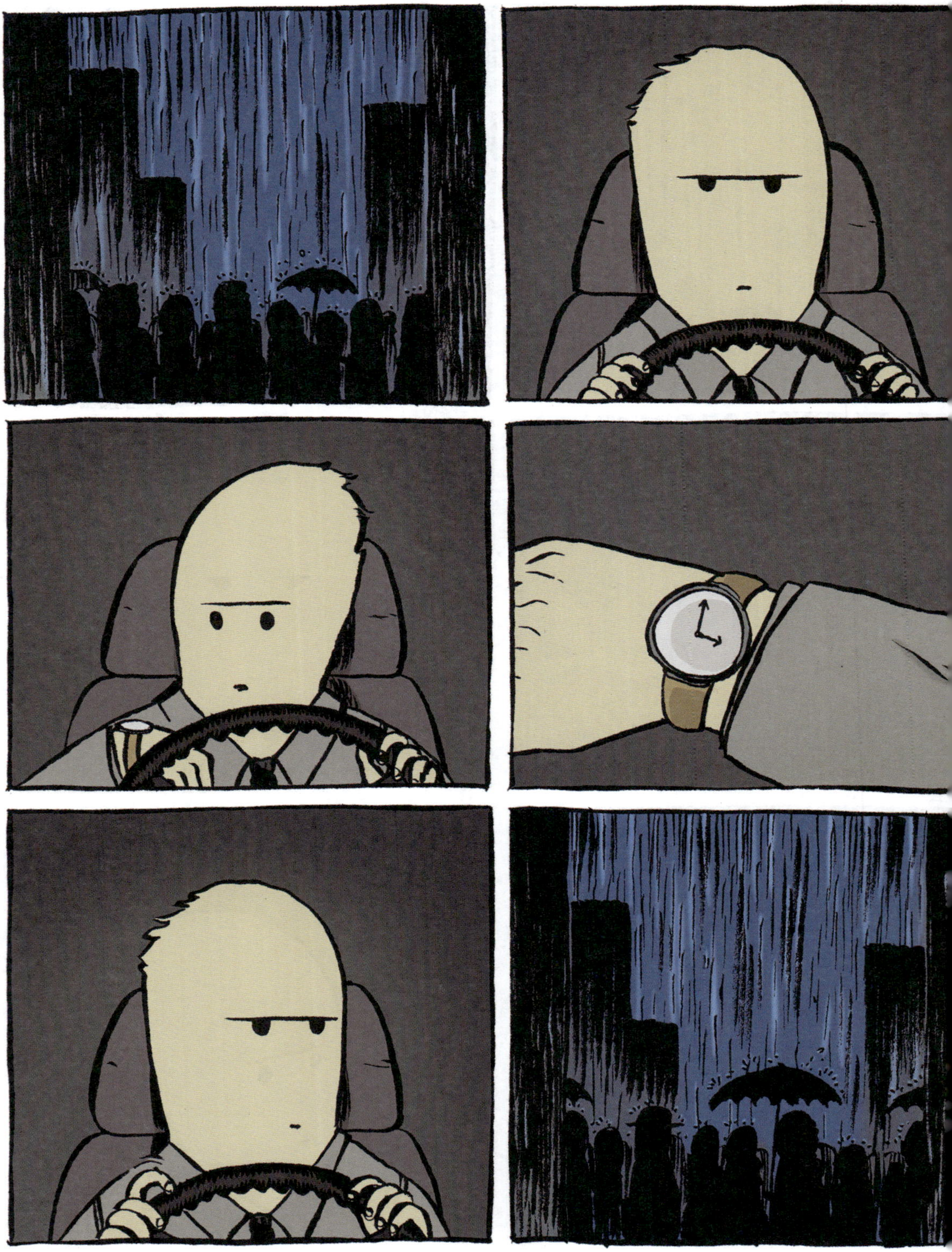

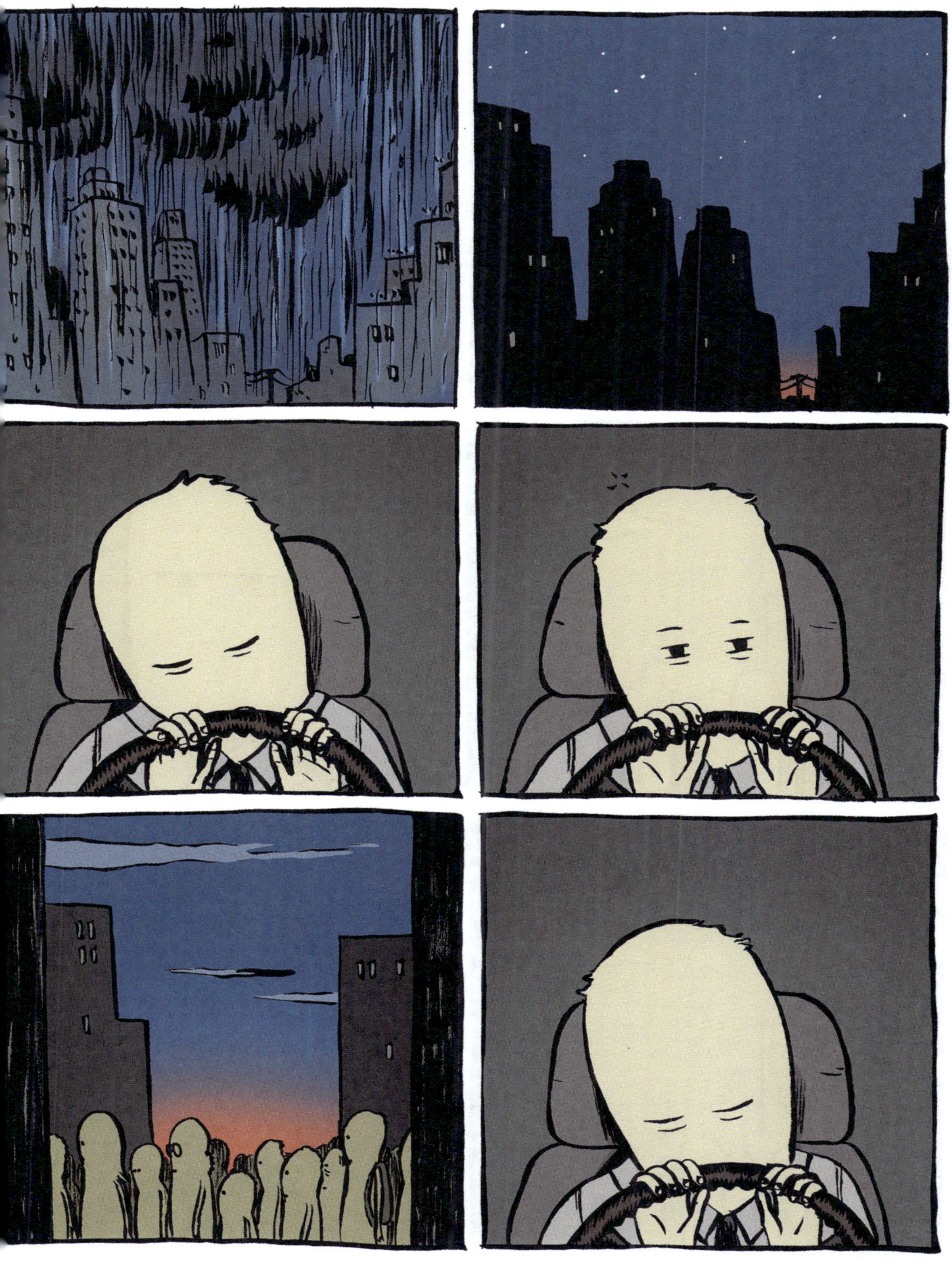

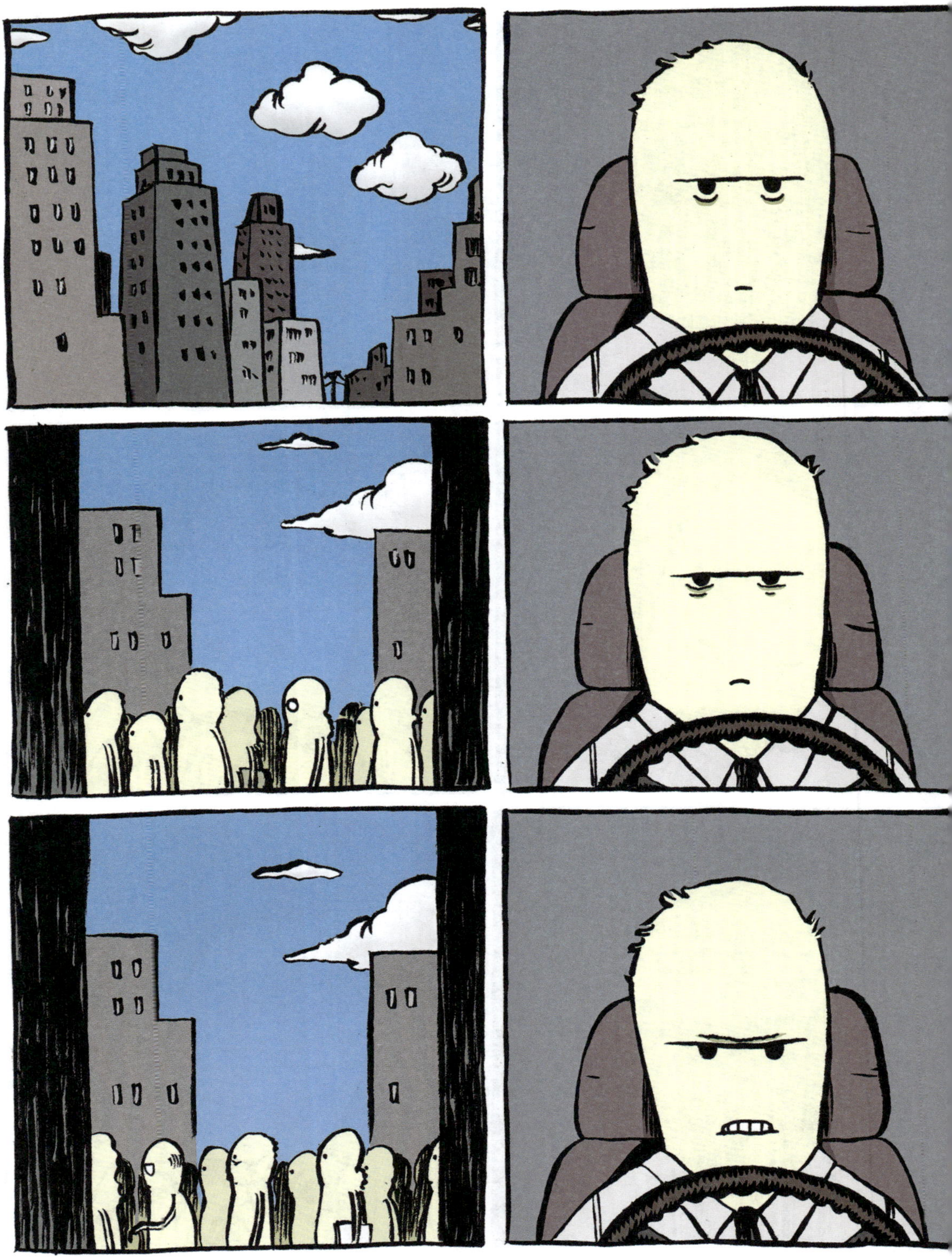

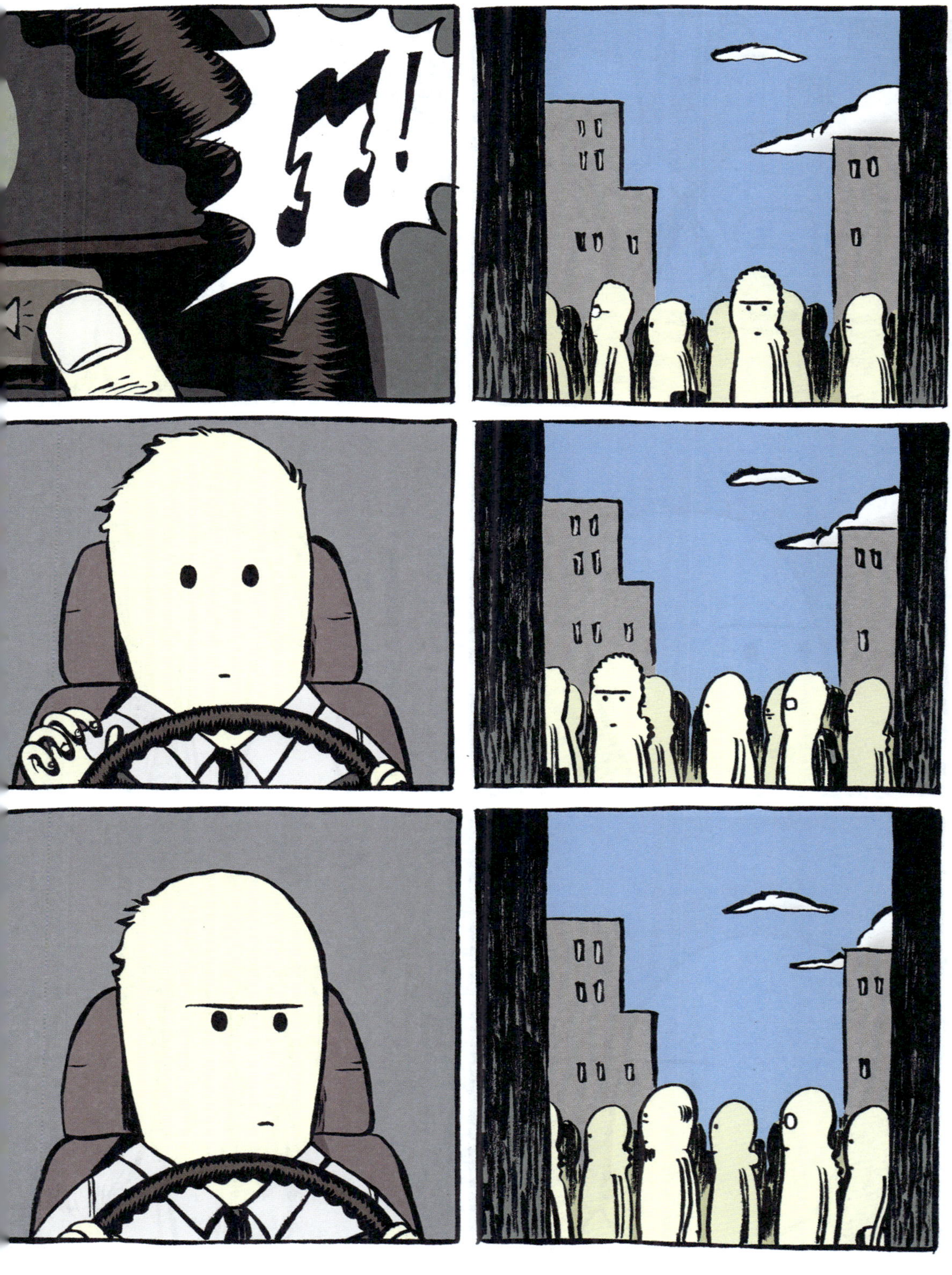

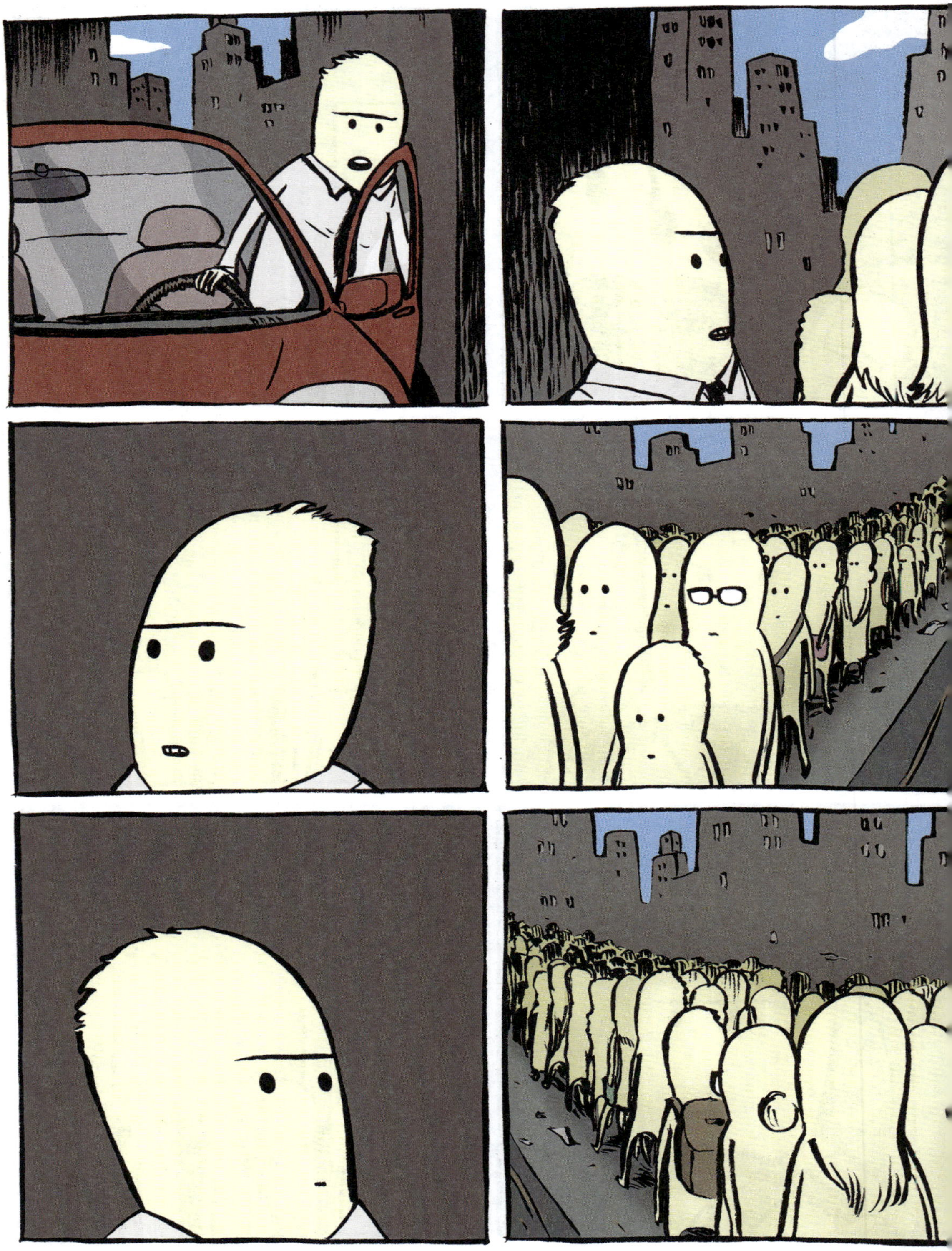

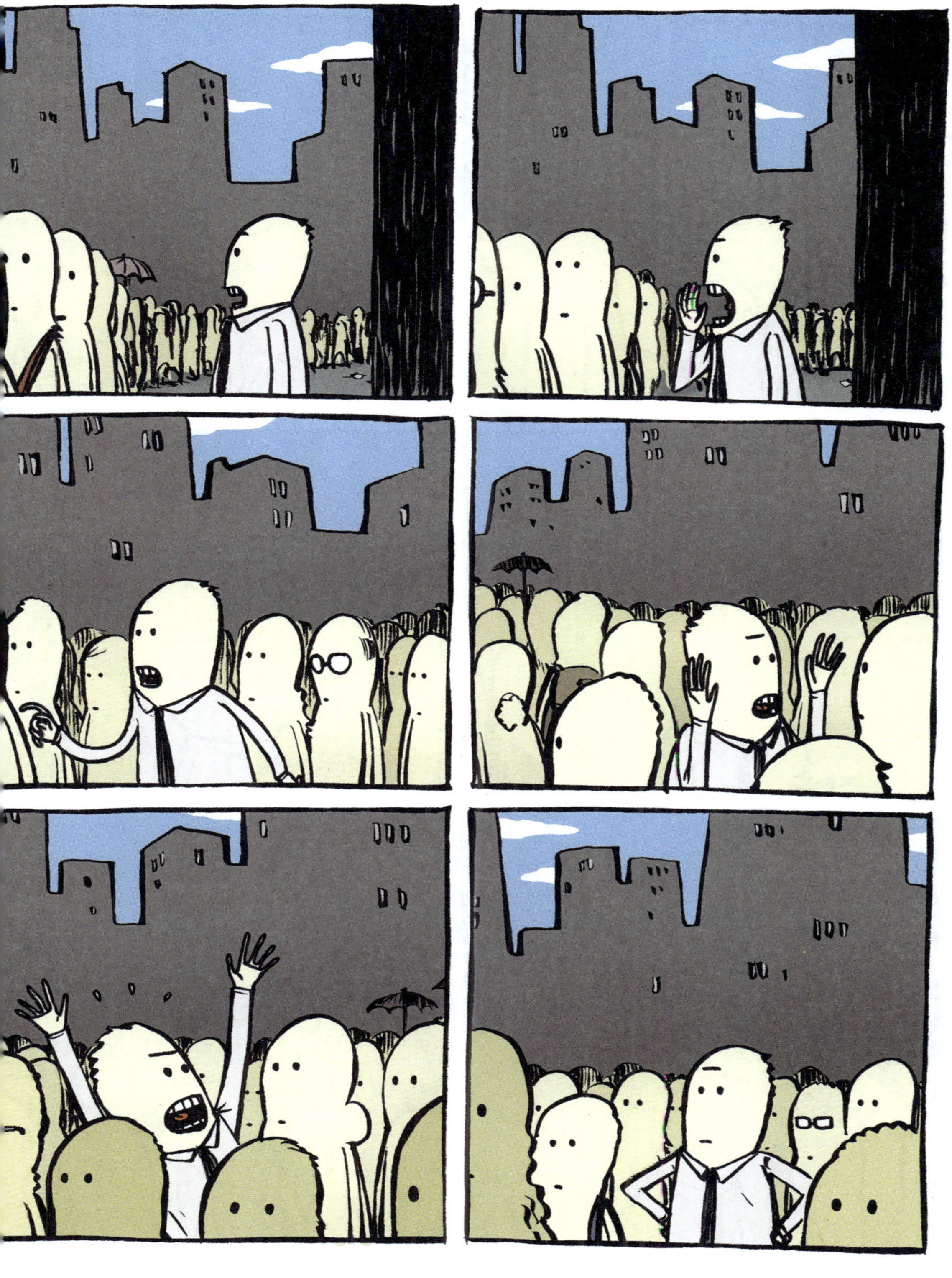

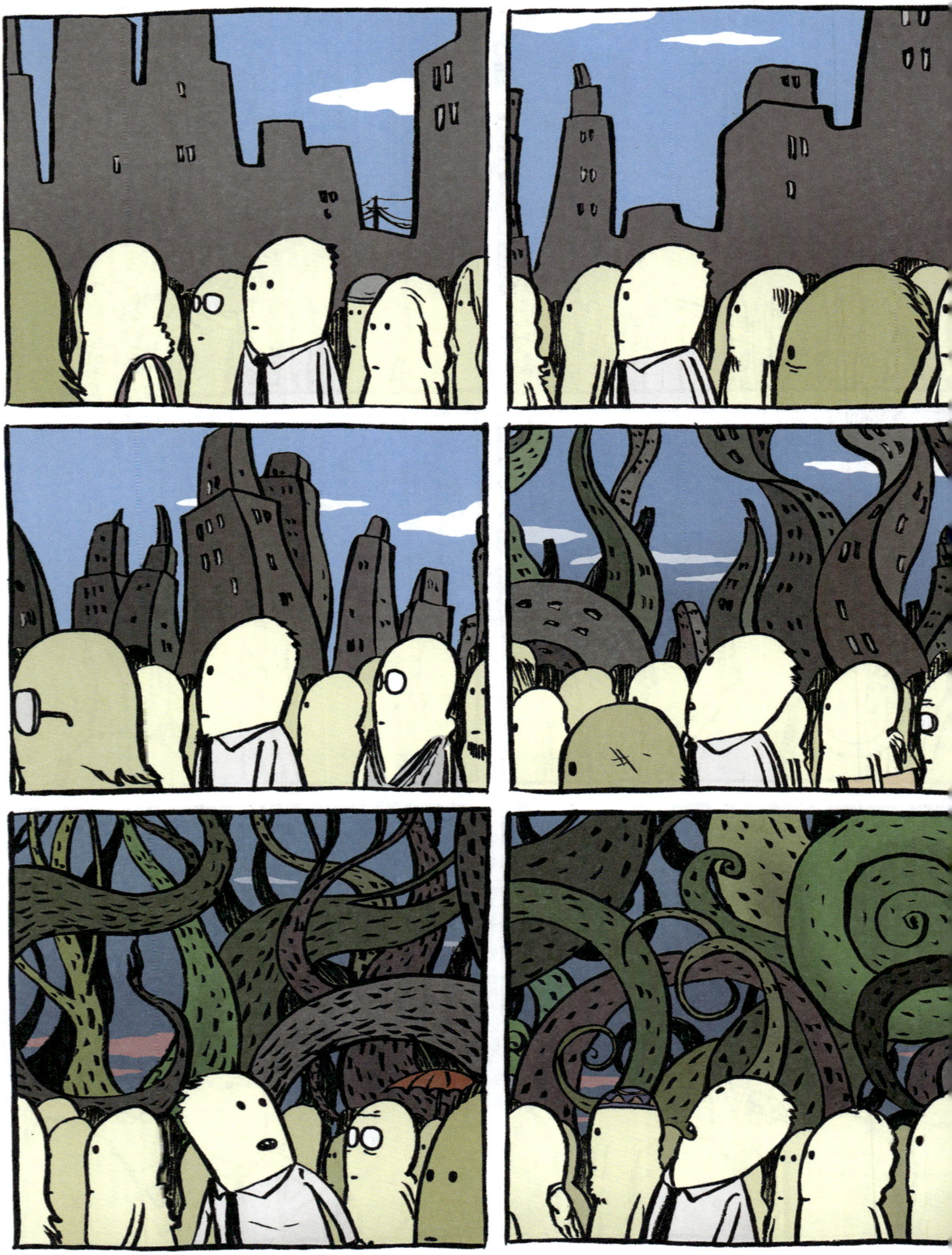

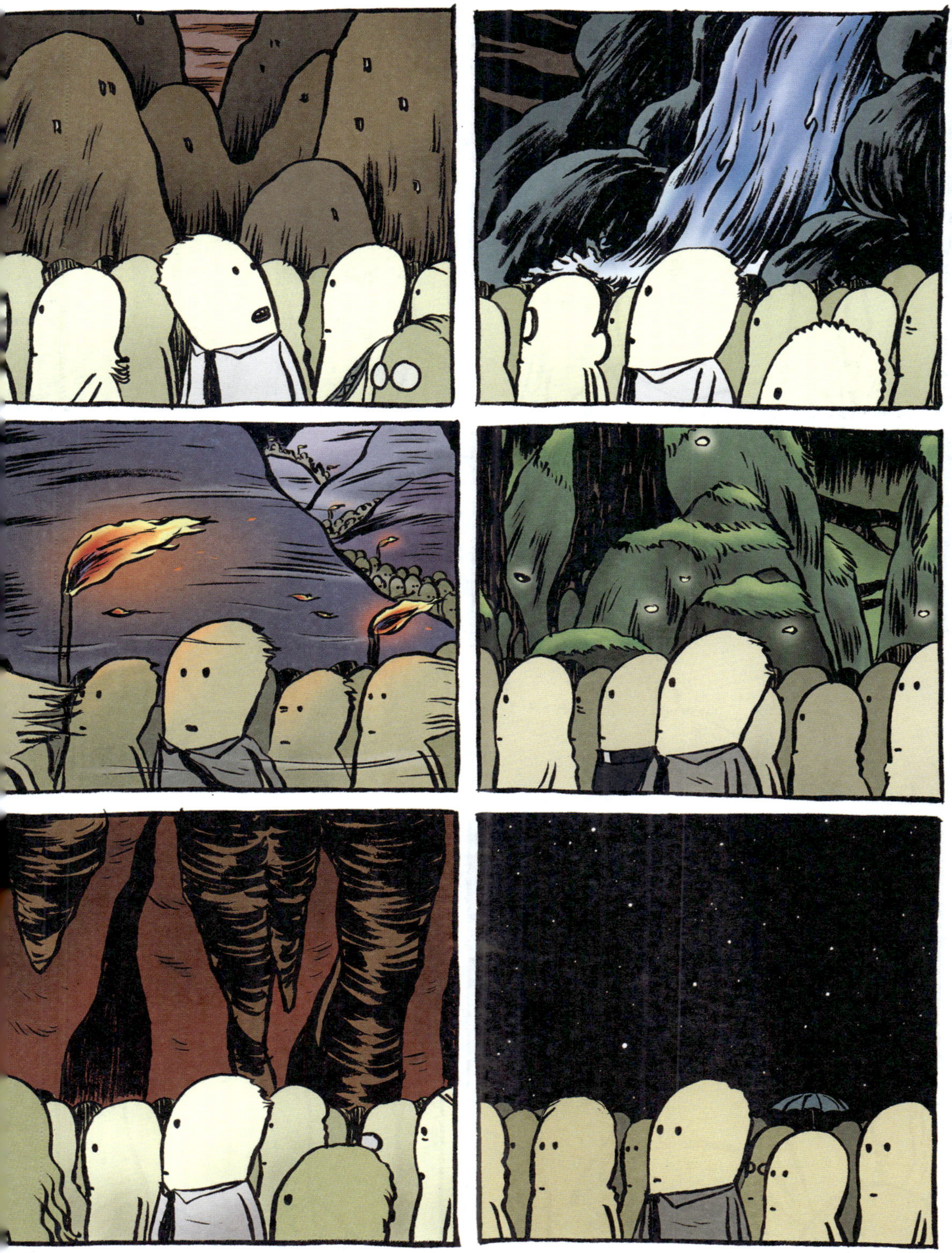

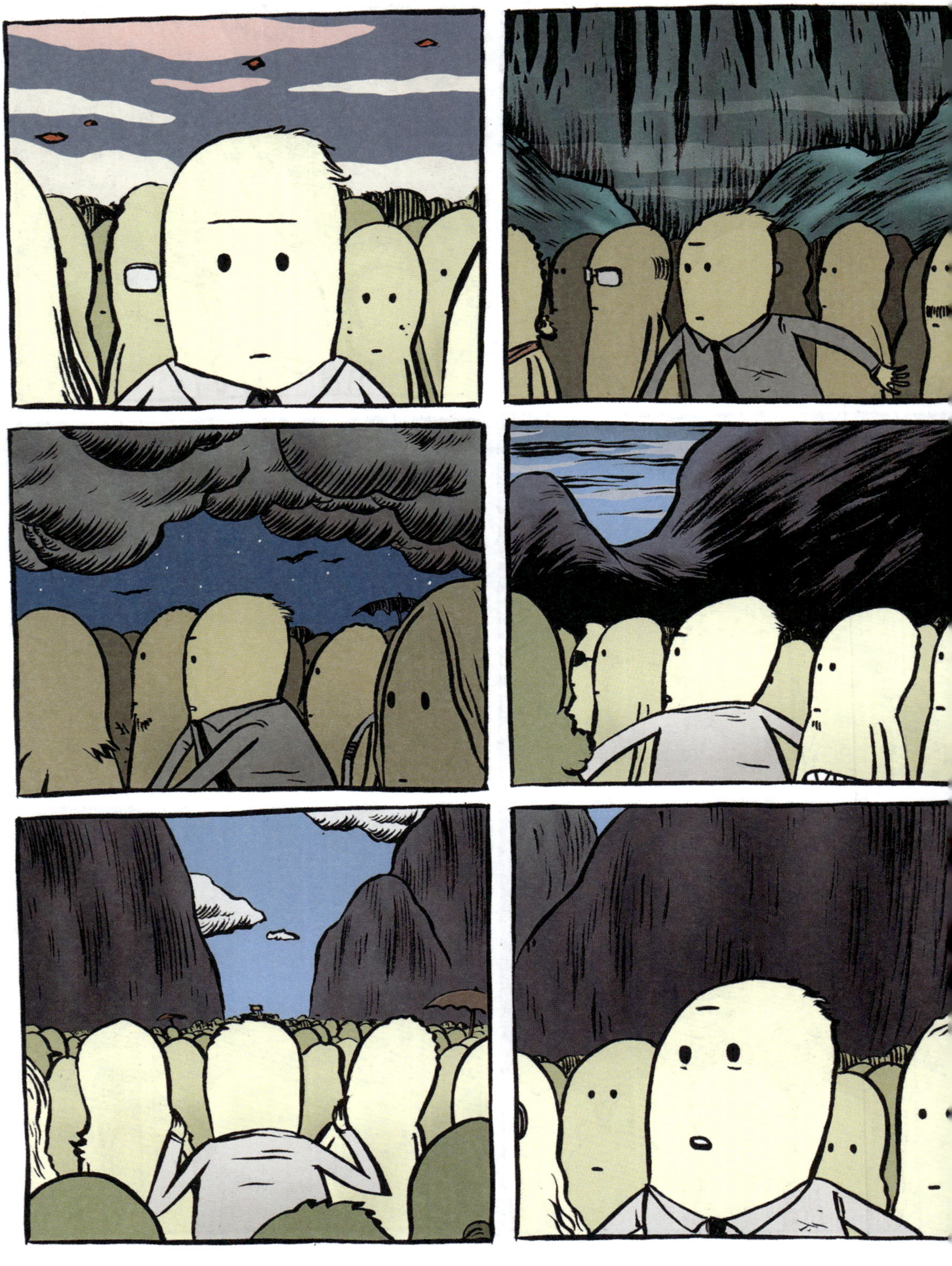

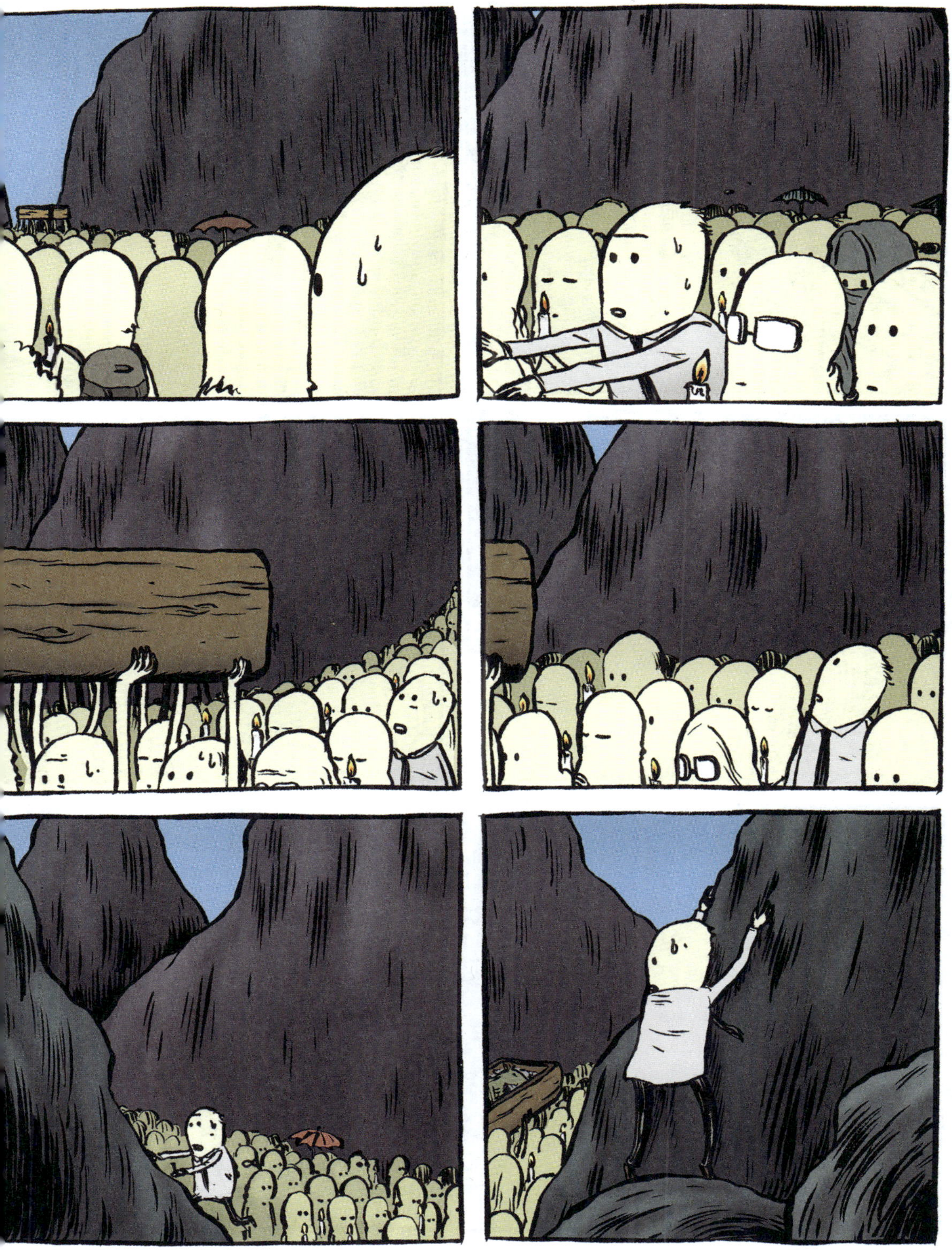

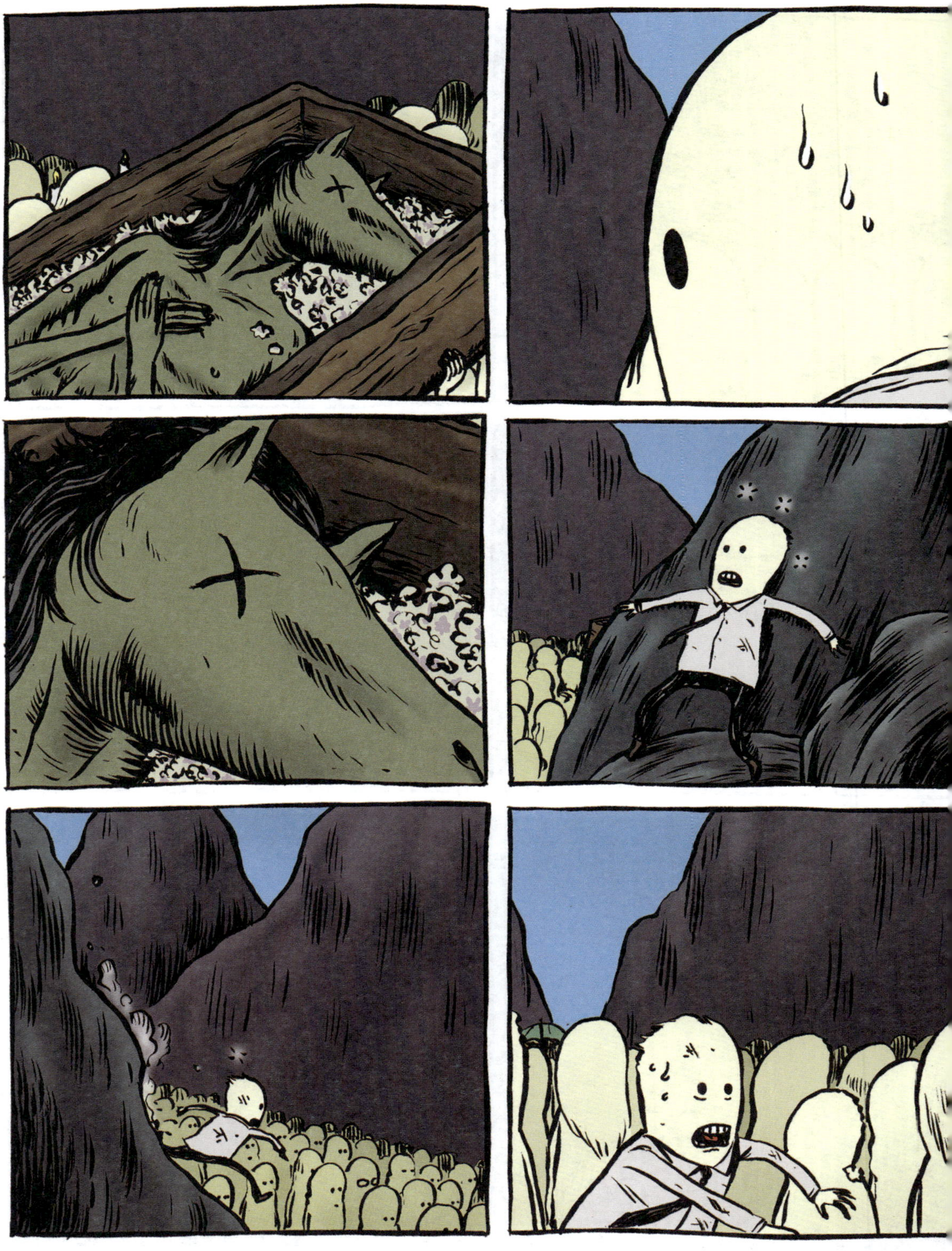

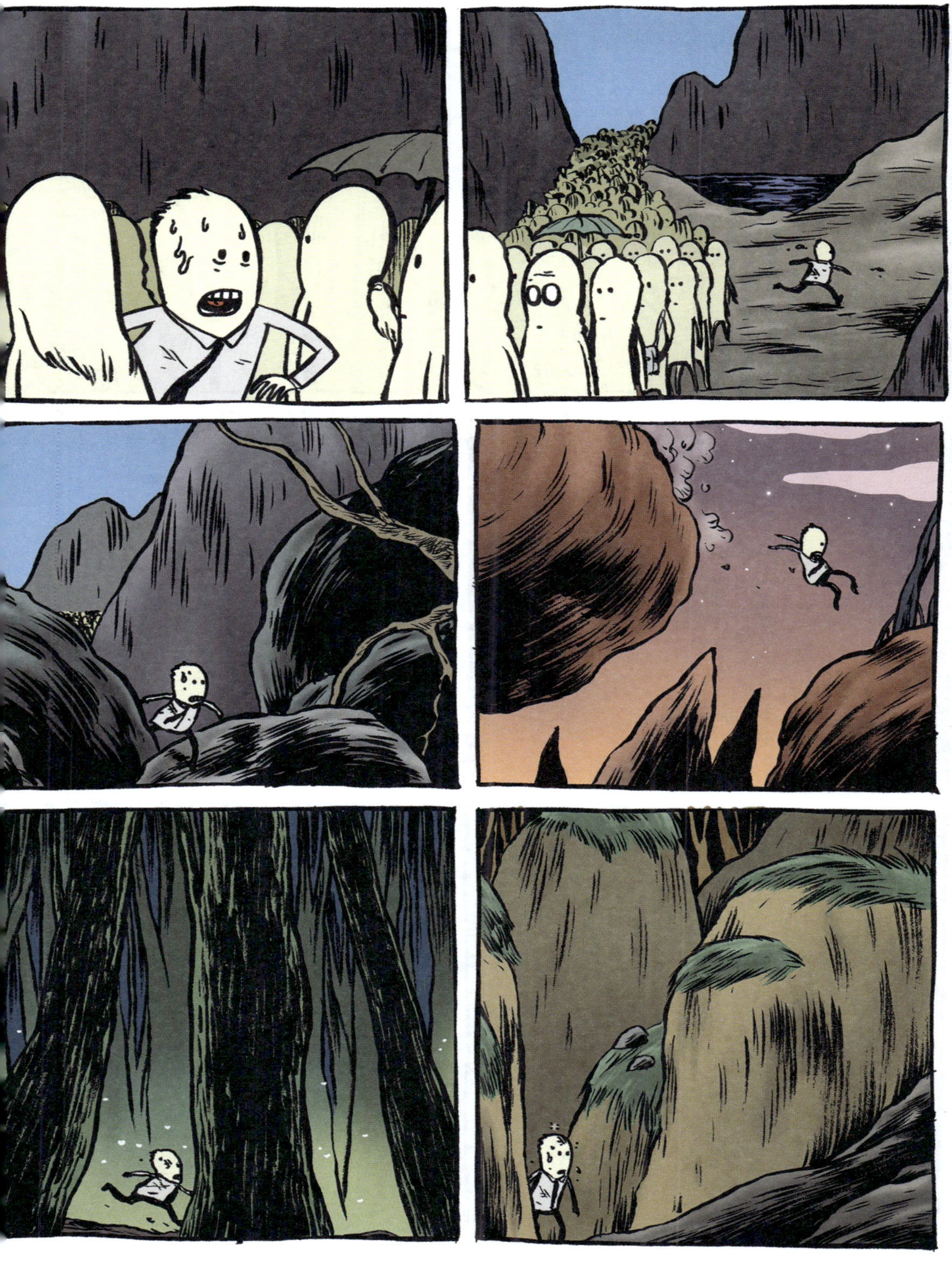

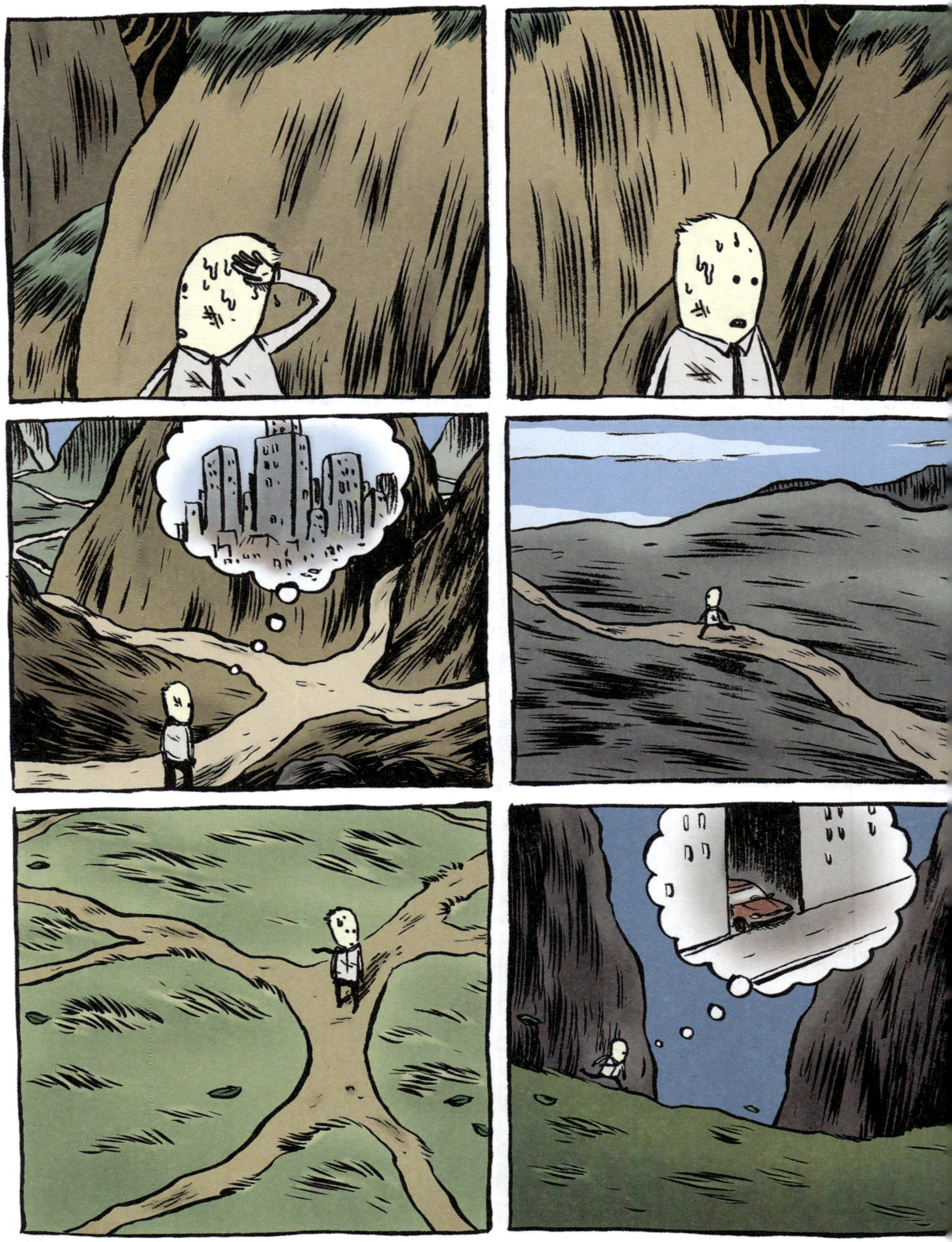

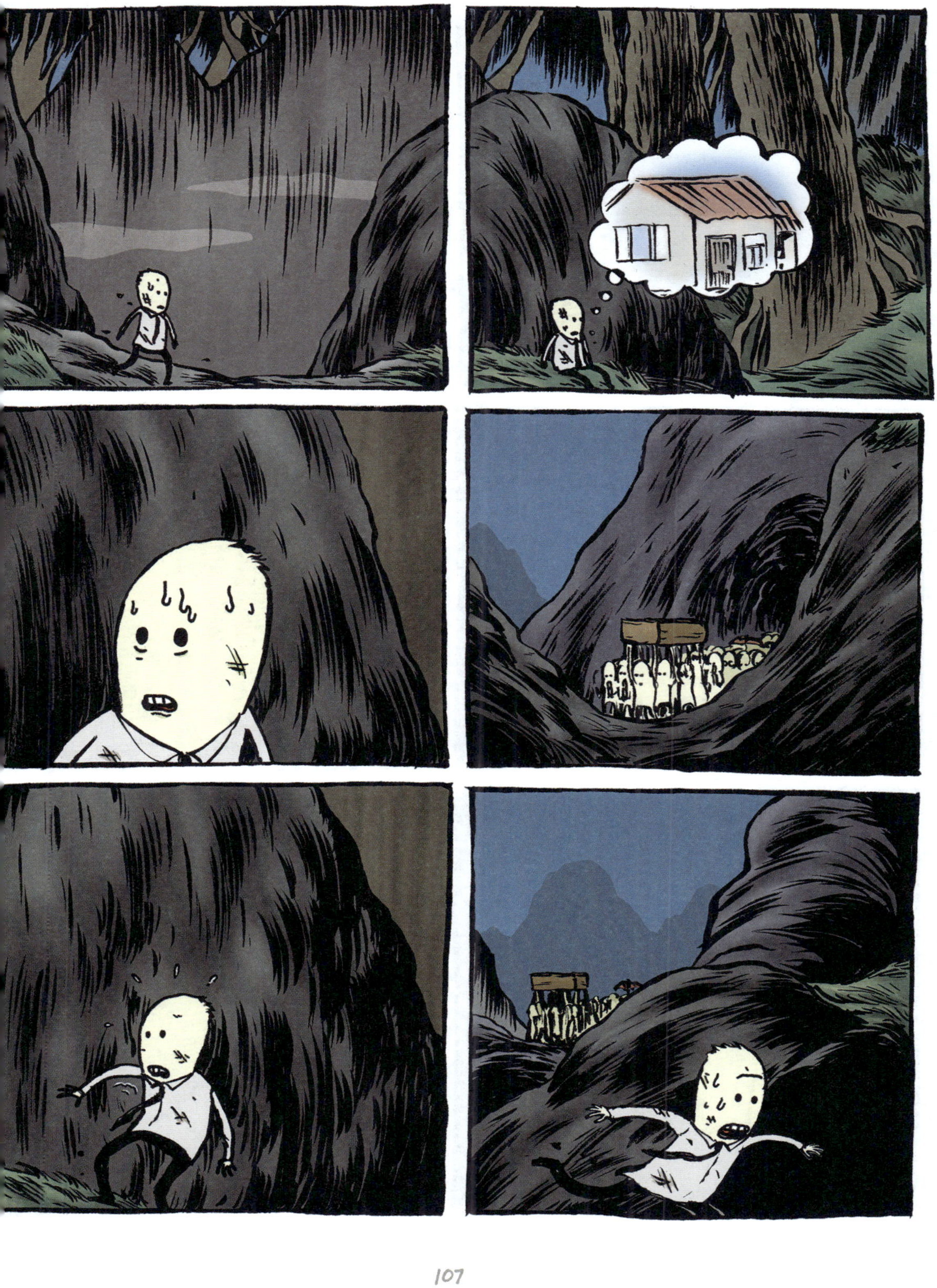

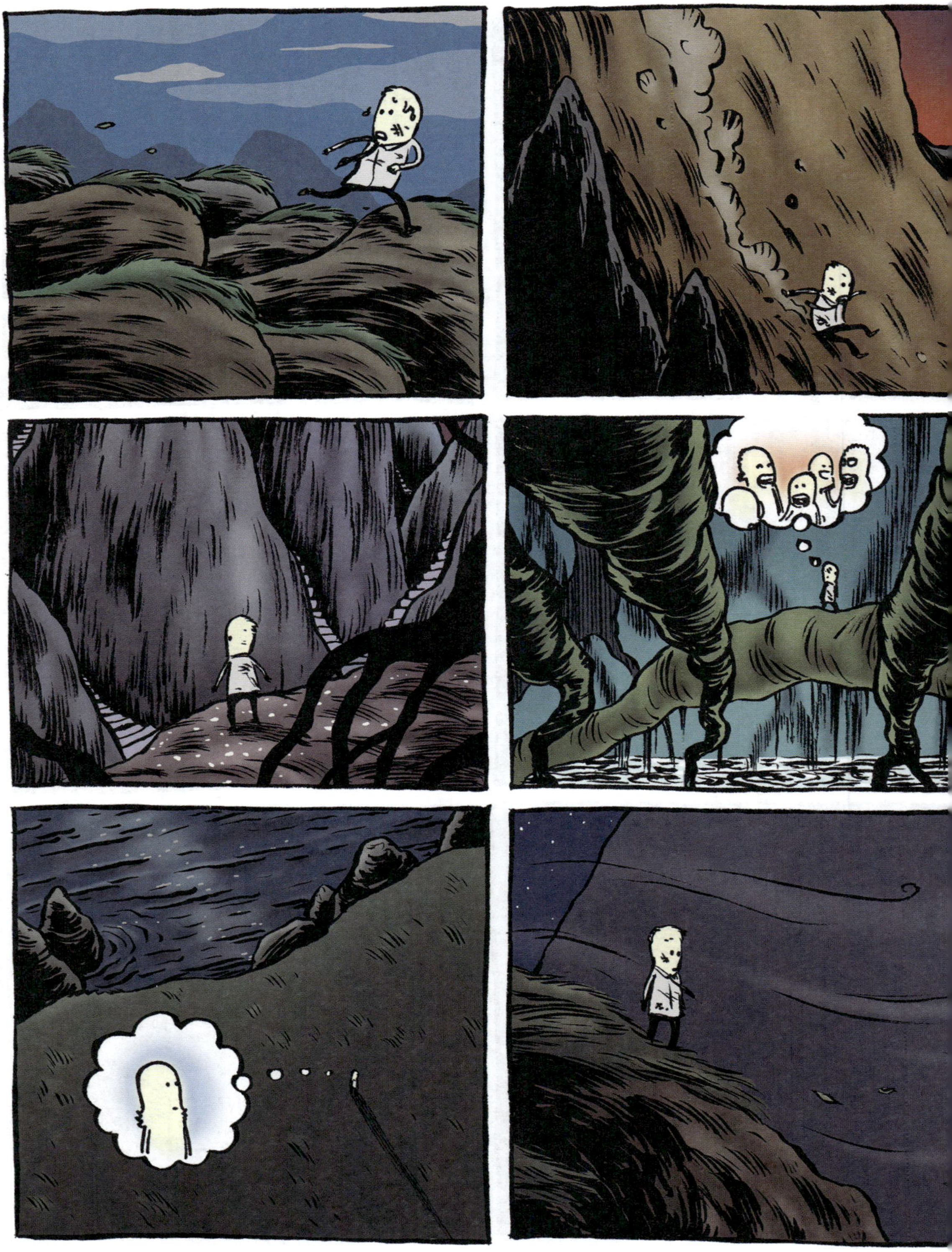

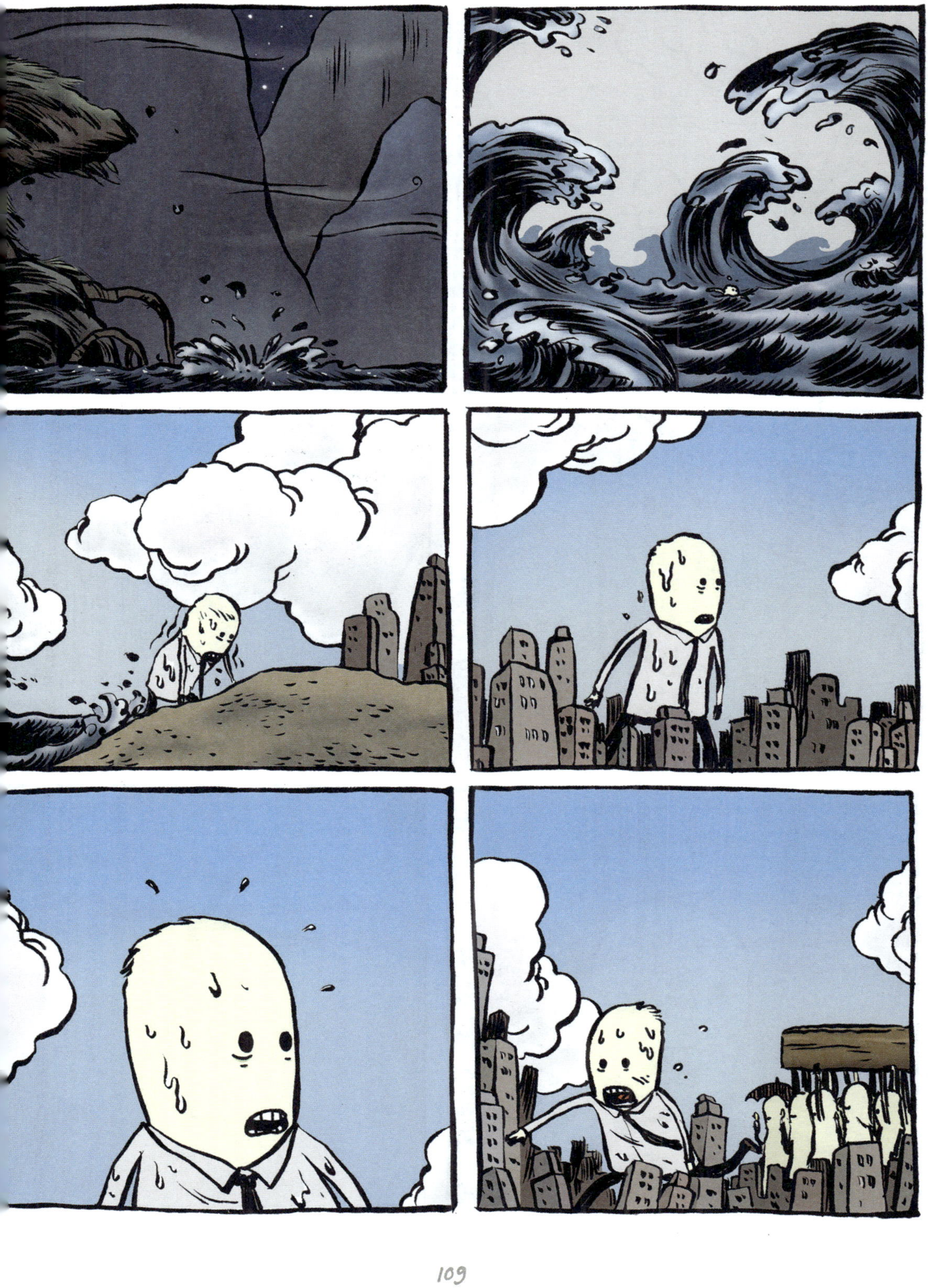

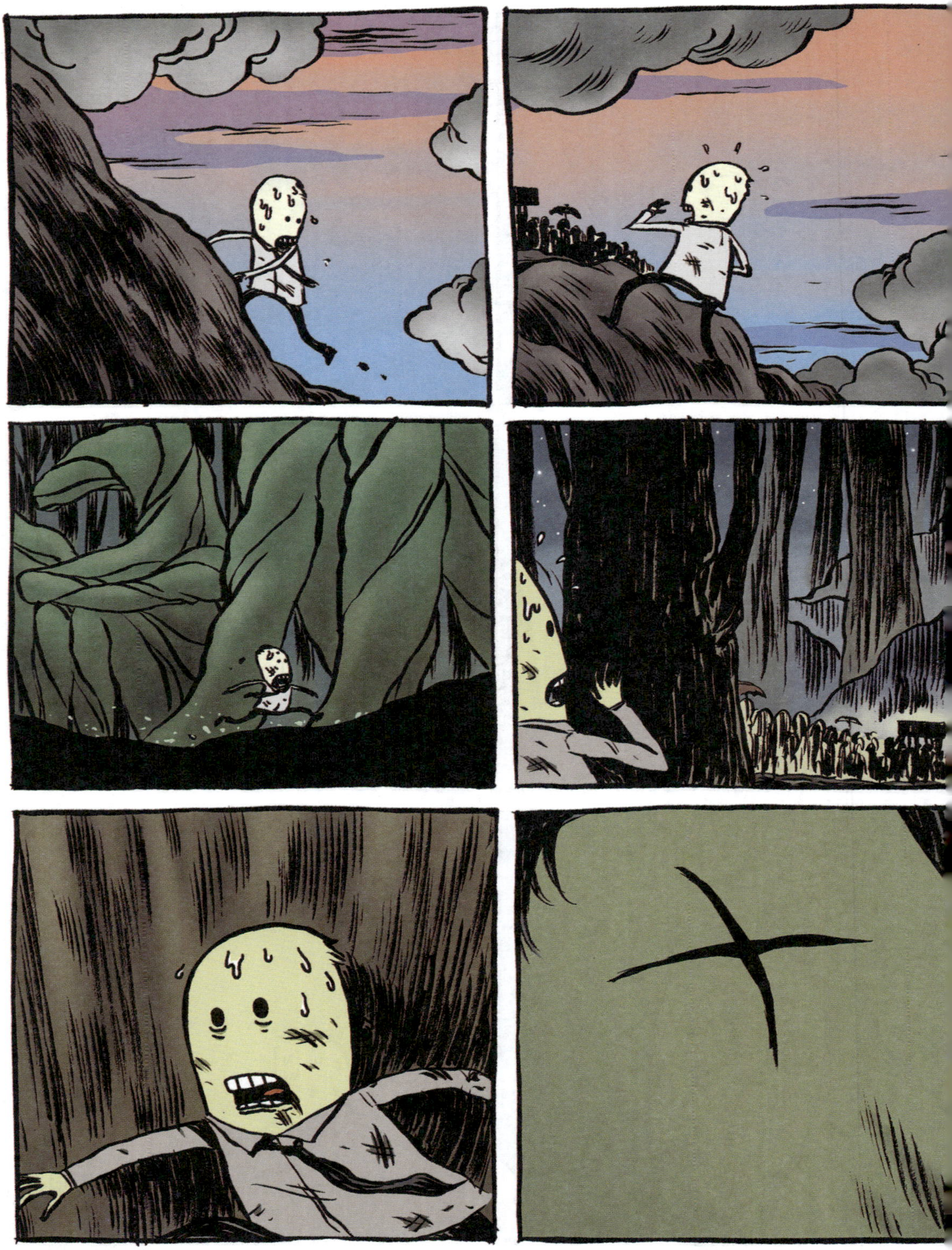

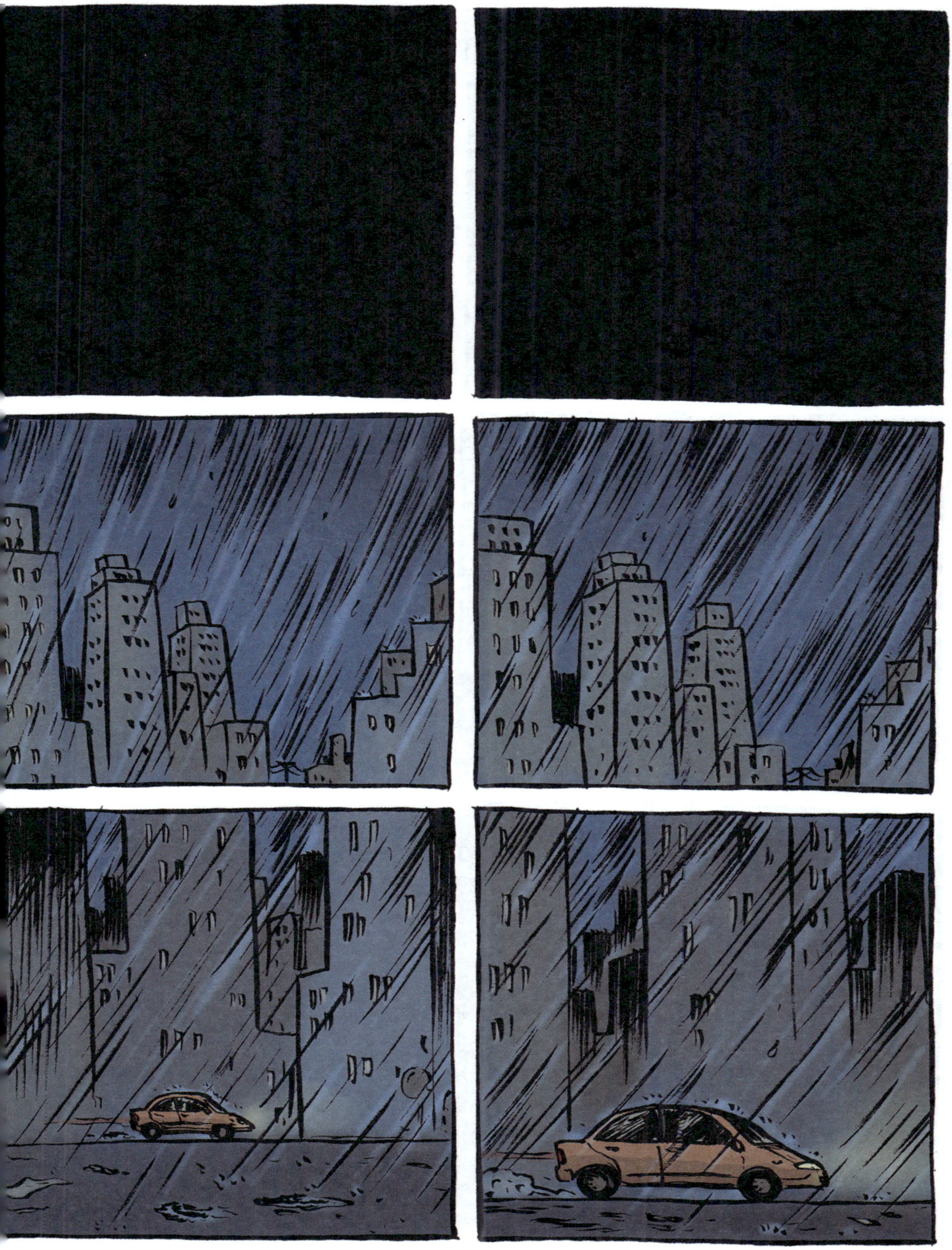

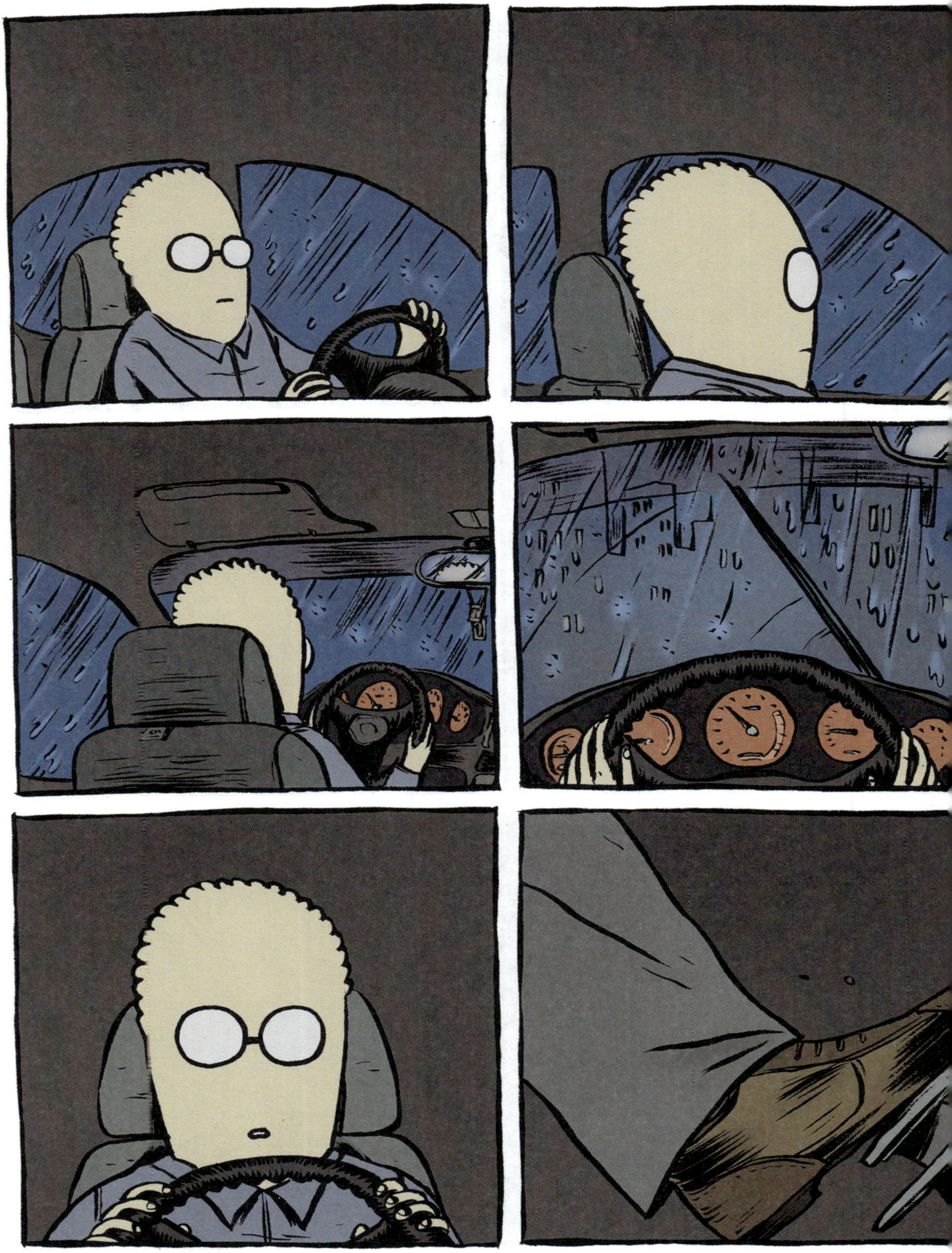

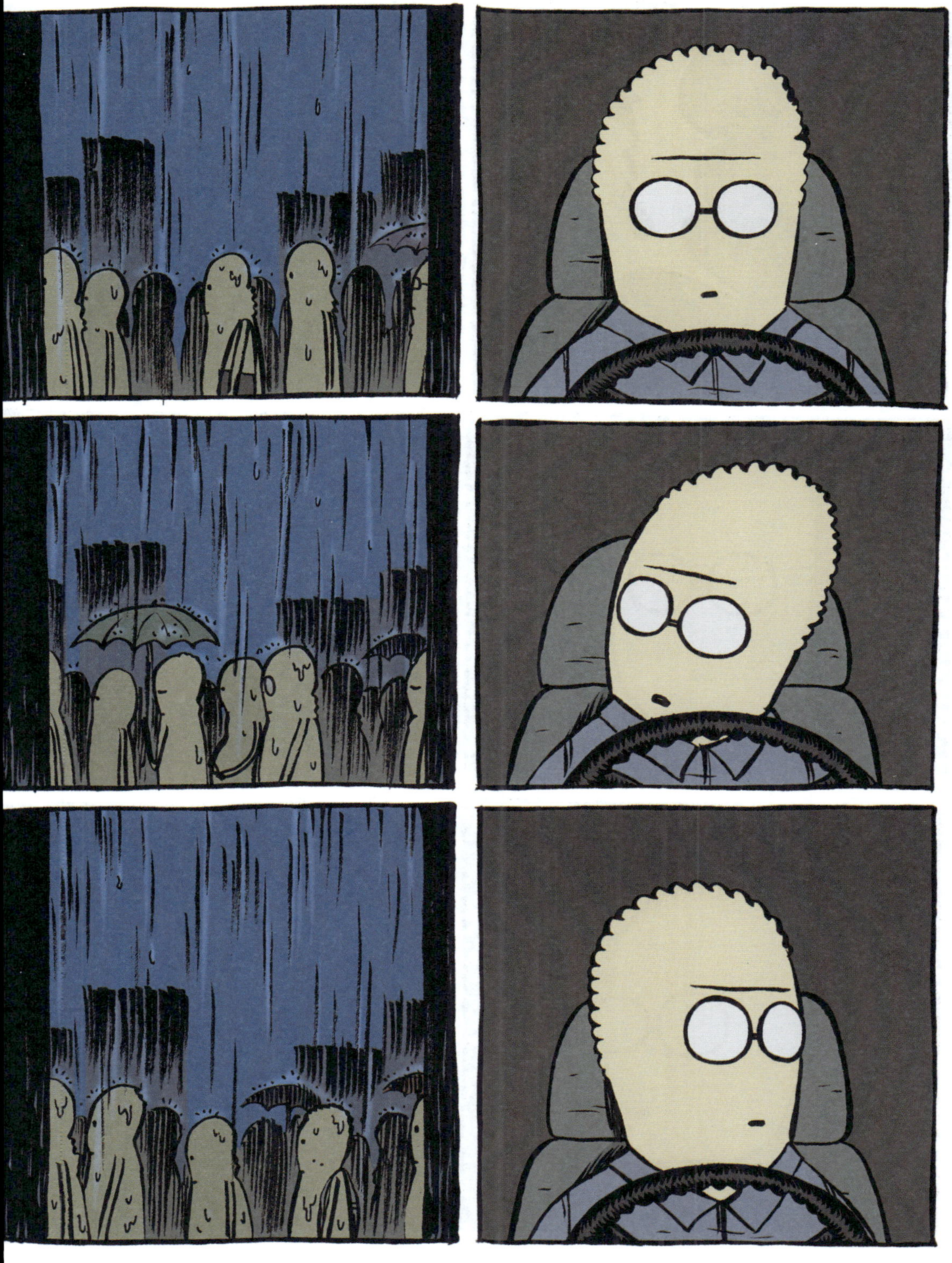

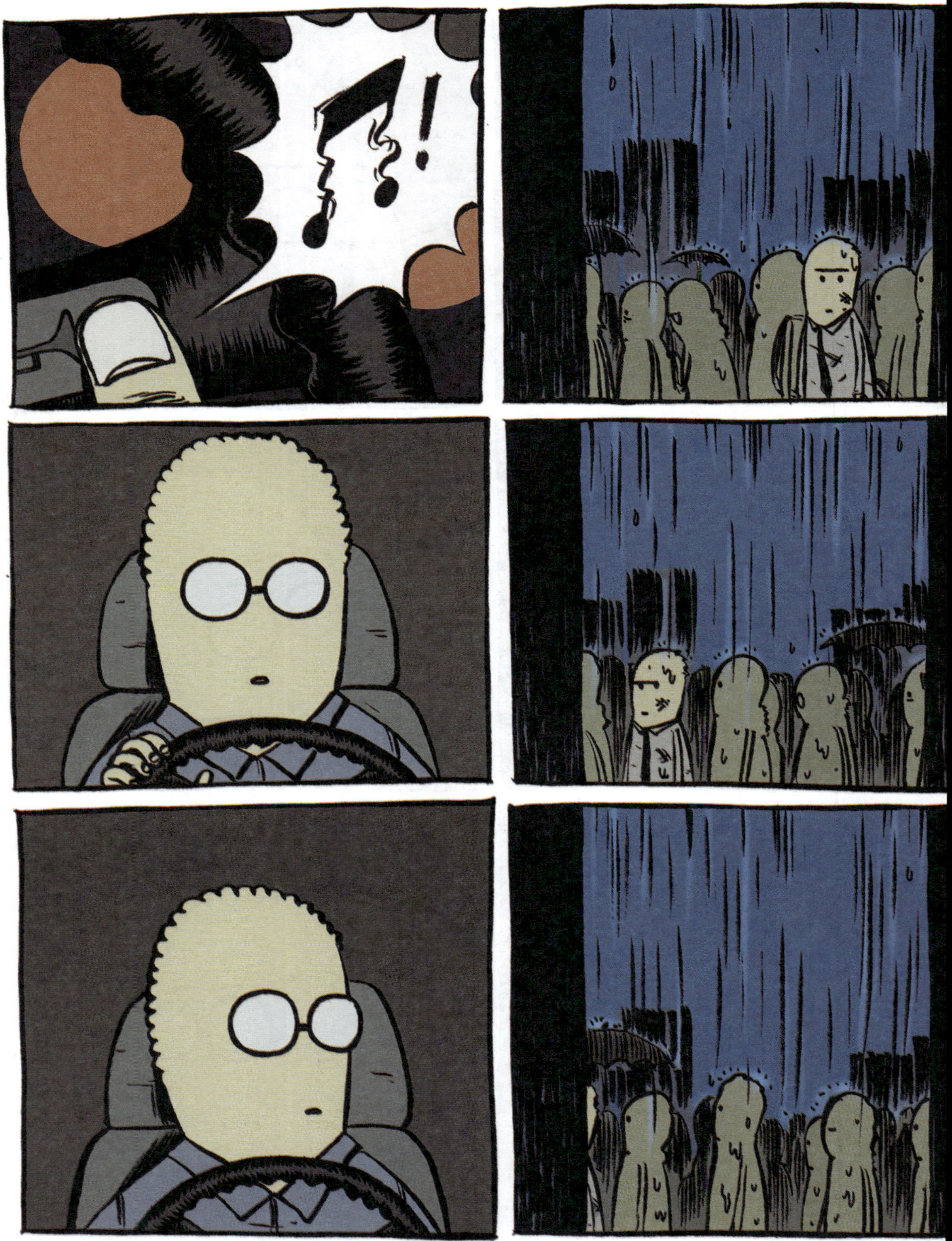
?!

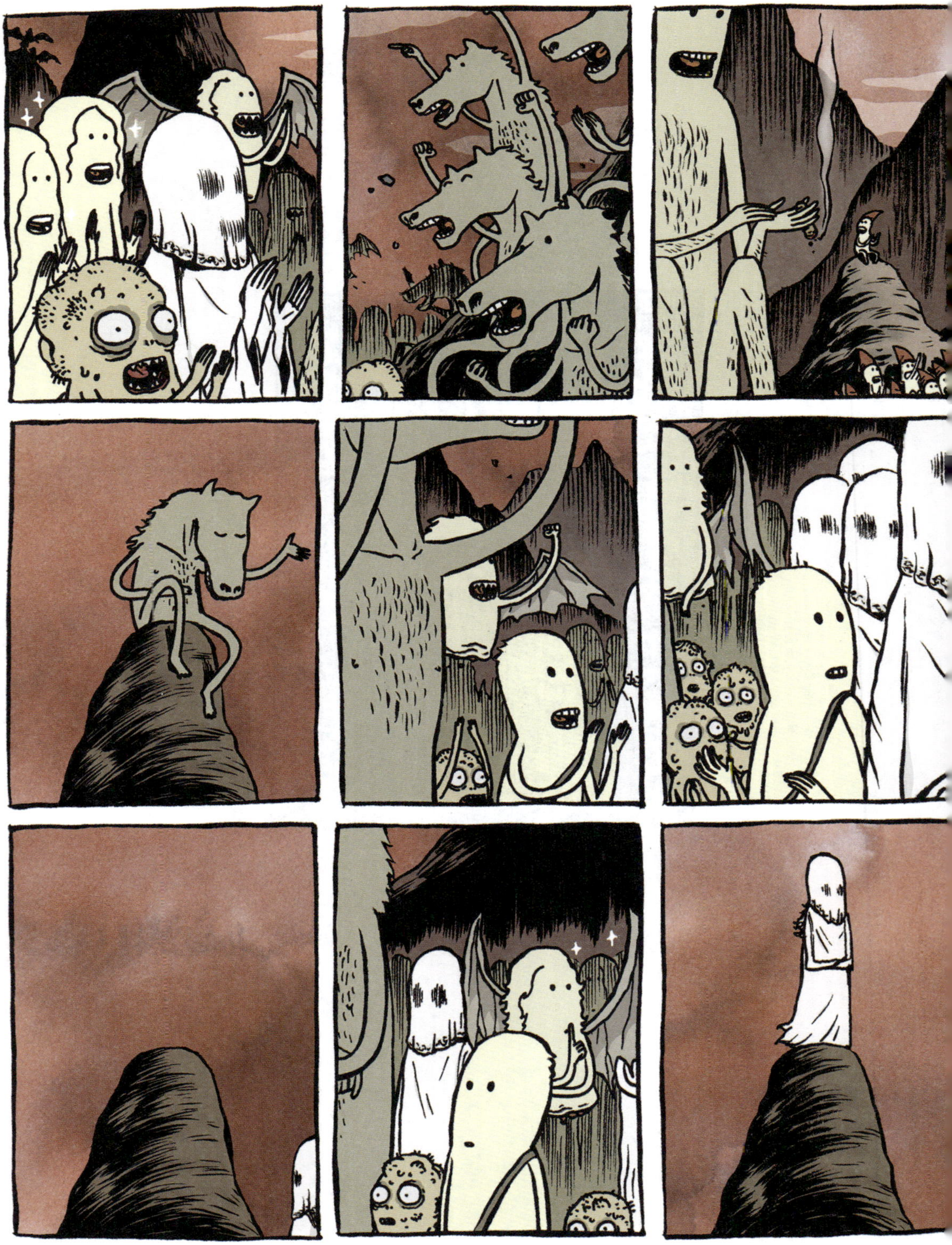

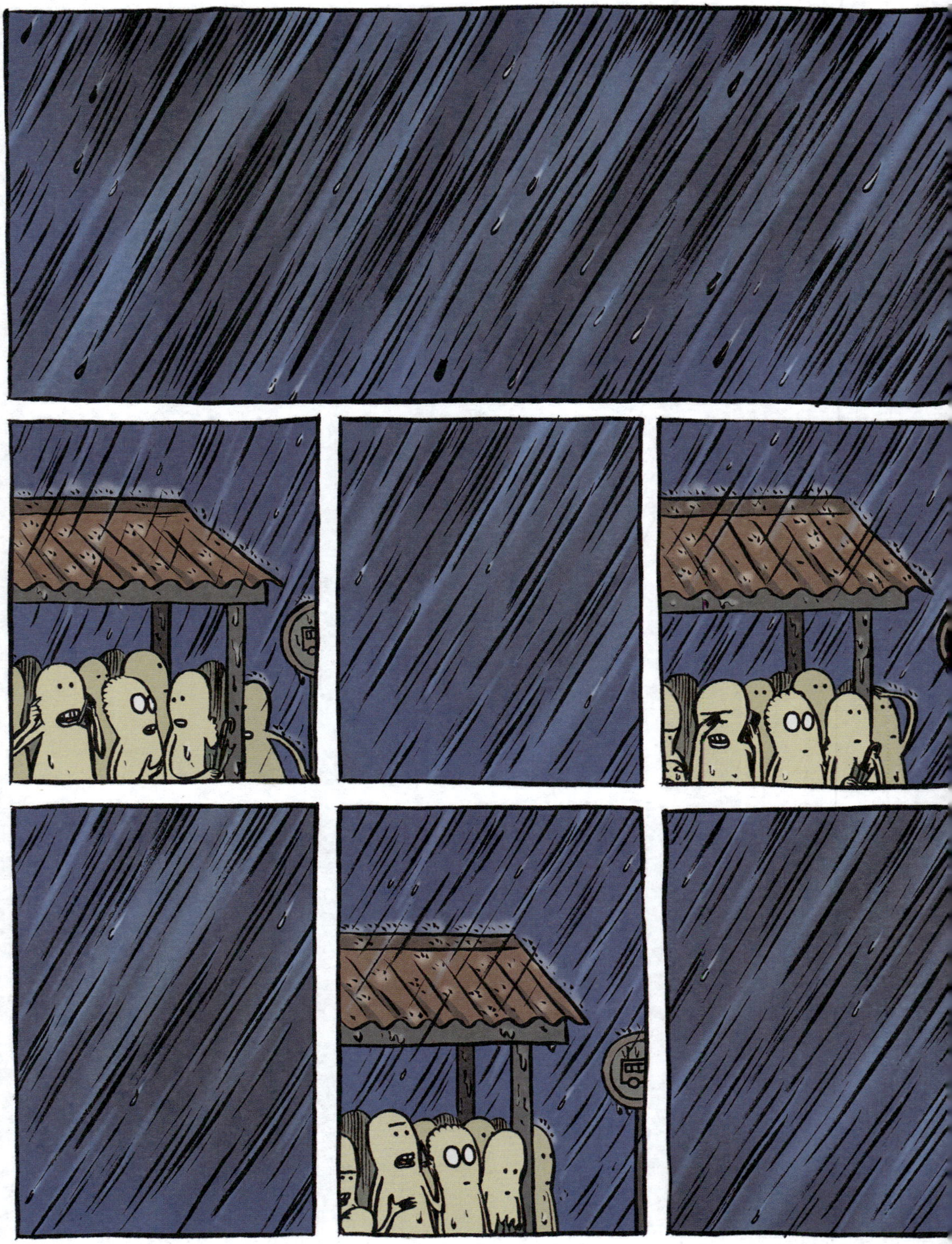

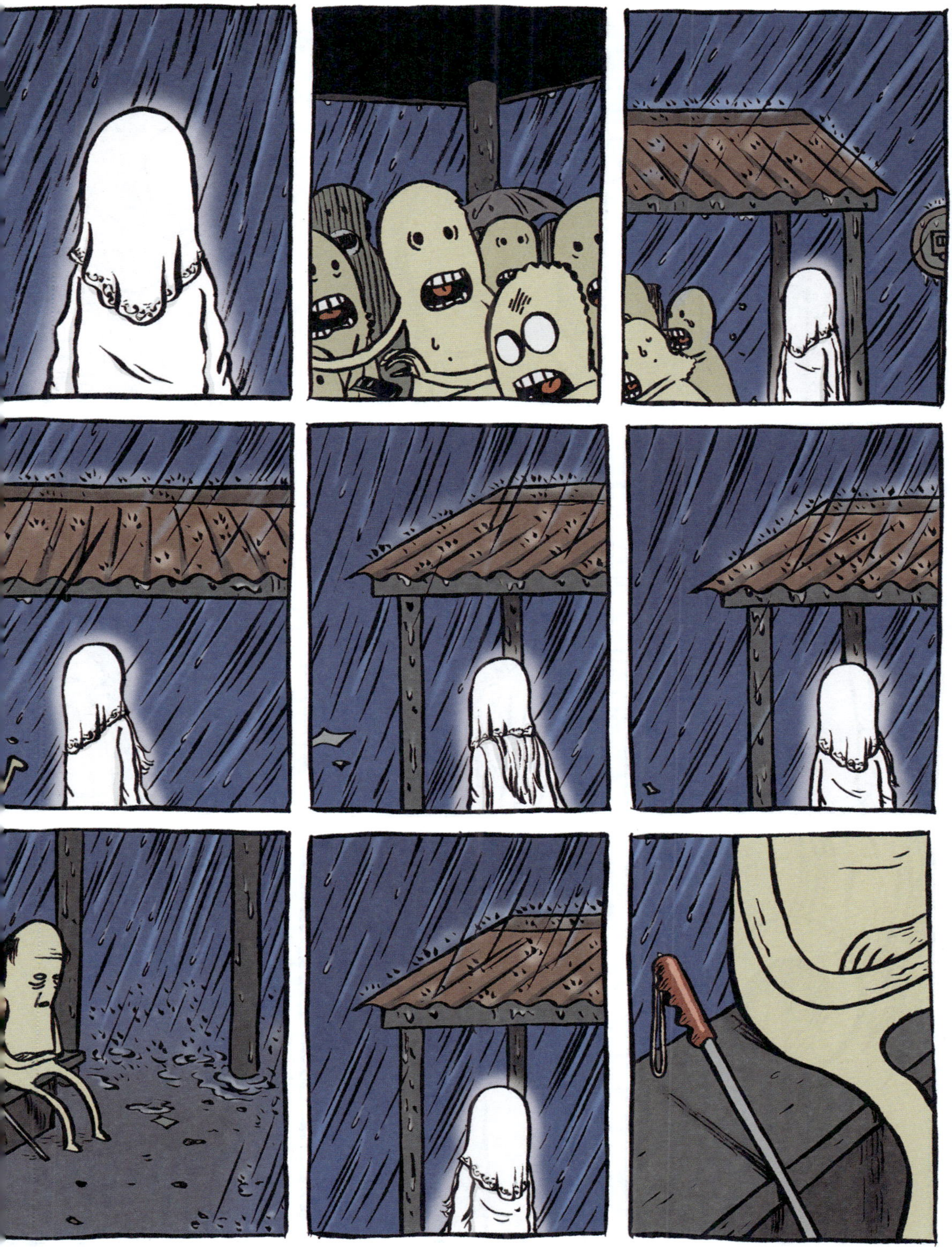

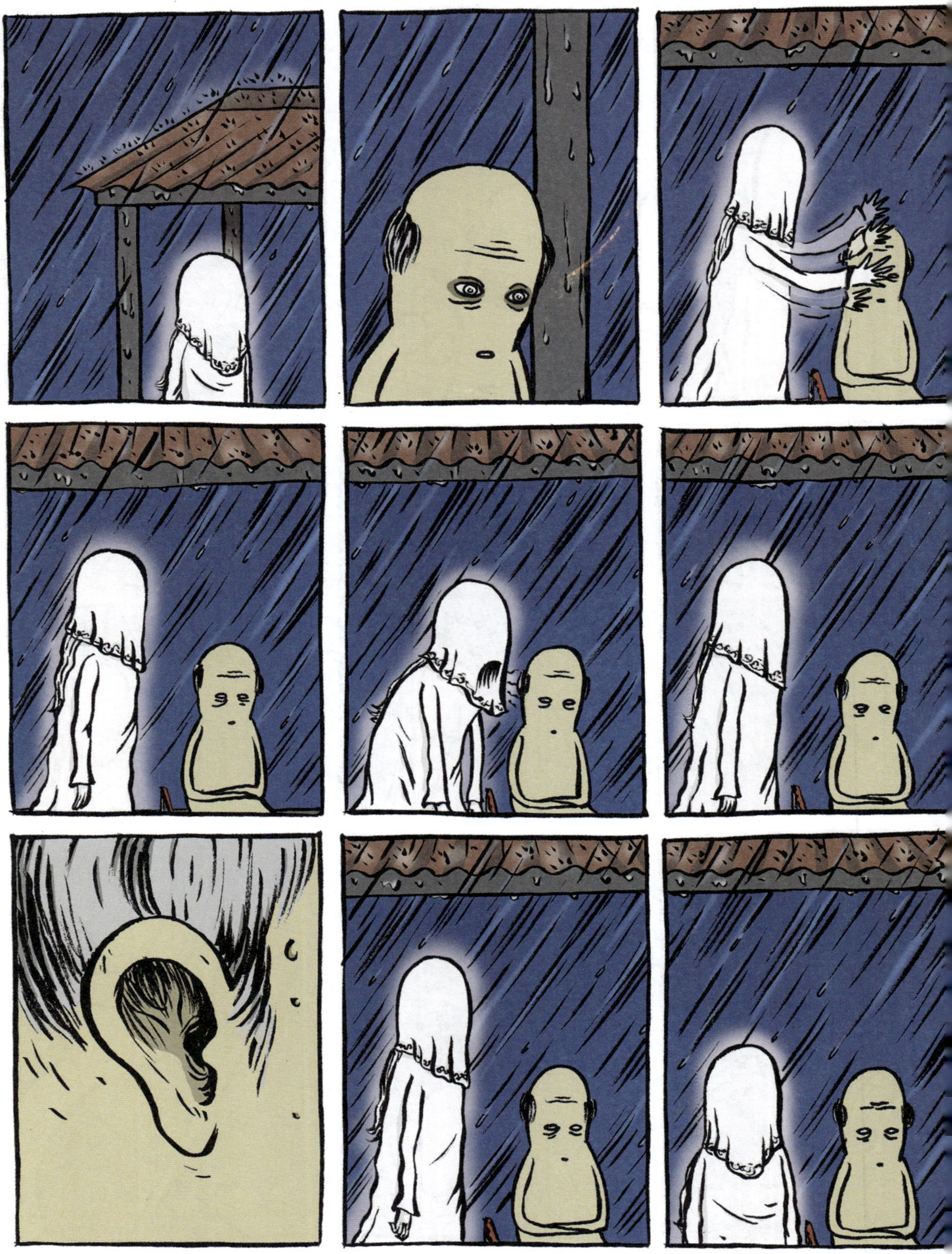

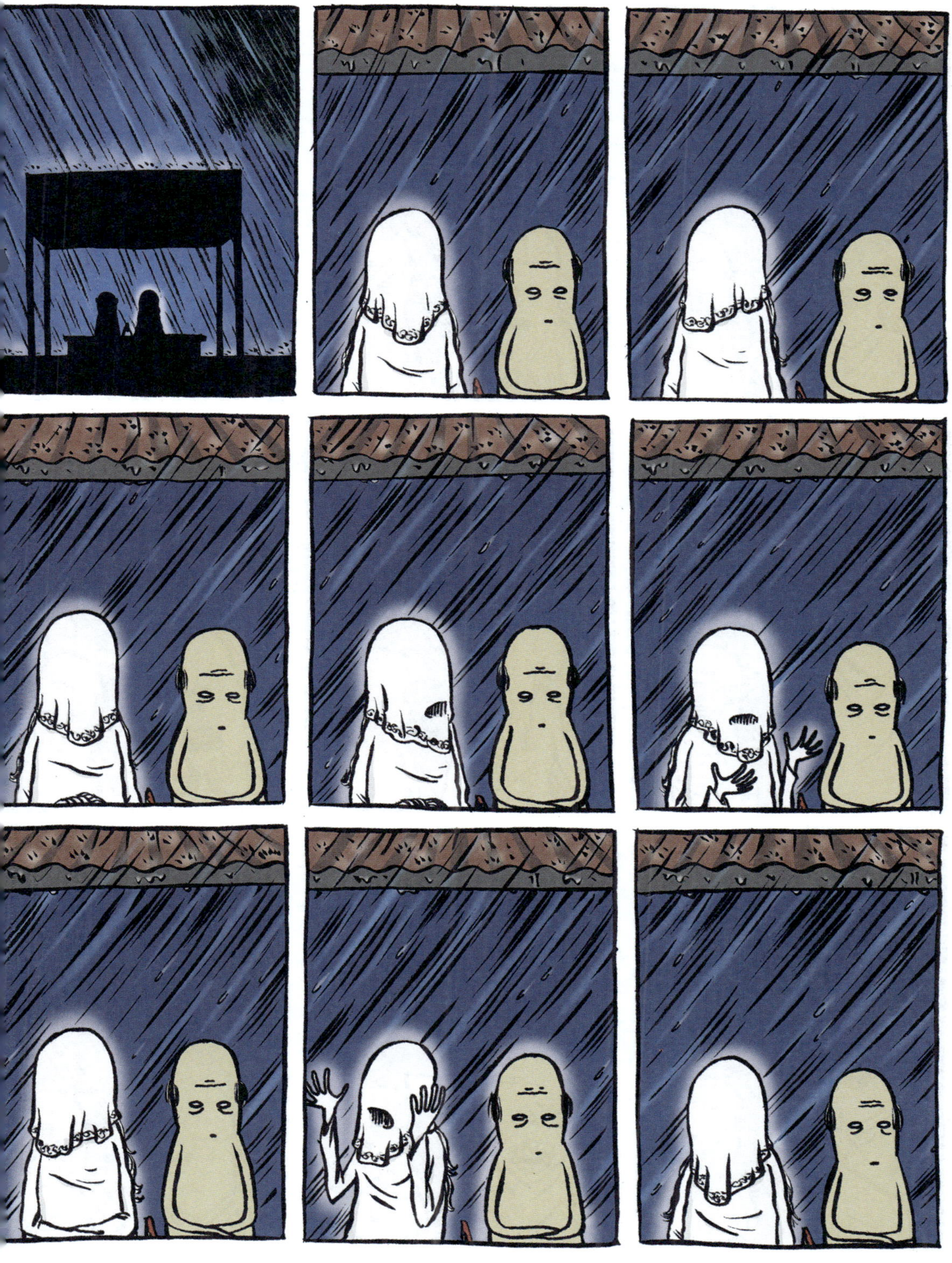

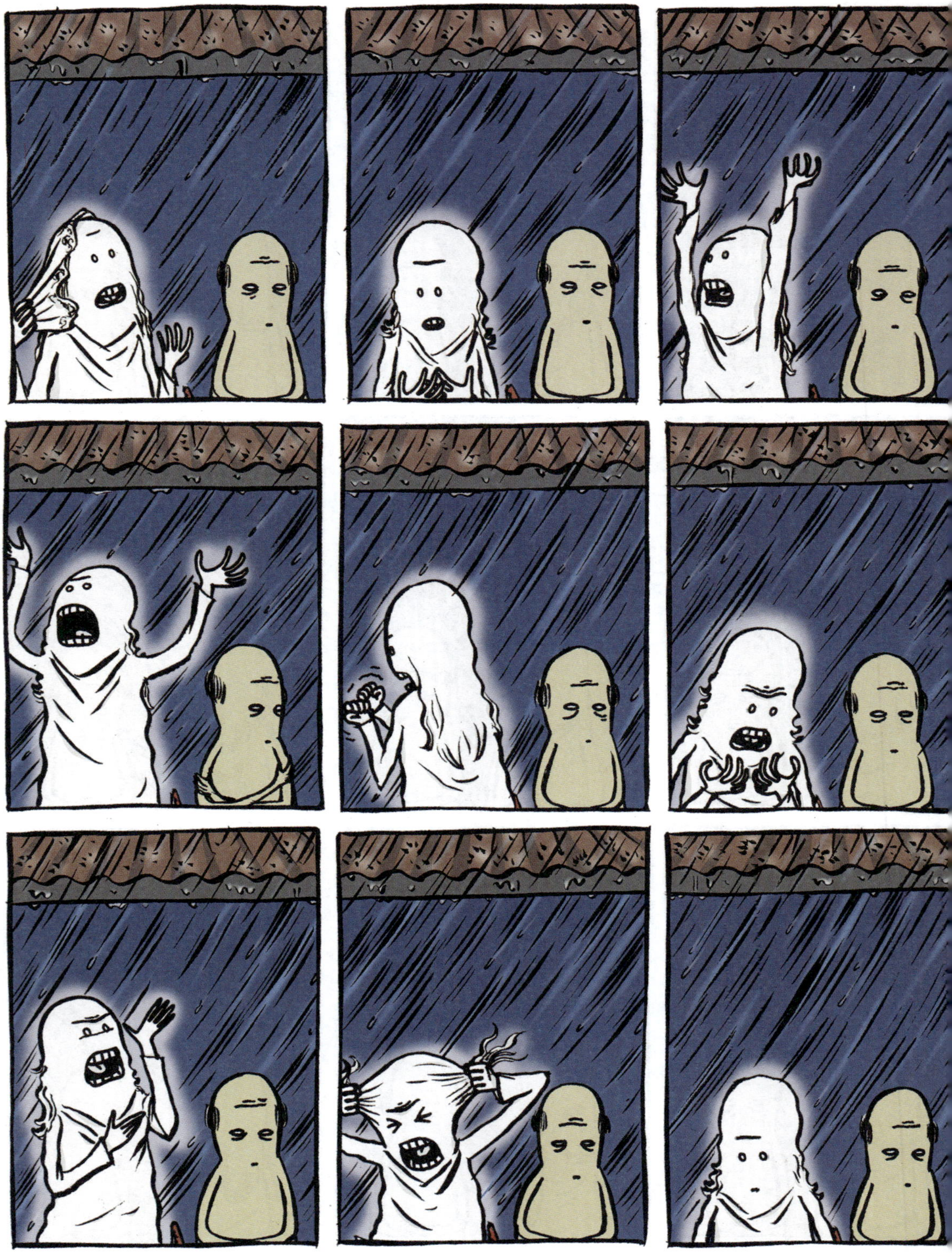

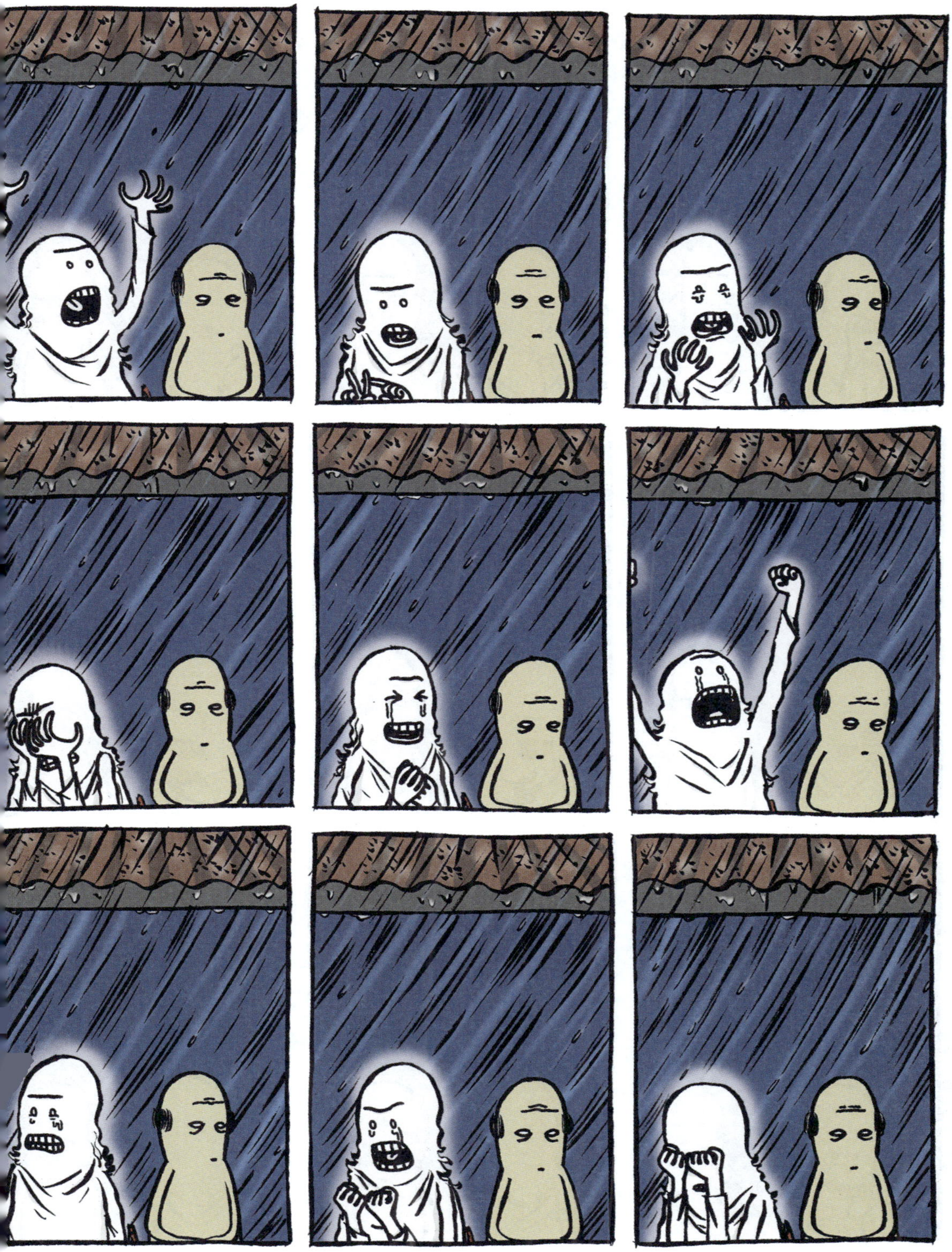

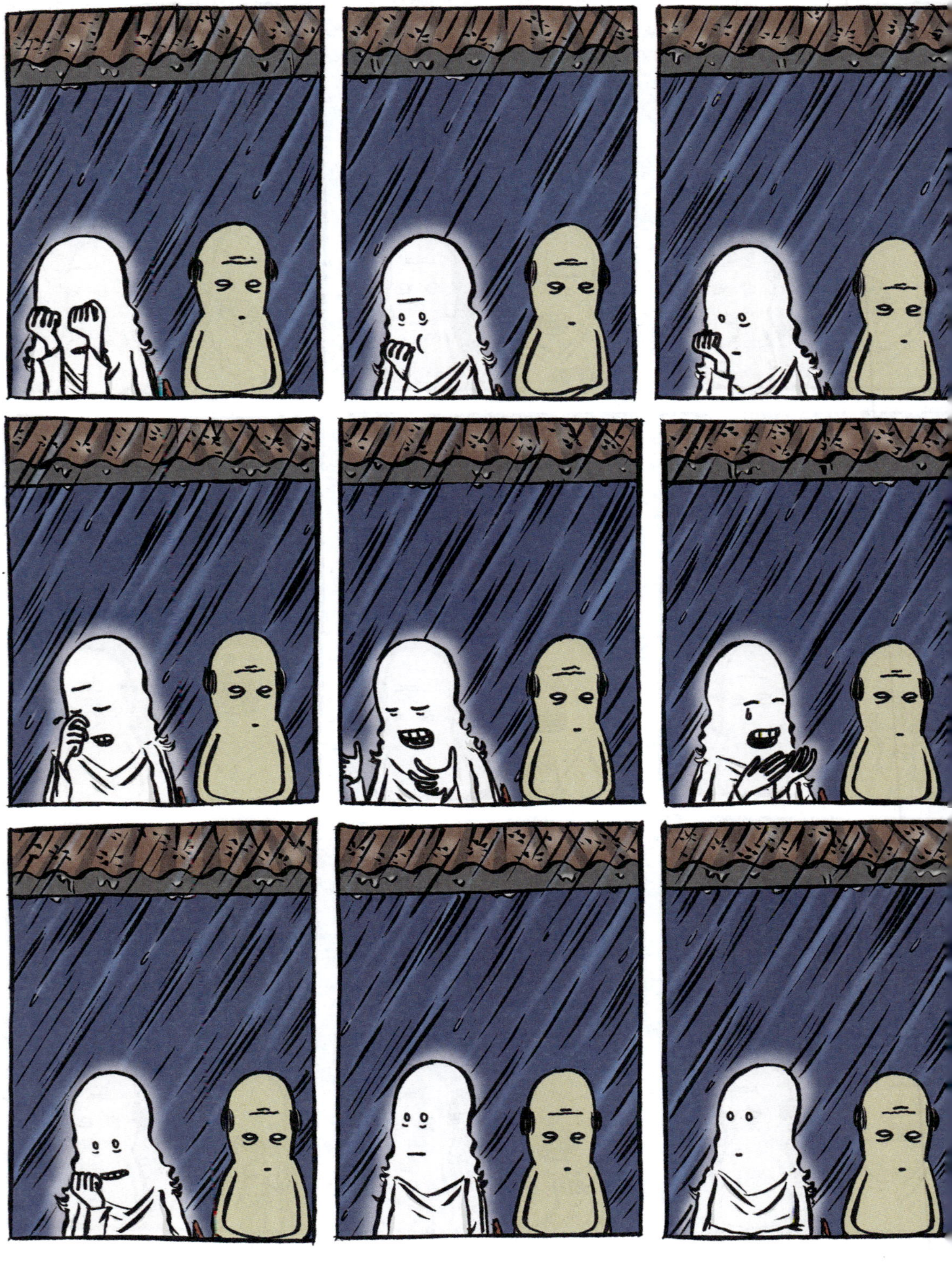

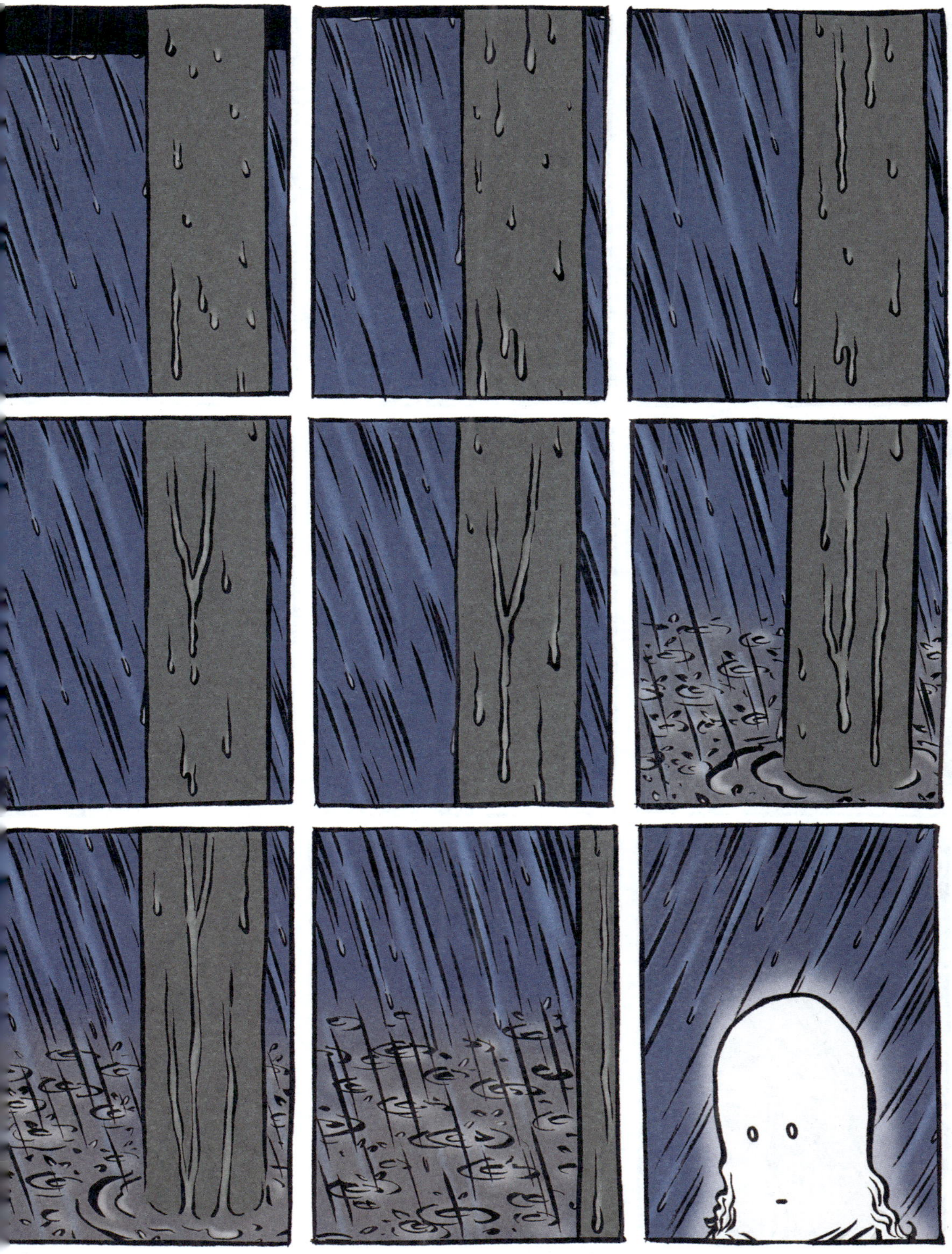

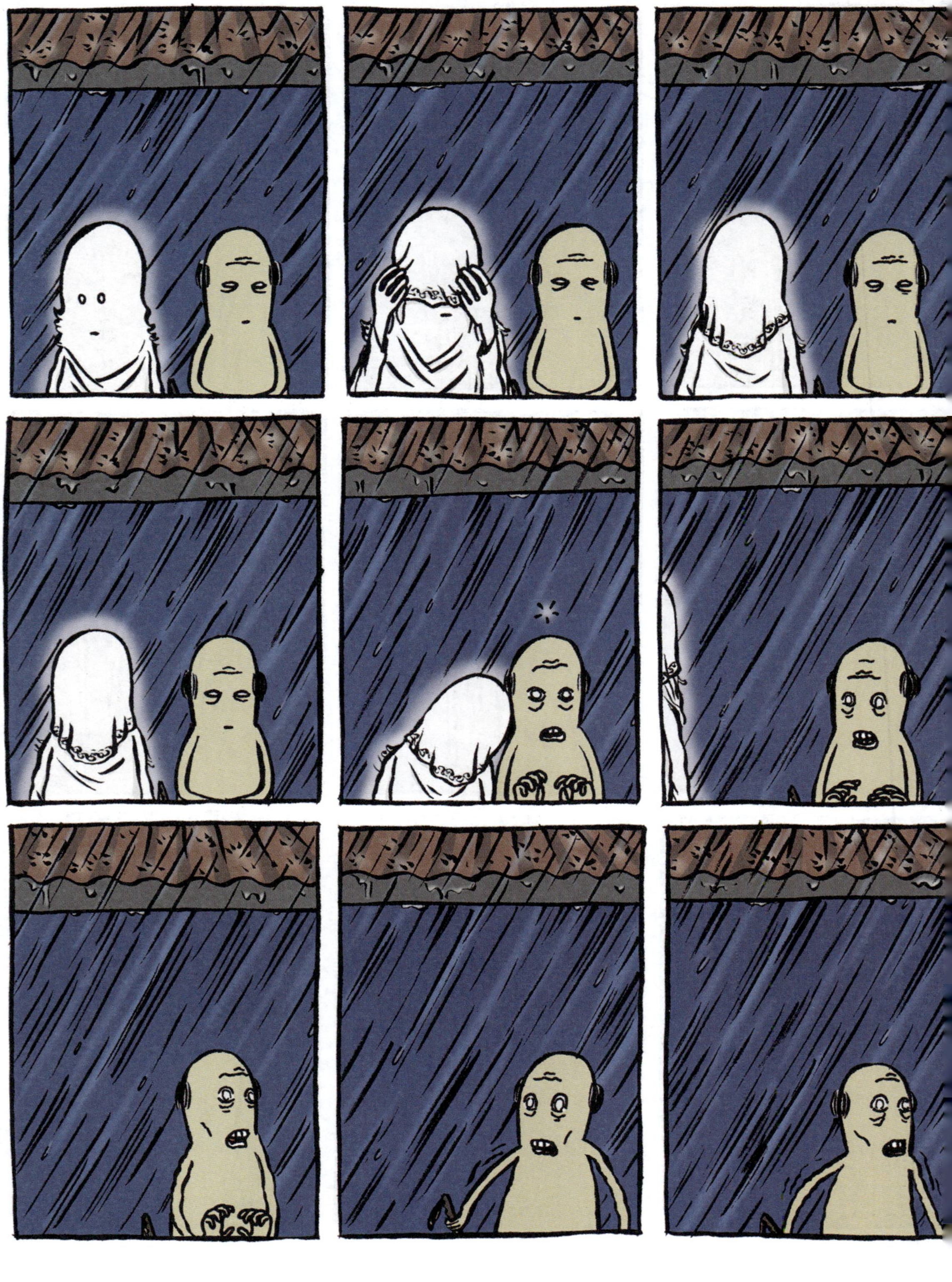

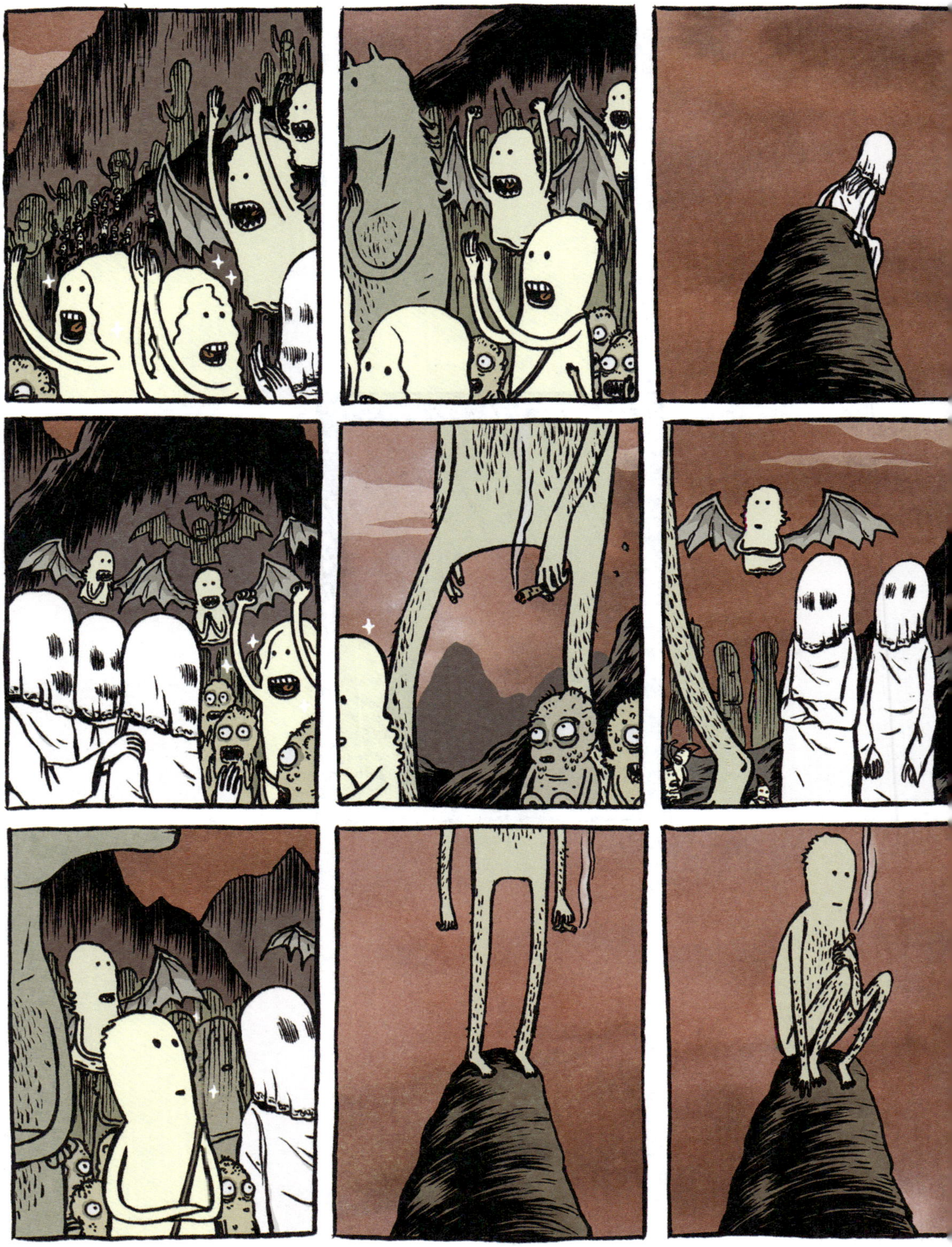

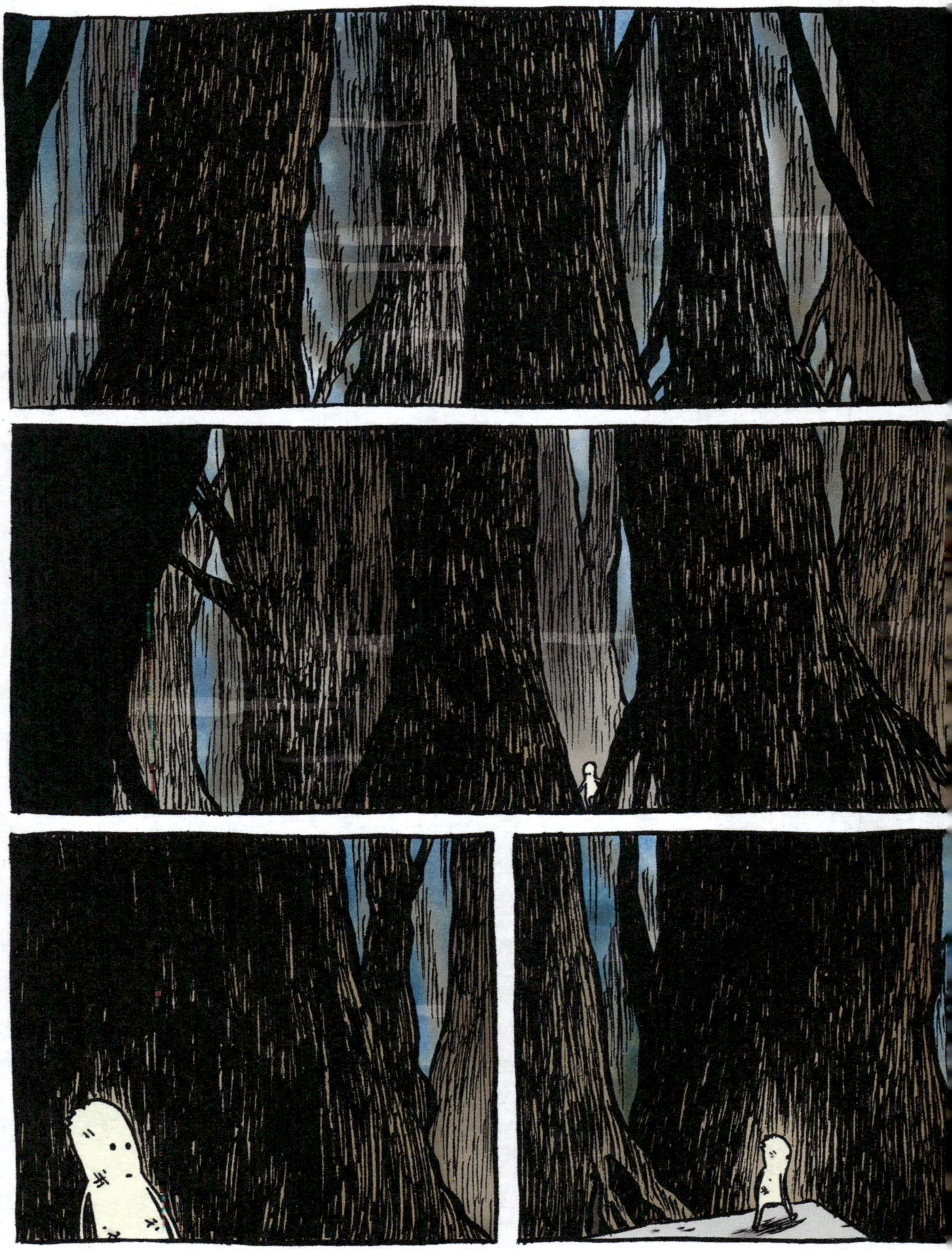

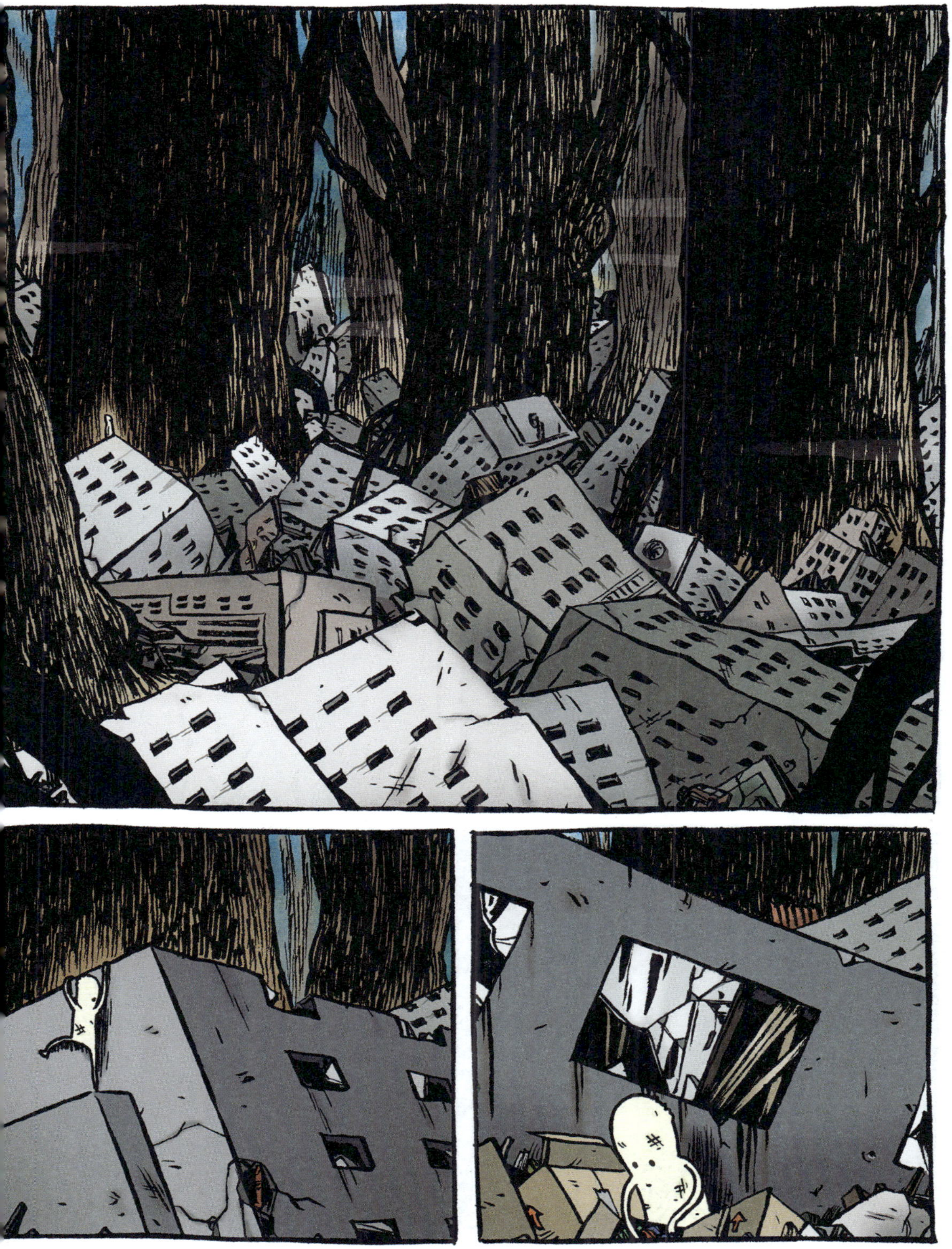

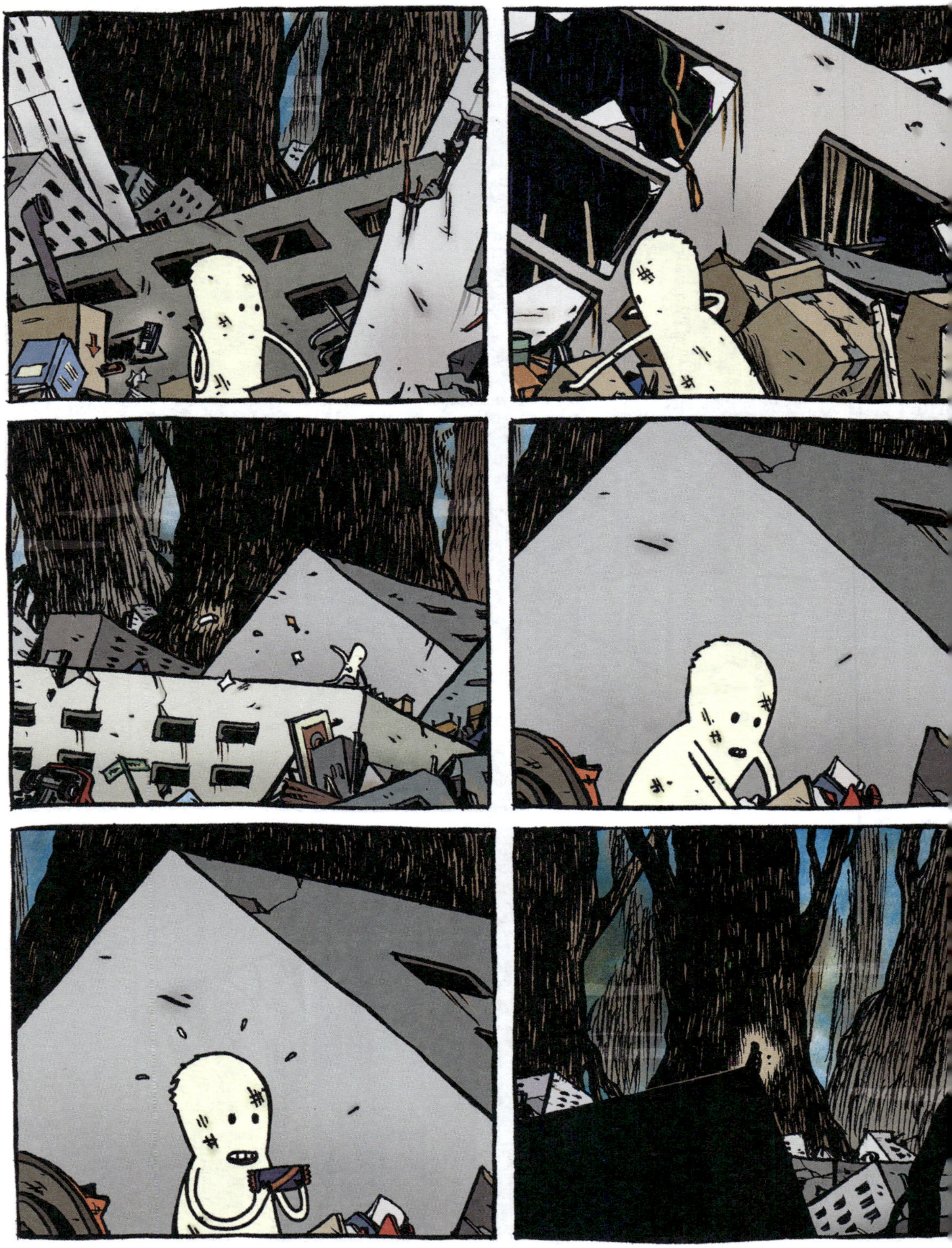

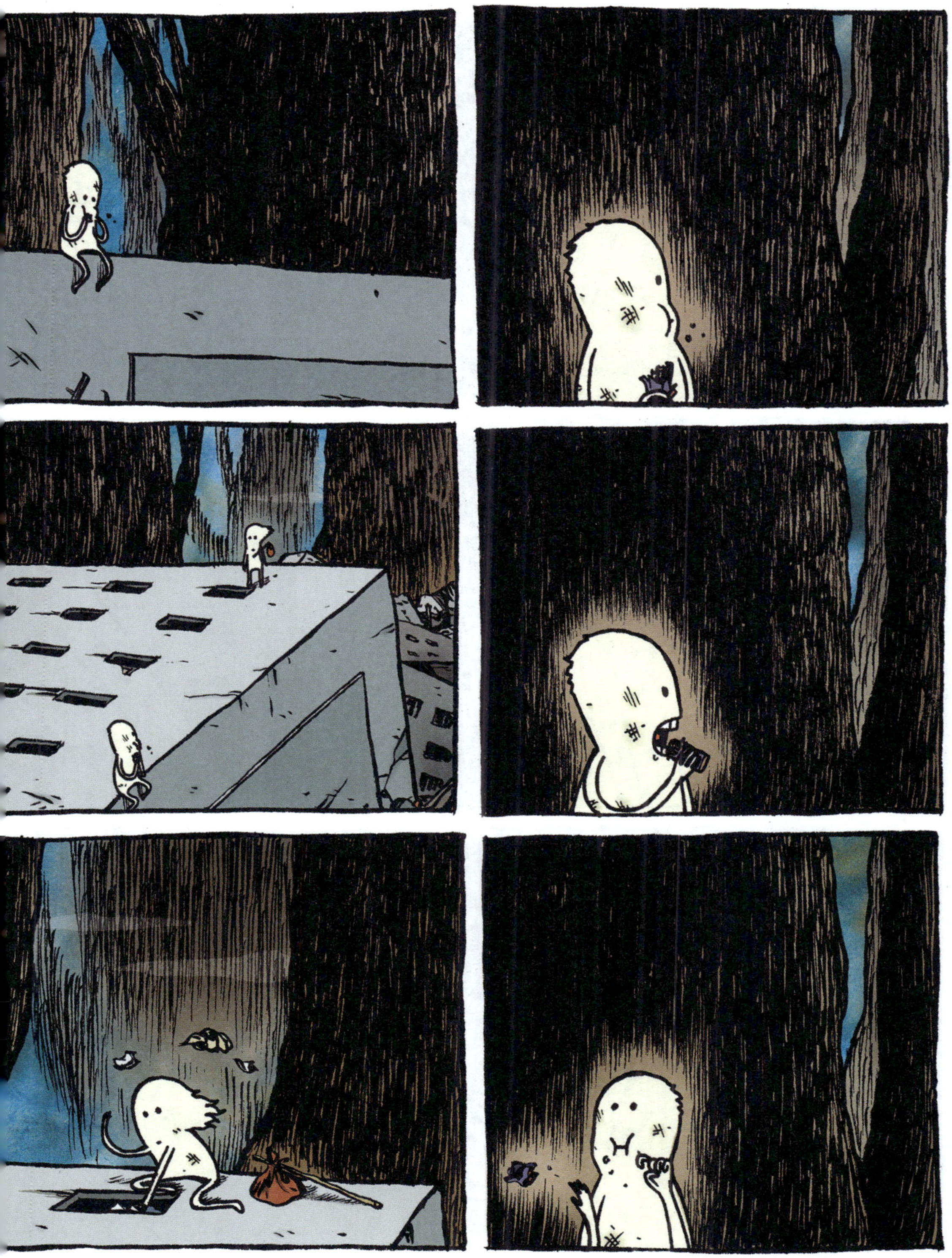

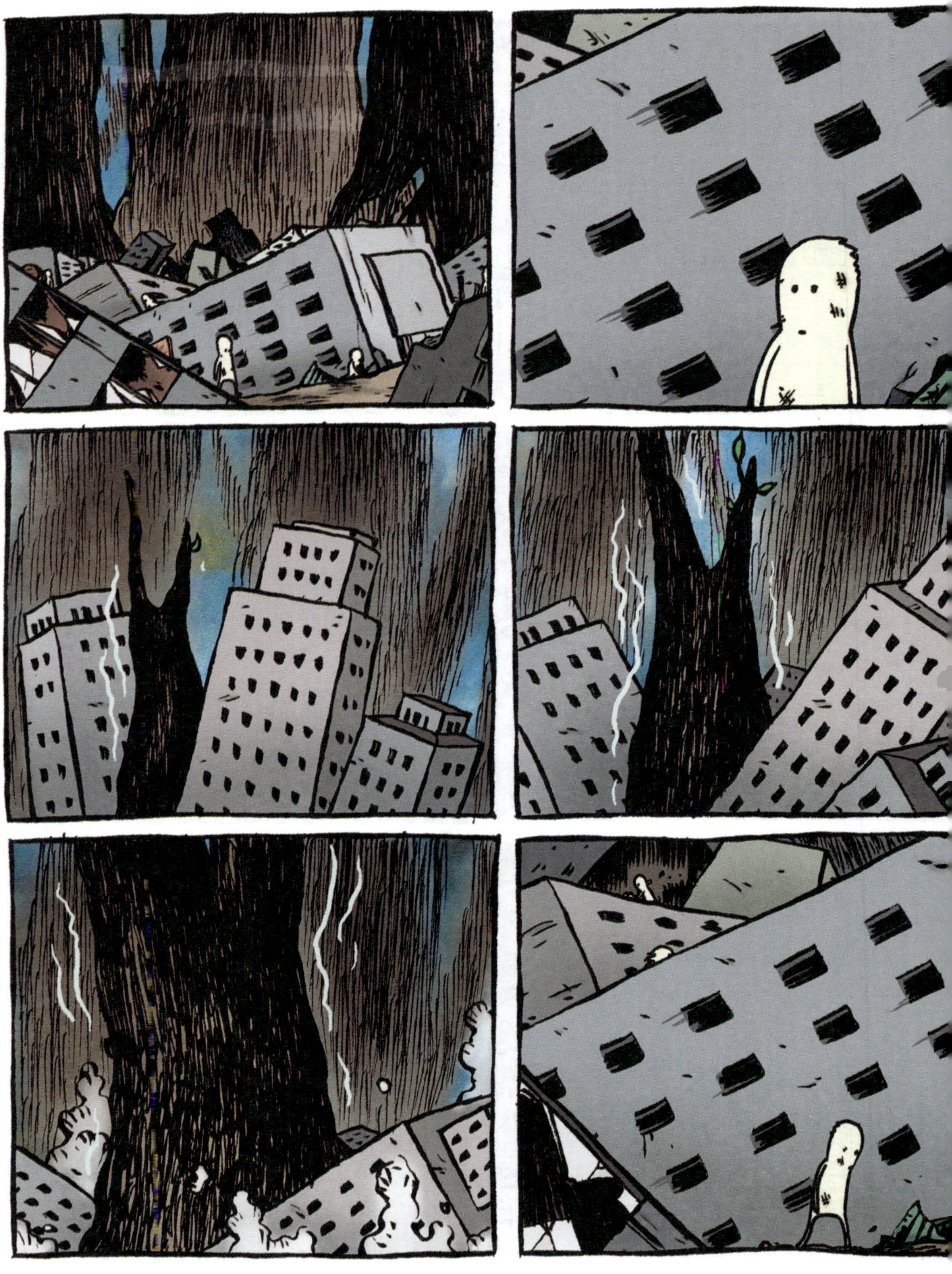

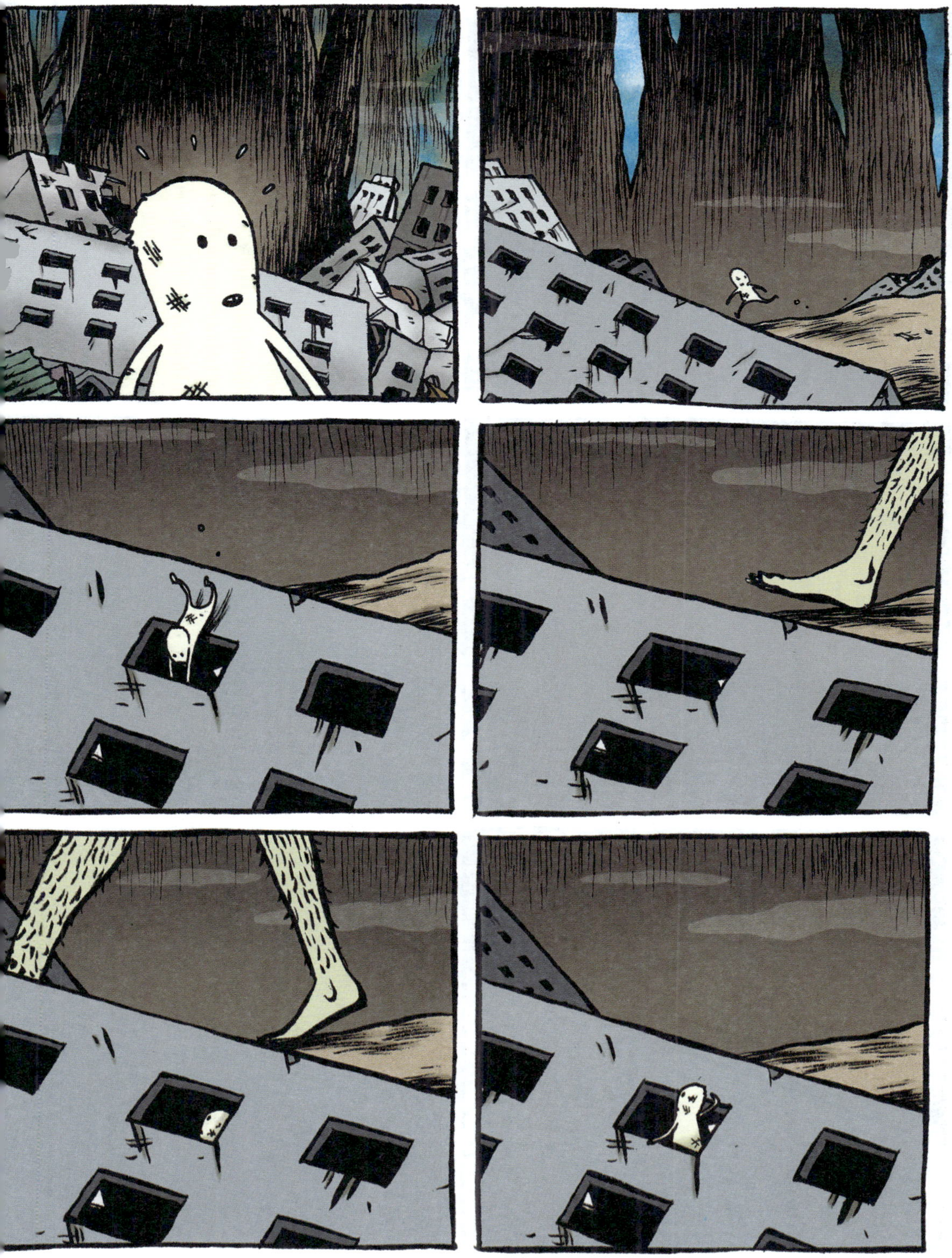

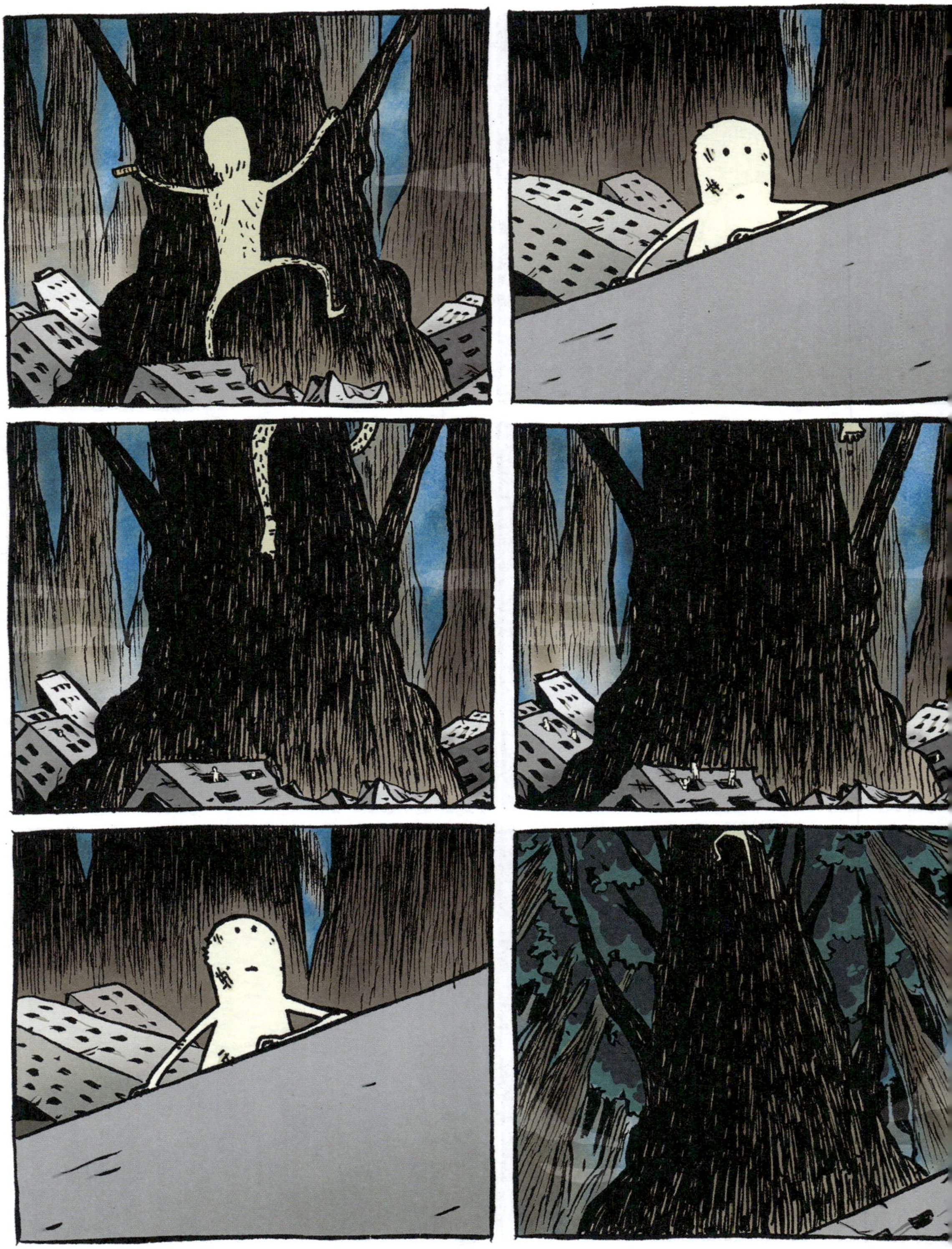

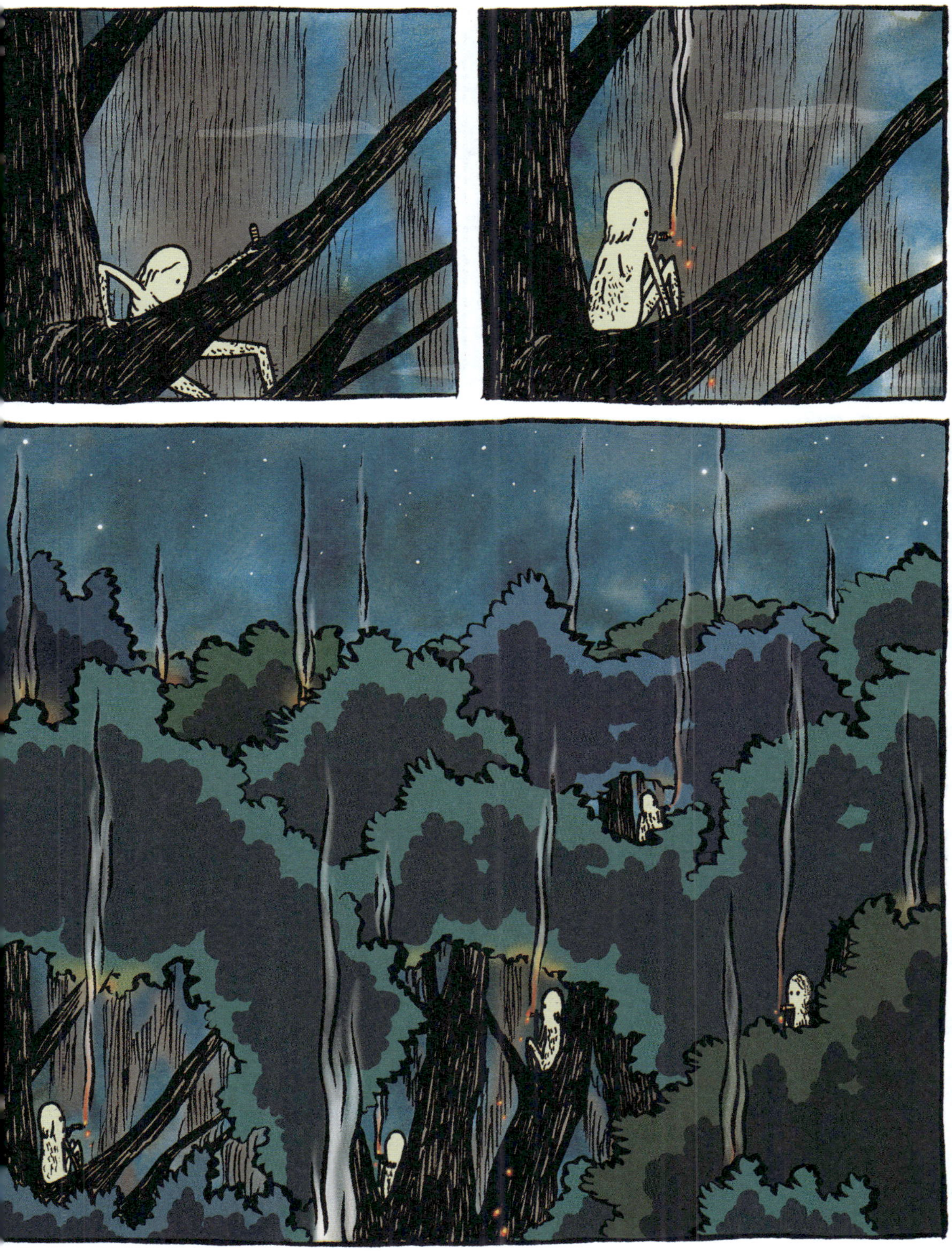

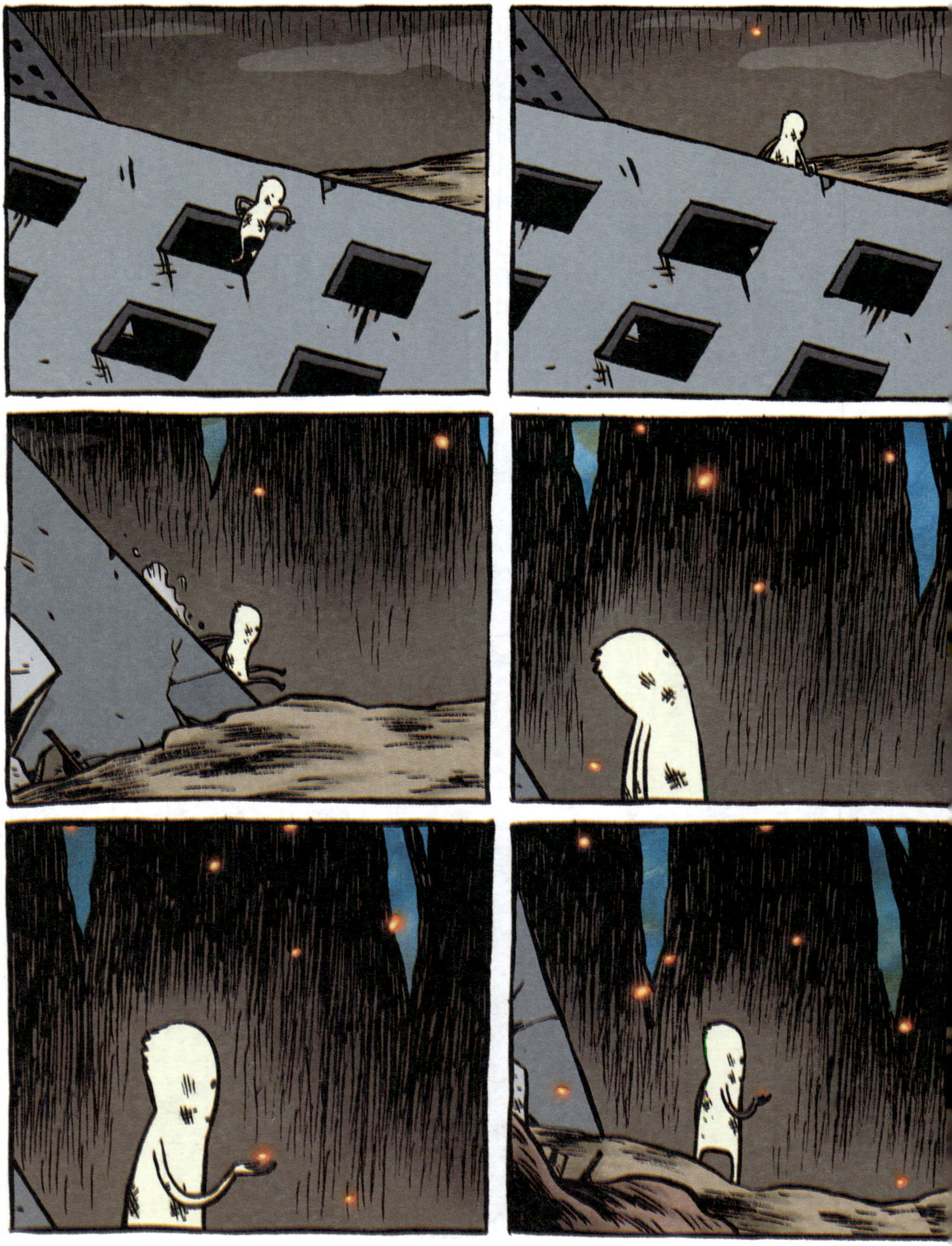

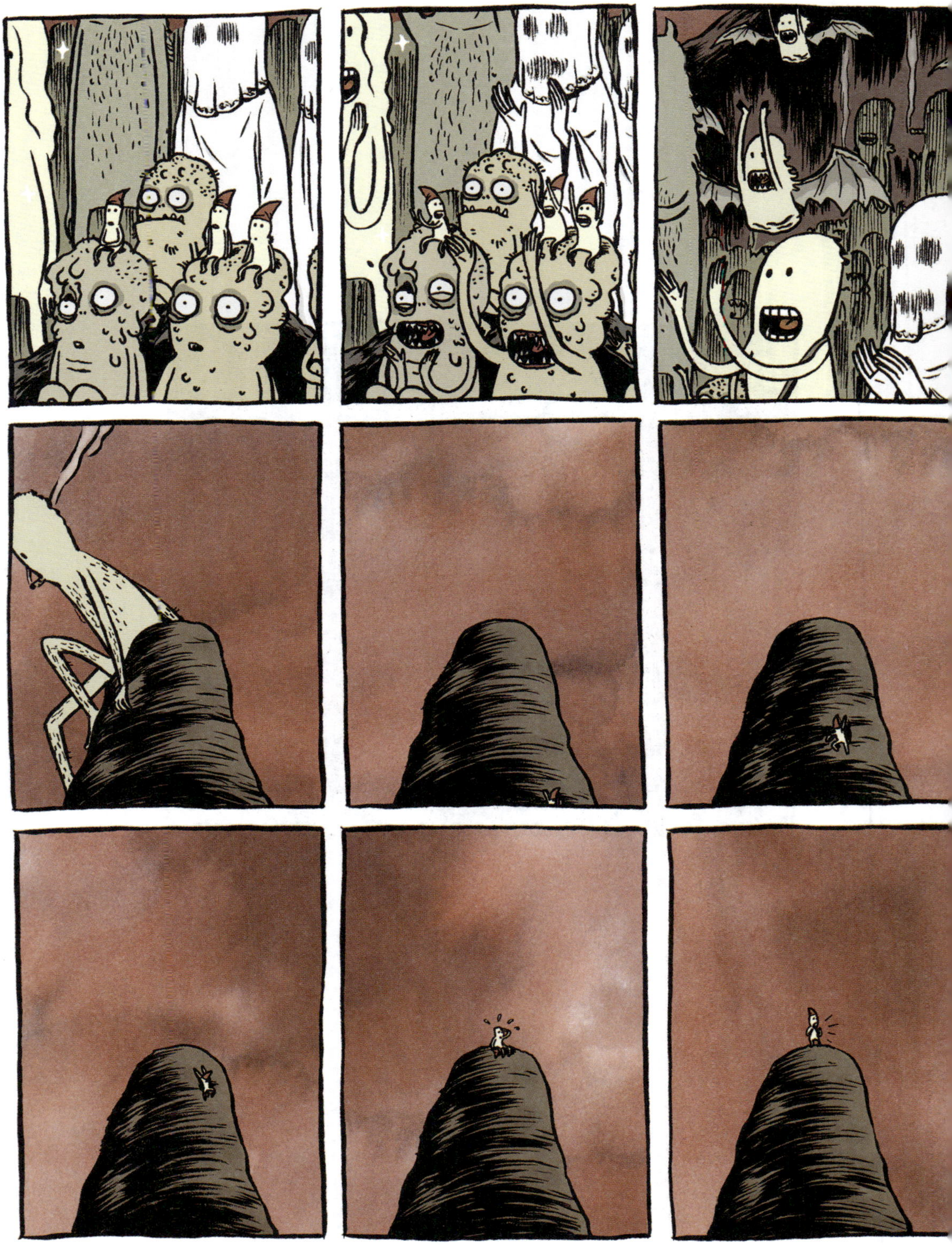

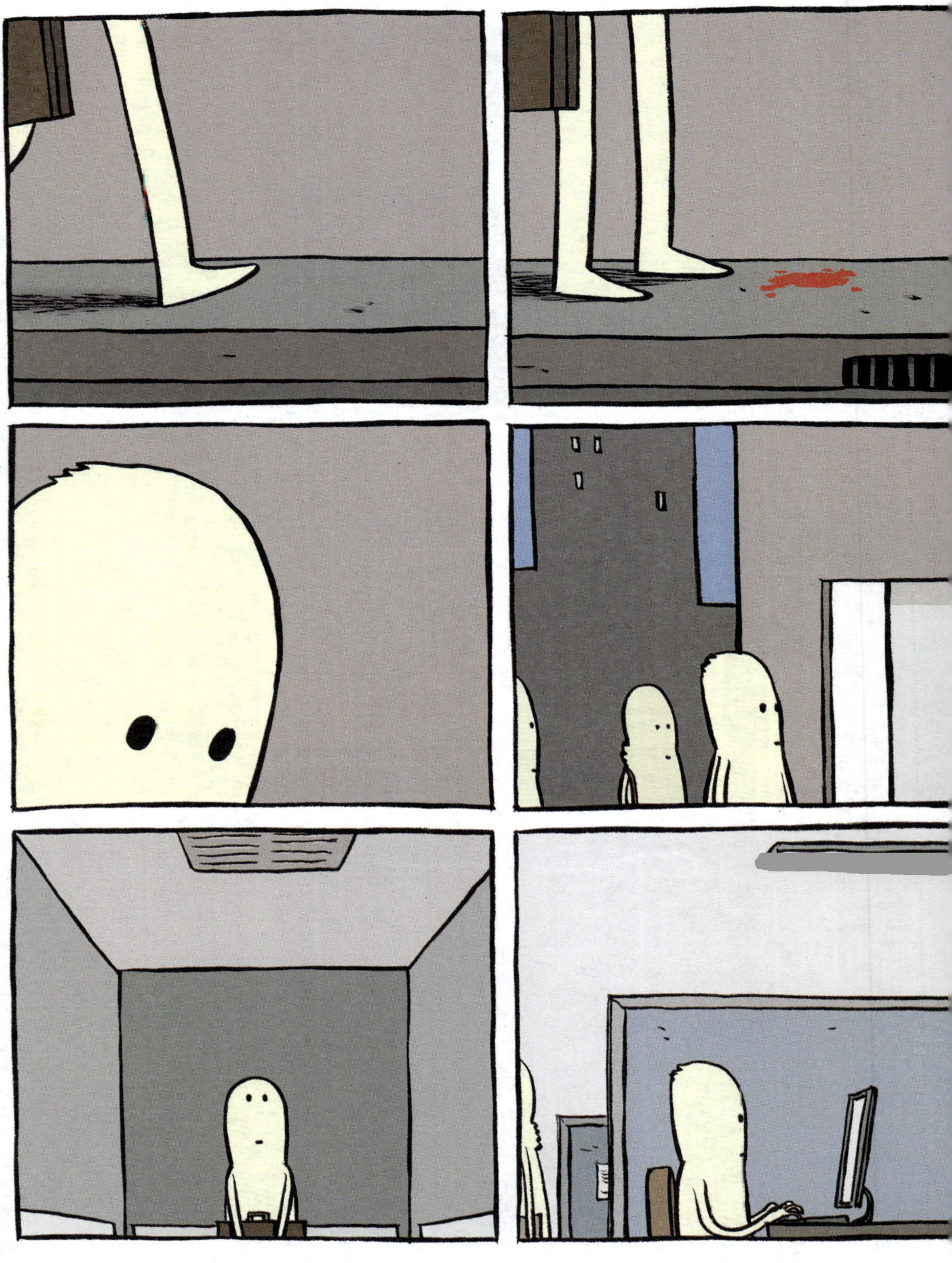

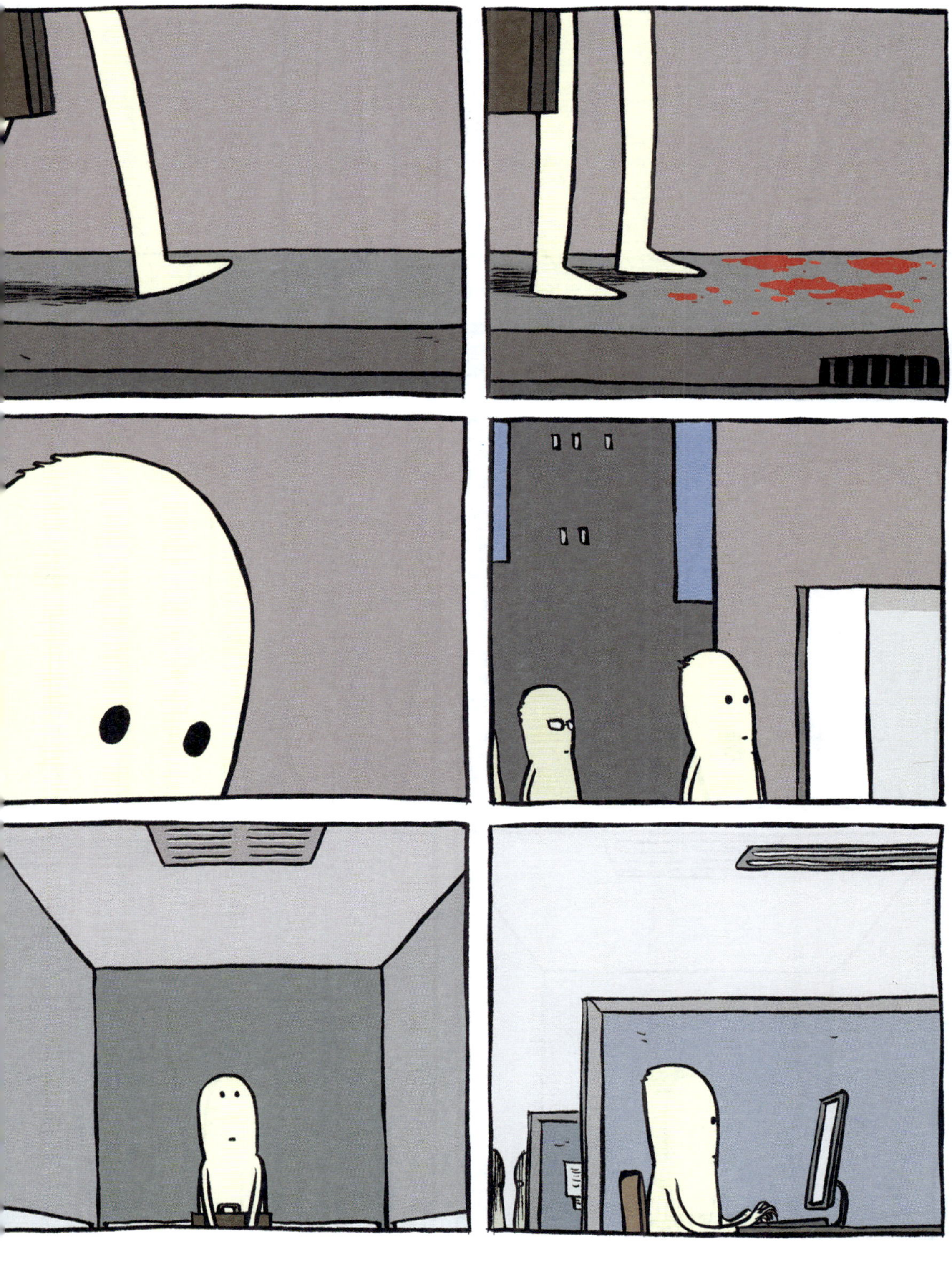

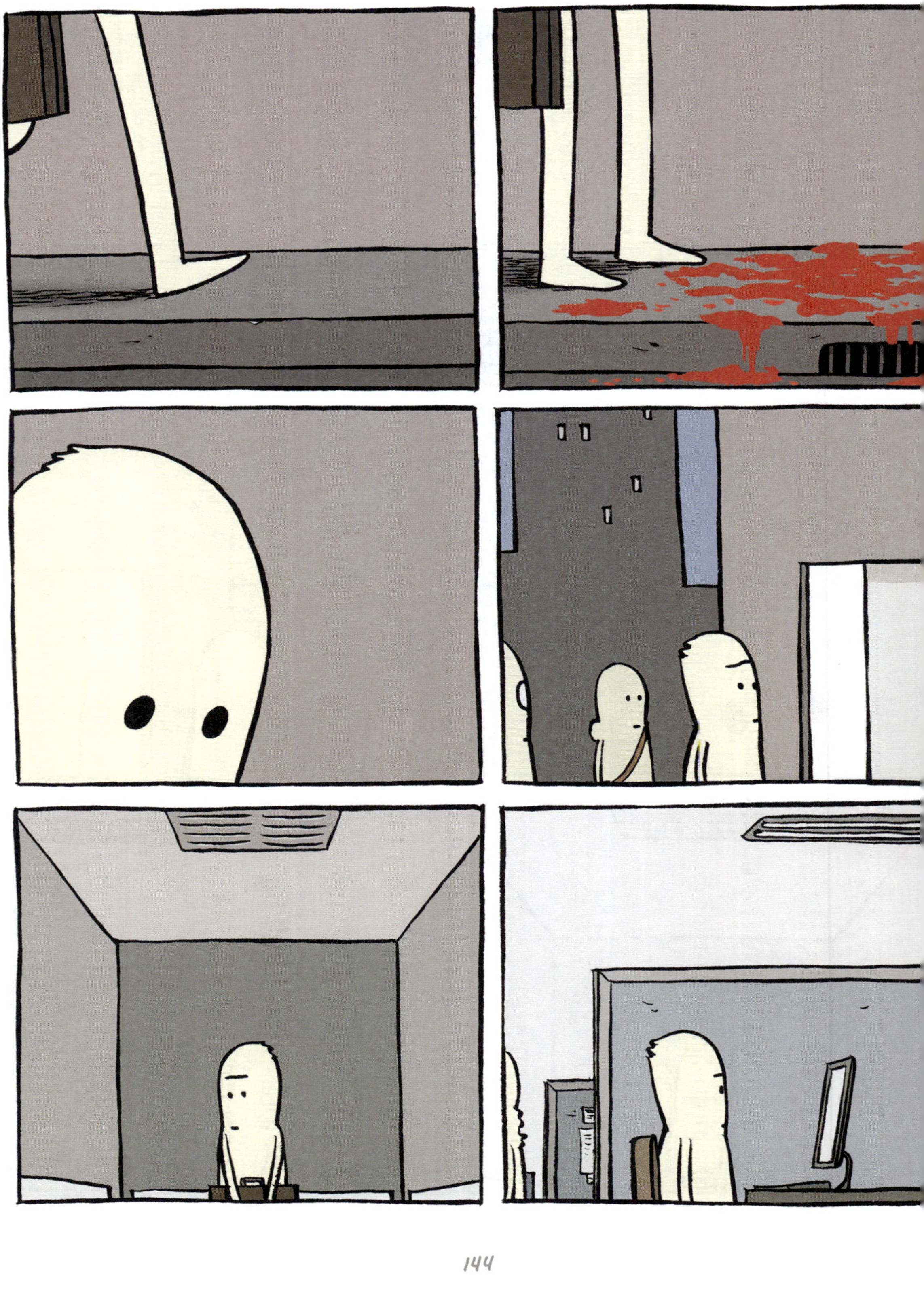

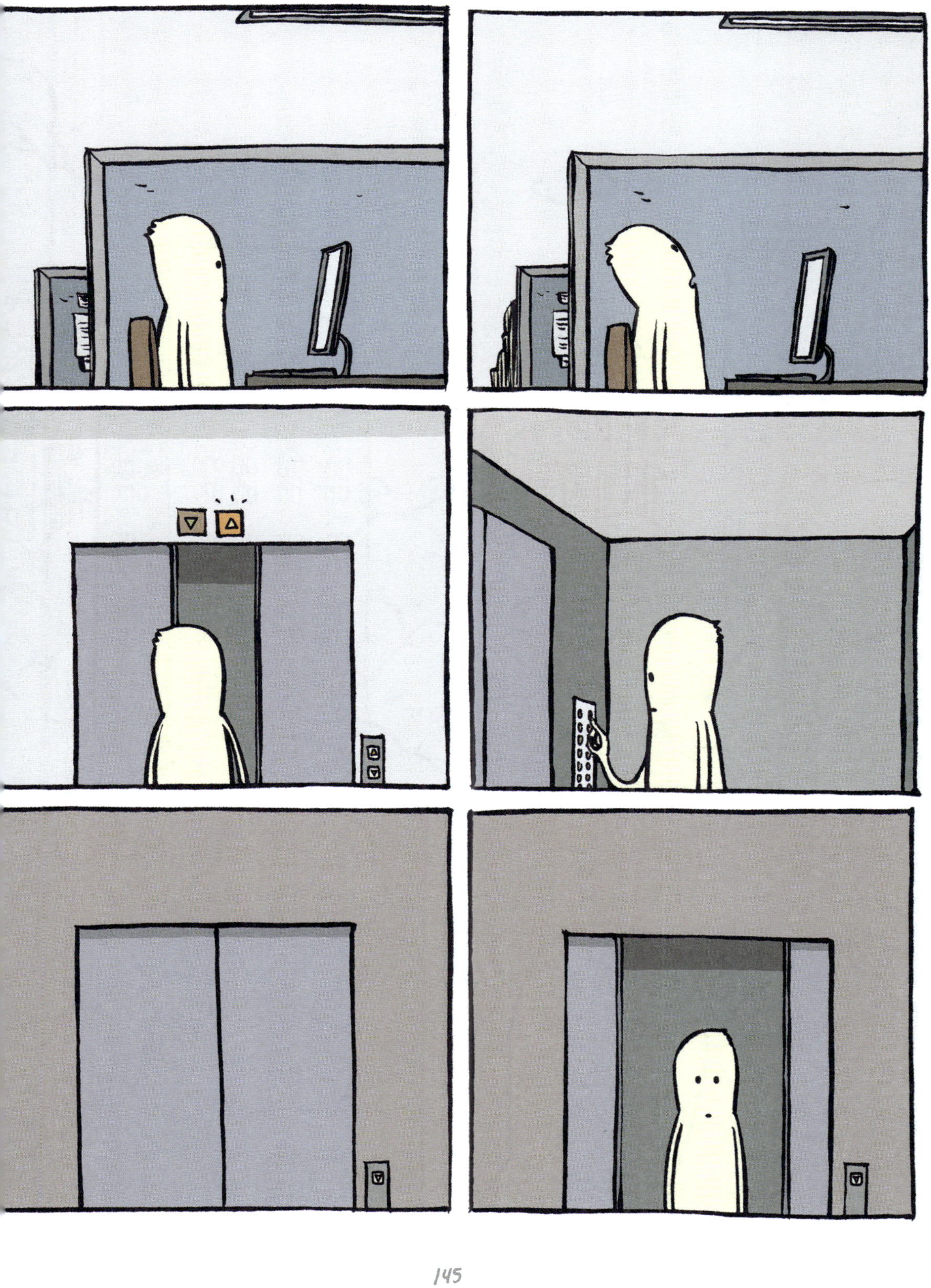

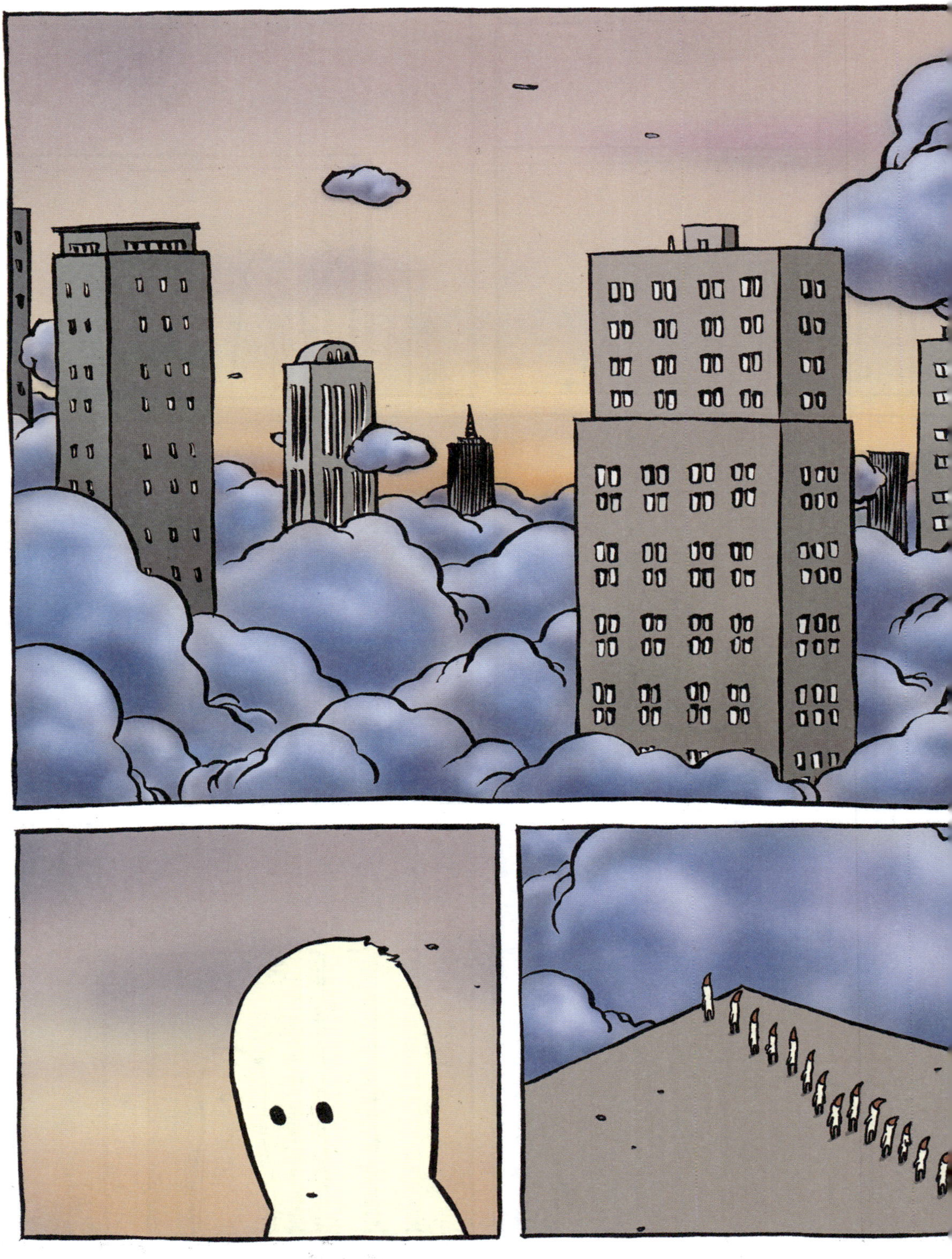

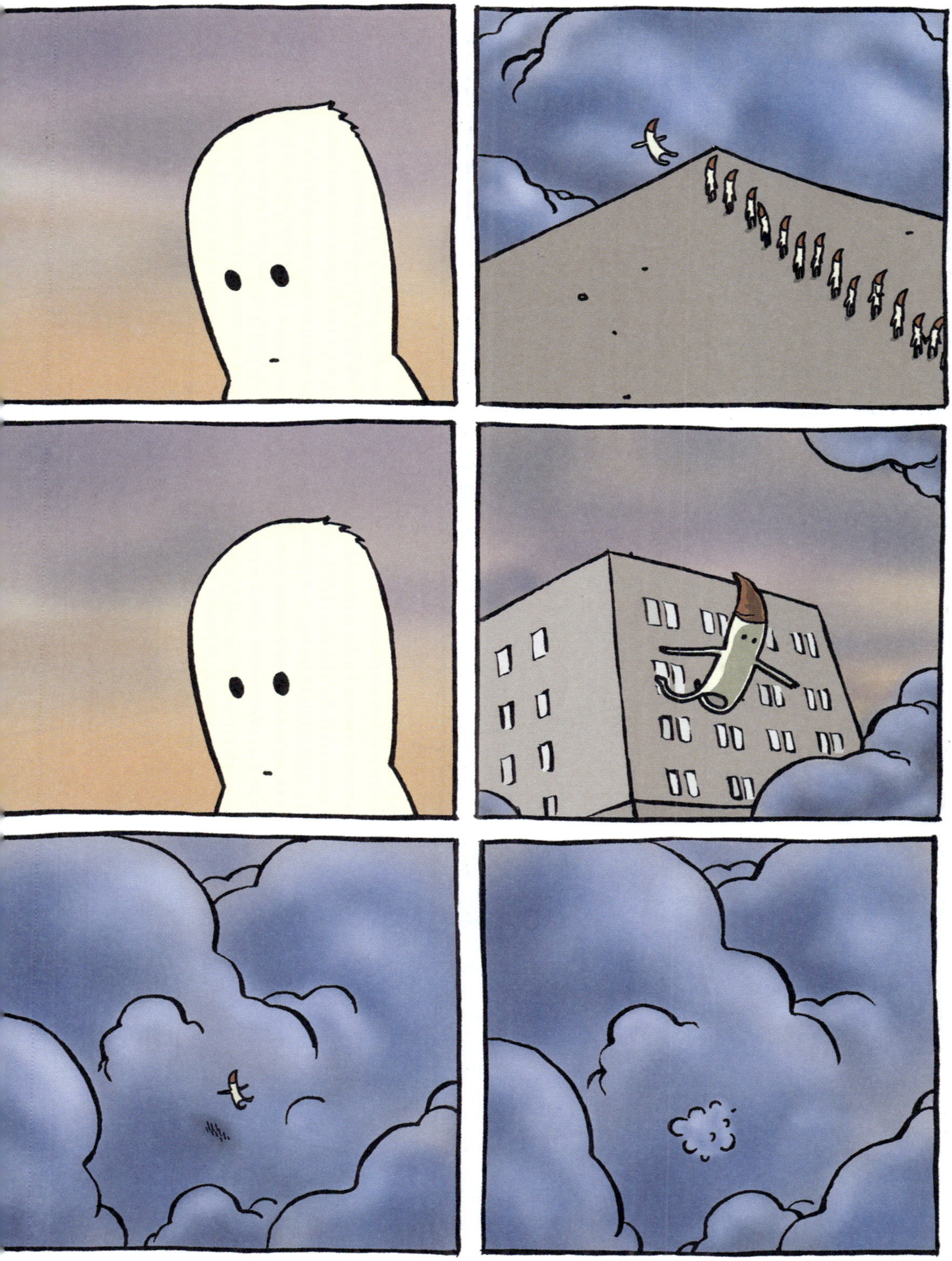

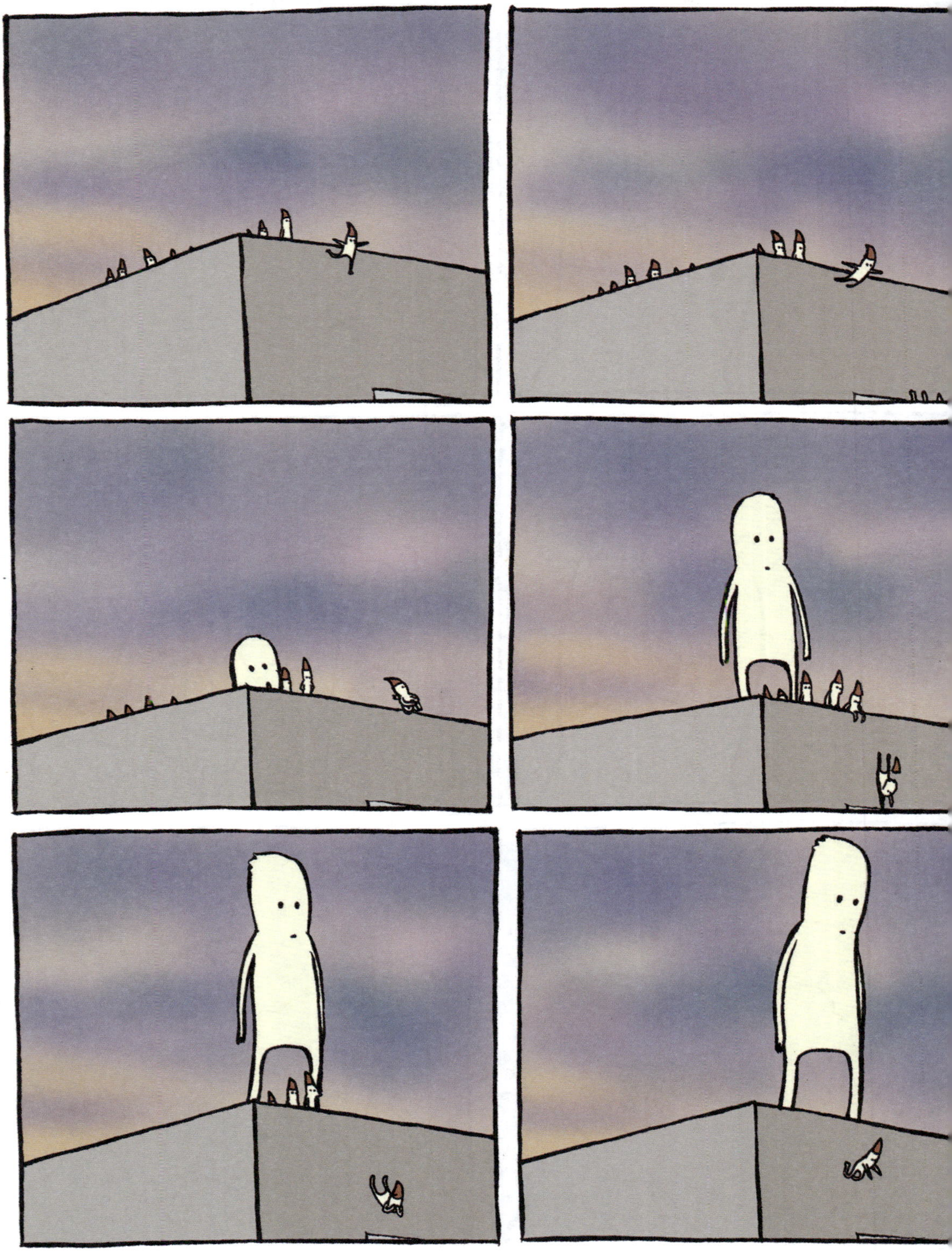

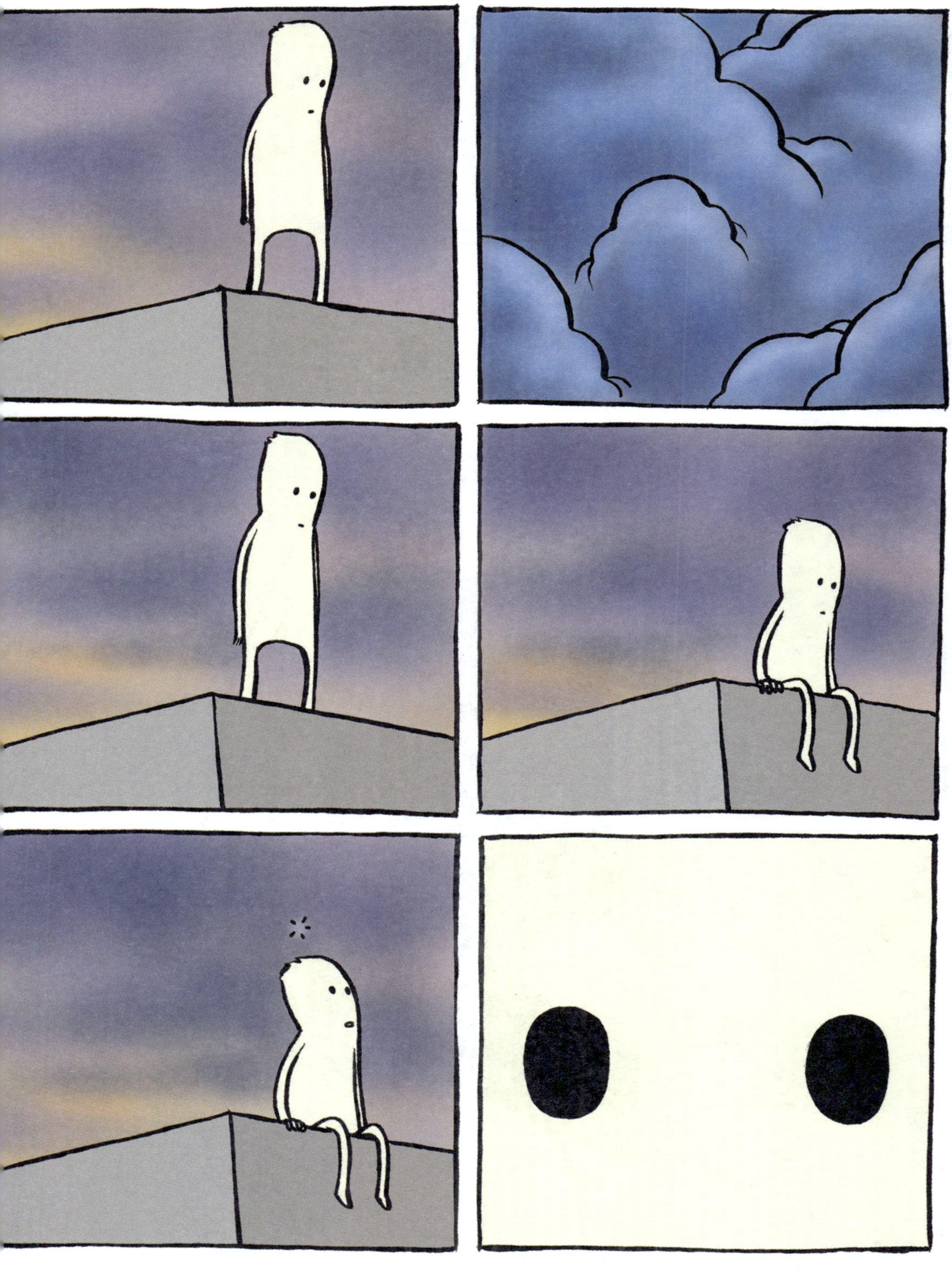

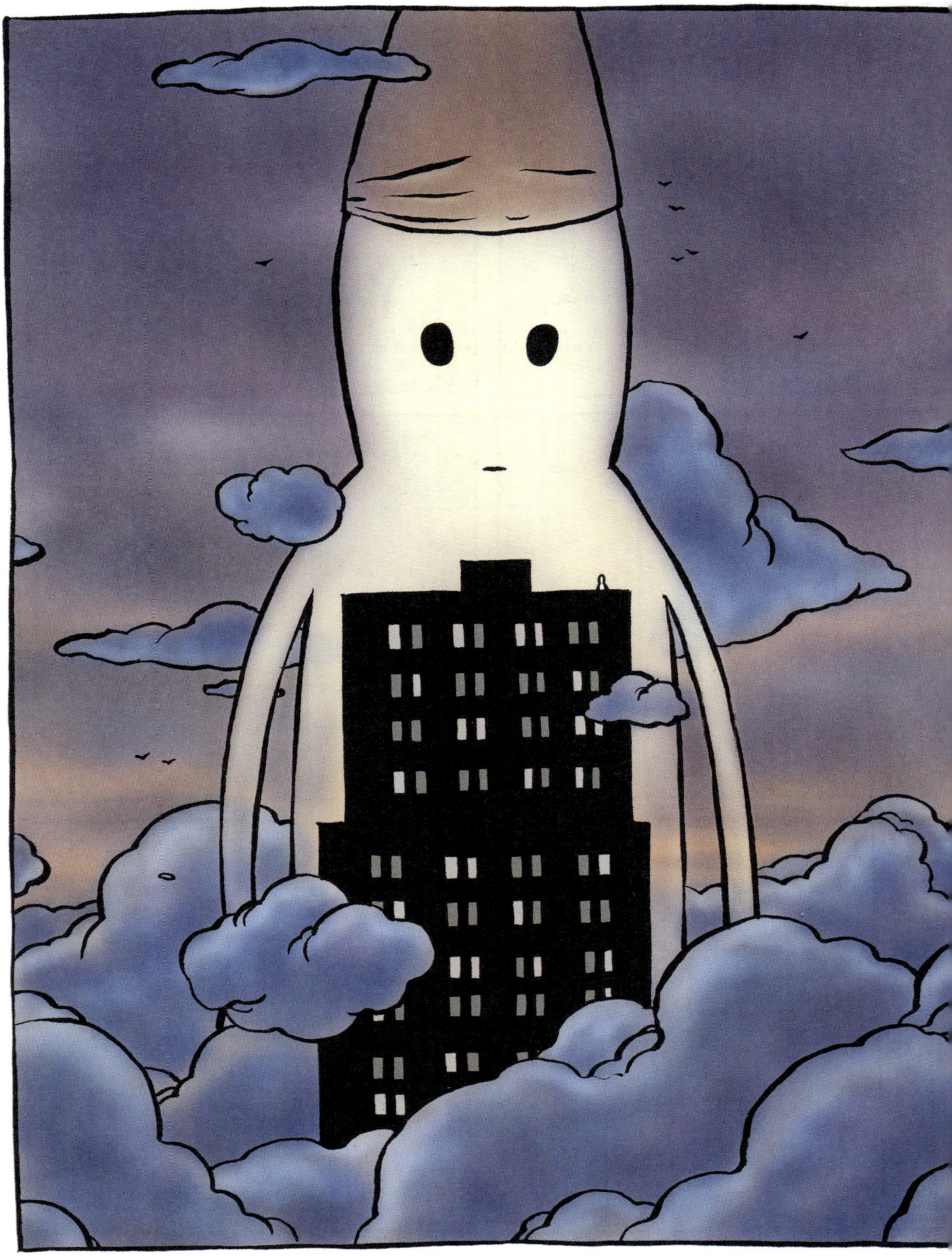

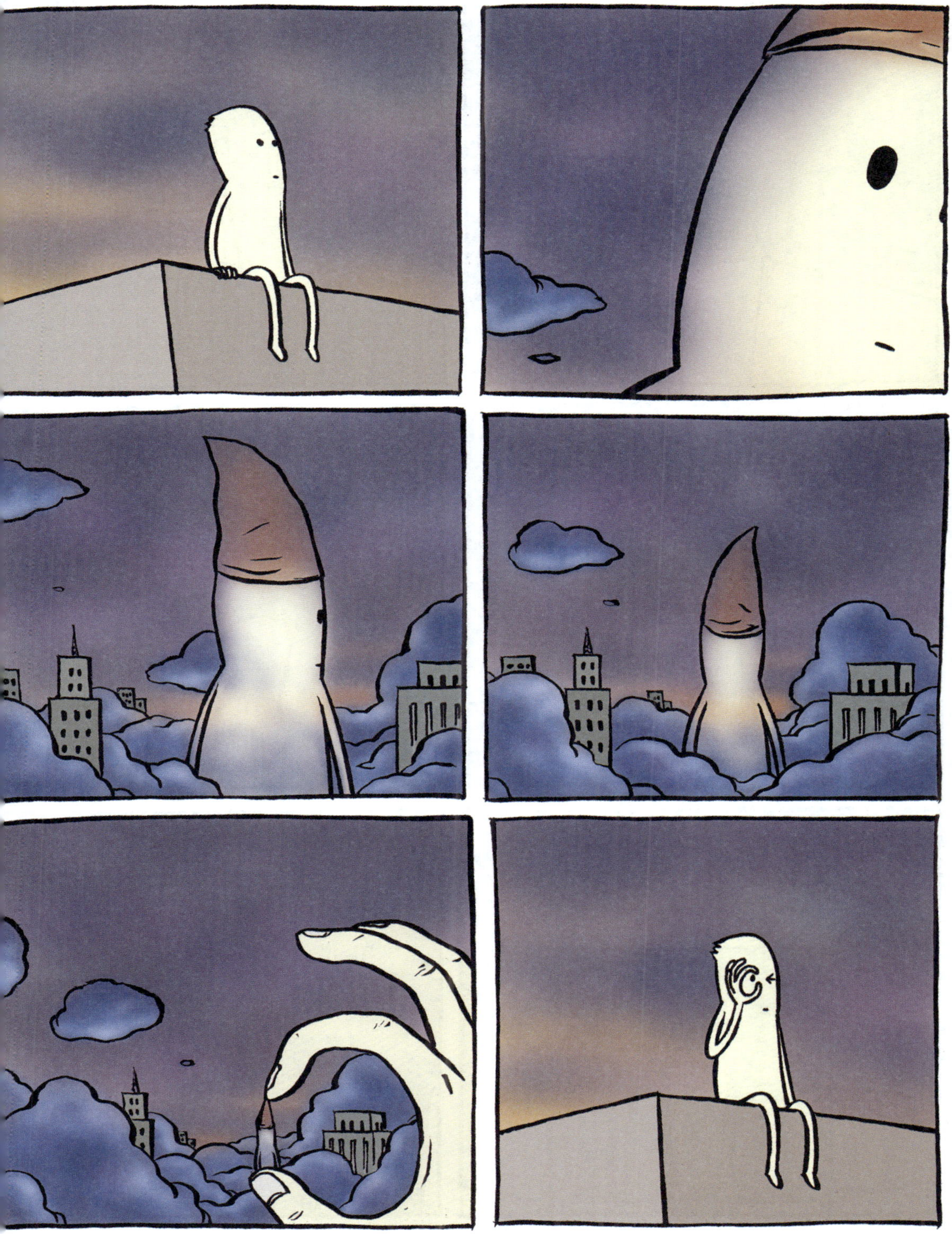

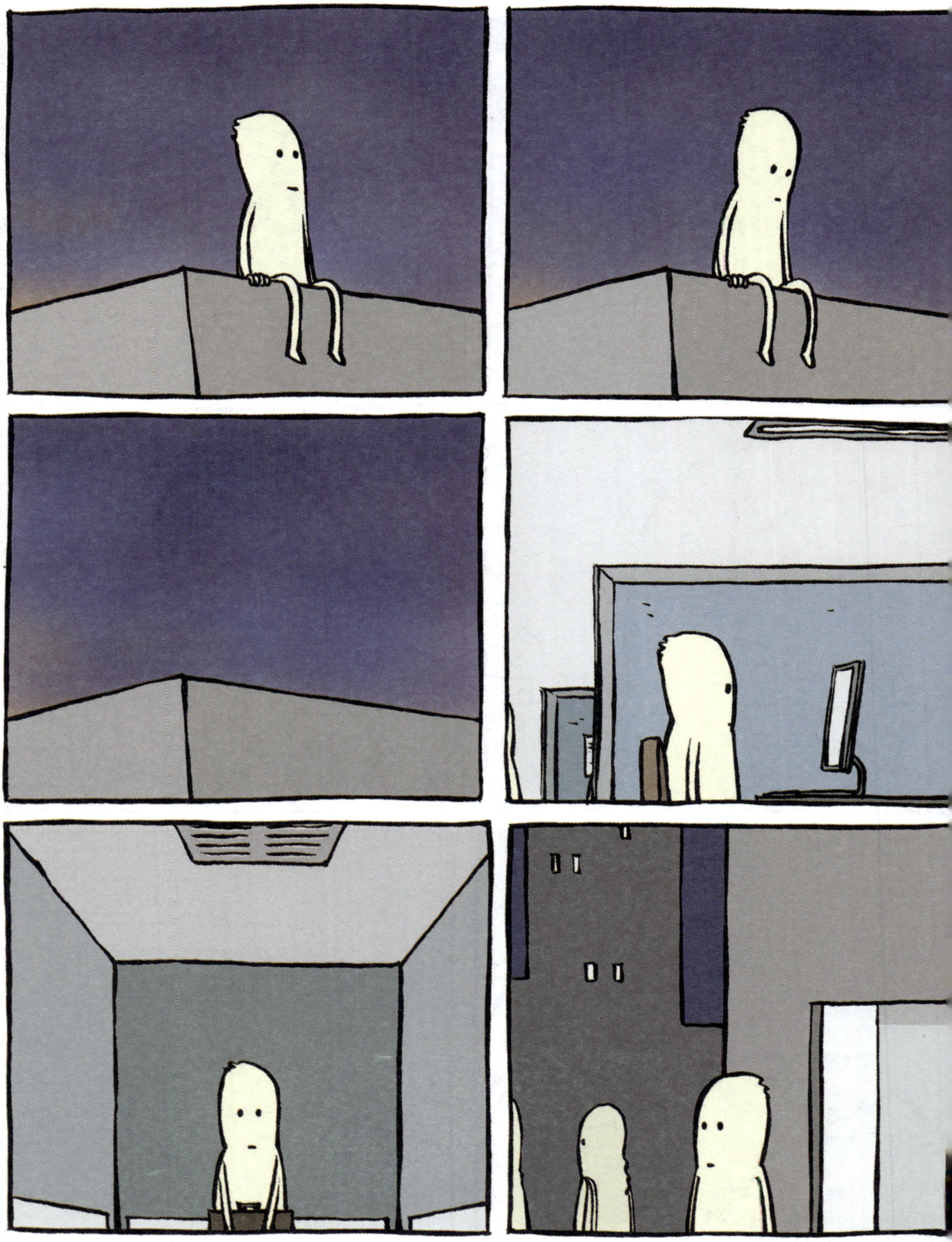

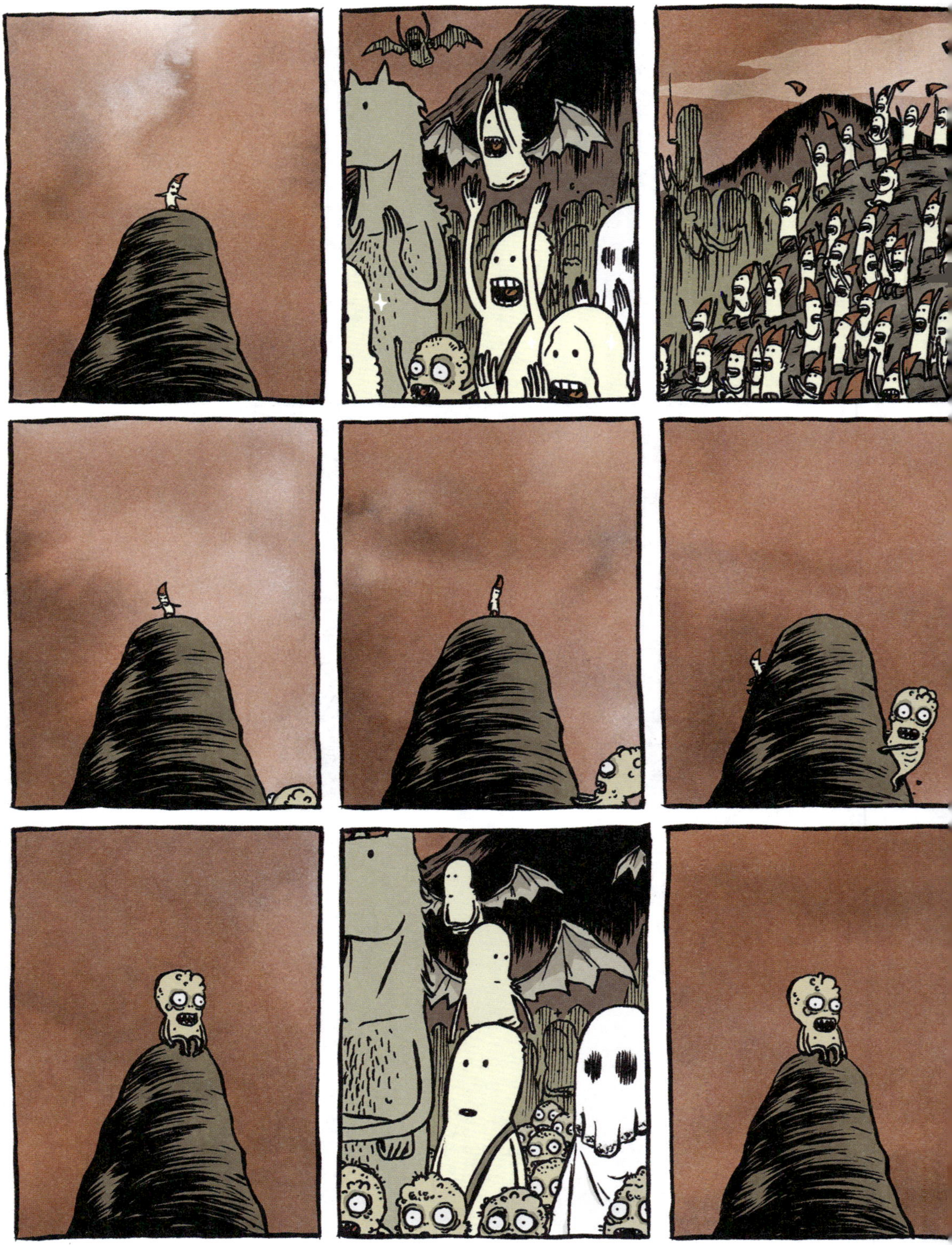

I

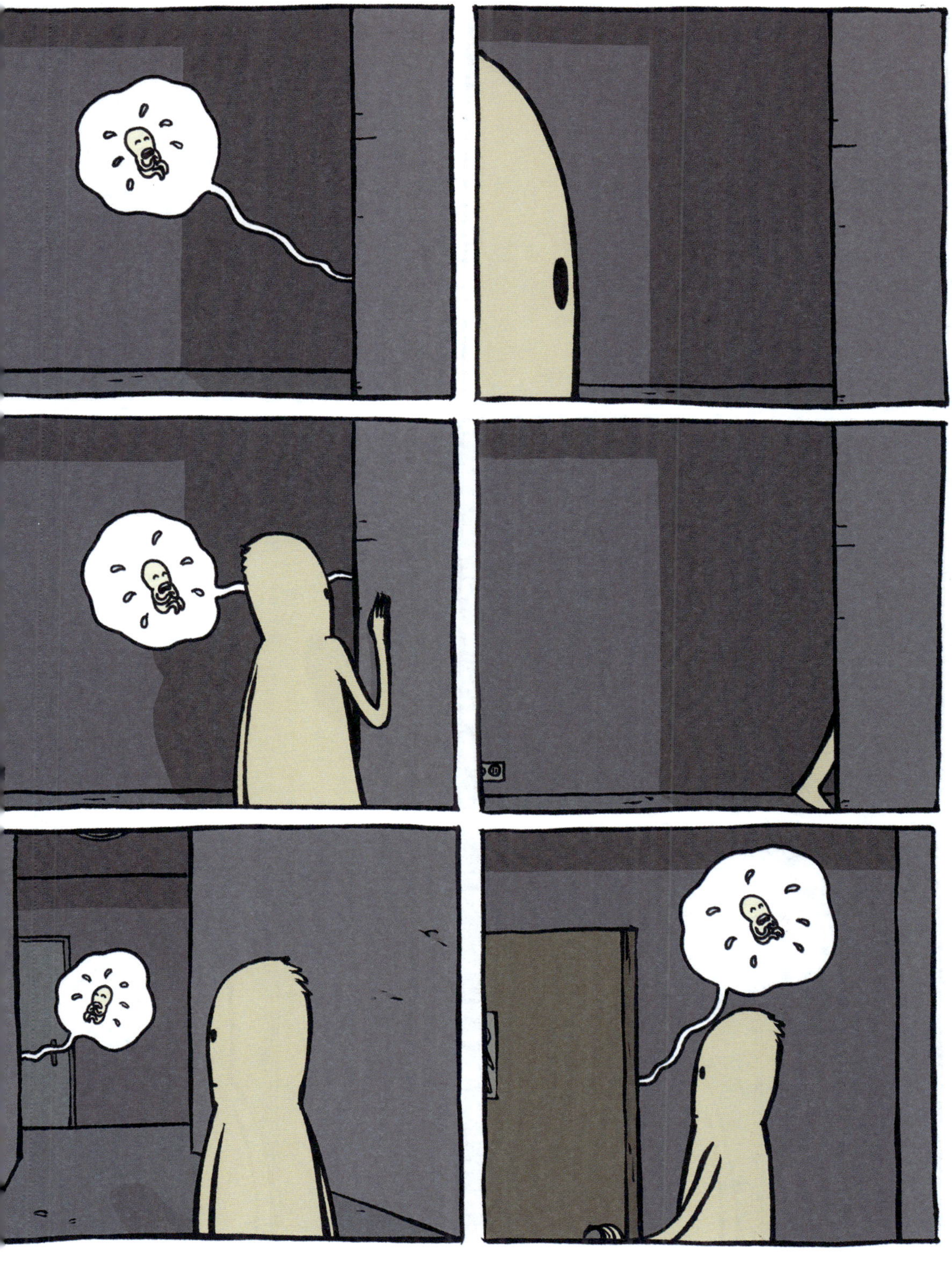

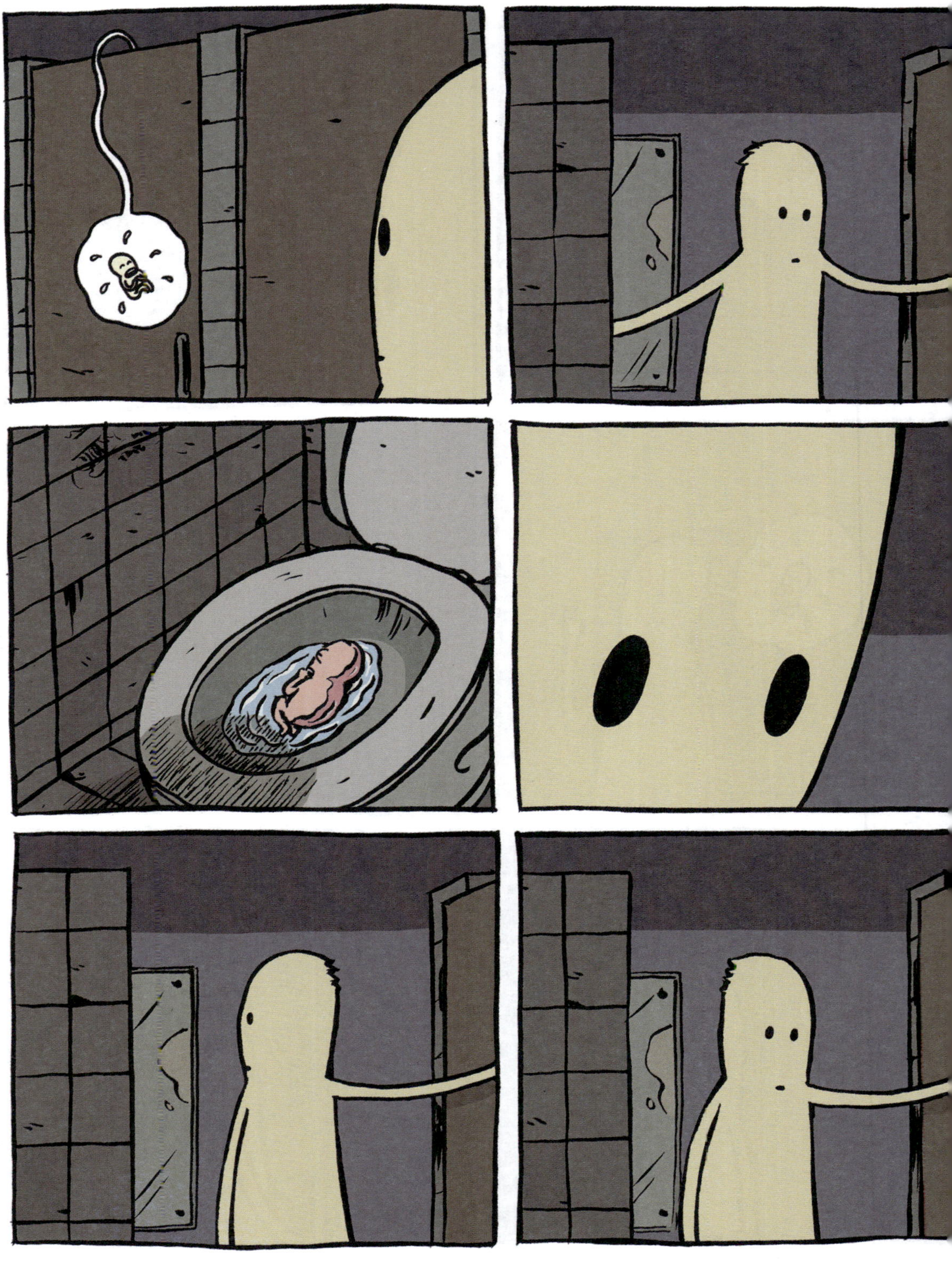

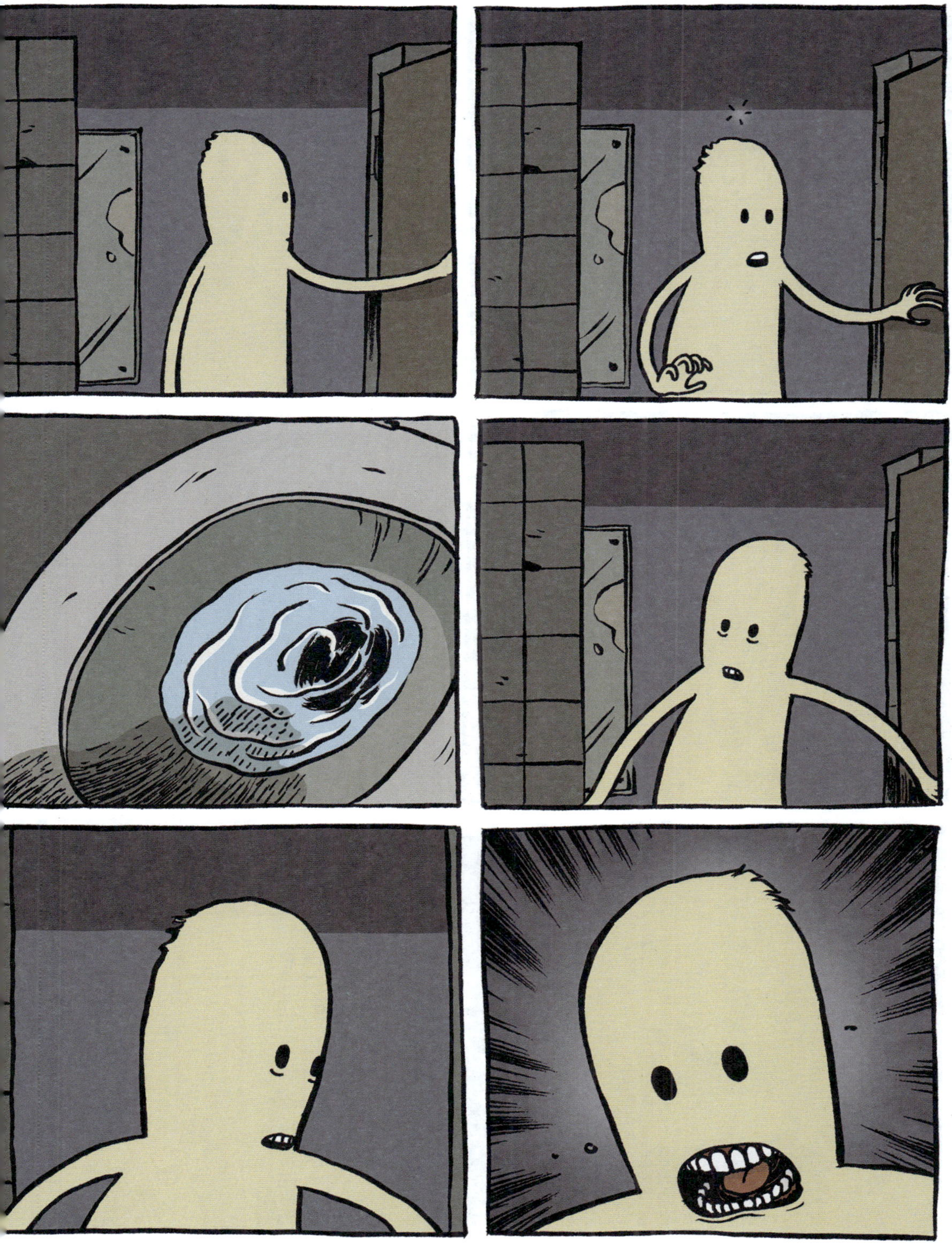

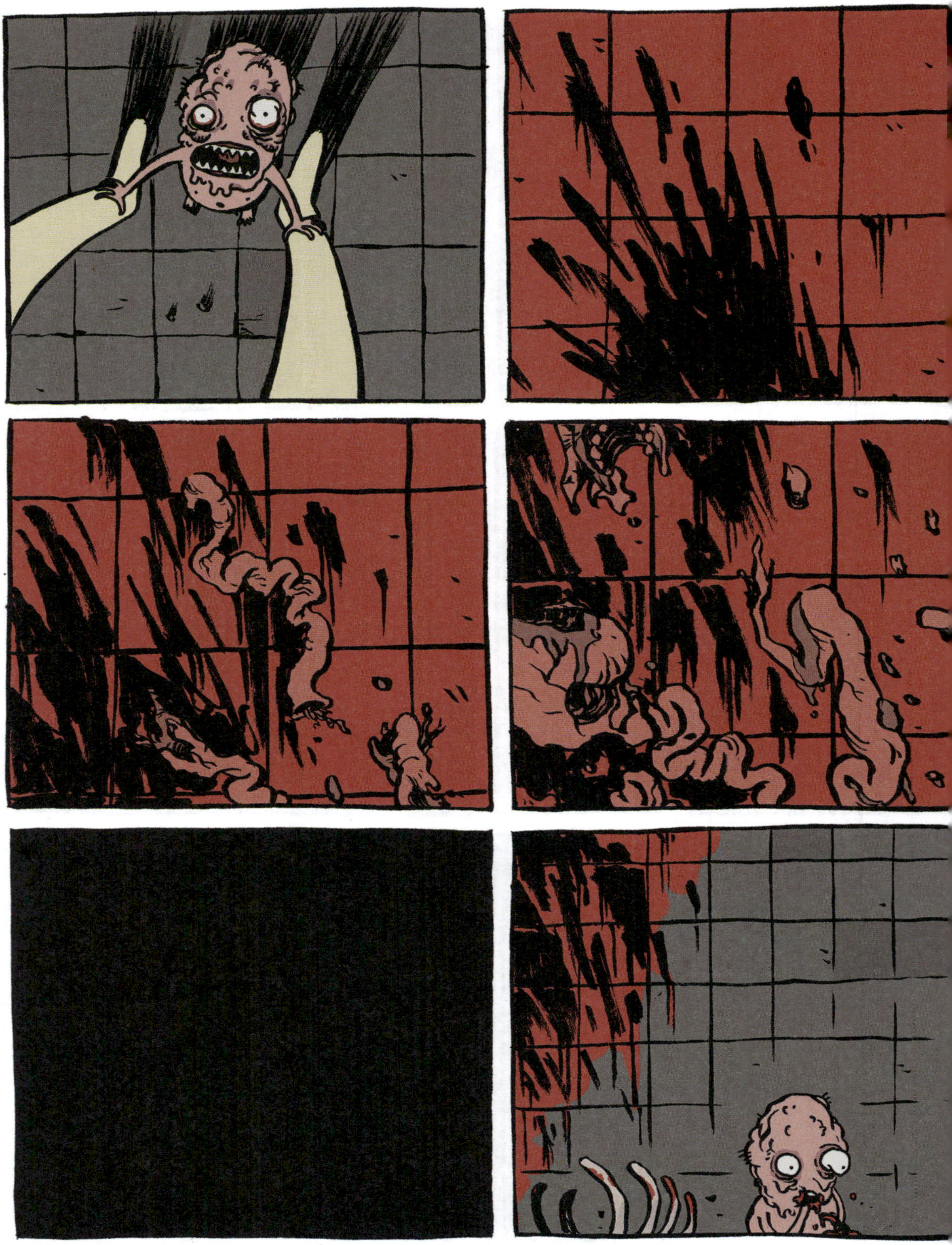

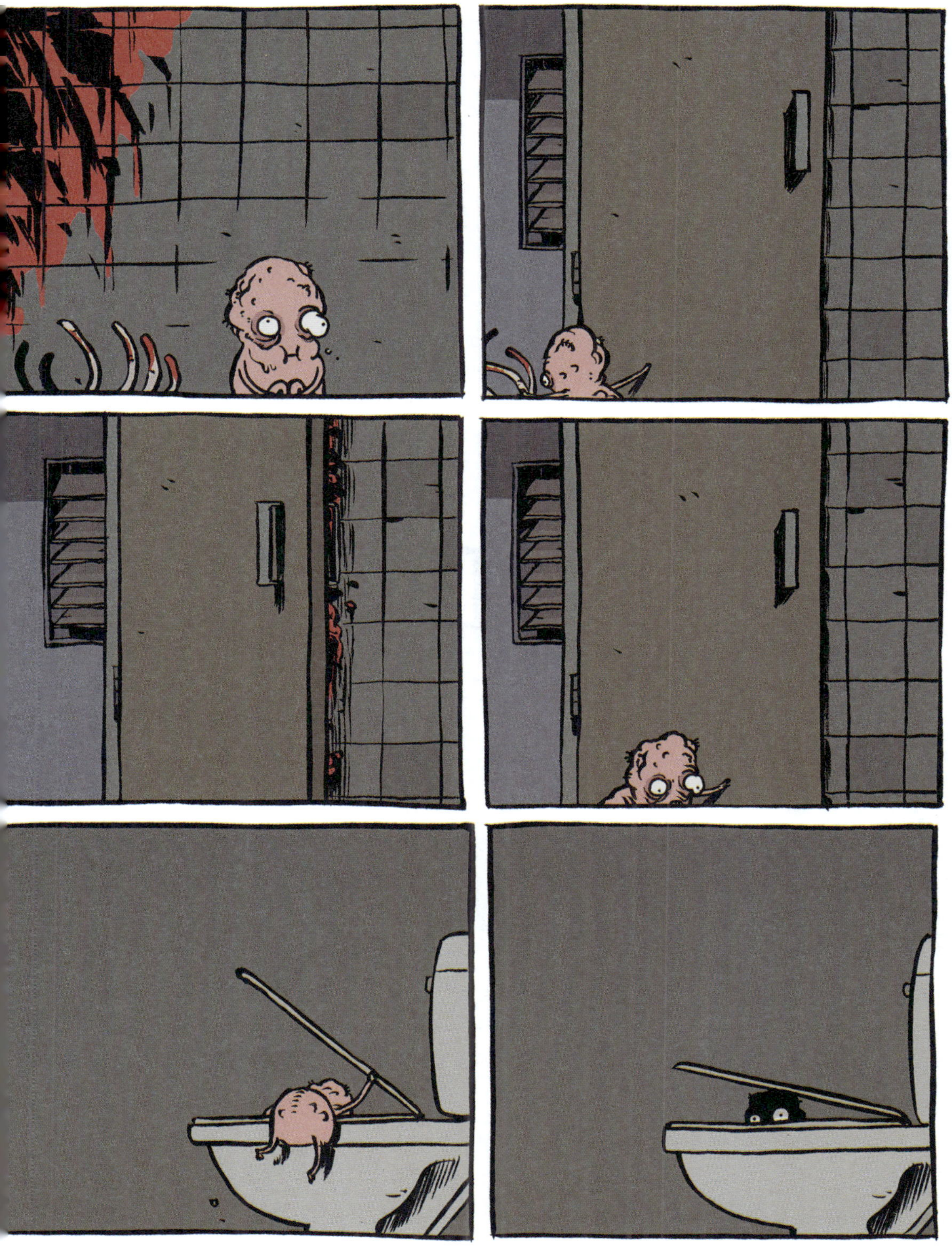

II

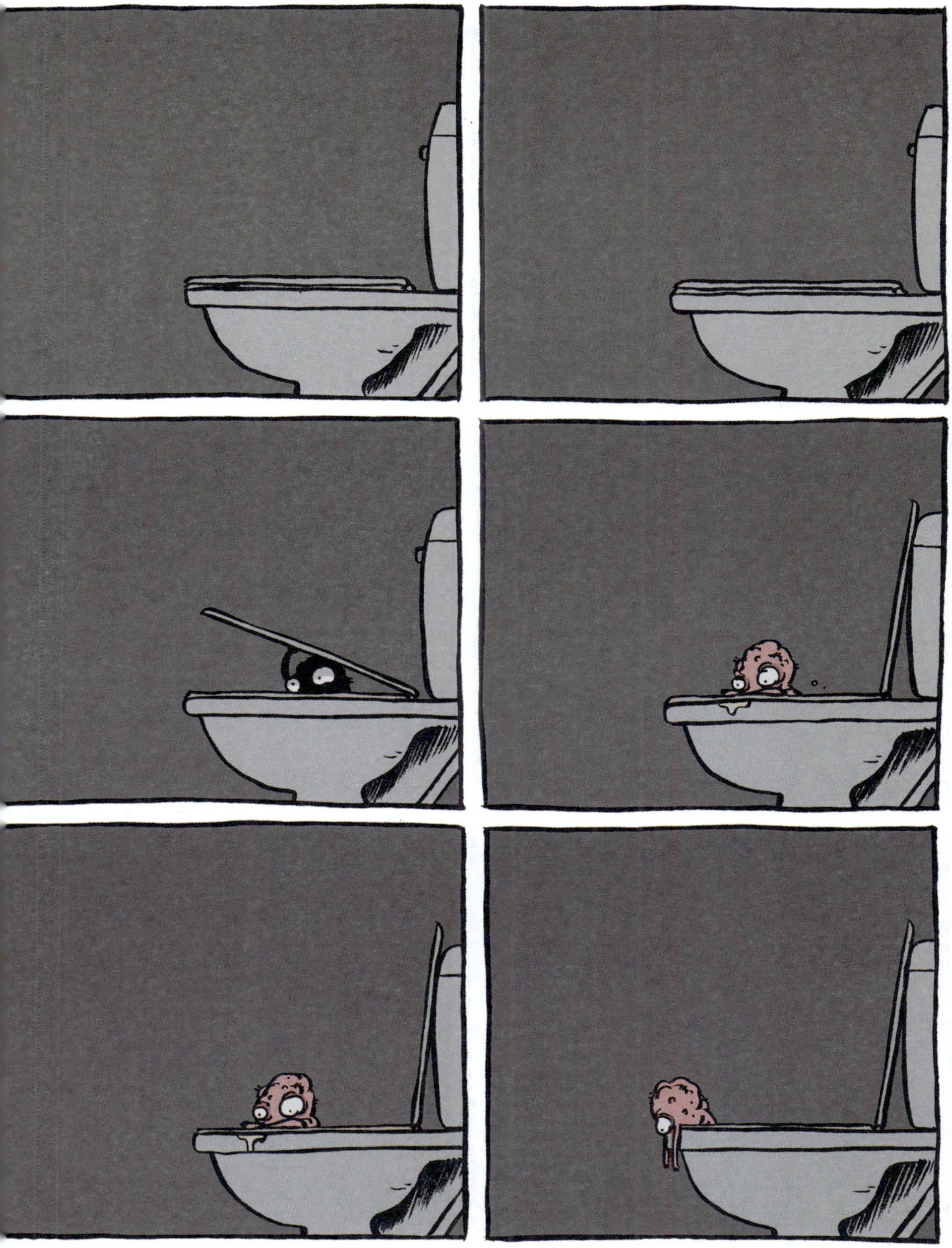

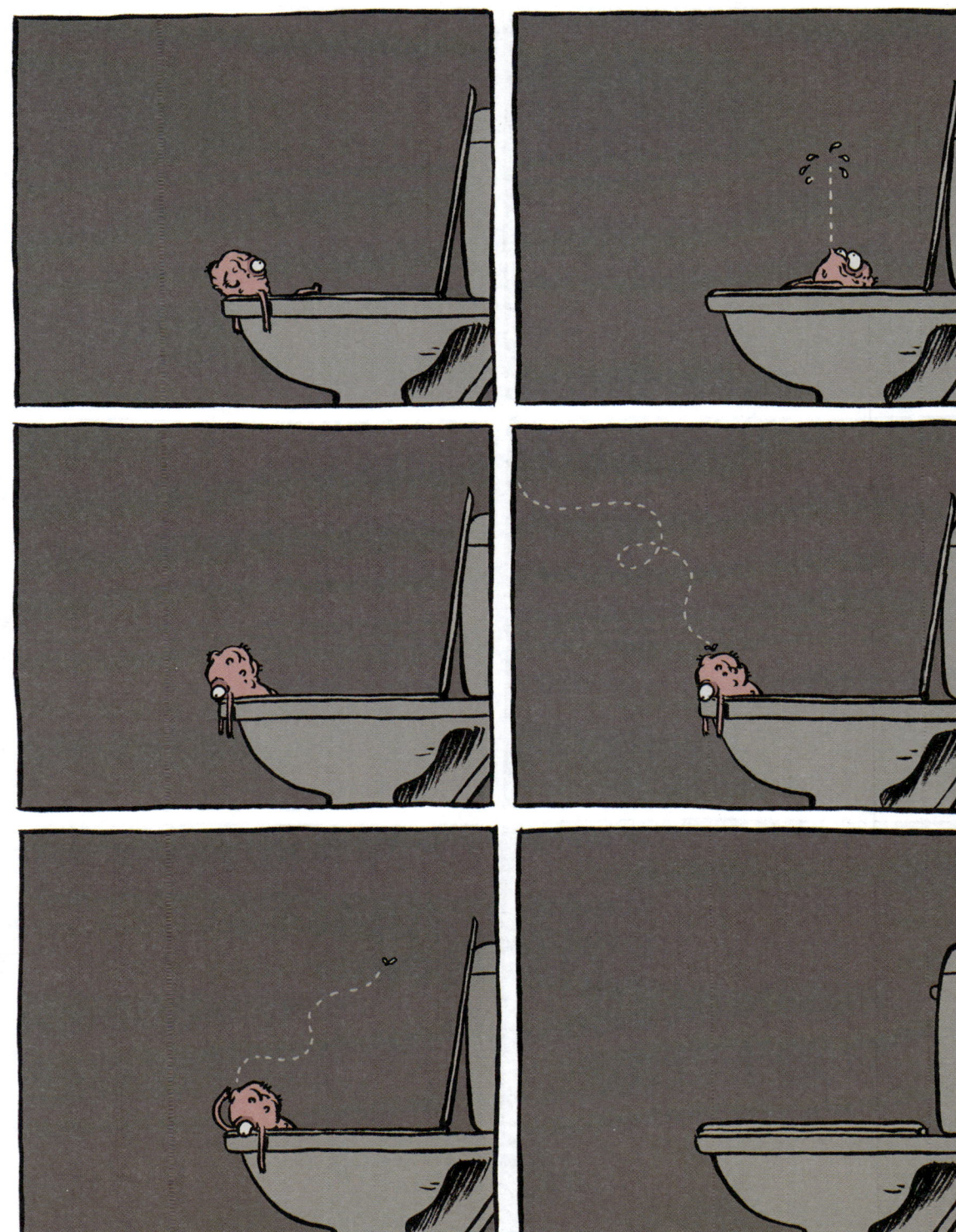

III

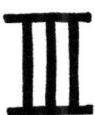

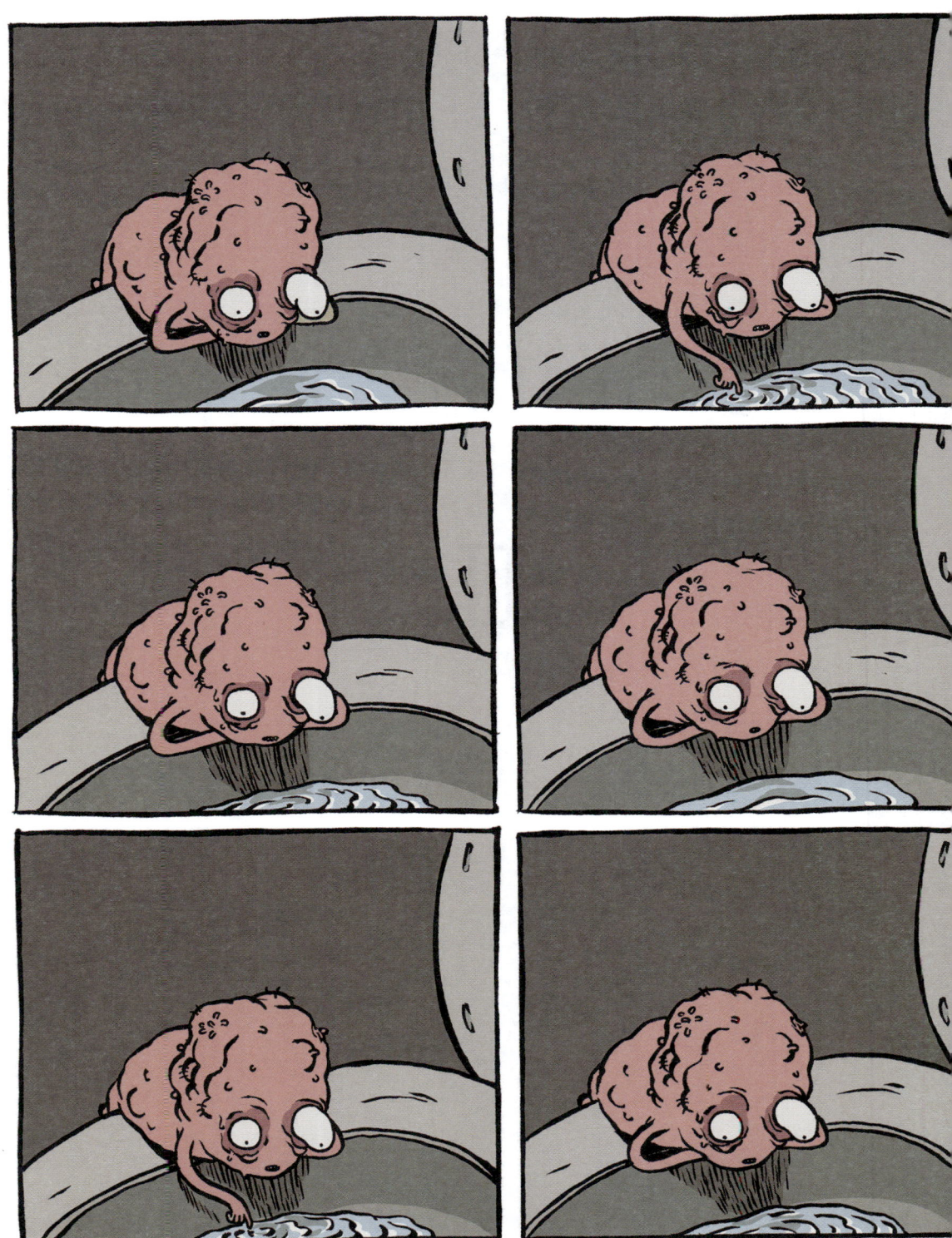

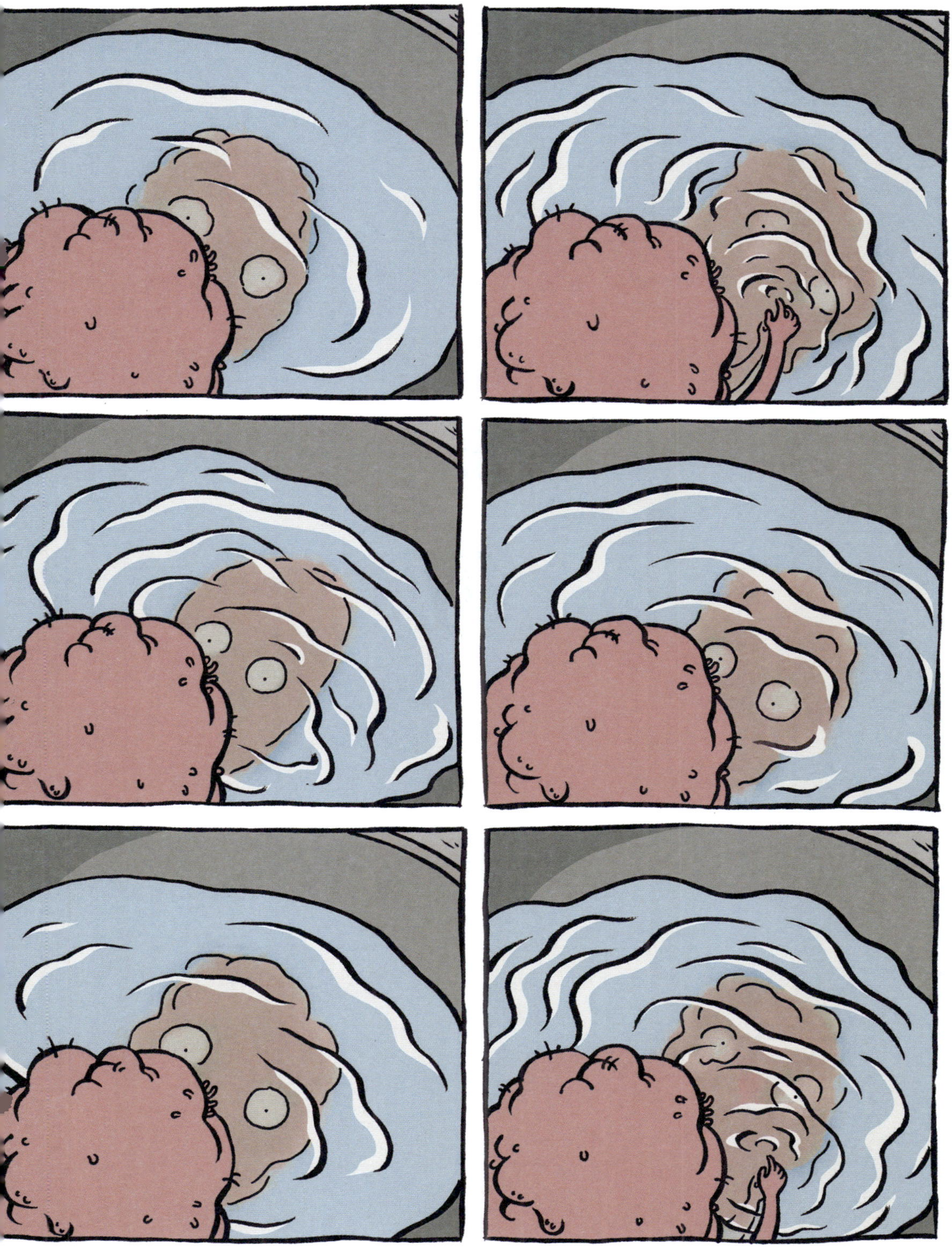

IV

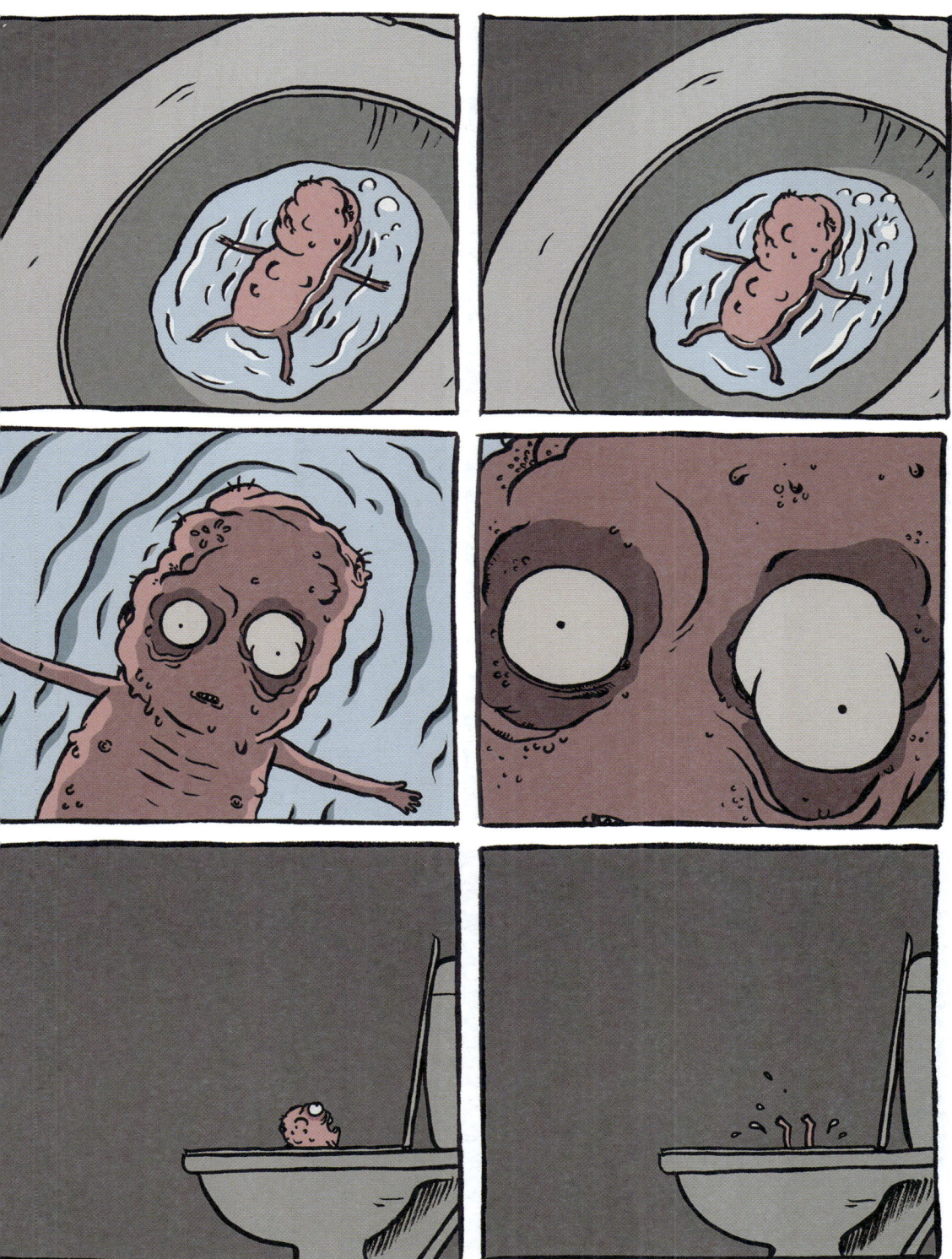

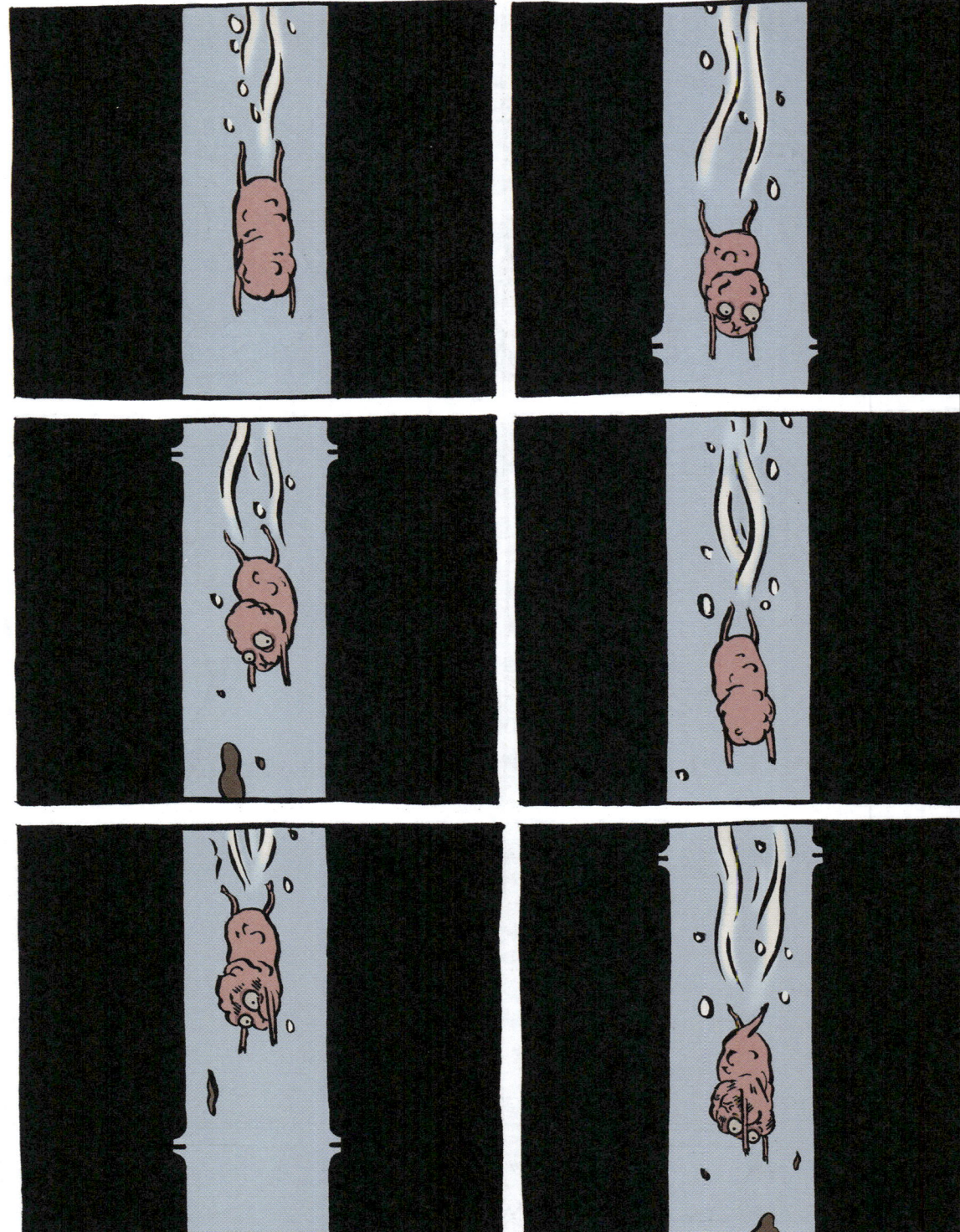

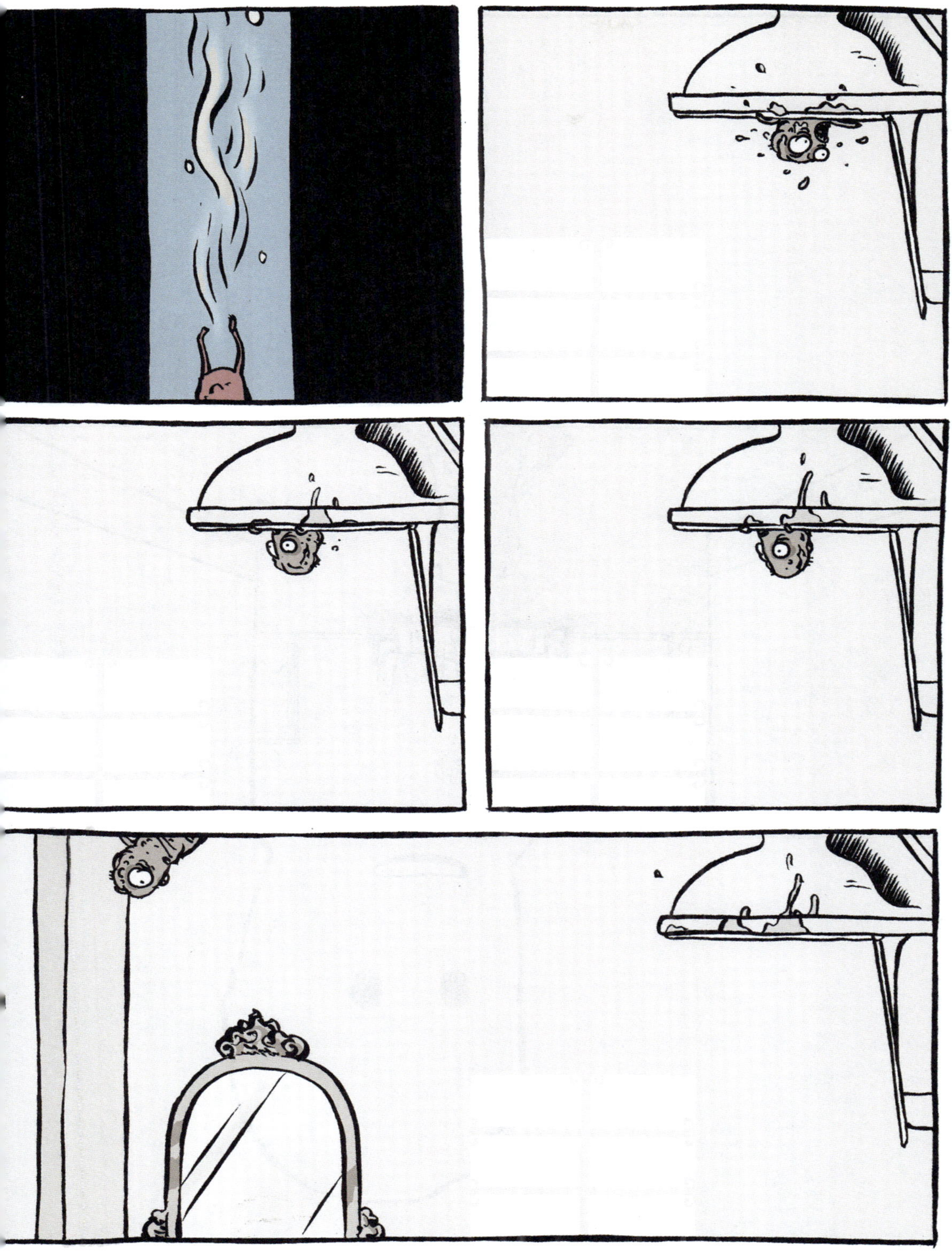

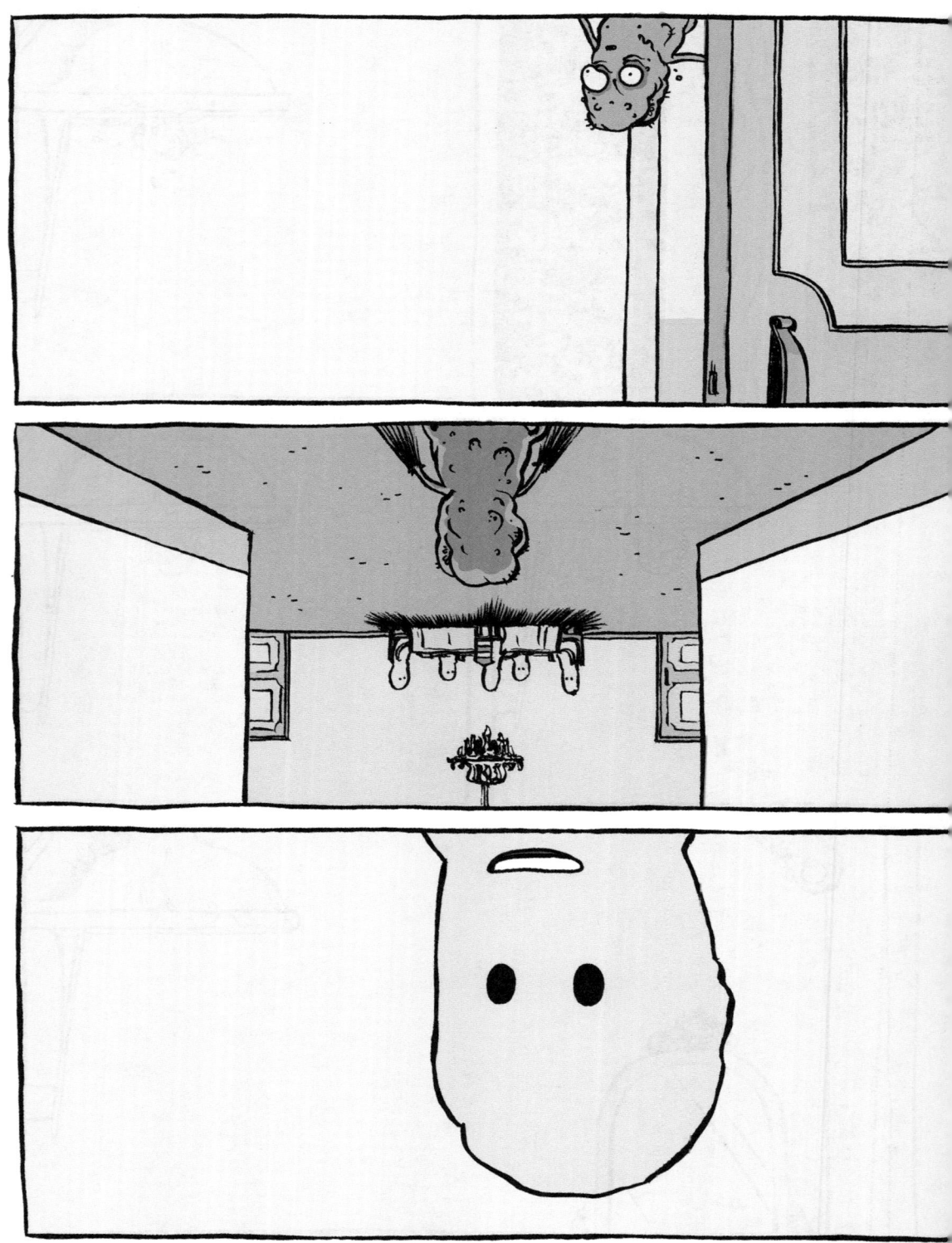

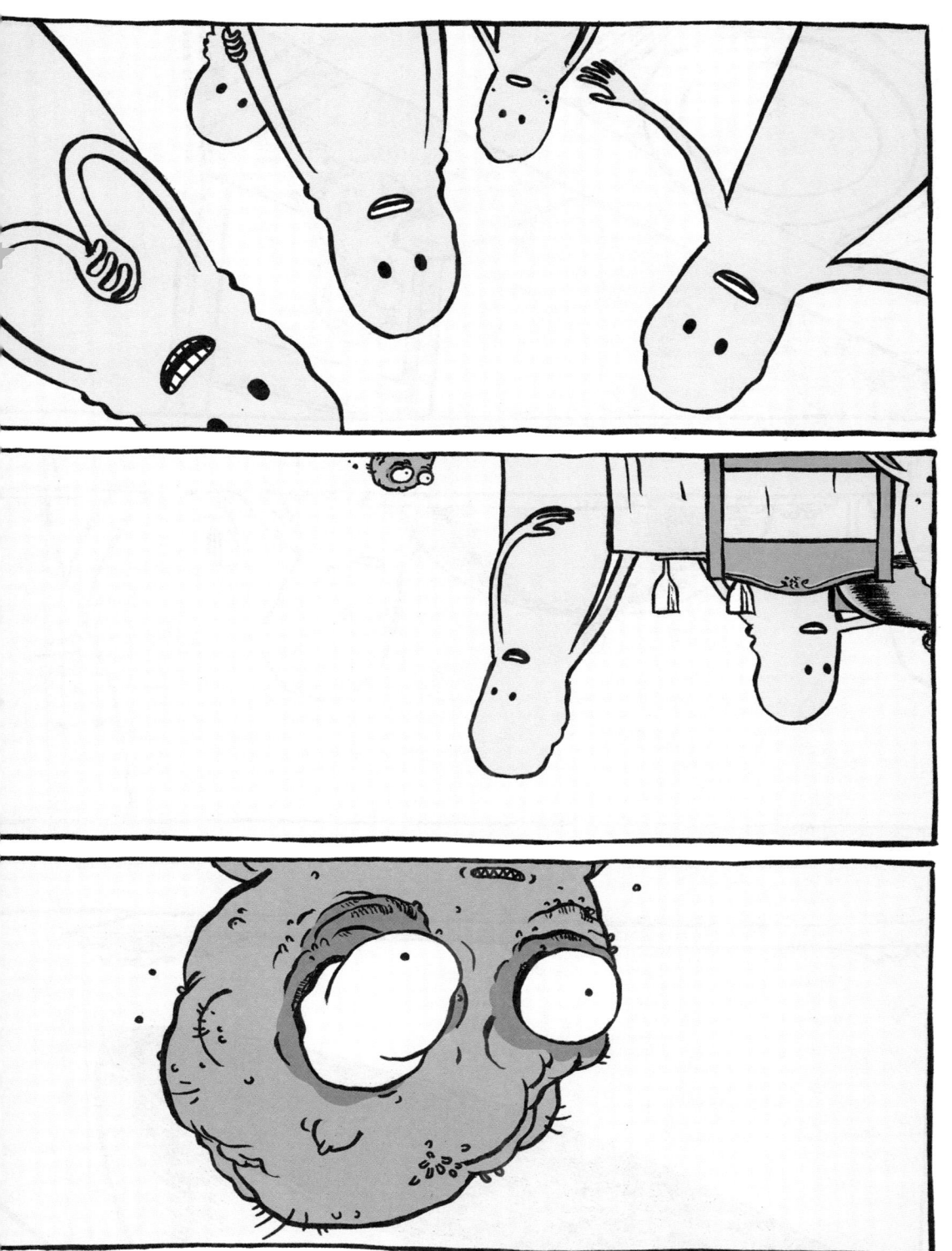

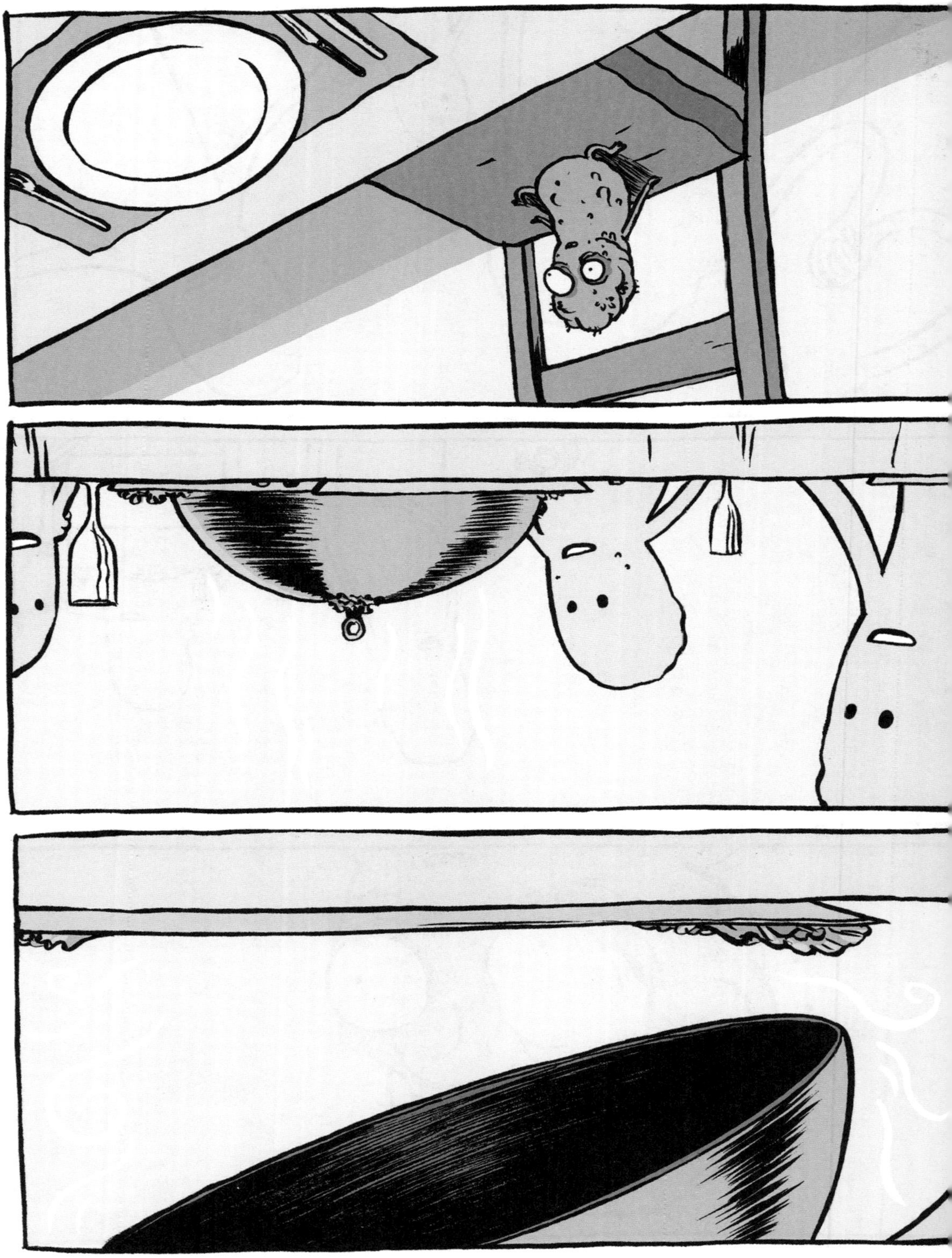

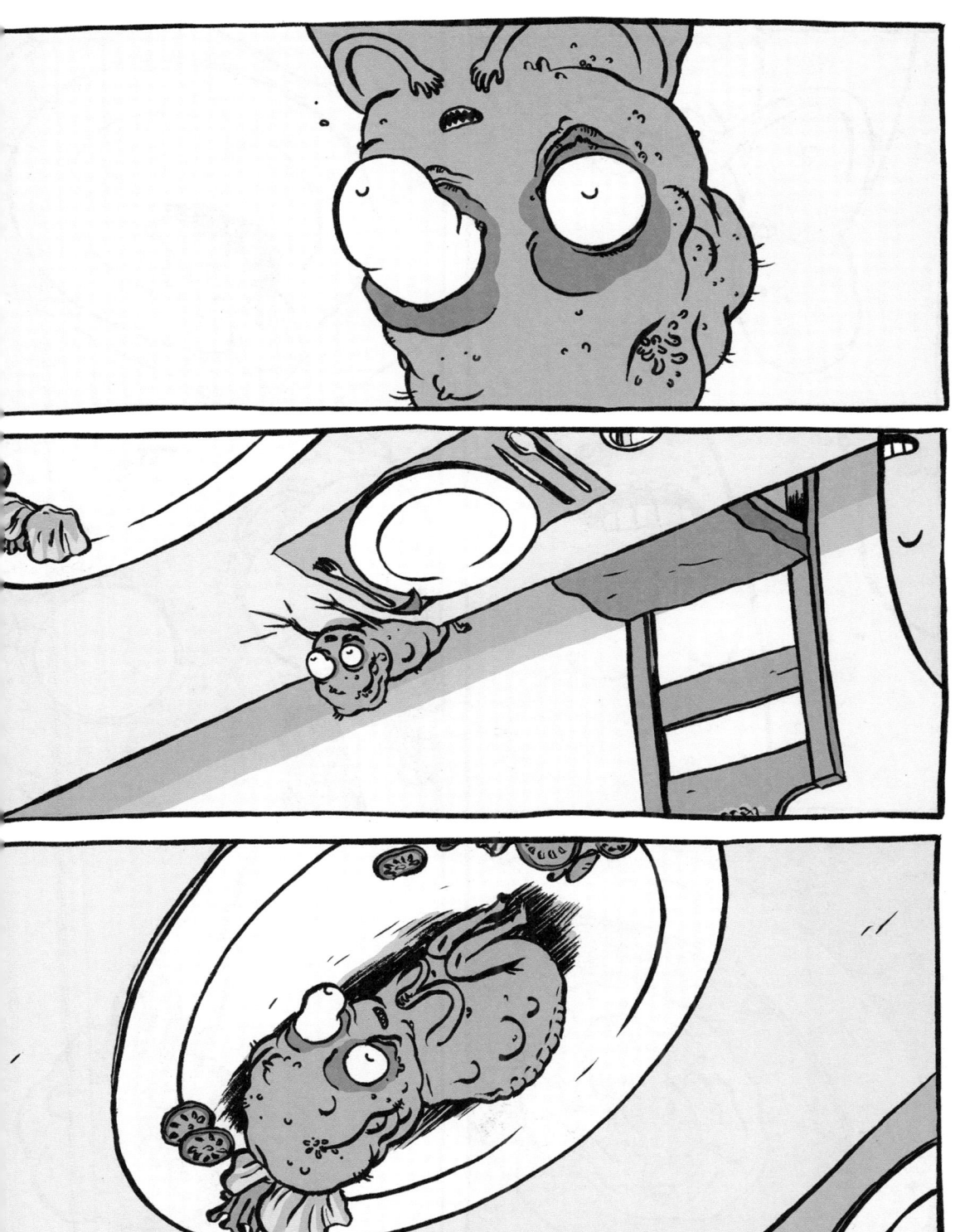

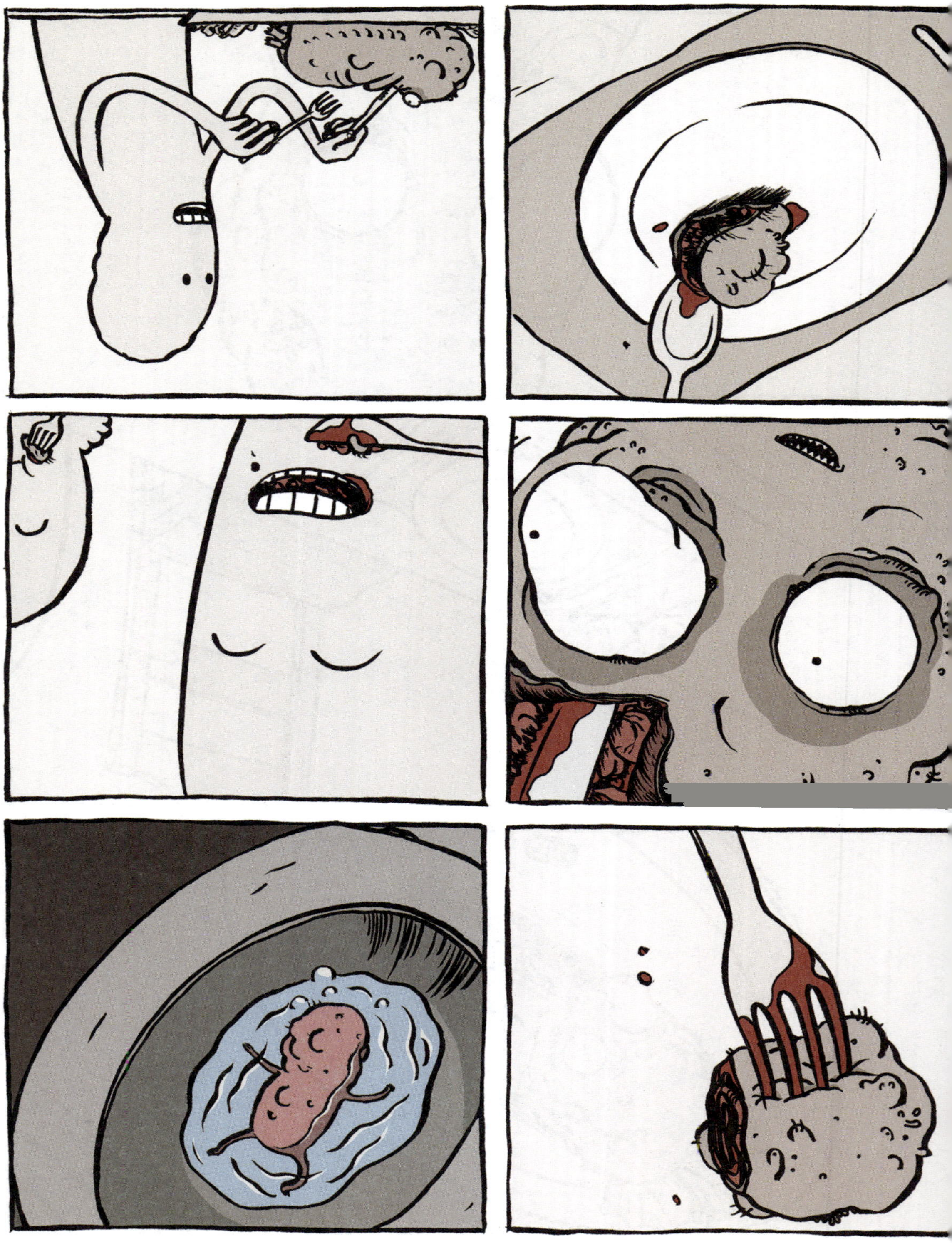

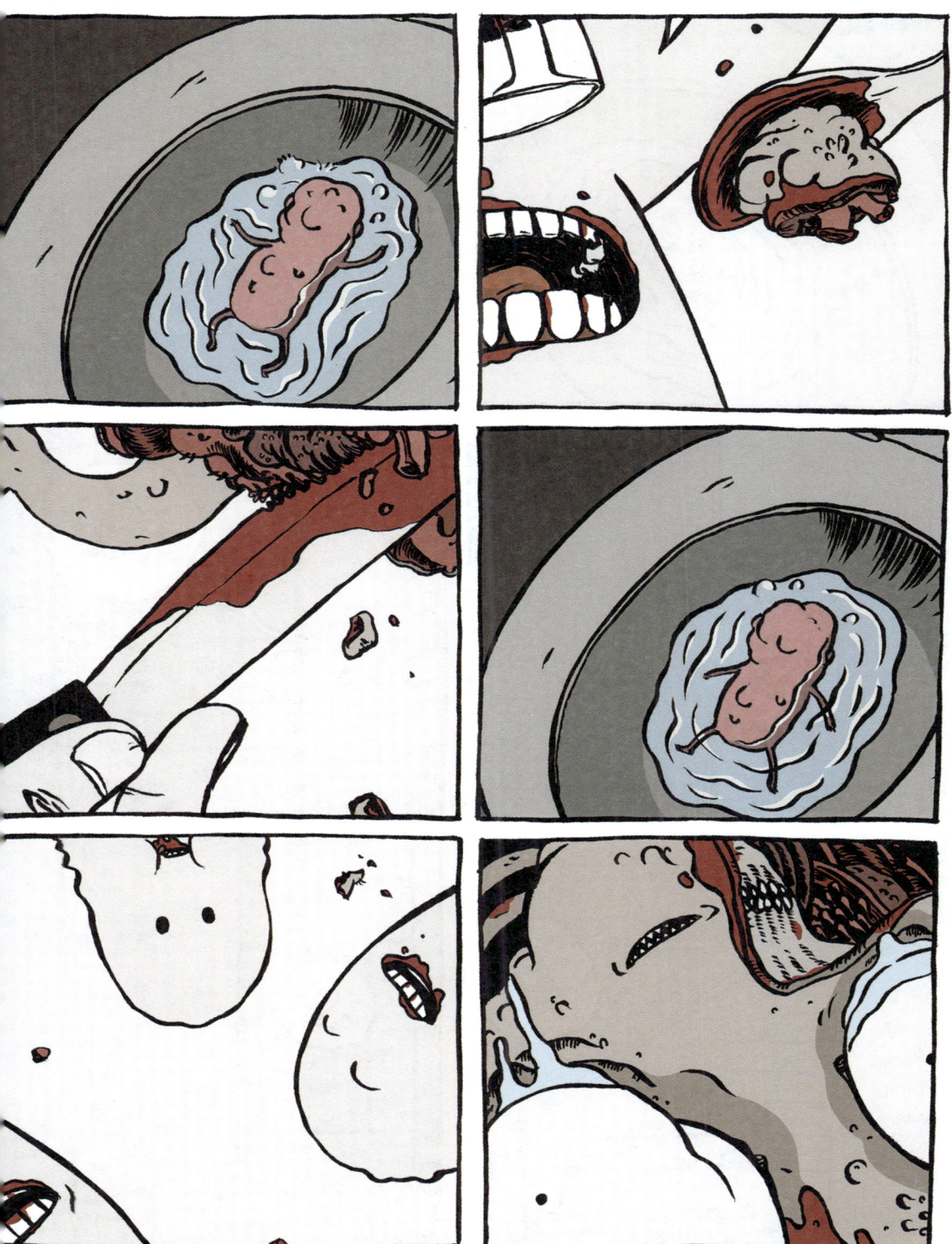

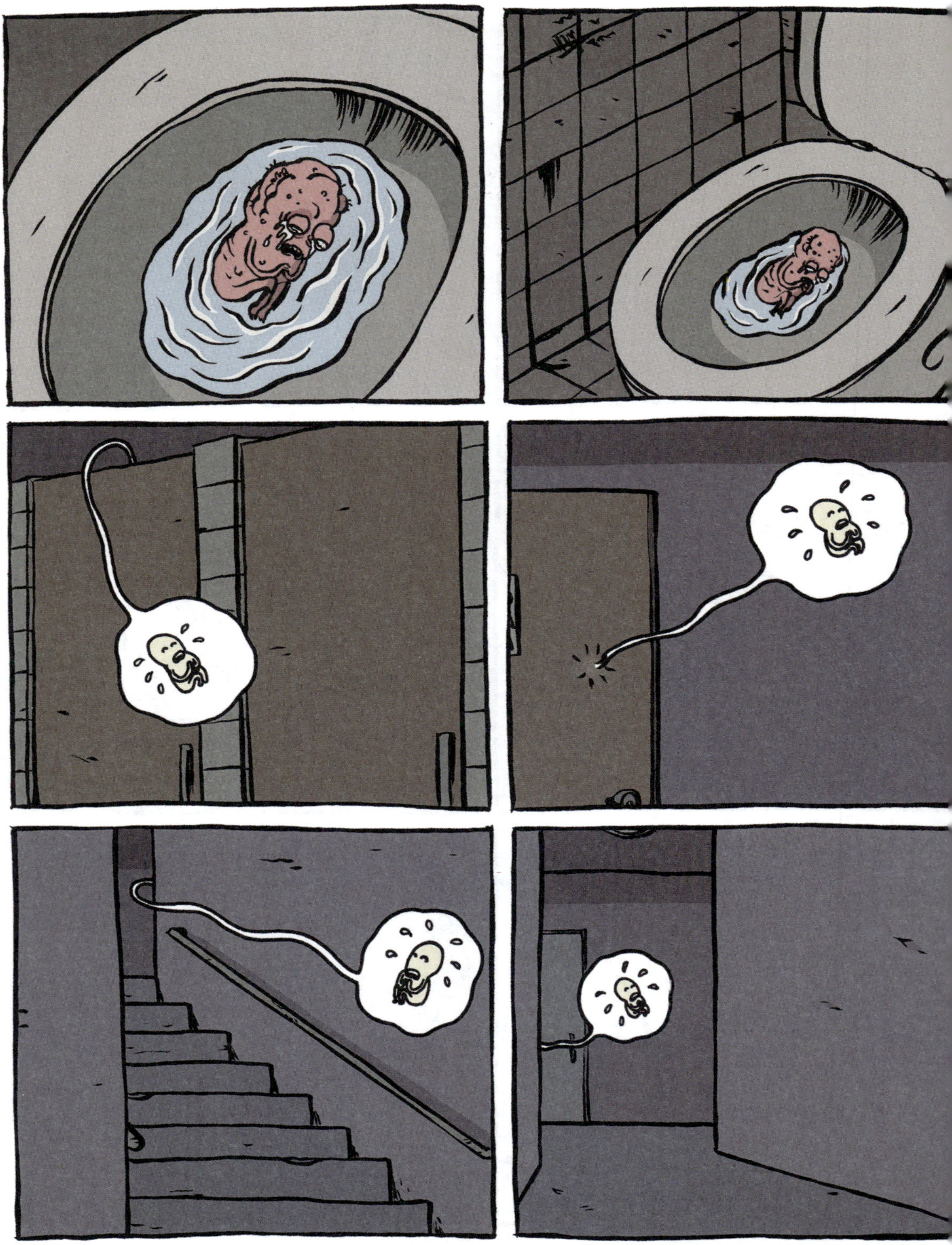

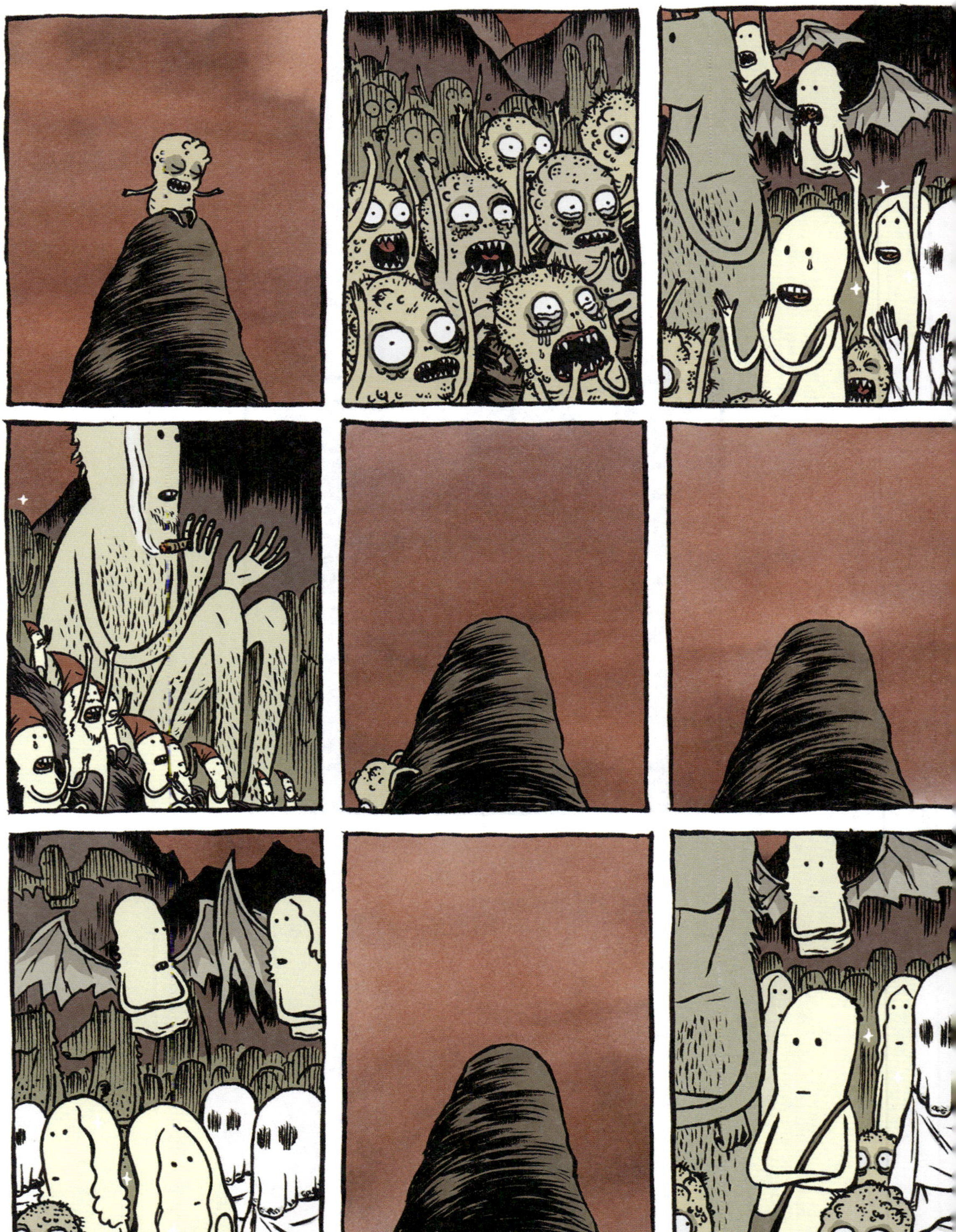

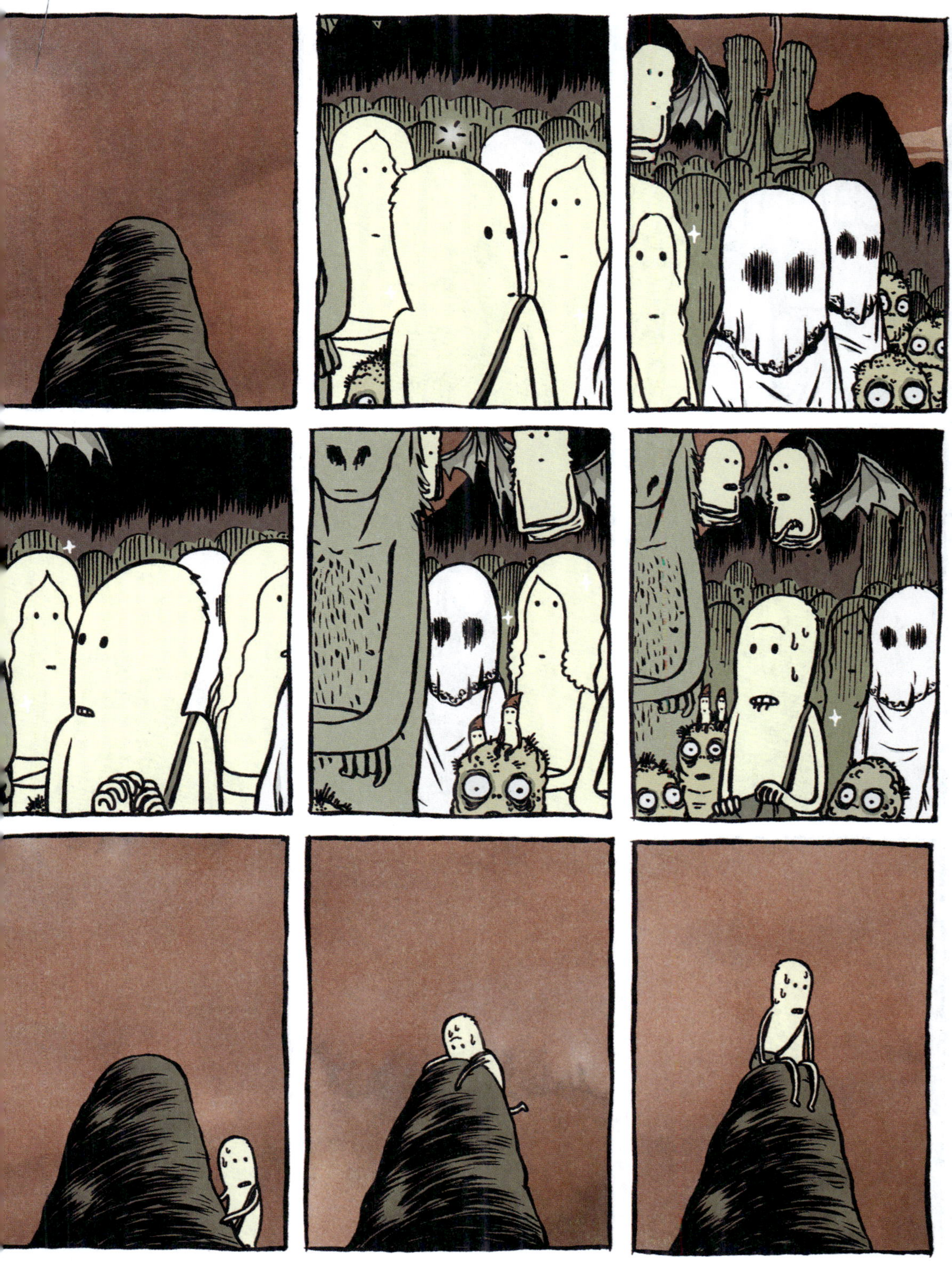

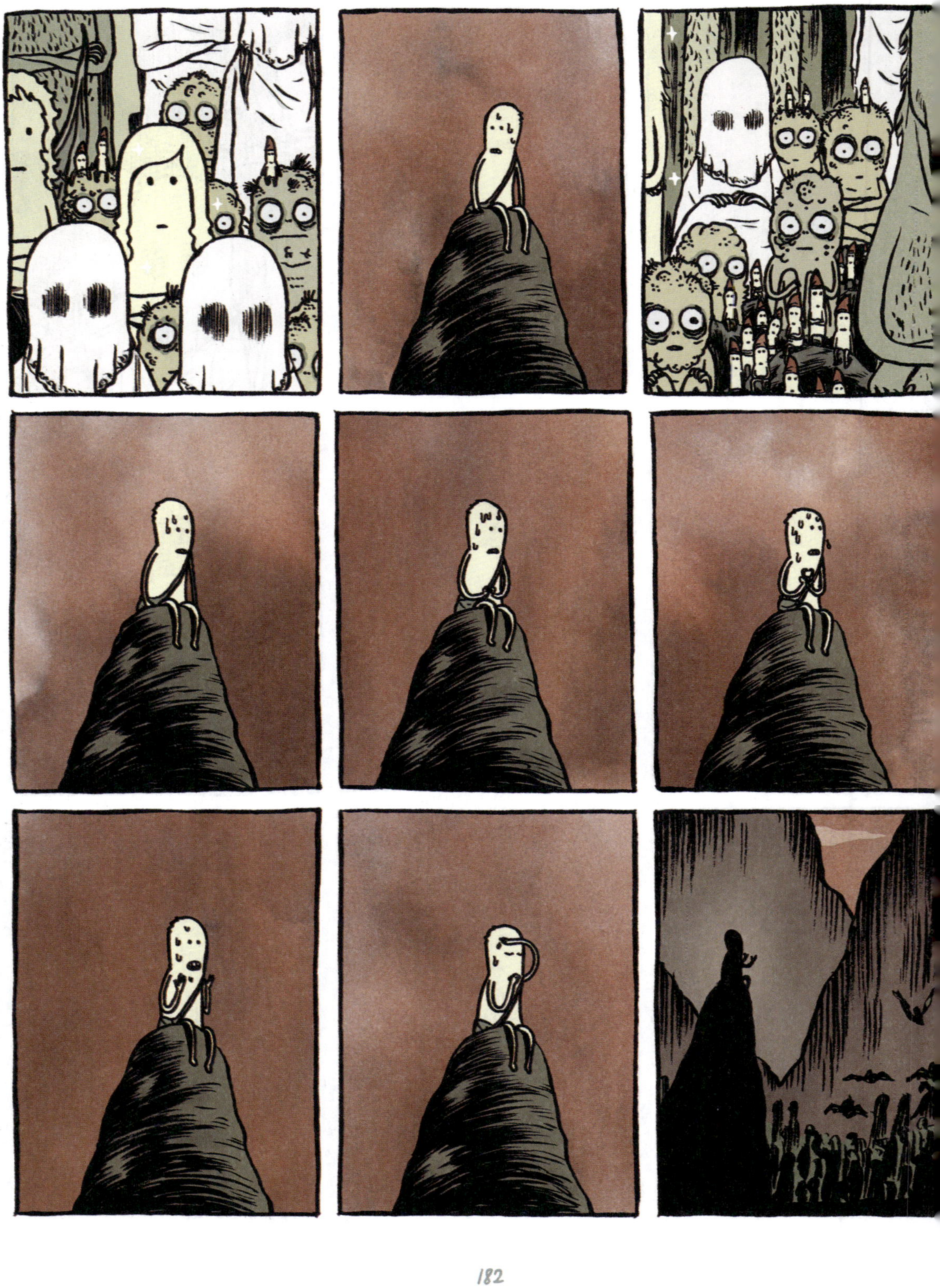

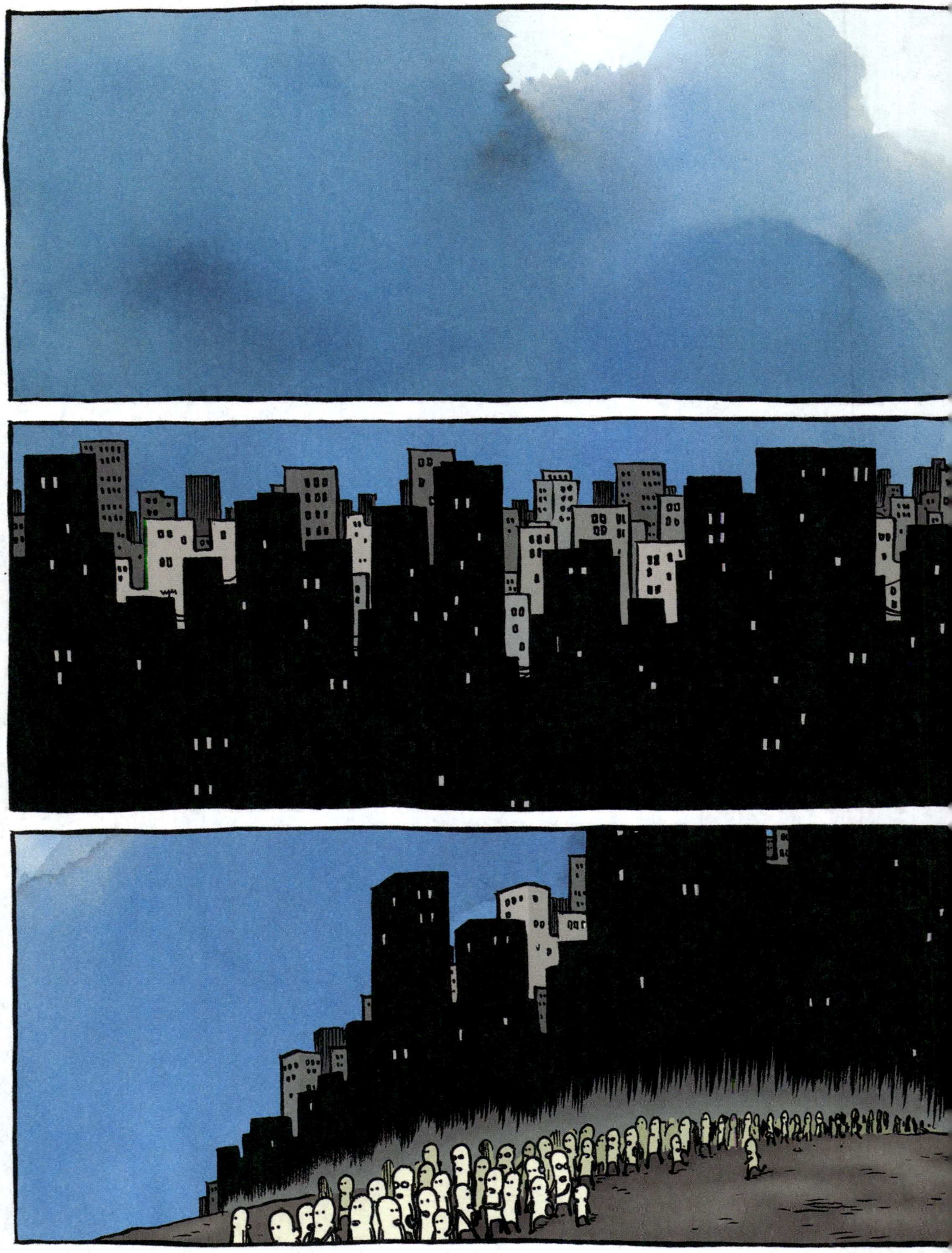

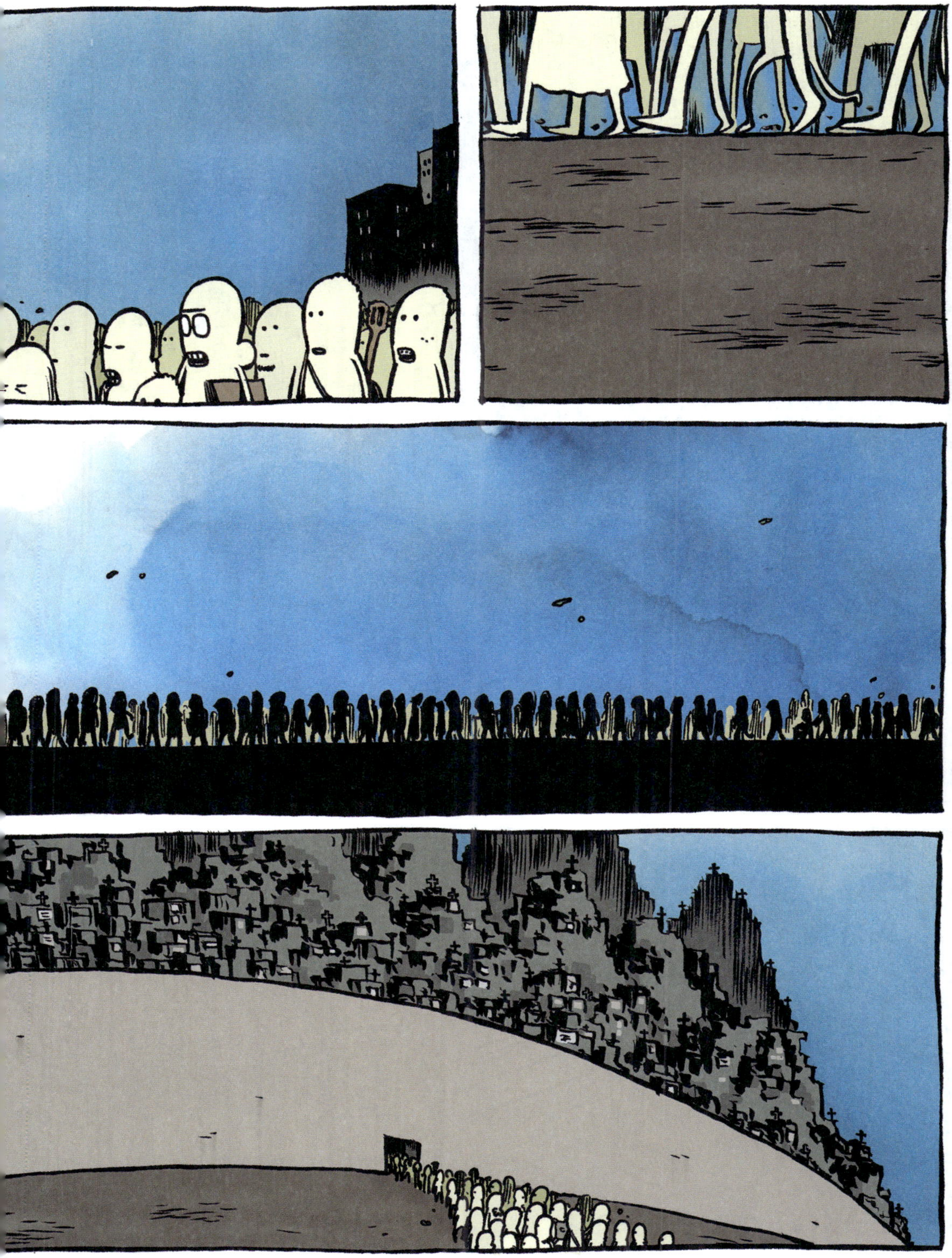

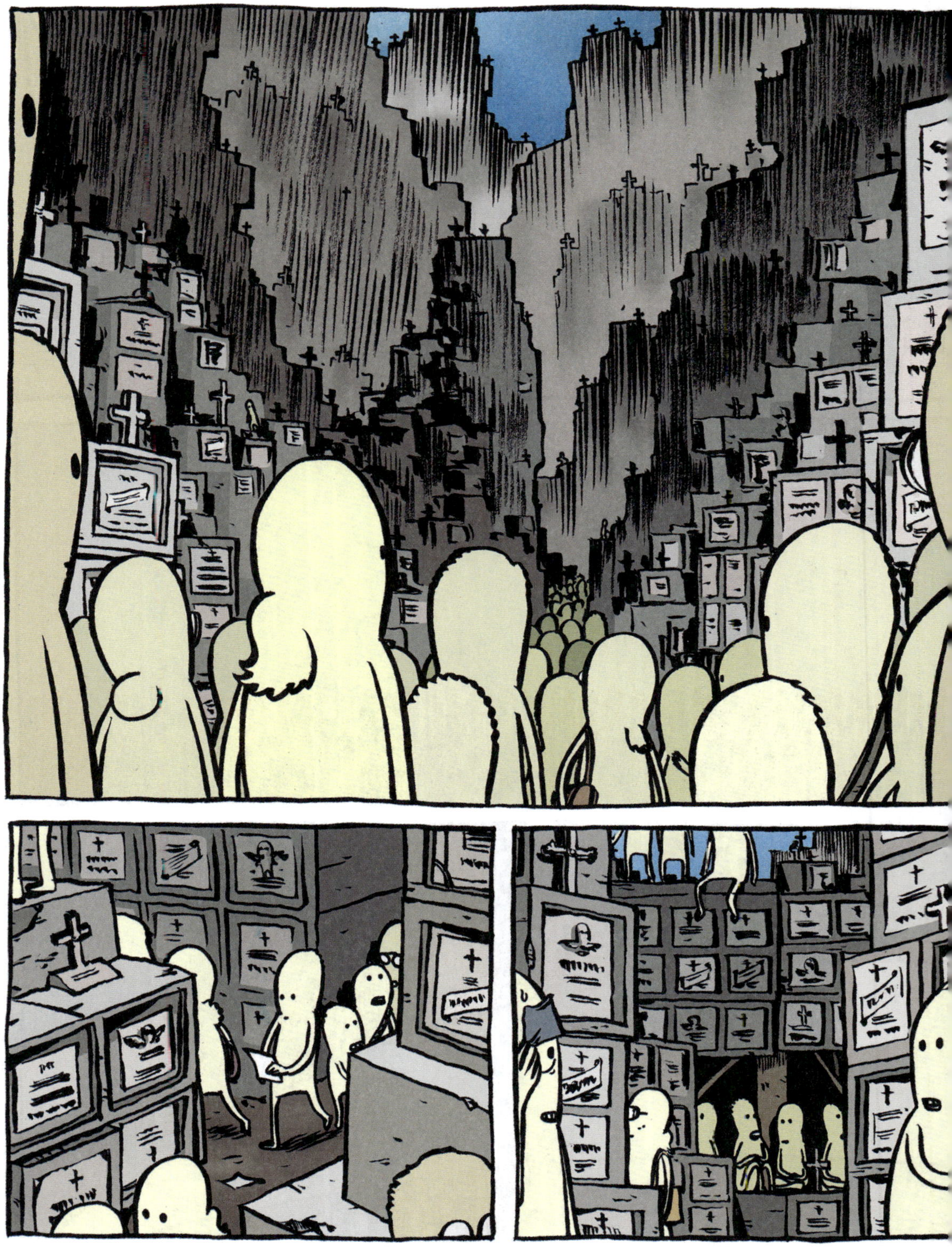

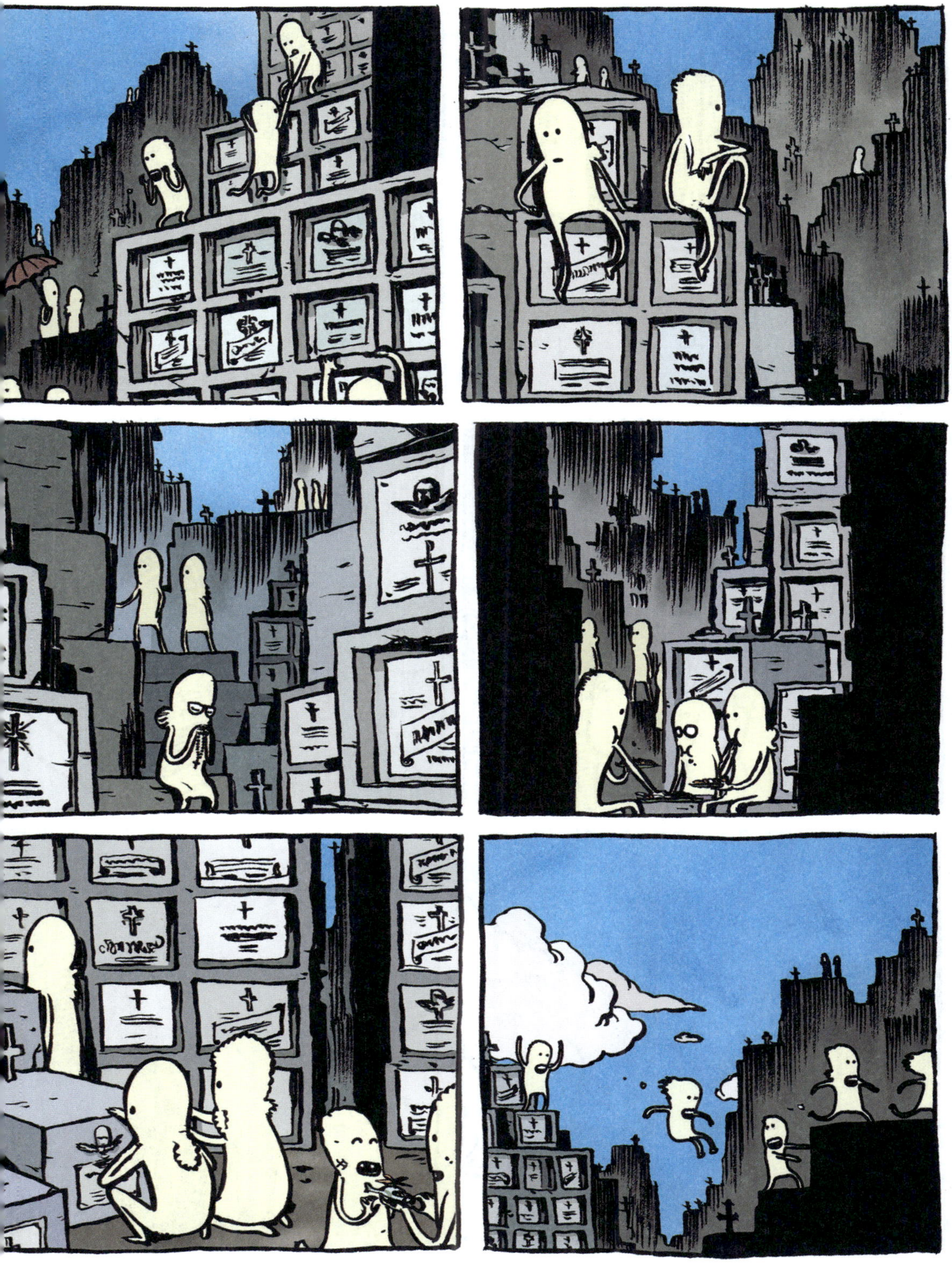

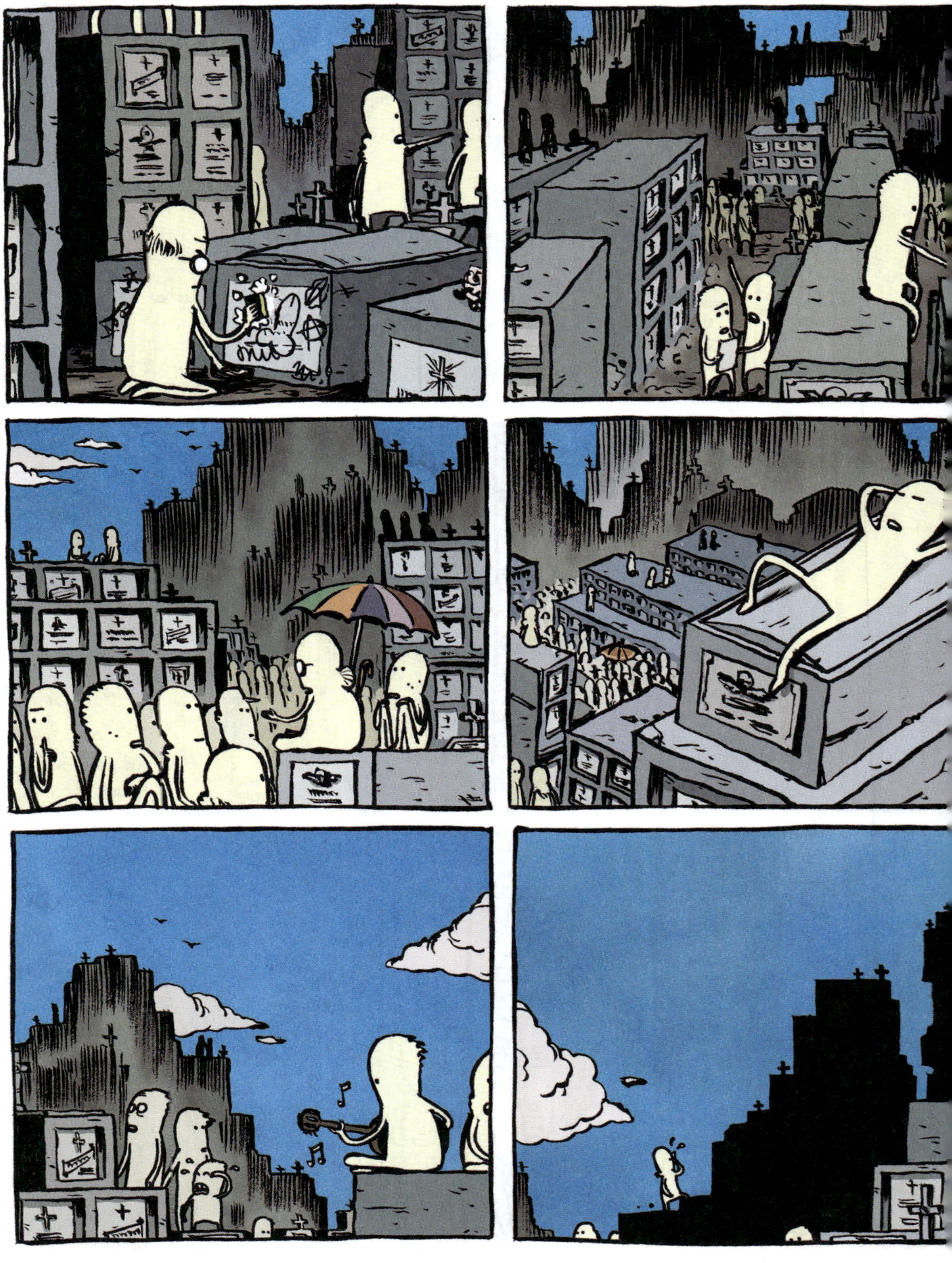

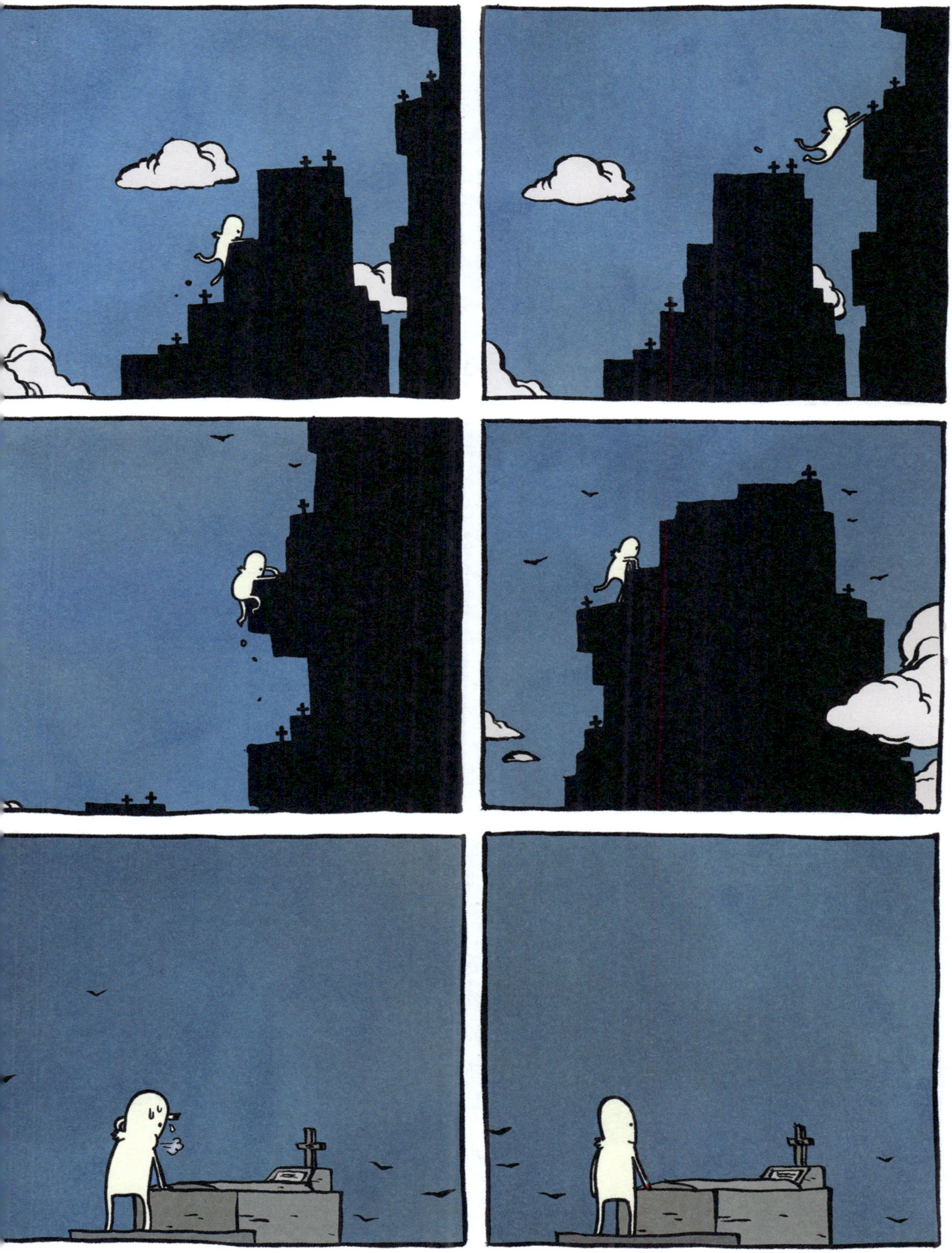

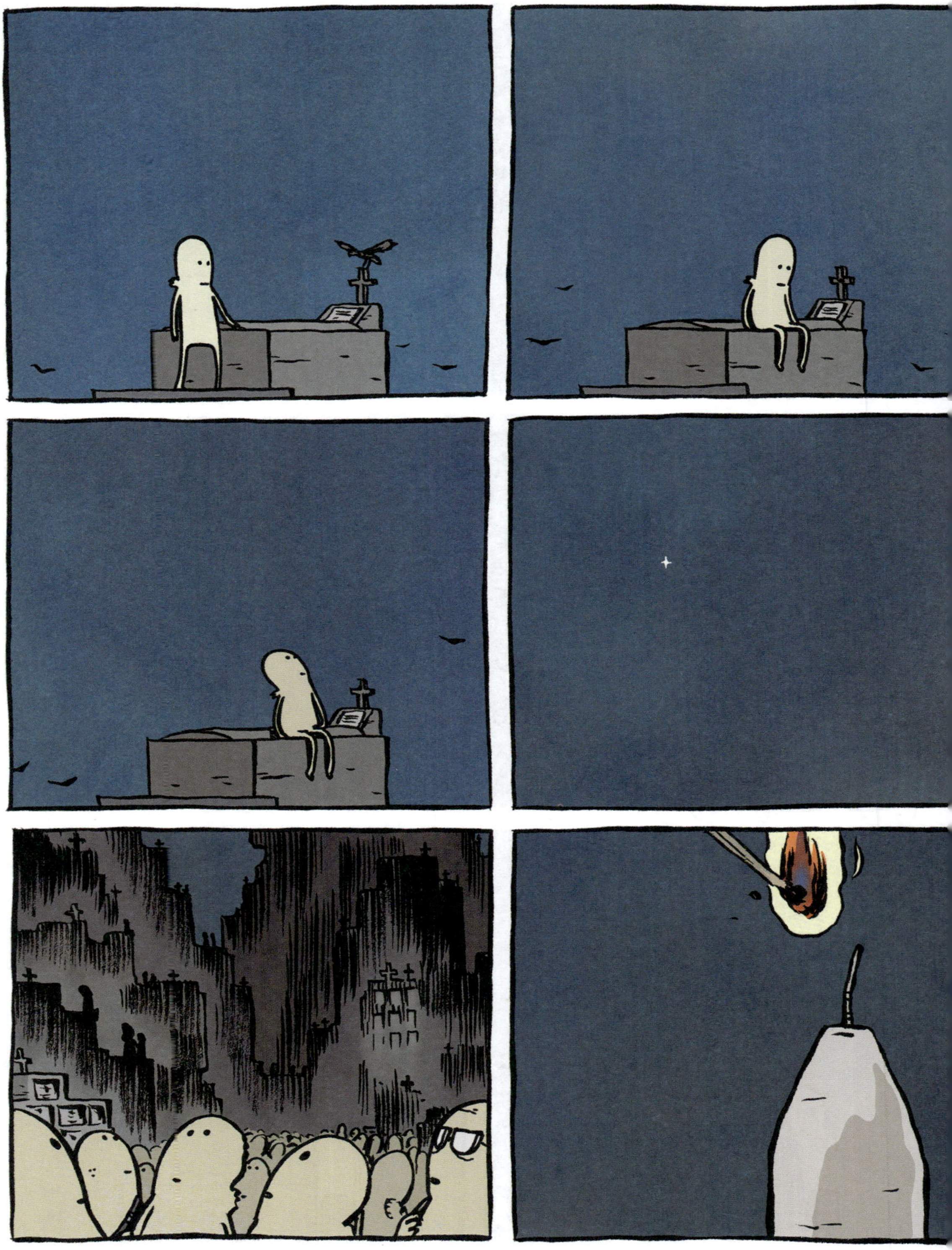

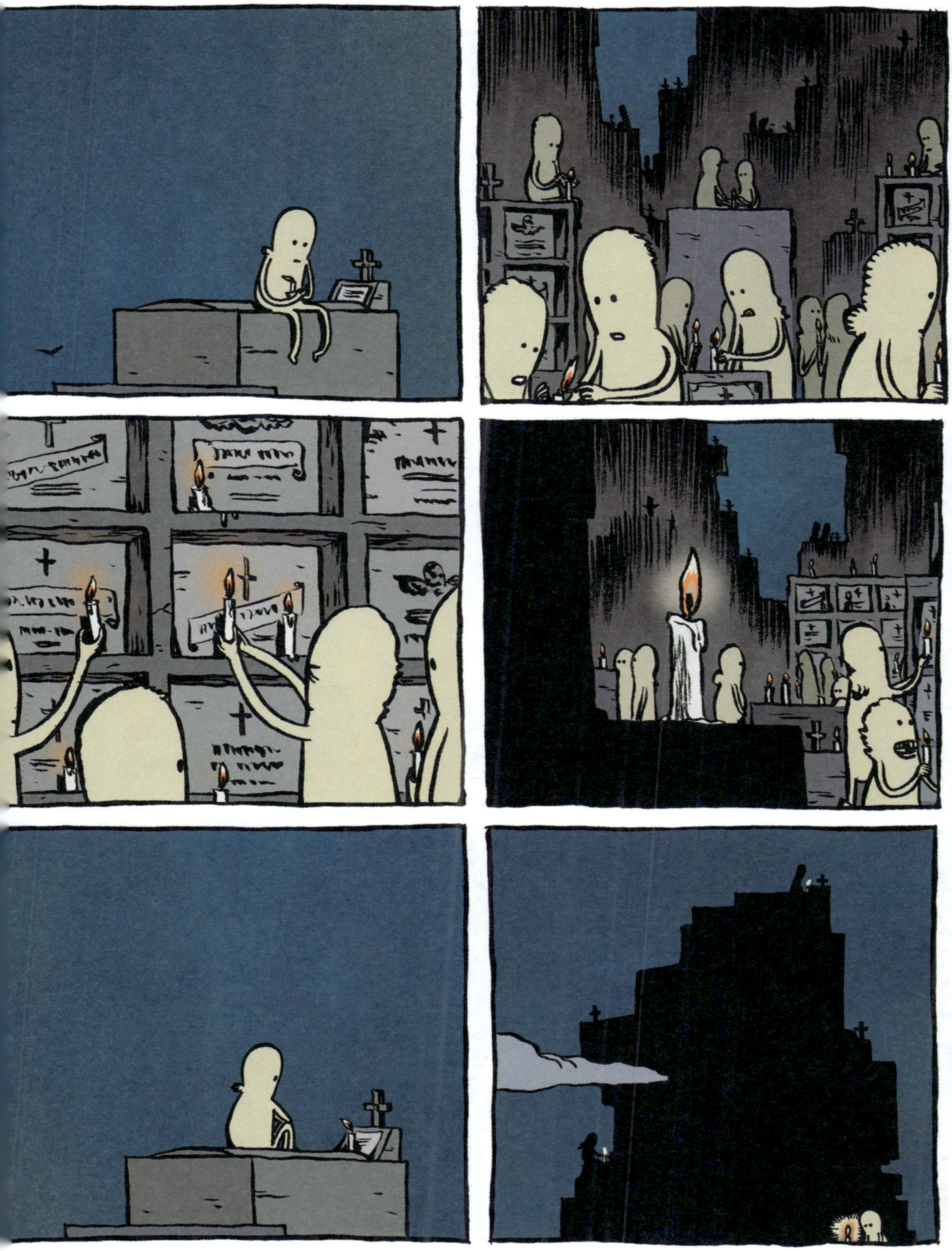

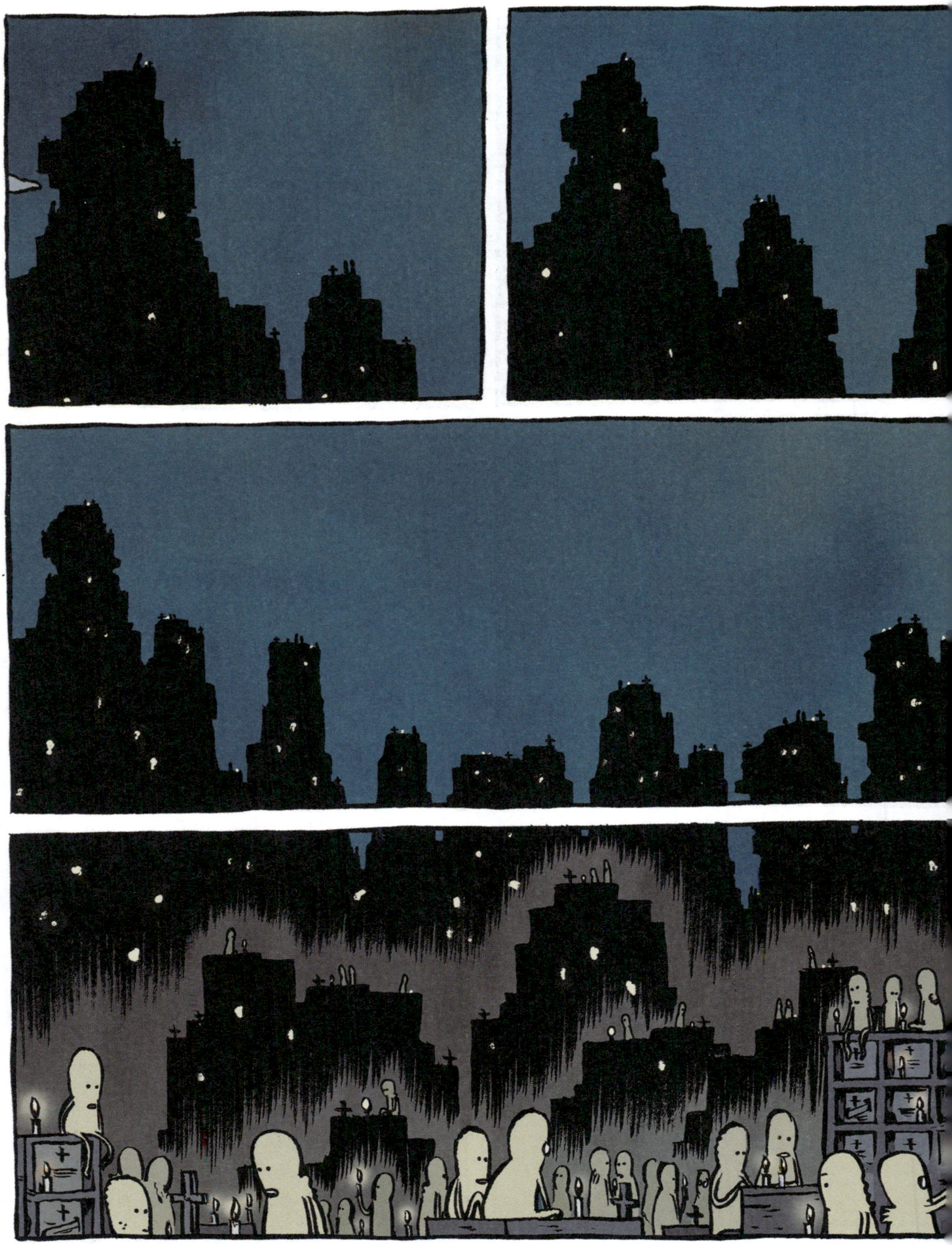

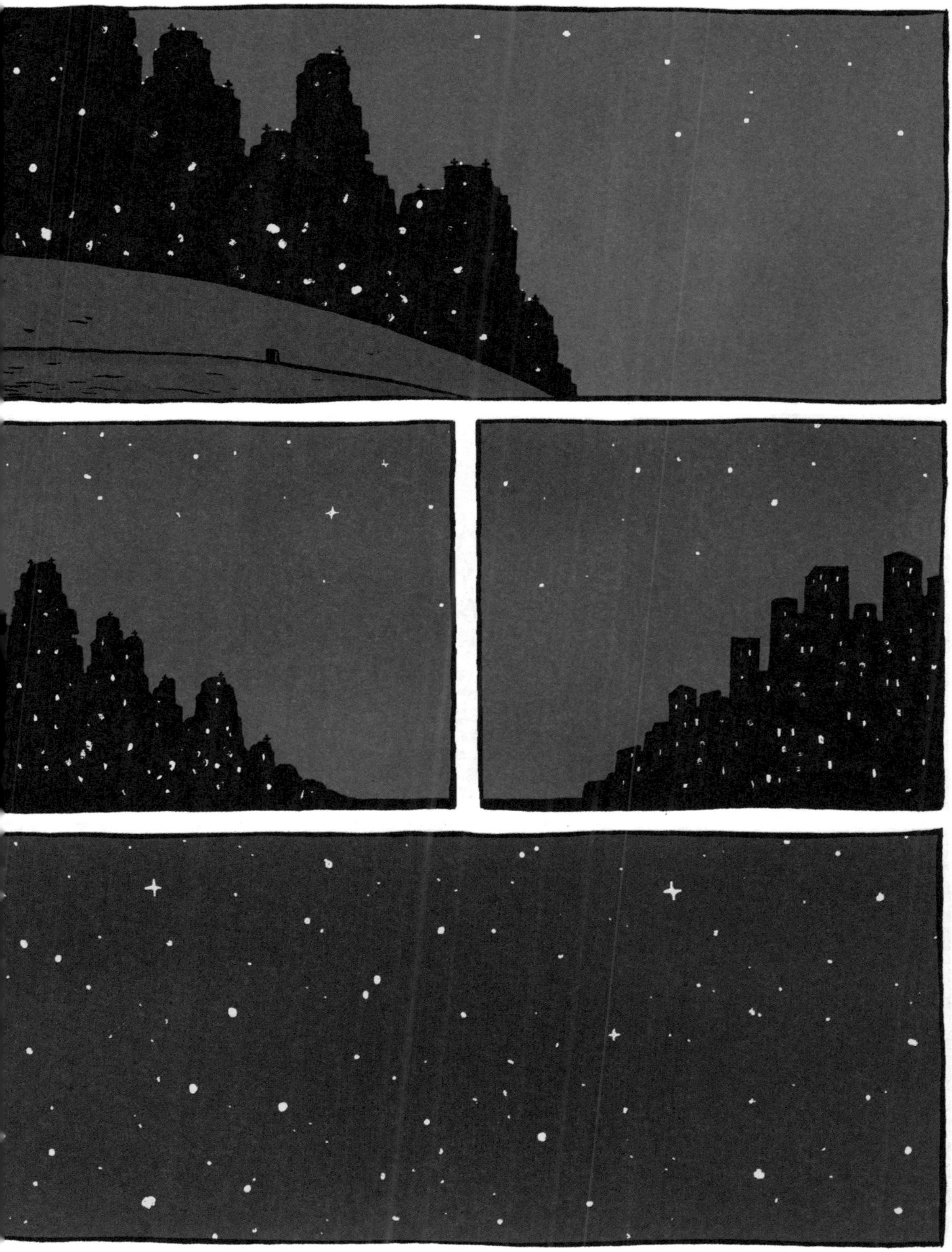

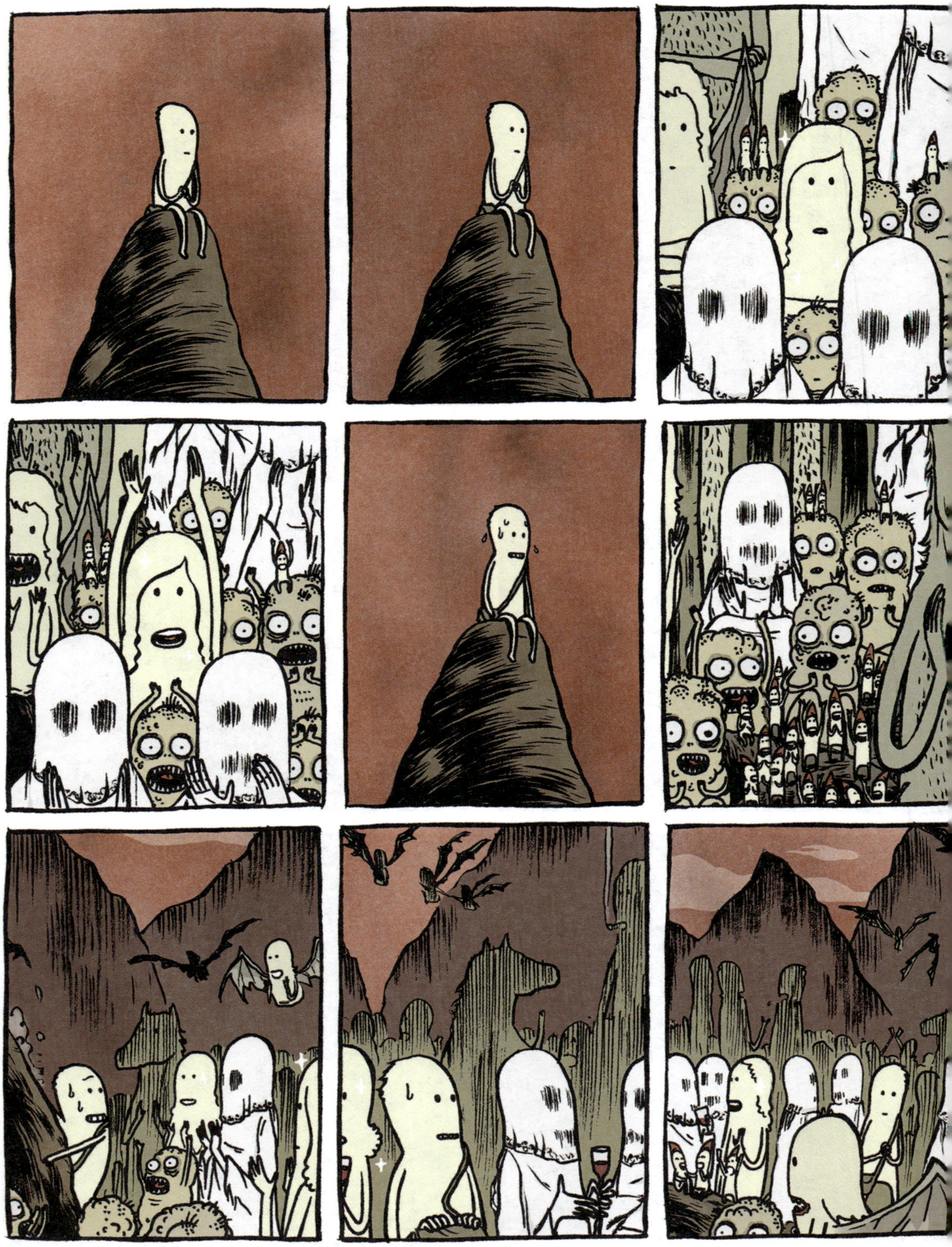

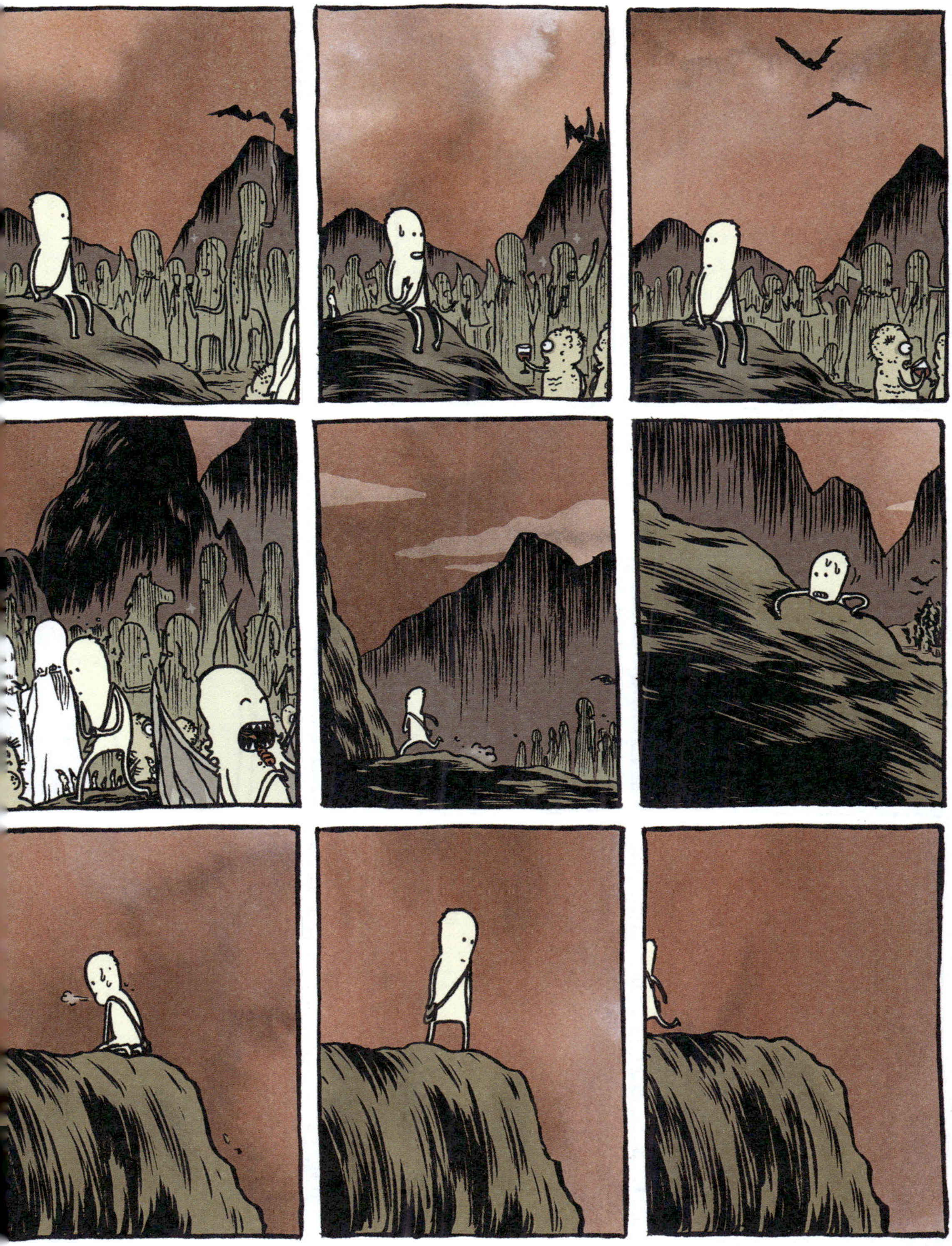

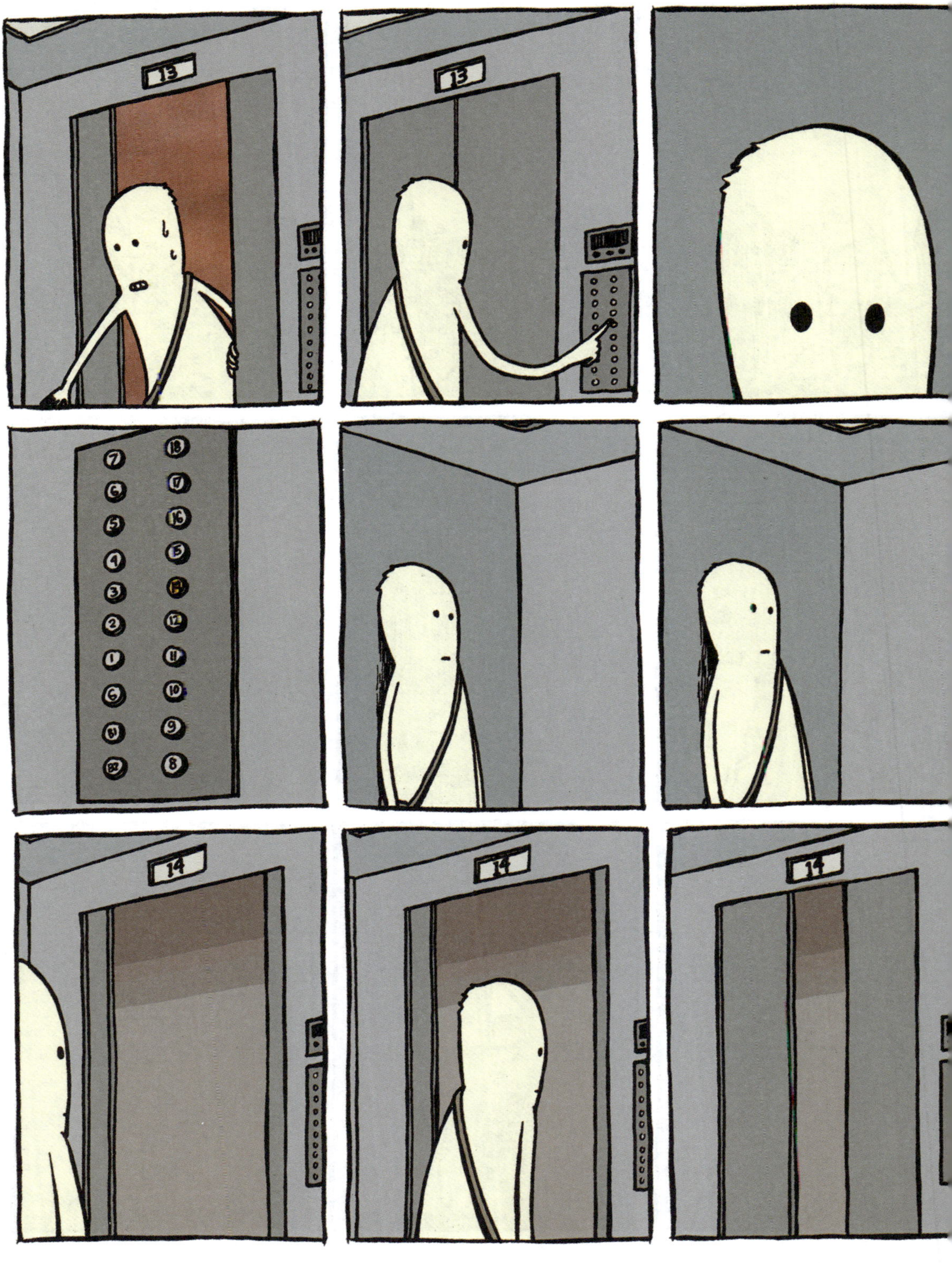
13
13
14
14
14

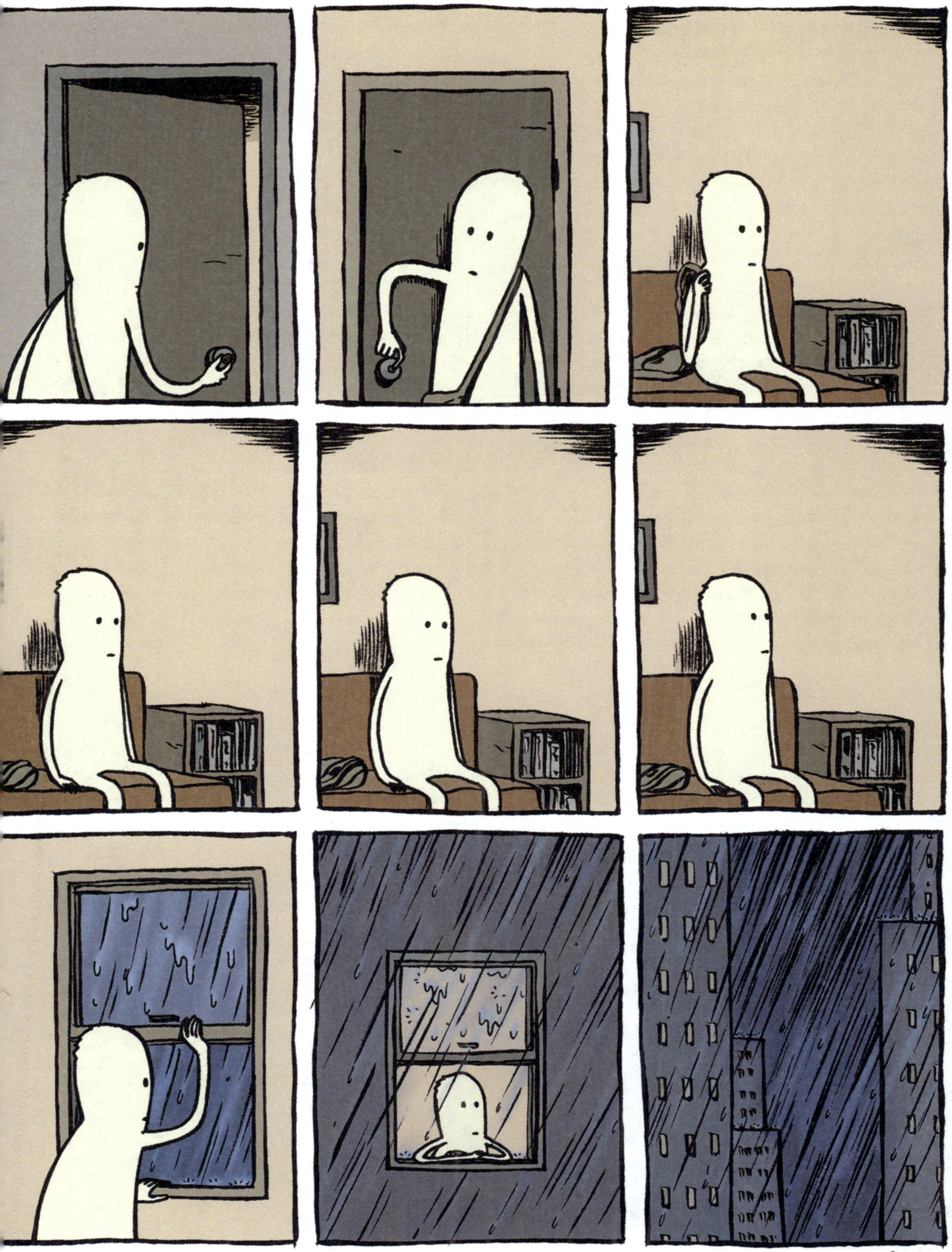

manix :)

Author's Note

I grew up listening to a lot of stories about different mythological creatures of Philippine folklore. Whenever we go to the province, my parents and grandparents would initiate stortelling sessions, gathering all the kids as the narrate horror stories about these creatures of the night, mavbe to keep us all quiet at first, then spook us later for the rest of our lives. :D

This is where I got the idea for 14, where a storytelling session takes place, but the creatures are the ones sharing their stories, and their longingness to belong and become accepted.

In this book, I included my favorite creatures from the Filipino underworld:

Chapter 1: "Manananggal"
The Manananggal is a creature that can detach its upper body from its lower half. She grows wings and fangs, and flies into the night to prey on sleeping victims (often pregnant women), using a long tonque to suck their blood and eat their visceral organs.

Chapter 2: "Diwata"
The Diwata is a good-looking deity, that often guards a forest, or an enchanted place It is believed that the Diwata can charm humans and trap them in the underworld forever.

Chapter 3: "Hunyango"
The Hunyango is a doppelganger who can deceive people by imitating another person's face and whole identity.

Chapter 4: "Tikbalang"
The Tikbalang is a tall creature, having the head of a horse, human-like torso, and long lower limbs with hooves. Tikbalangs are known for playing tricks on travellers, often leading them astray. I reimagined that when a Tikbalang dies, all travellers could be lost forever.

Chapter 5: "White Lady"
The White Lady is a female ghost, dressed in white, known to be a vengeful spirit and causes misfortunes. I had this idea, what if she only wants her struggles to be heard?

Chapter 6: "Kapre"
The Kapre is a giant that lives on trees. Thev usually smoke big tobaccos and play mischievous tricks on humans. I pictured a future where people have forgotten their beliefs, and the embers falling from the trees are a reminder that once, not too long ago, they believed in mythological entities, and even in dreams.

Chapter 7: "Duwende"
The Duwende is a very small, dwarf creature, believed to have magical powers that can bring good luck or misfortune. I imagined what if people continue to forget their existence. they suddenly show us that they are larger than life?

Chapter 8: "Tiyanak"
The Tiyanak is a demon baby who eats humans. I am told that when you hear one crying and you get near, it will eat you up. I felt that what if this Tiyanak is crying because it simply wants to belong, at whatever cost?

Chapter 9: The human
After witnessing all these underworld creatures converse, the human also shares his views about life, death, and dreams.

All these stories show that even if we might all be different, each one of us has a heart and a will to dream. Everyone has stories to tell and has undergone transformations in life because of experiences that are almost human, sometimes supernatural, often mysterious.

I wanted 14 to show that even if the stories about these mythological creatures trigger our innermost fears, they can also ignite our hopes and dreams.
So I hope, dear reader, that you may always have wonderful stories and dreams, whether in this dimension or beyond.

manix

About the Author

Growing up, Manix Abrera loved to watch his father draw editorial cartooons and comics for the Philippine Daily Inquirer. In 2001, while Manix was still a Fine Arts student at the University of the Philippines, he landed a gig in the same newspaper and started contributing his daily strips, Kikomachine Komix. Since then, he has produced over twenty comic book compilations, including two wordless graphic novels entitled “12” and “14”.

Manix is a three-time National Book Awardee for his works, “14”, “News Hardcore”, and “Kikomachine Komix Volume 14: Alaala ng Kinabukasan”. He has mounted several solo exhibitions at Galerie Stephanie and Vargas Museum. Some of his works were also staged in a group exhibition at the Metropolitan Museum of Manila.

Manix loves to ride his bike, hike, swim, and dive. He lives in Manila, Philippines with his family.

manixabrera.com

@kikomachinekomix

@manix_abrera

@manix_abrera

For Ablaze

Managing Editor
Rich Young

Editor
Kevin Ketner

Designers
Rodolfo Muraguchi
Cinthia Takeda

Publisher's Cataloging-in-Publication data

Names: Abrera, Manix, author.
Title: Manix Abrera's 14 / Manix Abrera.
Description: Portland, OR: Ablaze, 2022.
Identifiers: ISBN: 978-1-68497-061-2
Subjects: LCSH Folklore—Philippines—Comic books, strips, etc. | Mythology—Philippines—Comic books, strips, etc. | Short stories, Philippine—Comic books, strips, etc. | Graphic novels. | BISAC COMICS & GRAPHIC NOVELS / General
Classification: LCC PN6790.P5 .A37 2022 | DDC 741.5—dc23

MANIX ABRERA'S 14. First printing. Published by Ablaze Publishing, 11222 SE Main St. #22906 Portland, OR 97269. "14" © Manix Abrera. All rights reserved. For the English edition: © 2022 ABLAZE, LLC. All Rights Reserved. Ablaze and its logo TM & © 2022 Ablaze, LLC. All Rights Reserved. All names, characters, events, and locales in this publication are entirely fictional. Any resemblance to actual persons (living or dead), events or places, without satiric intent is coincidental. No portion of this book may be reproduced by any means (digital or print) without the written permission of Ablaze Publishing except for review purposes. Printed in China. For advertising and licensing email: info@ablazepublishing.com

10 9 8 7 6 5 4 3 2 1